The First Modern Comedies

The First Modern Comedies

THE SIGNIFICANCE OF ETHEREGE, WYCHERLEY AND CONGREVE

By Norman N. Holland

HARVARD UNIVERSITY PRESS
CAMBRIDGE, MASSACHUSETTS, 1959

Publication of this book has been aided by a grant
from the Ford Foundation

Distributed in Great Britain by Oxford University Press

Library of Congress Catalog Card Number 59-7654
Printed in the United States of America

Acknowledgments

Far too many people created the atmosphere of ideas and encouragement that enabled this book to come into being for me to thank them all individually. Friends, colleagues, students, librarians, readers, editors, and many others have in one way or another helped. It would be equally impossible for me to name the many, many scholars whose writings have prepared the ground of factual knowledge that any book on Restoration comedy must grow from. I should mention, however, my especial thanks to Professors Herschel Baker and Reuben Brower, who with great patience and solicitude guided the manuscript in its first early and difficult period of growth. They very carefully weeded out many of my excesses; those that remain serve as a warning of what might have been had the book not had the benefit of their insight and judgment. I owe most, however, to the marvelously durable support of my wife Jane, who, like the talented editor and gardener she is, has pruned much in this book that the rest might flower.

N. N. Holland

Cambridge, Massachusetts
April 1959

Contents

1. Ground Rules 3
2. Scenes and Heroes 9
3. *The Comical Revenge; or, Love in a Tub* 20
4. *She Wou'd If She Cou'd* 28
5. *Love in a Wood; or, St. James's Park* 38
6. Disguise, Comic and Cosmic 45
7. *The Gentleman Dancing-Master* 64
8. *The Country Wife* 73
9. *The Man of Mode; or, Sir Fopling Flutter* 86
10. *The Plain-Dealer* 96
11. A Sense of Schism 114
12. *The Old Batchelor* 131
13. *The Double-Dealer* 149
14. *Love for Love* 161
15. *The Way of the World* 175
16. The Critical Failure 199
17. From Charles to Charles 210
18. Forms to His Conceit 231

Notes 243

Index 263

The First Modern Comedies

In primitive times the blind man became a poet . . . because he had to be driven out of activities all his nature cried for, before he could be contented with the praise of life. . . . The poets of the ages of silver need no refusal of life, the dome of many-coloured glass is already shattered while they live. They look at life deliberately and as if from beyond life, and the greatest of them need suffer nothing but the sadness the saints have known.

—W. B. Yeats

1 · *Ground Rules*

"That miserable, rouged, tawdry, sparkling, hollow-hearted comedy of the Restoration," as Thackeray called it,[1] has almost always been the darling of audiences, but a strumpet to critics. Restoration comedy, or what literary people rather loosely call "Restoration" comedy — English comedy from the restoration of Charles II in 1660 to about 1710 — disappeared from the stage only during mid-Victorian times. In the eighteenth century and early nineteenth, and increasingly in the twentieth, revivals of Restoration comedy have succeeded beyond any expectation reasonable for a drama so consistently maligned.[2] "Neither is it a fact that the comedies of the last age are no longer played or enjoyed," wrote Leigh Hunt in 1840. "Whenever an actor comes who is equal to them . . . they are always played and enjoyed; nor do the present audiences of Covent Garden object to them in the least, in the spirit of a pedantic morality. A critic here and there may do so; but it is neither the feeling of the press in general, nor of the play-going public." [3] There is scarcely an important actor or actress of our day who has not starred in some Restoration comedy. Yet, ever since the seventeenth century, critics almost without exception have damned or belittled Restoration comedies: damned them for bad morals or belittled them by saying they deal only with "manners." Before going any farther, I had better clarify my position on these two ideas: I think they are both silly.

The notion that Restoration comedy is immoral confuses immorality with indecency. In what sense is literature moral? The purpose of literature is to me simply pleasure, the pleasure of understanding, first, the coherence and structure of the work itself and, second, the relation of the work to the reality it represents. The first kind of understanding involves such things as contrast, parallelism, images, or symbols; the second deals with lifelikeness, "character," probability, motivation, and the like. In both cases, "understanding" involves apprehending through a total activity of mind, emotions as well as discursive intelligence. If a play is true to its purpose, the pleasure of understanding, then I think it cannot be called immoral. The "morals" critics have made much of the fact that the dissolute rake-heroes of Restoration comedies marry the delectable heroines. The plays, they say, are immoral because vicious persons are rewarded. Unfortunately, vicious persons are sometimes rewarded in life, too, and delectable young ladies have been known to marry rakes. Indeed, rakes, I am told, have a certain charm. A play cannot be called immoral because it shows a rake rewarded, for it is not immoral to represent the truth.

A play can be, however, and most Restoration plays are, indecent. A play that is so indecent in language or subject matter, or in which the characters are so morally imbecile, or in which immorality is treated so lightly that the pleasure appropriate to a play, the pleasure of understanding, is destroyed — such a play is untrue to its purpose and hence, I think, "immoral" as well as indecent. In this sense, the Victorians were perfectly right in calling these plays immoral — for their age. Macaulay could hardly have received the pleasure of understanding from *The Country Wife*. For the age of Freud and D. H. Lawrence, however, there must be a great deal of indelicacy indeed before it blots out the pleasure of understanding. These plays, then, are not immoral, first, because they are meaningful, as the remaining chapters will show, and second, because they are not so indecent as to block our pleasure of understanding. If anyone these days is so thin-skinned that the comedies' indecency does block the pleasure they can give, then we had best part company here.

The notion that the plays are immoral confuses superficial smuttiness with the real meaning of the plays; in the same way, the notion that these plays simply describe the manners of upper-class life in the late seventeenth century substitutes superficial details for the larger substance of the plays. Manners are the stuff of comedies, as protoplasm is the stuff of men, but manners are not the whole of these comedies. Inevitably, a play must use realistic details, but those details are not necessarily what the play is "about." The eleven comedies with which this book deals are about the conflict between "manners" (i.e., social conventions) and antisocial "natural" desires. It is this dialectic between inner desires and outward appearance — not instincts alone or manners alone — that informs the comedies with masks, play-acting, disguise, intrigue, and perhaps most important, creates their language.

This is the one theme shared by the eleven comedies with which this book deals, the discrepancy between "appearance" and "nature," and the theme is distinctly and specially a Restoration theme. As Chapter 6 shows, the conflict between appearance and nature is one of the basic assumptions of Restoration politics, court pranks, literary criticism, cosmology, in short, of every phase of Restoration life. Medieval and Renaissance men tended to feel there was normally no conflict between appearance and nature. We in the twentieth century so habitually assume a conflict that we are almost unconscious of it: we inherit the feeling as part of our post-seventeenth-century, scientific world-view. Thus these comedies, as Chapter 17 shows, mark the distinction between Renaissance and "modern" drama.

I should explain that by "appearance" in this context, I mean simply that part of reality which we perceive by our senses or that part of ourselves which we let the world at large see. By "nature" I mean the part of reality that appears only to the understanding and, in particular, the part of our lives that we call personal, that we think of as no one's business but our own, or those we choose to reveal it to; that is, "nature" as we use it in the phrase, "the nature of things." I am in effect contrasting two kinds of perception. Wycherley called them "Eye Sight" and "reason's insight," or "outward sight" and "inward discerning." I have not used the ordinary critical rubric of "appearance and reality" because that implies, I think, that the appearance is in some sense not real. To the Restoration writer appearance was very real, indeed, a particularly important reality. It included not only the manners to which earlier critics have paid such deference, but almost all of daily life as well. As one of Congreve's heroes says, "I know no effectual Difference between continued Affectation and Reality." Also, I think, these two words, "appearance" and "nature," are the ones seventeenth-century writers used to describe the kinds of reality I am distinguishing, and they are as well the words that most readily convey the distinction to twentieth-century readers. Although the eleven comedies deal with other themes, too, this contrast between appearance and nature is the most important, and in a narrow sense this study can be taken as simply an analysis of this one theme in the eleven comedies of Etherege, Wycherley, and Congreve.

There are three, at least three, objections that might be made to this kind of study, and I should, I suppose, do my best to answer them before proceeding to the eleven plays. The first is that this is an essentially literary study of essentially dramatic works. This objection proceeds from the peculiar notion that what is good reading cannot also be good theater; in particular, that what English teachers and critics find interesting must be excessively dull on a stage. On the contrary, the producer or director is almost certain to produce a dull performance unless he understands the play *as literature*. As G. Wilson Knight, a distinguished producer — and critic — of Shakespeare, says: "The producer should be aware of the play's metaphysical core; that is, of its wholeness. . . . Close intellectual interpretation must come first."[4] True creativity on a stage involves *bringing out* the play (that is what *production* literally means), re-creating it from the static text into dynamic theater. In the hope of making this literary study more dramatic, I have included as a kind of come-on a final chapter suggesting ways of giving life on a stage to some of the abstractions involved in these plays.

A second objection that might be made is that this is a very serious and solemn treatment indeed for rather light and frothy comedies. This kind of objection proceeds from a Romantic notion of which we are all, consciously or unconsciously, victims: that laughing cannot be "serious." "Compassion" or "pity," to use the Romantic vocabulary, is a nobler emotion for an audience than pure laughter. "The instruction of Comedy," said the elder Schlegel, "is . . . the doctrine of prudence; the morality of consequences and not of motives. Morality, in its genuine acceptation, is essentially allied to the spirit of Tragedy."[5] Many great comic writers (Chekhov, Gogol, Shaw, Sheridan, for example) have rebutted this idea, but I suppose we all still tend to assume, as a leading literary history does, "Comedy represents in a ridiculous light the aberrations from the social norm." We have forgotten what Socrates told his drunken friends early one morning at the house of Agathon, "that the genius of comedy was the same with that of tragedy, and that the true artist in tragedy was an artist in comedy also."[6] We have perhaps never learned what Kierkegaard wrote: "If you wish to be and remain enthusiastic, then draw the silk curtains of facetiousness (irony), and so hide your enthusiasm."[7]

Comedy is the creation of perspectives. We are asked to look at an event from at least two points of view, acceptance and rejection, and to recognize not that one is right but that both are. We are asked to combine in ourselves the solemn idealist and the cynic (or mystic), both the Don and Sancho. "In humour," wrote Coleridge in the wisest statement I have read on the subject, "the little is made great, and the great little, in order to destroy both, because all is equal in contrast with the infinite."[8] We are asked to recognize that all we know is foolish and trivial, but that it is all we know, and therefore worth caring about — in this world. My answer then to the objection that this study treats comedy too seriously is that comedy is basically a very serious business indeed.

The third objection that might be made to this book is the scholarly one: the author, while he repeats many things long known to scholars, at other times takes a radical approach, ignoring ideas well established in literary history. It is true that I have dealt roughly with some of the standard assumptions of literary history — where I felt a close reading of the plays showed they were in error. It is true also that I have tried to include enough of the plot of each play and enough background from the Restoration so that the book would be intelligible even to someone who has not read the plays and does not know the period. I can only plead to my colleagues that I have included these things that, were I writing for scholars only, I could take for granted, in the hope that the book might thereby reach a wider audience. Frankly, I am trying to stir up interest in Restoration comedy, not just among professional scholars and critics, but among people interested in the comic or in the theater or just in good reading.

The somewhat unorthodox plan and method of the book is also designed to stir up interest. Most books on Restoration comedy treat a great many plays; one, for example, deals with 282. I felt that, to show the very real merits of these comedies, I should deal fully with each one the book touched. The book, therefore, had to deal with a smaller number of plays, or else it would become the work of a lifetime and a half. The comedies of Etherege, Wycherley, and Congreve, totaling eleven, provided a neatly defined sample, including some very good and some not-so-good plays. Furthermore, by dealing with only three writers, I would, I hoped, be able to give the reader a feeling for the way each of them developed. I also abandoned the conventional grouping — first the comedies of Etherege, then Wycherley's, then Congreve's — as deceptive: it gives the impression that Etherege was the earliest writer and developed the form which Wycherley varied and Congreve perfected. Actually, of course, Etherege and Wycherley developed together; the difference in their final styles suggests that there is no such thing as an archetypal "comedy of manners" represented by Etherege's last play *The Man of Mode.*

The eleven chapters dealing with the plays are "readings," that is, attempts to show first how the various parts of each play — plots, characters, events, and language — all fit together into one unified whole, and second, to show how that whole reveals certain aspects of reality. To me, a play is an analogue to reality. It has a life of its own as reality does; it embodies certain laws of operation; its various elements correspond to people and events we meet in life. At the same time, art is clearer than life. Confusing and superfluous details are stripped off in the act of creation; the details that are left are fused together in a richer, more meaningful way than the details of everyday life. The analogue is thus a metaphor for reality, not a literal, photographic rendition. In reading, therefore, I proceed from the hypothesis (which usually turns out to be correct) that everything in the play is there for a purpose, and go on from there to develop the relations between the parts, that is, the unifying principle that informs the whole. In seeing this unity, I have tried to be over-ingenious rather than conservative, because I think the reader would rather have something he disagrees with than complete silence on a particular topic. That way, my suggestions, even if they are in themselves wrong, can at least raise questions.

These "readings" deal, therefore, rather closely with the texts of the several plays, and to avoid trailing clouds of footnotes for all the necessary quotations, I have slipped into the text the page numbers for the quotations in the standard editions.

Chapters 6 and 11, spliced into the chapters on the plays themselves, relate what the plays "say" to certain ideas current in the sixteenth, seventeenth, and eighteenth centuries. The purpose of these chapters is not to show "sources" for the ideas in the plays, but to reinforce the readings themselves and to refute the idea that Restoration comedy is merely a coterie fad, relevant to nothing but itself. These chapters show, I think, that there is real intellectual substance in these plays and indeed that that substance comes surprisingly close to our twentieth-century world-view.

After discussing the plays I go on in Chapters 16 and 17 to suggest that the reason critics have dismissed these plays as immoral or as merely about "manners" is that we tend to think of them in Elizabethan terms, when they are really at bottom "modern." In the final chapter, I suggest some ways to realize these literary points of view by dramatic devices in the *viva voce* theater.

Such is the modest plan and arrangement of this book, but behind it lurks a shamelessly grandiose hope — I would like to see a total revaluation of these plays. The critics have always disliked them, but to me, and evidently to generations of players and audiences, they form the silver age of English comedy. In the nature of things, however, I cannot guarantee any such revaluation. An influential modern critic has made the ultimate objection — that these plays are "trivial, gross and dull," and to that I can make no answer. Much as I would like to persuade you that they are riotously funny and rich with meaning, there is a normative realm beyond all analysis where *expertise* is excluded. There each reader decides for himself. The only way to determine whether these plays please or not is to read them, and to that end, the remaining seventeen chapters of this book can do no more than serve as a somewhat prejudiced and crotchety guide.

2 · *Scenes and Heroes*

To appreciate a style it is probably not necessary to know its contexts, but it is certainly helpful, particularly in the case of a style so generally misunderstood as that of the "comedy of manners." There are five significant facts. First, Restoration comedy, coming at the end of the seventeenth century, marks the finish of a great dramatic period and the beginning of the abysmally bad drama of the eighteenth and nineteenth centuries. Second, Restoration comedy represents the "theatre of a coterie." Third, Restoration comedy embodies new, though not radically new theatrical techniques, which in turn reflect a new approach toward the audience: the spectator is not to be drawn into the action; he is to "judge" it. Fourth, the so-called "comedy of manners" is a new genre in the English theater. Fifth, in its early stages, Restoration comedy is "anti-heroic." Let me amplify.

The golden age of English drama lasted scarcely more than twenty years. Shakespeare's writing career (from the early 1590's to 1611 or 1612) spanned it. The preparation for this high plateau was long, reaching back to the ninth-century *Quem Quaeritis* trope; the tapering-off, however, was more rapid. It is safe to say that by 1700 the English theater had passed through its silver age (the Restoration). It had ceased to appeal to the population as a whole and catered largely to the upper middle class. Also, the theater was less and less thought of in terms of aesthetic pleasure and more and more in terms of moral instruction or "vehicles" for some noted actor or producer.

All through the long building-up to the Elizabethan period, the popular theater had appealed to all classes, there was something in it for the lowest apprentice, the most bookish scholar, or the highest nobleman — indeed the Virgin Queen herself seems to have been almost inordinately fond of the popular drama. However, as Professor Harbage[1] has pointed out so thoroughly, two traditions had evolved. The "theatre of a nation" was one, the popular drama of Shakespeare, Marlowe, Dekker, or Heywood, which emphasized bourgeois values, wedded love, patriotism, hard work, national unity, and moral responsibility. The other tradition, the "theatre of a coterie," that of Chapman, Jonson, and Marston, appealed only to aristocrats and intellectuals. It was much more consciously "literary" and academic; it questioned established values and often dealt with sexual abnormalities, satire, wealth, the need for ease, the animal nature of man, and the difficulty of ethical behavior. It often attacked middle-class groups, particularly Puritans and merchants. We look back to both traditions as great achievements; we tend today to favor the popular drama a little, but in the days after Shakespeare left the stage, it was the coterie drama that survived. Greater profit and greater prestige drew players and writers away from the popular theaters; more important, Puritan opposition drove audiences away. When, in 1642, a Puritan parliament forbade stage plays, the only important theaters were Blackfriars, the Phoenix, and Salisbury Court, all "priuat" theaters. The drama had ceased to be a popular medium. When Charles II returned and in 1660 the theaters formally reopened, they reopened as coterie theaters. Elizabethan audiences had kept as many as nine large popular theaters going; Restoration audiences supported two small private theaters. The theater had become distinctly an upper-class diversion, and monopolies granted by Royal Patents kept it that way.

Thus, Restoration comedy is part of the coterie tradition. Furthermore, Restoration comedy embodied new theatrical techniques. The theater itself had changed. The great Elizabethan popular theaters like the Globe and even the private ones had used a platform stage extending out into the audience with spectators on three sides of it. Very little, if any, scenery was used. The Restoration theater used a "picture" stage with a proscenium arch and a curtain and lots of scenery.[2] Elizabethan theatergoers were involved in an action: " 'Tis your thoughts that now must deck our kings," says one of Shakespeare's prologues. The Restoration theatergoer, however, watched a "scene," and prologues and epilogues by the dozens awaited his verdict of approval or disapproval. He was regarded as the dispassionate judge of a spectacle — not as someone to be drawn into the play. They make plays now, a Restoration critic wrote, "more for sight then hearing."[3] Actors and managers were, I suppose, more important than mere playwrights even in Elizabethan times, but now added to the playwrights' burdens were actresses allowed on stage for the first time by Charles's Royal Patents. For many ladies like Nell Gwyn, the stage was an avenue of advancement which led to walking over the play. An actress could have her way simply because a pretty girl could make any play a success. Thus Pepys on October 28, 1661, notes, "I to the Theatre, and there saw 'Argalus and Parthenia,' where a woman acted Parthenia, and came afterwards on the stage in men's clothes, and had the best legs that ever I saw, and I was very well pleased with it."[4] The language of the plays had also changed: comedies were, in the Restoration, unabashedly in prose; tragedies and tragicomedies were more and more often in rhymed couplets.

These differences between the Restoration stage and the Elizabethan-Jacobean stage led early commentators to conclude that Restoration drama represented an entirely new departure. It was thought that the act of the Puritan Parliament closing the theaters in 1642 was as definitive as the stroke of the headsman's ax that deprived the "royal actor" of "his comely head." English theatrical tradition was supposed to have died, and when theaters reopened in 1660 after almost twenty years of supposed silence, the returning Cavaliers demanded French genres, and brought into being heroic drama and the comedy of manners. Macaulay's criticism, for example, and Thackeray's, grow from the assumption that Restoration comedy is fundamentally un-English, its morals therefore suspect, and when compared with the hearty goodness of the native Elizabethans — well! More modern historical research,[5] however, shows that the play-going habit was too strong for even a Puritan edict to stifle. Plays were performed surreptitiously. There were private performances for the wealthy, and, particularly in the provinces, some clandestine public theatricals. The two most common kinds of entertainment were masques for the rich and for the poor, drolls — farcical scenes, such as the Falstaff episodes from *I Henry IV*, performed as one-act plays. People even wrote plays, mostly closet dramas, but some stage comedies too.[6] The picture is not that of a theatrical tradition killed in 1642 and a substitute taking its place in 1660; the theaters were sick after 1642, but the pulse held, and the patient recovered in 1660, or more properly, 1656, the date of Davenant's *Siege of Rhodes*.

Furthermore, the "innovations" that supposedly mark the "new" theater had taken place, more or less, before 1642. Women had appeared privately as actresses in court masques and publicly in visiting French companies. Indeed, Charles I's queen, Henrietta Maria, had herself acted in a masque, precipitating William Prynne's savage Puritan attack, *Histriomastix* (1632), and the loss of Prynne's ears as a seditious libeler. The use of scenery was common in private performances, sporadic in public — for financial, rather than aesthetic, reasons. Masques before 1642 commonly used a proscenium arch. Even the institution of a "theatre royal" controlled by a royal patentee took place in the thirties when Charles I appointed the Cockpit in Whitehall for the performance of plays at court. The blank verse in Caroline drama by the closing of the theaters had already become so amorphous as amply to justify the eighteenth-century epithet for it: "numerous prose." It was an easy transition to the actual prose of Restoration comedy, which, in the original editions, is often laid out like verse. Caroline drama, moreover, like Restoration drama, was written "by gentlemen for gentlemen." [7] Most important, the plays most often performed in the first few years the theaters were open were just revivals of Jacobean and Caroline dramas, tinkered with to suit Restoration taste.

Thus, in many respects, the Restoration theater represents simply a continuation of the coterie tradition of English drama. There are changes, but none is large enough to justify the notion that Restoration drama represents a radically new importation from Europe. There is one exception, the so-called "comedy of manners," which usually shows a dashing young rake-hero lured into marriage by a witty, wealthy young heroine. These comedies hold up fops, boors, country people, older, middle-class, or serious people for unfavorable comparison to the witty lovers. There is nothing in earlier English comedy quite like this, and it is the comedy of manners that has looked the most "foreign" to critics.

The term "comedy of manners" is, as Professor Bateson has pointed out,[8] a confusing misnomer of recent invention. Charles Lamb was the one who invented the term; George Meredith used it, but it achieved no particular currency until John Palmer's *The Comedy of Manners* appeared in 1913. In the seventeenth century, "manners" meant not only "custom" but "character," the total nature or essence of an individual, Greek ἦθος as opposed to ἔθος. The same ambiguity attaches to the Latin *moralis, -e* as opposed to *mos, moris,* and the French *moeur.* Virtually all seventeenth-century writers on Aristotle use as a translation of ἦθος, "manners." "The manners, in a poem," wrote Dryden, "are understood to be those inclinations, whether natural or acquired, which move and carry us to actions, good, bad, or indifferent, in a play; or which incline the persons to such or such actions." [9] The Restoration itself called its comedy "genteel comedy," meaning simply "comedy of the upper classes," as opposed to "low comedy."

The reason this "genteel comedy" seems such an innovation in the Restoration is that it is a reaction against the dramatic style that prevailed up to and after the Restoration. Professor Underwood has shown that, although English comedy before the Restoration dealt with somewhat the same intellectual conflicts as those that inform Restoration comedy, the tone was surprisingly moralistic.[10] "Surprisingly" because, as Professor Harbage points out, one would expect the gay delinquency of Cavalier lyricists like Lovelace and Suckling to have been accompanied on the stage by a genteel comedy quite like that of the Restoration. Actually, however, "Cavalier drama was prevailingly serious, sentimental, romantic." Restoration social comedy, he says, "can be explained only as reaction . . . [to] romance of the Cavalier mode." [11] Certainly it is true that the early phase of Restoration comedy is a reaction against this romantic Cavalier sentimentality. On the other hand, the comedies ultimately go far beyond mere reaction, and to understand that growth and development probably takes some understanding of the starting point, heroic drama.

The heroic drama, though one of the silliest creations of the human mind, had at least the saving grace of being quite thoroughly English — it had had a long nurturing in England before it finally appeared, fully ripe, on the Restoration stage. Professor Harbage's *Cavalier Drama* traces its ancestry from Greek romances to Elizabethan fiction and the "heroic poem," from thence to John Fletcher's comedies, and through Caroline court dramas to Dryden and Davenant, the first two Restoration playwrights to turn out a heroic play.[12] The heroic plays were "serious," that is, they were either tragedies or tragicomedies: laughable elements were usually excluded according to Aristotle's rule against mixing tragedy and comedy. The plays were ordinarily written in heroic couplets (thought to be the English equivalent of Greek, Roman, or French hexameters), but surely a most unhappy choice for dramatic dialogue — only a master can keep heroic couplets from lapsing into a jingle. The characters were almost all exceedingly stilted kings, queens, and other nobility, again according to the Aristotelian requirement of noble personages. The good people were sharply divided from the bad. The plots tended to be very schematic, melodramatic conflicts between love (i.e., desire) and honor (i.e., political, military, or domestic responsibilities). There was a propensity for neat, paired choices: the protagonist was apt to find himself standing on stage with his king on his left calling him to war and his lady friend on his right telling him to stay, each probably speaking alternate halves of neat little couplets. These pat — too pat — love-honor conflicts were generally resolved, no matter how artificial the means, according to the crudest notions of poetic justice. "Good guys" win; "bad guys" lose.

The heroic play was simply an attempt to put a heroic poem on the stage. The heroic poem — so neoclassic writers termed epic poetry — shared alternately with tragedy the distinction of being thought the "highest" genre. It included such apparently unrelated items as the *Iliad*, the *Aeneid* — Italian critics attempted to include *The Divine Comedy* — Tasso's *Jerusalem Liberated*, Sidney's *Arcadia*, *The Faerie Queene*, *Paradise Lost*, Dryden's *Annus Mirabilis*, and seventeenth-century French prose romances such as Mademoiselle de Scudéry's *Le Grand Cyrus*. While some of these "heroic poems" have no heroes and others are not in verse, they all have at least one thing in common: they idealized their subject matter. "Admiration is the proper object of Heroic Poesy," wrote Dryden, "just as laughter is the proper object of Burlesque, the opposite of Heroic Poesy. One shows nature beautified, the other shows her deformed." [13] In one of the earliest formulations of the heroic style, Tasso concluded that, while the hero of a tragedy, as Aristotle had said, should be a man neither perfectly good nor perfectly bad, the reader of a heroic poem did not have before him the visible action of the stage: to be equally stimulated, he must be shown a hero who is the height of virtue. The irony of the heroic play is that a style evolved specifically as an alternative to drama was put on the stage.[14]

Not only was it put on the stage — old plays were rewritten to fit the new style, and these alterations throw the heroic manner into high relief. Nahum Tate's *King Lear* (1681) proved one of the most durable of these heroic adaptations.[15] He drops Shakespeare's wonderful fool, because the pseudoclassical rules forbid mixing comedy and tragedy. In the heroic manner, he splices a love plot into the political story. Edgar and Cordelia are in love, and thus Cordelia has a motive for answering her father coldly in the three sisters' love contest: she *wants* to lose her dowry so she won't have to marry her royal suitor Burgundy. Edmund lusts after her and sends two ruffians to kidnap Cordelia when she goes out to her father in the storm, but the loyal Edgar drives them away. Tate makes much more than Shakespeare does of the love interest implicit in Edmund's affair with Goneril and Regan. All these changes serve to make the patterns of the play much neater and more symmetrical. That is, the play in this version is divided not just into high plot and low, but into political plot and love plot. Cordelia chooses between Burgundy and Edgar; Edmund chooses between the good woman (Cordelia) and the bad (Goneril and Regan); he has a further choice between the two bad women — which he never gets around to making. In the interests of symmetry, Cordelia is even given a confidante. Tate's most important changes, however, are in the interests of poetic justice. He fixes up the play so that the "good guys" win and the "bad guys" lose; Lear achieves a "blest Restauration" and Edgar marries Cordelia, saying:

> Thy bright example shall convince the World
> (Whatever Storms of Fortune are decreed)
> That Truth and Vertue shall at last succeed.

Our bardolatrous age may laugh, but this unwholesome mutant has had a stage history almost as long as its original. The last time it was played — seriously — on the London stage, was in 1838.[16] By contrast, the one or two revivals of the real *King Lear* shortly after the Restoration were singularly inconspicuous.[17] The success of the adaptation suggests, if nothing else, the remarkably bad taste in drama of Restoration and eighteenth-century audiences. Even the greatest of neoclassic critics, Dr. Johnson, seems (though somewhat hesitantly) to have preferred Tate's version:

> A play in which the wicked prosper and the virtuous miscarry, may doubtless be good, because it is a just representation of the common events of human life: but since all reasonable beings naturally love justice I cannot easily be persuaded, that the observation of justice makes a play worse; or that, if other excellencies are equal, the audience will not always rise better pleased from the final triumph of persecuted virtue.
>
> In the present case the public has decided. Cordelia, from the time of Tate, has always retired with victory and felicity. And, if my sensations could add any thing to the general suffrage, I might relate I was many years ago so shocked by Cordelia's death, that I know not whether I ever endured to read again the last scenes of the play till I undertook to revise them as an editor.[18]

The idea of poetic justice, the "happy ending," dies hard; indeed, it is still flourishing in Hollywood.

Poetic justice is simply one of the ways the writer of heroic drama idealized his subject matter so that, in Dryden's phrase, "Images and Actions may be rais'd above the life." Both in plot and language, the basis of the style is the attempt to outdo nature. Much earlier in the seventeenth century Sir Francis Bacon wrote:

> Because the acts or events of true history have not that magnitude which satisfieth the mind of man, poesy feigneth acts and events greater and more heroical. Because true history propoundeth the successes and issues of actions not so agreeable to the merits of virtue and vice, therefore poesy feigns them more just in retribution, and more according to revealed providence. Because true history representeth actions and events more ordinary and less interchanged, therefore poesy endueth them with more rareness, and more unexpected and alternative variations.[19]

Although this passage concerns nondramatic literature and was written long before true heroic drama appeared, Bacon's wording suggests a number of the stylistic traits of heroic drama. In particular, "more just" suggests the idea of poetic justice and "more . . . alternative" suggests the artificial antitheses between love and honor and the artificial parallelism between the hero and his confidant.

The fact that it is Sir Francis Bacon writing hints at the quasi-scientific basis for the idealizations of the heroic style which made the style so congenial to the scientific spirit of the late seventeenth century. The neatness of the love-honor conflicts reminds one of the neatness of scientific descriptions, particularly that most characteristic of seventeenth-century inventions, the two-dimensional coordinate system for the graphical representation of processes. The happy ending embodies a facile Leibnitzian faith in an ordered, scientific universe where "everything is for the best." The heroic drama also emphasizes a crude but scientific psychology: the characters discuss quite transparently their own reactions to the choices and stimuli presented to them by external reality. They are, *ad nauseam*, "motivated." In short, the idealizations and simplifications of the heroic style corresponded to the first steps the new science was taking.

Bacon's description, however congenial it was to the scientific spirit of the age, had a bona fide literary ancestry. He was probably following Sidney, who, in turn following the Italian critics of the Renaissance, had set forth the same idea: "Nature never set forth the earth in so rich tapestry, as divers Poets have done. . . . Her world is brasen, the Poets only deliver a golden." [20] The faith in idealizing that underlies the heroic style seems ultimately to come from a misunderstanding of Aristotle. "Since tragedy," he wrote, "is a representation of men better than ourselves we must copy the good portrait painters who, while rendering the individual outline and making likenesses, yet paint people better than they are." "Since the poet represents life, as a painter does or any other maker of likenesses, he must always represent one of three things — either things as they were or are; or things as they are said and seem to be; or things as they should be." "In the Characters there are four points to aim at. First and foremost, that they shall be good." All three of these passages are hard to translate. In the first, from the context, it would seem that Aristotle was saying that the poet must give his personages a quality that would make the audience identify themselves with them. In the second, "they should be," could equally mean, "as it is necessary (for the sake of the poem) for them to be." The Greek for "good" in the third passage is δικε, which could equally well be interpreted as "good for some purpose." [21]

These nuances of translation, however, slipped right by the theorists of heroic drama. "Heroick *Poesie,*" wrote Rapin, its great apologist,

> proposes the Example of great Virtues, and great Vices, to excite Men to abhor these, and to be in love with the other.
>
> The Value of *Heroick Poesie* is yet more *high* by the *Matter,* and by its *End,* than by its *Form;* it discourses not but of *Kings* and Princes; it gives not *Lessons* but to the Grandees to govern the People, and sets before them the *Idea* of a *Virtue* much more perfect than *History* can do; for *History* proposes not *Virtue,* but *imperfect* as it is found in the *particulars;* and *Poetry* proposes it free from all *Imperfections,* and as it ought to be in *general,* and in the *abstract.* This made *Aristotle* confess, *That* Poesie *is a better School of Virtue, than* Philosophy *it self,* because it goes more directly to Perfection by the verisimility, than Philosophy can do with the *naked Truth.*[22]

He misreads and distorts Aristotle toward idealization. The passage to which Rapin refers appears in the *Poetics,* cap. ix, and says:

> The poet's function is to describe, not the thing that has happened, but a kind of thing that might happen, i.e. what is possible as being probable or necessary. The distinction between historian and poet . . . consists really in this, that the

one describes the thing that has been, and the other a kind of thing that might be. Hence poetry is something more philosophic and of graver import than history, since its statements are of the nature rather of universals, whereas those of history are singulars. By a universal statement I mean one as to what such or such a kind of man will probably or necessarily say or do — which is the aim of poetry, though it affixes proper names to the characters.[23]

Rapin saw the poet picturing ("by the verisimility") the image ("Idea") of virtue, "more *perfect,*" "*general,*" and "*abstract,*" than the historian. This is quite a different thing from Aristotle's "universal statement" which is about the actual nature of man, not a "more perfect" ideal.

Oddly enough, not only critics like Rapin, but dramatists seem to have taken this kind of quibble very seriously. Professor John C. Hodges' exciting literary detective work has brought to light the contents of William Congreve's library, which show rather graphically the importance of literary criticism and theory to a practicing dramatist.[24] Congreve owned three texts of Aristotle's *Rhetoric* (in Greek, Latin, and French) and three texts of the *Poetics* (in Latin, French, and English) with the leading commentaries of his day, that of Dacier and that of Rapin (translated by the English critic Thomas Rymer). I quoted from Rymer's Rapin's Aristotle in the preceding paragraph, but Congreve read at least two of the other critics mentioned in this chapter: Dryden (notes 9 and 13) and Corneille (note 26). His library of about 620 works contained thirty-eight titles of general literary criticism, and, if commentaries on specific books and authors are counted, the list grows to nearly one hundred. Thus, in a library mostly composed of poetry, plays, fiction, and books of voyages and history, nearly one book in six was literary theory or criticism.

This period is almost unique in the importance that practicing writers gave to critical theories. For the first time in England, practicing dramatists read, took to heart, and even wrote dramatic criticism.[25] The same thing was true in France. Thus, for example, the great tragic dramatist, Pierre Corneille, has left us what amounts to a picture of himself making exactly the misreading of Aristotle I have described.

[As for] the second part of a poem, which are the Characters [ἤθη] . . . Aristotle prescribes four requirements for them, that they be *good, appropriate, like, and consistent.* These terms he has explained so little that he leaves us considerable room for doubt as to what he meant.

I cannot see how some people have understood by that word *good* that they must be virtuous. Most poems, ancient just as much as modern, would be left in a pitiful state, if one took from them any characters one found that were evil, or vicious, or touched with some weakness that does not go well with virtue. . . . If I may state my own guesses as to what Aristotle requires of us in this respect, I think that it is a splendid and exalted character of a virtuous or criminal nature [*le caractère brillant & élevé d'une habitude vertueuse ou criminelle*] whichever is appropriate and expedient for the person being put on. . . . At the very moment one despises his actions, one admires the source from which they come. [My thought] is based on a passage in Aristotle that follows shortly after the one I am trying to explain. *Poetry,* he says, *is an imitation of people better than they are, and as painters often make flattering portraits, which are better looking than the original, but keep in every way the resemblance, so poets who represent angry or lazy men must draw an exalted idea* [haute idée] *of those qualities they give them, so that one will find there a good example of equanimity or sternness. It is thus that Homer made Achilles good.*

Still another thought occurs to me concerning what Aristotle meant by that goodness of character that he imposes as its first requirement. It is that it should be as virtuous as it can be, so that we will not show anything vicious or criminal on the stage if the subject we are treating does not require it. . . .

I find in Castelvetro a third explication that may be satisfactory, which is that this goodness of character applies only to the chief character who must always be likable and therefore virtuous, not to those who persecute him or cause him suffering: but since that is to limit to one what Aristotle said for all, I prefer, in understanding this first requirement, to limit myself to that elevation or perfection [*élévation ou perfection*] of character of which I have spoken and which can apply to all who appear on the stage.[26]

Corneille, both in his own words and his misquotations from Aristotle, reveals the tendency we have been talking about: poetry should show things as better than they are, as exalted and splendid. Moreover, Corneille spoke not just of tragedy, as Aristotle had, but of poetry generally.

Whether out of misunderstanding or simply because of the scientific temper of the times, Renaissance and neoclassical writers took Aristotle as justifying — even requiring — the improbable kind of exaggeration and idealization that was the heroic style. In the search for a technique of idealizing, English poets of the seventeenth century turned to their own ideals, the two literary models they admired most — classical literature, particularly the *Aeneid,* and contemporary French writing. Less obvious, but equally important as a source of style, was the scientific thought of the day with its faith in logical structure, systematic classification into genera, and "clear and distinct ideas." [27] It was felt that all poetry — that was not intentionally comic — ought to adopt the heroic manner, and thus this misunderstanding of Aristotle had effect long after the heroic plays to which it gave rise had been laughed off the stage. In neoclassic poetry the heroic style took the form of periphrasis, a verbal idealizing, for example, of grass into an "enamelled green," or a brook into a "crystal stream." The individual blades and tufts of grass, the irregular surface of the brook, details thought unessential, were smoothed off in the manner of scientific abstraction or what was thought to be the manner of Virgil.[28]

The heroic play is a peculiar, even if logical aberration for an age that prided itself on "sense" and cynicism. The Restoration is without any question the most depraved period in English social history (at least among the upper classes); it is not a little puzzling, therefore, that the rakes of Restoration London found enjoyment in a stylized, exaggerated representation of ideal virtue. One answer, and one that is not as foolish as it sounds, is that the heroic drama, to some people at least, was a colossal joke. While some writers and some people in the audience took it seriously, possibly other members of the public saw the absurdity and other writers such as Etherege capitalized on it. I was privileged to see in the spring of 1954 a performance of Dryden and Purcell's *King Arthur* by the Lowell House Opera Society. The twentieth-century Harvard audience found the heroics almost intolerably ludicrous; it is hard to believe that an even more sophisticated seventeenth-century audience, composed of such rakes as Rochester, Sedley, or Dorset, took them seriously. "I have observed," says Dryden's Lisideius (Sedley) in *An Essay of Dramatic Poesy*, "that in all our tragedies, the audience cannot forbear laughing when the actors are to die; it is the most comic part of the whole play."[29] It seems at least possible that the only reason the heroic plays lasted as long as they did on the stage was the low acumen of the Restoration audience: to those members of the audience who were more astute these plays must have been rather funny.

In any case, whether or not the audience found the *plays* absurd, the heroic *style* was fairly bursting with absurd possibilities. A comic dramatist could write a funny play simply by exaggerating the heroic manner a little bit. He could add to the humor by providing a realistic low plot to contrast with the idealized heroic high plot. Finally, he could give his play some solidity by providing a golden mean about which the high and low plots could fluctuate. And that is precisely what Sir George Etherege did, in the first Restoration comedy to set a style which later writers followed.

3 • *The Comical Revenge; or, Love in a Tub*

By March 1664 the theaters had been open for well over four years following the so-called dramatic interregnum. Yet scarcely a half-dozen new comedies had emerged to interrupt the revivals of Fletcher, Shakespeare, and Jonson that filled the stages, and none of these had caught the fancy of Restoration audiences enough to set a new style. There survived only Dryden's device of witty lovers from *The Wild Gallant* (February 1663), probably suggested by Nell Gwyn and her then lover, Charles Hart, of the Theatre Royal. The first new comedy to provoke real imitation was Sir George Etherege's *The Comical Revenge.*

Of Etherege the man, little is known. A gay, handsome individual, who spoiled his looks with drinking, he was a wit of the court circle who turned his hand to playwriting as a gentlemanly thing to do and wrote no more than the gentlemanly number of three plays. James II appointed him envoy to the Diet in Ratisbon, where he misbehaved in a gentlemanly manner, complained of Lady Etherege (apparently a shrew whom he had married for money), and found solace with a young comedienne stranded in the Low Countries. After the Glorious Revolution, he was, of course, replaced. He cast his lot with the Stuarts, went to France, and apparently never returned to England. He died in the early nineties; neither the date nor the place are known. Although to modern eyes his first play looks anything but promising, "The clean and well performance of this Comedy," wrote the prompter, John Downes, "got the Company more reputation and profit than any preceding Comedy; the Company taking in a month's time at it 1000£." [1]

The Comical Revenge has three plots, high, low, and middle. The high plot, in neat couplets and even neater patterns of love, honor, and confidants, follows the crossed loves of Lord Beaufort and Colonel Bruce for Graciana, and the unrequited love of Graciana's sister, Aurelia, for Bruce. In the middle plot, Sir Frederick Frollick, Beaufort's cousin, lackadaisically pursues the Widow Rich, Graciana and Aurelia's aunt. The low plot shows Wheadle, a rogue acquaintance of Sir Frederick's, and Palmer, a card-sharper, swindling a Cromwellian knight named Sir

Nicholas Cully. In the incident — one cannot call it a plot — that gives the play its title, Betty, the widow's maid, lures and locks Sir Frederick's valet, the Frenchman Dufoy, into a tub. (A sweating-tub was the usual seventeenth-century remedy for Dufoy's "French disease.")

Most commentators on this play dismiss the heroics of the high plot as irrelevant — "obviously out of the picture," or "out of keeping with the rest of the play." "We turn from one to the other," says one critic of a similarly bifurcated play, "as a music-hall audience will welcome the alternation of bawdry and sentiment." [2] More important, however, is the fact that the high heroic drama and the low farce interact, each making the other more meaningful. "The clash," Mr. Empson notes of Dryden's similarly hybrid *Marriage à la Mode*, "makes both conventions less unreal; . . . it has a more searching effect, almost like parody, by making us see they are unreal." [3] Certainly the high plot is not the main plot, as many writers seem to think. On the contrary, more than twice as many scenes and two and a half times as many lines are given to the low plots as to the romantic, heroic plot. The play opens and closes with Sir Frederick.[4]

The high plot of *The Comical Revenge* idealizes and exaggerates in pure heroic style. The story concerns Cavalier bravery and romance. Both Lord Beaufort and Colonel Bruce love Graciana, while Graciana's sister Aurelia loves Colonel Bruce. The colonel returns from imprisonment by the Roundheads to find Graciana in love with Beaufort. He therefore challenges Beaufort; on the field, these gallant enemies unite to drive off some treacherous Cromwellian assassins pursuing Bruce and then return to their fight. Beaufort wins the duel but spares the colonel's life. The colonel, then, despairing of Graciana, falls on his sword and the doctor pronounces him certain to die. Graciana decides she ought to be in love with Colonel Bruce and therefore spurns Beaufort, who despairs. Meanwhile Aurelia reveals her love for Bruce and he reciprocates, at which point "the wound/ By abler Chyr'gions is not mortal found," and confessions match the proper pairs.

It is somewhat puzzling that a man of "easie" George Etherege's urbanity could write this sort of thing. Etherege was a comic writer, and nothing could be farther from the multiple perspectives of comedy than the single-minded admiration of the heroic manner. Possibly, as I suggested in the preceding chapter, Etherege and his friends found the heroic manner funny in and of itself. But whether they did or not, Etherege plays the high plot of *The Comical Revenge* off against the lower plots to develop Sir Frederick Frollick's role as a realistic but golden mean.

Frollick, being somewhat of a roisterer, beats up the widow's quarters with a drunken serenade by way of showing his affection; she puts him off, however. He acts as second for Beaufort in the high-plot duel, and has himself carried in as though dead to make the widow reveal her love, but she sees through his ruse in time. He then pretends to be arrested for a debt and the widow pays it, thus committing herself. After much verbal play and pretended indifference, Sir Frederick and the widow are finally matched. As a ludicrous parallel to their courtship, Betty, the widow's maid, locks the neck of Sir Frederick's valet into a great tub, which Dufoy must then carry about with him like a snail's shell.

Strange as it may seem, Sir Frederick is the one breath of common sense in the high plot, as, for example, when, after Colonel Bruce has fallen on his sword, he prevents Bruce's second from doing the same so as to complete the stylized heroic pattern. Sir Frederick says simply, "The Frollick's not to go round, as I take it" (55).[5] "I mistrust your Mistresses Divinity," he answers to one of Beaufort's exalted love-speeches. "You'l find her Attributes but Mortal: Women, like Juglers Tricks, appear Miracles to the ignorant; but in themselves th'are meer cheats" (7). "What news from the God of Love?" he cries to Beaufort's servant, "he's always at your Master's elbow, h'as jostl'd the Devil out of service; no more! Mrs. *Grace!* Poor Girl, Mrs. *Graciana* has flung a squib into his bosome, where the wild-fire will huzzéé for a time, and then crack; it fly's out at's Breeches" (3). The hint that Beaufort knew the wench Grace somewhat better than his high-flown heroics warrant (see also 7) and these various contrasts — physical sex as opposed to spiritual love, the devil as opposed to the god of love, firecrackers as opposed to the flames of love, Grace the wench as opposed to Graciana the heroine — run throughout the play and make up the antiheroic humor.

Sir Frederick is also the one who straightens out the complexities of the low plot. Wheadle, an acquaintance of Frollick's, and Palmer, another crony, disguised as a sheep-farmer, cheat Sir Nicholas Cully at cards. Cully refuses to pay his losses, and Palmer challenges him. In the field, Cully's cowardice forces him to sign a judgment for the amount. Wheadle, at this point, promises to mend his fortunes by introducing him to the Widow Rich (actually Wheadle's mistress Grace in disguise). Cully, however, blunders in on the real Widow Rich, roaring like Sir Frederick. The real Sir Frederick rescues both her and Sir Nicholas by blackmailing the sharpers out of the debt and into marrying: Wheadle to Grace, and Palmer — and Sir Nicholas — to his own ex-mistresses.

Just as Sir Frederick is contrasted by his common sense and earthiness to Beaufort, his counterpart in the high plot, he is, as an urbane, brave, amorous Cavalier, the opposite of the countrified, Cromwellian knight

Cully, the fake Frollick of the low plot. Just as Sir Frederick wittily reveals the unreality of the high plot with his skepticism, he brings to the intrigues of the low characters a semblance of honor and mercy. " 'Tis fit this Rascal shou'd be cheated; but these Rogues will deal too unmercifully with him: I'le take compassion upon him, and use him more favourably my self" (73), he says, as he decides to marry Cully off to his ex-mistress. The fact that it is Sir Frederick who puts Cully in his place, Professor Underwood points out, establishes a sense of "degree" between "hero and dupe, wit and fool, gentleman and fop." The applicability of the word "degree" here shows how this typical trick of Restoration comedy relates to traditional medieval and Renaissance values.[6]

Even so, lest Sir Frederick be taken too seriously, there is always his own ludicrous counterpart, Dufoy, who puts a comic perspective on even the golden mean. Not all the antiheroic contrasts are channeled through Sir Frederick, moreover. Palmer ironically pretends to be a virtuous Loyalist like Colonel Bruce (32), and Wheadle compares the dueling-field to a sheep-field (29). Palmer can speak the heroic cant of the high plot as he complains of his lack of business:

> I protest I had rather still be vicious
> Then Owe my Virtue to Necessity. (9)

The widow (who "must needs have furious flames," 16) is a comic compromise between the virginal heroines of the high plot and the wenches of the low — a woman sexually experienced, but not immorally so. High and low scenes are contrasted individually: III. v, the cowardly duel, to III. vi *et seqq.*, the honorable duel; the incident of a letter supplies a bridge between low I. iii and heroic I. iv; the mention of love-wounds brings the audience from Aurelia's unrequited worship in I. iv to Dufoy's syphilis in II. i.

As all this talk of wounds suggests, the whole play is a set of variations on the theme of hostility. Sir Frederick's debauches set the keynote; as described in the opening scene they consist of brawls with watchmen and constables, "beating up" a lady's quarters, breaking windows, and the like. Counterattacks take place in the morning: "De divil také mé," announces Dufoy in his French dialect, "if daré be not de whole Regiment Army de Hackené Cocheman, de Linke-boy, de Fydler, and de Shamber-maydé, dat havé beseegé de howsé" (3). Love, in particular, is compared over and over to fighting. In the high plot, the metaphor takes the form of a stale Petrarchanism — the victory of the mistress' eyes over the lover (17, 34, 46, 56, 57, 63). "Beauty's but an offensive dart; / It is no Armour for the heart" (76). In the low and middle plots, however, the metaphor becomes an anti-ideal, a reference to the sexual duel: "I have not fenc'd of late," says Sir Frederick, "unless it were with my Widows Maids; and they are e'en too hard for me at my own weapon" (47). Grace, when she is trapping Sir Nicholas, must "lye at a little opener ward" (78). Sir Frederick mocks the convention when he raids the widow's home in the middle of the night: "Alas, what pains I take thus to unclose/ Those pretty eye-lids which lock'd up my Foes!" (31). In the high plot, love is the heart-wound inflicted by the mistress' conquering eyes (63, 64), but Dufoy's wound is far more realistic. He expains it in a dialogue with Beaufort's servant:

Dufoy. . . . it be de voundé dat my Metresse did give me long agoe.
Clark. What? some pretty little English Lady's crept into your heart?
Duf. No, but damn'd littel English Whore is creepé into my bone begar. (14)

This colloquy is immediately preceded by a soliloquy in the high plot in which Aurelia mourns the wounds Bruce has inflicted on her heart (13), wounds she later refers to as her "disease" (22).

Hostility exists not just between lovers: love itself and all passions are essentially hostile influences, flaming arrows (63) or flames (46) that burn and torture the heart (63). Passions assault (19); they raise a tempest in the mind (44) that tosses and tumbles the individual until difficulties are resolved and love reaches its expression in marriage:

Thus mariners rejoyce when winds decrease,
And falling waves seem wearied into Peace. (82)

Nor is dueling the only metaphor in the lower plots for the hostilities associated with love. Sir Frederick describes his courtship of the widow as fishing (8) and the sharpers in the low plot use exactly the same metaphor for their swindle (11), and refer to it also as trapping (9, 78). The ideas of tricking and courtship are linked again when Sir Frederick disguises fiddlers as bailiffs and tricks the widow into bailing him out, thereby swindling her: "Nay, I know th'art spiteful," he laughs, "and wou'dst fain marry me in revenge; but so long as I have these Guardian Angels about me, I defie thee and all thy Charms: Do skilful Faulkners thus reward their Hawks before they fly the Quarry?" (82). (The pun on "angels" as coins is only one of many parodies of the religious imagery in the high plot.) Instead of revenge taking the form of a duel, as in the high plots, in the middle plot the widow retains her estate when Sir Frederick marries her for it; that is one "comical revenge" (Epilogue) and Betty's locking Dufoy into a tub is another.

With marrying for money in mind, Etherege supplies his characters with gambling, as well as swindling, as a metaphor for courtship and marriage. "Do you imagine me so foolish as your self," the widow asks of Sir Frederick, referring to the money of which he has cheated her, "who often venture all at play, to recover one inconsiderable parcel?" (83) Sir Frederick's debt is a parody of the obligations ("debts," 64, 65, 77, 85) of love and honor in the high plot. Just as Beaufort can speak of his "claim" or "title" to Graciana (45), so Wheadle can call his illicit relationship with Grace, making "bold, like a young Heir, with his Estate, before it come into his hands" (80). This "conversion downward" of abstractions to matter, of people to things — Sir Frederick's former mistresses to furniture (84) or old gowns (85), the soul to body (42), reputation to a possession (5), and the like — becomes a major component of the antiheroic jokes of Restoration comedy, a metaphorical form of hostility.

Love, in the high plot, is divine, a kind of religious devotion to the loved one (45), directed by the god of love (12, 45, 81), for passion is too much for mere mortals to control (43). By contrast to this febrile neoplatonism, the low plot takes place in the "Devil" inn (10), using the "Devil's bones" (27), i.e., dice. The "hell" of the low plot is dramatized as complete pretense. One disguise follows another and the basest motives are tricked out as love, friendship, or honor. The high plot lacks any pretense. Every emotion is on the surface, to be talked about, analyzed, displayed. It is as though Etherege were trying "to express the motions of the spirits, and the affections or passions whose center is the heart," trying "in a word, *to make the soul visible.*" (These phrases come from a treatise on painting that Dryden translated for its insights into poetry.)[7] In the high plot, there is no body; the fact that "the Parenchyma of the right lobe of the lungs, near some large branch of the *Aspera arteria*, is perforated" must never intrude upon "Those flames my tortur'd breast did long conceal" (63). As opposed to the low plot, the heroics are only a different kind of incompleteness.

Between this bodiless heaven and soulless hell stands Sir Frederick Frollick, complete because he partakes of both sides. He cuts through the pretenses of both high and low, but is in turn capable of both kinds of conduct, honorable dueling or drunken battles with constables and bailiffs, which are called his "Heroick actions" (6).

Thus, an elaborate set of contrasts and parallels establishes the somewhat doubtful merits of Sir Frederick Frollick as a golden mean and casts a comic perspective on the doings of all the characters, both high and low. There are the parallel duels, one the paragon of honor, the other of dishonor. There are the parallel near-deaths, Bruce's real and Sir Frederick's pretended one, both of which result in declarations of love later recalled. There are the parallel "revenges": Betty the maid taunts Dufoy the valet for his disease as the widow taunts Sir Frederick for his promiscuity; the maid drugs the valet and locks him in a tub, while the mistress makes her admirer fall in love, and locks him into marriage. All four plot lines are united by the faintest hint of a comic version of death and resurrection. Each one of the men must be laid low before the final matches can take place: Sir Frederick has himself brought in as though dead; Sir Nicholas falls into a drunken stupor and wakes to find himself about to receive Sir Frederick's Lucy in marriage; Dufoy is drugged so Betty can lock him into the tub; and Colonel Bruce is nearly killed before Aurelia declares her love. These absurd deaths-and-rebirths fit into what Professor Underwood sees as the basic comic action of Restoration comedy, which, he says, Etherege developed in this play: the protagonist (Sir Frederick — or Sir Nicholas or Colonel Bruce or Dufoy) aspires to a love or libertinism beyond his "degree," falls (dies) through this pride, and is regenerated by compromise.[8] We might say the hero dies and is reborn at a more reasonable level.

Thus, in the much-maligned scene (IV.vii) where Sir Frederick pretends to be dead to trick the widow into declaring her love, the action runs the whole gamut from utter heroic down to utter antiheroic and comes up again to the middle note. The intrigue is admittedly not very sophisticated, but the scene is central to the structure of the play. In the scene immediately preceding it, Betty locked the drugged Dufoy into the tub. A messenger from the field of honor goes before Sir Frederick's corpse to announce in solemn poesy the "bloody consequence" of the duel. The widow drops social restraint and reveals her love. "The World's too poor to recompense this loss," she cries, but just as Sir Frederick is about to be elevated to the role of Everyman, Dufoy enters, grotesquely locked in his tub, and frightens everyone away with *his* cries of distress at his master's death. Sir Frederick starts up, and the fact of death against which the widow's pretense of indifference had collapsed shrinks again to comic size: "Farewell, Sir;" laughs the widow, "expect at night to see the old man, with his paper Lanthorn and crack'd Spectacles, singing your woful Tragedy to Kitchin-maids and Coblers Prentices," and the love-duel resumes. The scene ranges in fifty-six lines from high plot to low.

As this sample shows, the play seems neither overpoweringly funny, nor startlingly new. It uses a number of Restoration devices developed before 1664: the witty lovers, the concentration upon the upper class, and the cynical, competent rake-hero. In many ways, moreover, it stands closer to Tudor-Stuart dramatic techniques than to those of the Restoration, particularly in the religious imagery of the high plot and the extended use of parallelism and analogy. Nevertheless, the play did, for those who first saw it, define a new comedy. Although the dominant humor of this new comedy was to be antiheroic, its techniques grow from the same sense of schism that shows in the rigid patterns of love and honor in heroic drama and the antithetical structure of heroic verse. Its cynicism is that of a disappointed idealist. Things are either perfect or awful: the hero, if he cannot be a heroic Cavalier, becomes a rake.

This antiheroic comedy found three characteristic devices of language and action. First, love is shown with a strong component of hostility or reluctance (a comic and truer version of the artificial love-honor conflicts of heroic drama). The lovers engage in a verbal duel, pretending indifference and comparing themselves to adversaries. Second, abstractions and ideals are converted downward into physical realities: love into sex, reputation into a possession, and so on. Finally, the outer appearance of a thing or person and its inner nature are shown as separate, indeed, inconsistent, and this division is seen as usually true, not an aberration that the action of the play corrects. The cuckold is not given justice as he would be in an Elizabethan play; rather Cully must set out to pass Frollick's ex-mistress off as an honest lady to his country neighbors.

Although *The Way of the World,* written nearly forty years later, is a far more subtle and complex piece, these three elements of Etherege's first play still pervade it. "The Coldness of a losing Gamester lessens the Pleasure of the Winner," says the villain in what is almost the opening speech, "I'd no more play with a Man that slighted his ill Fortune than I'd make Love to a Woman who undervalu'd the Loss of her Reputation." First, there is the sarcastic sense of hostility: love is a winning against the woman-opponent. Second, the speaker converts reputation downward into something monetary that can be priced and wagered. Third, he tacitly assumes that reputation (an appearance) is normally inconsistent with the woman's "natural" desires. Unpromising as it is, *The Comical Revenge* sounded the authentic triad.

4 • *She Wou'd If She Cou'd*

It was nearly four years before Etherege brought out his second play. In his entry for February 6, 1668, Pepys describes the opening run:

I to the Duke of York's playhouse; where a new play of Etherige's, called "She Would if she Could;" and though I was there by two o'clock, there was 1000 people put back that could not have room in the pit: and I at last, because my wife was there made shift to get into the 18 *d.* box, and there saw; but, Lord! how full was the house, and how silly the play, there being nothing in the world good in it, and few people pleased in it. The King was there; but I sat mightily behind, and could see but little, and hear not at all. The play being done, I into the pit to look [for] my wife, and it being dark and raining, I to look my wife out, but could not find her; and so staid going between the two doors and through the pit an hour and half, I think, after the play was done; the people staying there till the rain was over, and to talk with one another. And, among the rest, here was the Duke of Buckingham to-day openly sat in the pit; and there I found him with my Lord Buckhurst, and Sidly, and Etherige, the poet; the last of whom I did hear mightily find fault with the actors, that they were out of humour, and had not their parts perfect, and that Harris did do nothing, nor could so much as sing a ketch in it; and so was mightily concerned: while all the rest did through the whole pit, blame the play as a silly, dull thing, though there was something very roguish and witty; but the design of the play, and end, mighty insipid.[1]

A rival playwright, though, Thomas Shadwell, wrote in the preface to his own *The Humorists* (1671), "I think (and I have the Authority of some of the best Judges in *England* for't), [it] is the best Comedy that has been written since the Restauration of the Stage."[2] Even though Shadwell was writing before Restoration comedy had reached a very high level, I fear that Pepys, for once in his life, was right in his critical judgment.

Nevertheless, Etherege had come a step closer to what was to become the final Restoration style. That is, *She wou'd if she cou'd* does not make its point by the contrast between high and low plots as Elizabethan or Jacobean drama — or *The Comical Revenge* — did. Instead, it concentrates on the one plot of matching two pairs of witty lovers. Further, *She wou'd if she cou'd* presupposes a fundamental split in human beings between appearance and nature, between social requirements and "natural" desires. The basic theme of the play, its sense of humor, thus becomes the contrast between liberty and restraint. "The Town" in the play stands for a place big enough, offering enough opportunities for anonymity, so that social restrictions do not really interfere with natural desires. Conversely, the country stands for a place where close observation makes social restrictions impinge directly on natural desires. In the town, private self and social self can be quite separated; in the country they cannot. The town thus suggests liberty, and the country, restraint. Similarly, gallantry and flirtation are associated with the town and liberty; marriage becomes associated with confinement and the country. Country restraints are permanent; one only lends oneself to such town requirements as clothing, conversation, or disguise. Thus, plot, symbols, and action all grow from the fundamental assumption that there is a deep division between social and "natural" man.[3]

As the play opens, two young gallants, Courtall and his friend Freeman, are interrupted in their search for "new game" by Mrs. Sentry, who tells Courtall that her mistress, Lady Cockwood, has come back to town and is eagerly looking forward to seeing him. Courtall has so far managed to avoid satisfying the lady's importunities, and to escape her attentions this time he pleads an engagement to meet her henpecked husband, Sir Oliver Cockwood, and his drinking companion, Sir Joslin Jolly, both of whom are eager to run riot after their release from the country. While Courtall and Freeman are on their way, they meet and are charmed by two witty and handsome girls in masks. When the two gallants are brought to Lady Cockwood's by the two drunken country knights, they find these young ladies are Sir Joslin's nieces Ariana and Gatty, who, also feeling suddenly liberated from the restraints of the country, had been taking the liberty of the town. After a number of meetings during Sir Oliver's alternate drinking bouts and penances and Lady Cockwood's schemes to consummate her relation with Courtall, the two gallants become thoroughly enamoured of the girls. Lady Cockwood sees that they are and angrily realizes why she and Courtall never seem to find an opportunity. She sends forged letters to antagonize the couples, meanwhile assuring Sir Oliver that Courtall has made her dishonorable proposals. Despite the confusion, Courtall adroitly figures out what is going on, and maneuvers Lady Cockwood into a position where she is forced to let the young romances take their course. The girls finally agree to accept their suitors on a month's probation.

As one might surmise from the plot, there is one "natural" desire which is constant for every character — almost the only one: the desire for sexual gratification. And this desire is constant regardless of outward differences between town people or country people, between Lady Cockwood's pretenses to honor or Sir Joslin's frank vulgarity. It is conspicuously true of all the women in the play, to any one of whom the title *She wou'd if she cou'd* applies. Moreover, each character assumes that sexual desire is the major motive in any action by another. Ariana and Gatty suspect Lady Cockwood's affair with a gallant as she does theirs; Sir Oliver assumes Lady Cockwood is motivated by desire—his only mistake is that he thinks he is to be the instrument of her gratification; Sir Joslin introduces the lovers to each other on strictly physical terms; Lady Cockwood even suspects Sentry of trying to take Courtall away from her. The characters express this indiscriminate sexuality in animal terms. A lover is to his mistress as a spaniel (155) or as horses are to a coach (98).[4] A jealous woman is like a bloodhound (142). "I was married to her when I was young, *Ned*," sighs the restless Sir Oliver, "with a design to be baulk'd, as they tye Whelps to the Bell-weather; where I have been so butted, 'twere enough to fright me, were I not pure mettle, from ever running at sheep again" (137).

Birds are the most common symbol for this animality. Thus, Courtall describes himself as an "old Fowler" (151), and Gatty compares him to a kite looking for poultry (154). The belligerent little oldsters, Sir Oliver and Sir Joslin, think of themselves as game-cocks (101, 131) and Sir Joslin even swears: "If I ever break my word with a Lady, . . . she shall have leave to carve me for a Capon" (100). Like Courtall, Lady Cockwood pursues and is a "kite" (59), and "old Haggard" (122), even an old hen, to whom the girls are chicks (130). The girls themselves are birds in a cage (103), whereas whores are "ravenous Cormorants" (140). Courtall calls the pursuit of Ariana and Gatty going "a birding" (155); "Are you so wild," asks Freeman, comparing the masked girls in the park to falcons, "that you must be hooded thus?" (107). The play makes this one joke over and over—its theme, insofar as this play has a satirical theme: the absurdity of a two-legged animal's pretending its animal desires are something better. A curious comparison presents itself at this point. As Professor G. Wilson Knight points out in an entertaining appendix called "The Shakespearian Aviary," Shakespeare also uses birds frequently.[5] "Such images and impressions," writes Professor Knight, "occur mainly in direct relation to all essences which may be, metaphorically, considered ethereal and volatile. Bird-life suggests flight and freedom and swiftness: it also often suggests pride." For Etherege, birds are just another two-legged animal. The difference, in a sense, epitomizes what had happened to English drama.

Etherege portrays love in this play, as in *The Comical Revenge,* as various antagonisms. Thus, the love-chase is a naval battle (106) or land war (118): the gallants are military strategists (105) and the girls mere soldiers (105) to whom they ultimately surrender (109). Even Sir

Oliver and Sir Joslin are "mighty men at Arms" ready to "charge anon to the terrour of the Ladies" (132), for whoring requires courage (138). In this terminology, a billet-doux is a challenge, an assignation a duel (156), and so on. In another form of sex-antagonism, the pursuit of the opposite sex is "hunting" (91, 101, 104, 106, 107) or hawking or horse-breaking (92) or fishing, the girls being "young Trouts" (121). In a set of monetary comparisons, sex is a "trade" (91, 119, 131, 175), "gambling" (98, 128, 168), swindling (104), or lawsuits (150): thus, Courtall speaks of Lady Cockwood's sexual forwardness as trying to arrest him for debt (153). Etherege so proliferates this kind of unfavorable comparison that it almost seems to lose any kind of pattern or direction: love (or sex) is acting a part in a play (121), alchemical projecting (151), an execution (131), a stain (168), or a fever (169); a woman is something to be eaten (153, 178), or even read (155). The same disparagement applies to marriage: it is a duel (176) to which the proposal is the challenge. It is a business enterprise (103, 174), a mortgaging of one's person to acquire an estate; courtship is simply negotiating the contract (174). Nevertheless, these comparisons, even as varied and as proliferated as they are, do show a pattern. In every case, the basis for the comparison is that the individual is about to accept an apparent restraint in order to satisfy his real natural desires. In a sense, he must obey "the rules of the game" to achieve satisfaction: in this respect, love and marriage can be thought of as acting or bargaining or lawsuits, even as alchemy. Etherege is simply saying metaphorically that a fine gallant hates falling in love, for then he must restrain his liberty: "All the happiness a Gentleman can desire, is to live at liberty" (174).

This theme of liberty and restraint — the most basic theme of the play — is organized about various contrasts. One such contrast is that between sexual animality and falling in love. Another such contrast is that between town and country. Indeed, the action of *She wou'd if she cou'd* is simply that of country people (the Cockwoods, Jolly, and his nieces) adventuring into the wider scope and complexity of London. The difference between town and country shows itself in the form of intrigue. "There is some weighty affair in hand, I warrant thee: my dear *Ariana,* how glad am I we are in this Town agen," cries Gatty as she infers an intrigue from Lady Cockwood's behavior (102). "A man had better be a vagabond in this Town, than a Justice of Peace in the Country," says Sir Oliver, summing up the difference between them. "If a man do but rap out an Oath, the people start as if a Gun went off; and if one chance but to couple himself with his Neighbours Daughter without the help of the Parson of the Parish, . . . there is presently such an uproar, that a poor man is fain to fly his Country" (93). The difference, in other words, is that the country allows little or no scope for a personal life. There is no privacy: observation is so close that one's nature cannot be given free play, but is bound in tightly by social restrictions. Petty pretenses, like a child's, are the only escape.

In the town, on the other hand, pretenses become large and graceful responses to convention, ends in themselves because the town is large enough and anonymous enough for a person's outward appearance and private life to be quite separated. By being separated, each becomes important in and of itself. Clothing, for example, assumes a new importance in the town. Lady Cockwood can severely restrict Sir Oliver's activities by locking up all but his "Penitential Suit" (127ff.) A face is like a hat (107); an affair to Freeman is like putting on a new suit (97); and a lover, to the girls, runs in one's head like a new gown (168). A woman is known simply as her mask and her petticoat (103, 131). In the town, appearances, because they are separated from the private self, have a separate existence all their own.

The humor of the play lies in the contrast between what the young people do with the liberty of the town and what their elders do with it. Lady Cockwood makes herself ridiculous by pursuing Courtall, and Sir Oliver and Sir Joslin make themselves ridiculous by their sophomoric debauches, while the young people use their liberty to fall in love. Their doing so does not mean they are wiser. On the contrary, they have simply used their freedom to exchange it for confinement; they have ceased being "Tenants at Will" and have bound themselves to a "Lease for life" (174). Accepting confinement means letting oneself in for pretense, because confinement creates a tension between the "natural" self and the outward, social self, and that tension in turn creates a need to deceive others. Thus, Ariana and Gatty disguise themselves to flirt in the Mulberry Garden and resent the social rules that deny them the same liberties as men. Thus, too, Sir Oliver pretends fidelity to escape and resents Lady Cockwood who, by restraining him, creates the need for pretense. In this way, the Cockwood marriage operates not by love but power politics. Sir Oliver tries to establish himself as a monarch (114, 115) or "tyrant" (96) controlling the "politicians," his wife and Mrs. Sentry. Sentry's name, of course, is significant and Sir Oliver's might be a reminiscence of the Civil War. At any rate, domestic altercations are called "civil war" (137) and infidelities, whether Sir Oliver's or Courtall's, "treason" (139, 144). They are put down, however, and in the finale Lady Cockwood is cast as a restored monarch bestowing an "Act of Oblivion" (176) and marching Sir Oliver off to bed where "we'll sign the Peace" (179). Even the young lovers at this early stage of their relation are subject to power politics. Courtall and Freeman are to Gatty and Ariana as subjects are to rulers, or indeed to "absolute Tyrants" (103).

The play, however, develops one important difference between the old pretenders and the young. Sir Oliver and Lady Cockwood have been pretending so long and so hard that the inconsistency between their inner natures and outer appearances has confused them and corrupted the expression of their real selves. The two overtones in their name suggest this confusion, Cockwood, expressing sexual desire, and "woodcock," the bird proverbial for stupidity. Lady Cockwood, even in her private interviews with Courtall, cannot put aside her pretenses to honor (as in II.ii, for example.) Even when they are alone, she scolds Sentry for neglecting to chaperone her, and Sentry apologizes for her: "This is a strange infirmity she has, [but] custom has made it so natural, she cannot help it" (113). Sir Oliver's continual pretense of affection and respect to his lady has mixed his inner and outer selves, too, so that he can no longer satisfy his desires for other game. His riots are tainted with the impotency that his relations with Lady Cockwood bring out ("The very sight of that face makes me more impotent than an Eunuch"—114). Thus, his amours in the play are uniformly failures; even his desires are limited: "When we visit a Miss,/ We still brag how we kiss,/ But 'tis with a Bottle we fegue her" (141). He pretends to his wife (to whom he should not have to pretend at all) that he is more virtuous than he is and to the world that he is more vicious.

This, then, is what is laughable about the older people: that they let their social pretenses creep into private affairs where they do not belong. The difference between them and the young people shows in the two "hiding" scenes. In the first (I.i), Mrs. Sentry, who has come to tell Courtall of the Cockwoods' arrival, is forced to hide when Sir Oliver comes, and overhears him invite the young men to a wild evening. Only confusion results from Lady Cockwood's learning of this, because, since both Cockwoods are pretending to each other, she cannot admit to her knowledge. In the later hiding scene (V.i), when Courtall and Freeman overhear the girls solving the problem of the forged letters, the result is to give both sides the knowledge to break down the barriers Lady Cockwood put between them. The lovers can use their knowledge because they are completely aware of the line where social pretense leaves off and plain dealing begins. The young people use pretense without being dominated by it, and their sense of appropriateness is the screen against which most of the wit sallies are projected. The young people are as aware of their double selves as an actor in a part and, indeed, Gatty uses the metaphor: "I hate to dissemble when I need not; 'twou'd look as affected in us to be reserv'd now w'are alone, as for a Player to maintain the Character she acts in the Tyring-room" (170). "A single intrigue in Love," says Courtall, "is as dull as a single Plot in a Play, and will tire a Lover worse, than t'other does an Audience." "We cannot be long without some under-plots in this Town," replies Freeman, "let this be our main design, and if we are anything fortunate in our contrivance, we shall make it a pleasant Comedy" (121). Two acts of frankness in friendship are what break through the outer barriers of pretense and resolve the intrigue, such as it is. "Let us proceed honestly like Friends, discover the truth of things to one another," says Freeman, and the two gallants find to their good fortune that they are pursuing different women (152). Similarly, it is Ariana's and Gatty's frank talk (168) that clears up the business of the forged letters. In broader terms, the lovers know that appearance and nature are necessarily different; they know when one's inner nature can be converted into a social, outer fact and when it cannot be, and that is the key to their competence. The difference between old and young, then, is simply that pretense has taken over the old folks' personalities, but not the young lovers' — at least not Courtall's and Gatty's.

The lesser lovers, however, Freeman and Ariana, have begun to show the same confusion of selves that mars the actions of the older people. Freeman's explanation to Courtall of his beginning an intrigue with Lady Cockwood is not convincing (173), and suggests that he is playing his friend false. Similarly, Ariana rejects Gatty's frankness; Gatty demands, "Hast thou not promis'd me a thousand times, to leave off this demureness?" and Ariana answers, "If your tongue be not altogether so nimble, I may be conformable," suggesting that she, like Lady Cockwood, carries social pretense into a relationship where it ought not to be (102, see also 170).

The denouement resolves these contrasts between town and country, gallantry and marriage, old and young, liberty and restraint, by compromise. Early in the play, when Gatty and Ariana successfully trick Courtall, they speak of turning him into a "Country Clown" (126). At the end of the play, Gatty, speaking of marriage as a kind of confinement, ironically remarks, "These Gentlemen have found it so convenient lying in Lodgings, they'll hardly venture on the trouble of taking a House of their own." "A pretty Country-seat, Madam," replies Courtall gallantly, "with a handsom parcel of Land, and other necessaries belonging to't, may tempt us; but for a Town-Tenement that has but one poor conveniency, we are resolv'd we'll never deal" (174). The young men accept their confinement and agree to a month's trial before their final satisfaction: For Courtall, the ways of intrigue seem almost to have passed: "If the heart of man be not very deceitful, 'tis very likely it may be [a match]." For Freeman, however, the lesser lover, "A month is a tedious time, and will be a dangerous tryal of our resolutions; but I hope we shall not repent before Marriage, whate're we do after" (176). The month's trial, of course, continues the pattern of the various unfavorable metaphors for love and marriage: that one must obey "the rules of the game" to achieve satisfaction, submitting to a restraint to win in the end. There is a hint in Freeman's remark that these marital confinements will give rise eventually to the same pretense and hostility that mar the Cockwood marriage. The older people at the end of the play continue their pretenses unchanged. "I am resolv'd," piously says Lady Cockwood, "to give over the great bus'ness of this Town, and hereafter modestly confine my self to the humble Affairs of my own Family." "Pray entertain an able Chaplain," replies Courtall dryly (178). Sir Joslin and the unwitting Sir Oliver are just as restless as at the opening of the play as they prepare to return to country life, a morass of crabbed pretenses forced on them by the binding effect of social restrictions on natural desires.

Etherege's second play is quite different from his first, and the change measures his capacity for growth as a dramatist. Gone are the old devices of parallel plots and character groups. The entire action is built on a series of contrasts, each of which grows from one central idea: the felt conflict between social restraints and "natural" desires. The conception is thoroughly un-Elizabethan, and the form of the play has grown to meet the conception. While there is an occasional heroic note in Lady Cockwood's hypocritical cant about her honor, the highness of the high plot of *The Comical Revenge* is almost wholly gone, too. The supernatural element, present in a half-serious way in his first play, has now been almost eliminated. The Devil appears: everyone in the play is called a devil at one time or another (126, 129, 150, 151, 157, 158); Lady Cockwood, in particular, is an "Old Devil" (153, 158) or a "long-Wing'd devil" (121). But the epithet is not meant in any traditional religious way and there is hardly any heavenly counterpart in the finale; marriage is taken as a penance for the sins of the gallants (174), Lady Cockwood is urged to entertain an able chaplain, and that is about all. The new play is saturated with realism, real taverns, real parks, real stores, contrasted implicitly to the outlandish atmospheres of heroic drama. The play is antiheroic, but to heroics heard only in the mind's ear. So too, the low plot has been absorbed into the single, unified dramatic situation. Folly, in this play, has risen to the upper class, though it still is, as it was for Sir Nicholas Cully, allowing one's pretenses to take the place of one's real nature.

She wou'd if she cou'd is a study, still somewhat crude, of this kind of folly. The young people of the play face constantly the risk that their necessary and proper social pretenses, whether to honor or to vice, may obstruct their real feelings; they face, too, the warning example of the Cockwoods. Their success in avoiding this pitfall defines an ethic of pretense. Etherege's second play has little of the sheer doings of his first — there are neither duels nor slapstick — and this suggests a growing awareness on the part of the characters and their author that "*talk* is a very important kind of action." [6] Conversation is a performance; speech, clothing, manners, and other forms of appearance have importance in themselves because they are separate from the private life of the individual, his "nature." These appearances constitute the visible, apparent acquiescence to social and other restraints and are thought of as separate from the nature that rebels against restraint. But even the purely private actions of an individual — sexual conversation as opposed to verbal, for example — are felt to have this double nature, a visible, external performance and a personal, internal satisfaction.

The talk Etherege gives his characters bodies forth this sense in linguistic form. "Now shall I sleep as little without you," cries Courtall, in his curtain speech, as he is parting from his betrothed, "as I shou'd do with you: Madam, expectation makes me almost as restless as Jealousie." These comparisons, a late-seventeenth-century version of Donne's conceits, let a man be passionate but discuss his passion at the same time, as Donne's do. Impersonally, whimsically, the observer talks about things which he, by an odd coincidence, happens to be doing.[7] In later Restoration comedies, this figure of speech becomes a rhetorical device of extraordinary complexity: the speaker hides his feelings by the comic comparison at the same time that by discussing them at all he makes them more visible and himself transparent in the heroic manner. In *She wou'd if she cou'd* the device is not yet used with skill. When the events of the play move quickly, metaphor drops out. Where characters are acting or planning action, they speak normally, as when Sir Oliver or Sir Joslin plan their parties or Lady Cockwood an assignation or when the gallants hide in the Cookwood house. Figurative speech is reserved for the obvious occasions when talk is an action itself, such as the time in the park when the two young men meet the girls or when the final matches are made. Metaphor is still felt as a frothy formality opposed to the "weighty affairs" of the play, not yet a part of them. Nevertheless, Etherege has begun to weld action and language into a way of seeing. Town and country symbolize opposite poles of experience, liberty and restraint. Etherege uses this division to split his characters, to show how in response to the pressure to conform some respond by dissimulation and affectation, and some evolve a golden mean of a restraint, the acceptance of which is an expression of self — marriage for love. Both language and action represent human conduct split under the pressure of conformity into a visible, social appearance and a personal, private nature. Folly is the confusion of the two; wisdom is their separation and balance. *She wou'd if she cou'd* is a quasi-scientific exploration of divided man, and this was to be the Restoration comic mode.

5 • *Love in a Wood; or, St. James's Park*

When William Wycherley retired from the stage in 1676, everyone agreed that he had written the finest comedy since Ben Jonson: even today it would be hard to decide whether Congreve's polish ever really surpassed the achievement of "manly Wycherley." His first play is promising enough, though hardly as gratifying today as it evidently was to the audiences of the 1670's. The aging Wycherley told young Pope that he had written *Love in a Wood* when he was nineteen, that is, in 1659. While this was a perhaps pardonable attempt to retain "one-upness" in the large eyes of a rather nasty little genius, it has added one more straw to the burdens of modern scholarship. Wycherley left England at fifteen, and not even in the seventeenth century could a fifteen-year-old acquire such a knowledge of London. While he might have written a first draft when he was at Oxford and twenty, internal references and the accurate picture of London life in the play suggest that Wycherley subtracted eight years: the play was probably finished about 1670, and its first performance took place in the spring of 1671. Whenever it was, it suddenly brought Wycherley success — in the Restoration manner. Two days after the opening, the Duchess of Cleveland, circling the Mall in her chariot, leaned out and cheerily called to him: "You, Wycherley, you are a Son of a Whore." Starting from this novel conversational gambit, actually a reference to the song at the end of the first act: "Great Wits, and great Braves/ Have always a Punk to their Mother," Wycherley and the lady soon became lovers. The dramatist was thus drawn into a group that included such a varied assortment of people as Jacob Hall, the tight-rope dancer, the Duke of Buckingham, and the king himself. The lady's nobler lovers accepted him gracefully, and he quickly became one of the most noted wits of the court circle.[1]

Though Wycherley rose higher than Etherege, both in society and in the annals of literature, he grew as a dramatist in much the same way. Thus, Wycherley's first play shows the same crudity and use of high and low plots as *The Comical Revenge*. The seven years since *The Comical Revenge*, however, had made a big difference in dramatic technique. Wycherley reduced analogy to a minimal function: the high plot differs so little from the low that the contrast between them forms only a small part of the meaning of the play. Both plots are realistic. Neither is an absurd contrast to the other; rather, both show the same sort of action and the same sort of epistemological flaw. In both plots, there are crossed lovers, people who stray from their "proper" relationships, where consent is more or less mutual, because they confuse appearance with nature. In each plot, there is one character who "superintends" the action: Vincent, the helpful friend of the high plot, and Mrs. Joyner, the marriage broker of the low. Both stand in the position of matchmakers: Vincent's name refers equally to *vincere,* to conquer, and *vincire,* to bind. Just as Mrs. Joyner is the only one in possession of all the facts in the low plot, Vincent is the only one in the high plot to keep his faith in the misunderstood heroine. While there is analogy between the high and low plots, however, it is the form of the intrigues that brings out the meaning in the comical goings-on.

In the low plot, Mrs. Joyner is promoting various unions: Sir Simon Addleplot, a fool, has disguised himself as Jonas the clerk to enter Alderman Gripe's household, so he can marry (for money) either Lady Flippant, Gripe's sister, supposedly rich, or Mrs. Martha, his daughter; Lady Flippant wants to marry (for money) Sir Simon, but would prefer to have an affair with Dapperwit; Dapperwit wants to marry (for money) Martha, and keep his wench, Lucy; Lucy, however, finds Gripe more prosperous. Martha uses Sir Simon to help her elope with Dapperwit (to father the child she is carrying); Gripe marries Lucy to get heirs in revenge; Lady Flippant falls reluctantly into the reluctant arms of Sir Simon.

The low-plot intrigue grows out of the confusion of appearance and nature. Each of the men mistakes his own pretenses and those of others for reality. The foolish Dapperwit, for example, thinks that because he affects to be a wit he is actually charming, witty, and clever enough to deserve an heiress. Sir Simon thinks that because he wears a disguise he is clever, and that he is a gallant because he uses "the words in fashion, though I never have any luck with 'em" (84).[2] Gripe, a Puritan, pretends piety: he disguises his attempted seduction of Lucy as redeeming her from someone else (77). The men's names suggest this theme. "Sir Simon Addleplot" is, of course, one who cannot keep unconfused his disguised self and his real self. "Dapperwit" implies a comparison of clothes and wit, as though Dapperwit's pretensions to wit were a kind of padded shoulders to cover his actually feeble intelligence. Gripe's name implies one who clutches his real self close to him, who cannot let it go unless it be twisted into a distorted shape. Each of the men tricks himself by confusing his pretended self with his real self or by failing to look beneath the surface of the woman he pursues. Dapperwit thinks he is witty enough to charm an heiress; unaware of his own limitations — or hers — he is duped into fathering Martha's unborn bastard. Gripe, because he will not let his lechery appear as what it is, disguises it by marrying — a wench. Sir Simon also is hoist with his own petar: he is not allowed to cast off his disguise as Jonas, and he marries Lady Flippant only because he never finds out whether she was rich or not. Each of the three men confuses the appearance or pretense of the woman he seeks with her real nature through his own system of confusions: vanity (Dapperwit) or hypocrisy (Gripe) or folly (Sir Simon).

The women in the low plot are far more clever than the men at keeping their façades separated from their real selves. "Women," says one of the high-plot lovers, "are poor credulous Creatures, easily deceived"; but the wiser Vincent replies, "We are poor credulous Creatures, when we think 'em so" (81). Precisely this ability enables them to dupe the men: Martha's pretended love for Dapperwit traps him into marrying her; Lucy's pretense of innocence charms Gripe. Only Lady Flippant comes close to failing when she almost lets the lechery behind her pretenses betray her real nature to Sir Simon (121). This theme of affectation is neatly summed up when Dapperwit and Martha pretend not to recognize that Sir Simon's disguise as Jonas is a disguise (134–139): in a sense, every other character in the low plot does the same.

This facet of character mockingly develops the principal theme, the relation of appearance to nature; far more important, however, to the actual funniness of the play, is the wit at the expense of marriage. "Not a husband to be had for money," cries Lady Flippant in the opening lines of the play. Etherege had used the same motif in *The Comical Revenge,* but with nothing like the proliferation of *Love in a Wood.* Lady Flippant, Sir Simon, Dapperwit, and Lucy are all trying to marry for money. The opening scene of the play consists of Lady Flippant's complaint to Mrs. Joyner that she has failed to get her a husband even though the lady has constantly frequented all the "Publick Marts where Widows and Mayds are expos'd" (74). The constant metaphor for marriage — or even simple fornication — is gambling or swindling (117, 120, 124, 128, etc.) Dapperwit keeps Lucy, his wench, his "Jewel" in "a small House, in an obscure, little, retired street"; "the Cabinet" is hidden "with as much care as a Spark of the Town do's his money from his Dun, after a good hand at Play" (105). His efforts to sell Lucy to another man (108) are defeated only because her mother and Mrs. Joyner are resolved to get a higher price from Gripe (113). Gripe, in turn, marries her only because " 'tis agreed on all hands, 'tis cheaper keeping a Wife then a Wench" (148).

This sense of marriage as an outward form that represents no inner core of affection carries over even to the high plot. "Want of mony," drily remarks one of the high-plot ladies, "makes as devout Lovers as Christians" (117). The surest sign of the heroine's madness, her maid tells her, is that she is eager to marry a man without a penny (96). One of the high-plot gentlemen, learning of his beloved's fortune, sarcastically remarks, "Faith, I am sorry she is an Heiress, lest it should bring the scandal of interest, and design of lucre upon my love" (102).

The high plot is a less heroic version of Calderón's *Mañanas de abril y mayo.*[3] Christina, a young heiress, has shut herself in her house, away from the world, to await the return of her lover Valentine from hiding after he had won a duel to revenge her reputation. Suddenly, her friend Lydia bursts in on her. Lydia, while spying in the Park on her philandering fiancé Ranger, has been seen by him. He pursues her, and she persuades Christina to hide her. Ranger now bursts in, but on finding Christina promptly falls in love with her, much to the discomfort of the concealed Lydia. Valentine returns, overhears Ranger boast of his "conquest," refuses to believe his friend Vincent's protests on her behalf, and finally sees Christina appear at Vincent's house, apparently for an assignation with Ranger. All parties rush off in anger to the Park, where confusions of identity produce frank accusations and confessions. Both Ranger and Valentine thus learn that the jealous Lydia forged the note of assignation. Needless to say, the proper pairs are matched.

The humor of the high plot, like that of the low, grows from the confusion of appearance with nature, but in a much more heroic and less bestial — and less funny — way. Thus, Lydia watches Ranger's apparent faithlessness, and by testing him and spying on him, drives him in reality further away from her. The confusion of appearance and nature shows most in Valentine: he fails to rely on what should be his knowledge of Christina's impeccable character; instead, he deceives himself with the appearance of her infidelity and Ranger's pretensions. Ranger, too, fails to act on a proper knowledge of Christina's character and relies on appearances. Only Christina herself and Vincent manage to keep faith in her integrity and give proper importance to her real nature. "Open but your Eyes," cries Vincent to Valentine, "and the Fantastick Goblin's vanish'd" (141).

In the low plot, love undergoes the usual unfavorable comparisons: it is "midnight coursing in the Park" (87), fishing (74), hunting (81, 94), and birding (96), gambling (84, 125), fighting (125) with sexuality being courage (89), and a disease for which pimp and bawd are doctor and apothecary (84); flirting men are like soldiers (94), pursuing women like "Bayliffs" (92). "I never admitted a Man to my conversation," avows Lady Flippant, "but for his punishment certainly" (96). One love must cure another, says Dapperwit, as "one poyson expel another, one fire draw out another, one fit of drinking cure the sickness of another" (105).

In the high plot, love is more heroic. Dapperwit parodies it when he speaks of his wench's "conquest" of his heart (107) and Ranger corrupts it, calling his love for Christina his "plague" (98). Love takes the specific form of a duel: thus Lydia speaks of men as "the common enemy" (91); when she forges the note of assignation from Christina, she phrases it as a challenge (124–125), and the metaphor is carried through to the end (128, 132, 141). The duel, of course, recalls Valentine's initial difficulty, his fight with one Clerimont who boasted (falsely) of Christina's favors, another instance of excessive concern with forms and appearances (95). Disguise in the high plot takes the form of emotional disguise: "Your anger has disguis'd you," says Ranger to Christina, "more then your Mask" (131) and Christina too accuses Valentine of letting his anger disguise his real self (130).

Thus, the action and the metaphors, both in high plot and low, both funny and not-so-funny, set out the fundamental Restoration "slant" on reality. Man has an outward self and an inward, an appearance and a nature. His "nature," revealed in metaphors, is sexual, appetitive, and aggressive; it conflicts with the requirements of society. Man resorts, therefore, to the dissimulation, disguise, hypocrisy, affectation, and intrigue which make up the action and the characters of these comedies. In *Love in a Wood* (and in Wycherley's other plays) women are rather more successful at these social games than men. It is a woman, Christina, in *Love in a Wood* who establishes the ideal against which the other people are measured.

Christina (her name is, of course, significant) represents a very specific ideal, one that transcends the conflict between appearance and nature: she freely expresses her "natural" self. Her first appearance and conversation with her maid (95–96) establish the basic fact about her: that she will act openly on her love for Valentine regardless of what people will say. Ranger calls her "an Angel" (99). Mr. Bonamy Dobrée quite correctly points out that the contrast between her honest relation to Valentine and the dishonest affairs of the low plot defines a middle ground.[4] Lady Flippant's epithet for her, "faithful Shepherdess" (96, 99), and her maid's accusations of "madness" (95, 96) give her an air of pastoral unreality. But her serious attempt to keep herself above the comical cross-currents of society fails when Lydia and Lady Flippant burst in on her from a real park (not a pastoral one). She herself is forced, finally, to go out into the darkness to bring about the final enlightenment.

The Park is an important symbol. It is a piece of country within the

Town, and for Wycherley, the country stands for a place where one's inner nature is very close to the surface. So, among the deceptions and pretenses of the Town, the Park brings out one's hidden nature. For the ordinary light of day is substituted Phoebus' other light, the light of wit or judgment (91, 92). Surface attributes become invisible: "The Moon . . . scarce affords light enough to distinguish a Man from a tree" (142). "A Lady will no more shew her modesty in the dark, then a *Spaniard* his courage" (138). The three wits discuss the advantages of the Park in enabling one to show his real self:

Vincent. A Man may come after Supper with his three Bottles in his head, reel himself sober, without reproof from his Mother, Aunt, or grave relation.
Ranger. May bring his bashful Wench, and not have her put out of countenance by the impudent honest women of the Town.
Dapperwit. And a Man of wit may have the better of the dumb shew, of well trim'd Vest, or fair Peruque; no man's now is whitest.
Ran. And now no woman's modest, or proud, for her blushes are hid, and the rubies on her Lips are died, and all sleepy and glimmering Eyes have lost their attraction.
Vin. . . . No observing spruce Fop will miss the Crevat that lies on one's shoulder, or count the pimples on one's face.
Dap. And now the brisk reparty ruins the complaisant Cringe, or wise Grimace; something 'twas, we Men of virtue always lov'd the night. (87–88)

Even Gripe likes it: "I can conform to this mode of publick walking by Moon-light, because one is not known" (136). "I come hither," says Lydia, "to make a discovery" (89).

"In a wood," as an idiom, means "confused," and in the complexities of town life, confusion is exactly what results when the mask of pretense falls. The play begins, for all practical purposes, with a confusing episode in the Park and ends with an unconfusing in the Park. In the first scene, Ranger betrays his philandering, Lydia reveals she knows of it, and Lydia's flight precipitates the complications of the high plot. In the second, because Ranger and Christina each mistake the persons they are talking to, their frank remarks clear up the mistakes of Lydia and Valentine, respectively. This is a London pastoral.

For the people of the low plot, however, the bringing of their real selves to light is of no help. Their inner natures are so corrupted with pretense that only further confusion results, each one "Abus'd by him, I have abus'd" (149). In the low plot dissimulation continues; in the high, there is a hint that plain dealing will be the new order, as Ranger cries:

Of Intrigues, honourable or dishonourable, and all sorts of rambling, I take my leave; when we are giddy, 'tis time to stand still: why shou'd we be so fond of the by-paths of Love? where we are still way-lay'd, with Surprizes, Trapans, Dangers, and Murdering dis-appointments:

Just as at Blind-mans Buff, we run at all,
Whilst those that lead us, laugh to see us fall;
And when we think we hold the Lady fast,
We find it but her Scarf, or Veil, at last. (133–134)

Mere outward forms are not to control: in their curtain speech, all the high plot people agree that it is an imperfect world and marriage an imperfect institution. Ranger's final cynical couplet sums it up:

The end of Marriage, now is liberty,
And two are bound — to set each other free.

Marriage, the social form, should release the private life or nature. Ideally, the appearance should express one's nature: marriage should represent freedom within a form: "Two are bound — to set each other free." More likely, however, it will represent a freedom outside the form, and that is the comic sense of *Love in a Wood*. The world is a pretty imperfect place, and quasi-heroic perfectionists like Christina and Valentine have to be comically taught its imperfections by being dragged through its mire.

Wycherley's first play, like Etherege's, gives scarcely any indication of what is to come. We can see, however, that Wycherley's manner, even in this first crude play, is uniquely his. First, the force of the play comes not from analogy or parallelism, but from the actual events of the intrigue: the gatherings in the Park, marrying for money, disguises and pretenses; whereas in both of Etherege's plays, the actual events are not so meaningful as the contrasts and similarities among them. Wycherley, too, is far more acutely aware than Etherege of the difference between outer appearance and inner nature. His emphases on light and dark, visibility and invisibility, wit and judgment, show that he has the schismatic way of seeing that we will find the fundamental characteristic of the great Restoration comedies. Finally, Wycherley has a special feeling for compromise that creates his own special kind of comedy, in which idealists like Christina are forced to compromise their ideals. *Love in a Wood* is crude, but its nucleus of ideas is not. They are only partly realized, far more in the action than in the language, which Wycherley has not yet shaped to fit his own peculiarly mordant sense of the comic. But for a man who was to write the English *Misanthrope*, it was the right beginning.

6 · *Disguise, Comic and Cosmic*

Descartes, Bacon, Hobbes, and Locke, Purcell, Rembrandt, Rubens, Van Dyck, Wren, Vermeer, Bernini, the better parts of Shakespeare, Cervantes, and Lope de Vega, and Jonson, Donne, Milton, Herbert, Marvell, Dryden, Racine, Corneille, Molière, Calderón, Galileo, Kepler, Newton, Huyghens, Cromwell, Richelieu, and the gentlemen of the Plymouth plantation, all these the seventeenth century produced. Alfred North Whitehead called it the "century of genius"; if anything, an understatement. In these hundred years, England had her greatest periods of prose, comedy, and perhaps of lyric verse. The Restoration itself gave us *Paradise Lost* and *Pilgrim's Progress,* Sir Isaac Newton and the law of gravitation, and the greatest of all comedies of "manners." [1]

It would be surprising if these comedies did not share in the almost magical energy of the age. Yet critics of Restoration comedy have been almost unanimous in pronouncing these plays a meaningless coterie drama, appealing only to a tiny class, and therefore of no larger significance. Just the three that we have examined so far have been filled with disguises and pretenses, masks and affectations, all of which seem pretty trivial — and so the critics have assumed. I disagree. I think these comedies by their use of disguise (even if that use is frivolous) are probing some of the most basic assumptions of their age and ours. In the seventeenth century, disguise became a matter of cosmic significance, a fundamental element in ethical and metaphysical thought, largely as a result of the new physics. The writers of comedies were connected in various ways to the newly formed Royal Society and were thus exposed to this new scientific thought. It behooves us, therefore, at least to consider the possibility that disguise, even in the frothiest of these comedies, shared in this new importance. After all, their frothiness serves, as Mr. Empson would say,[2] for a kind of pastoral: the dramatist, by describing an idealized, simplified world, the "Utopia of gallantry" of which Charles Lamb spoke, gains a vantage point from which he can examine the more complex world of reality. The single most important element of this "pastoral" setting is disguise, and to see its implications involves us in an excursion into the seventeenth-century attitude toward dissimulation, affectation, pretense, and the like.

In Shakespeare's day, the general feeling was that appearance reflects nature, that "the body reflects the soul, and, ideally, the outward appearance and the inner reality are the same." [3] Thus, Kate in *The Taming of the Shrew* could argue,

> Why are our bodies soft and weak and smooth,
> Unapt to toil and trouble in the world,
> But that our soft conditions and our hearts
> Should well agree with our external parts? (V.ii.165–168)

and Enobarbus could see a lesson in Antony's decline:

> Things outward
> Do draw the inward quality after them
> To suffer all alike. (III.xiii.32–34)

The union of appearance and nature was, to a writer like Spenser, a theological bond:

> For of the soule the bodie forme doth take:
> For soule is forme, and doth the bodie make.
>
> . . . . .
>
> For all that faire is, is by nature good;
> That is a signe to know the gentle blood.[4]

The Elizabethans were not naïve on the point; Spenser goes on to qualify:

> Yet oft it falles, that many a gentle mynd
> Dwels in deformed tabernacle drownd,
> Either by chaunce, against the course of kynd,
> Or through vnaptnesse in the substance fownd. . . .
>
> And oft it falles (ay me the more to rew)
> That goodly beautie, albe heauenly borne,
> Is foule abusd. . . .[5]

The rule is by no means absolute; Spenser admits there are exceptions, but they represent "chaunce," they run "against the course of kynd," they are, in short, unnatural.

> Nothing so good, but that through guilty shame
> May be corrupt, and wrested vnto will.[6]

In other words, appearance either matches or ought to match nature. And such is the *mos* of the drama. People who find appearance and nature different in a Shakespearian play are either villains like Richard III, who says,

> No more can you distinguish of a man
> Than of his outward show; which, God he knows,
> Seldom or never jumpeth with the heart. (III.i.9–11)

or men like Duncan, who, deceived by a villain, says,

> There's no art
> To find the mind's construction in the face. (I.iv.11–12)

The normal situation is that appearance and nature accord. When they do not, the action of the play is to expose and remedy the discrepancy. Even in the rather more decadent plays for the aristocratic "priuat" theaters, the discrepancy leads either to satire — or tragedy. Rare indeed is the Elizabethan or Stuart play in which a difference between appearance and nature is sustained beyond the final scene.

The tradition, of course, went back to medieval times in the morality plays in which the chief attribute of Vice was his ability to deceive. And as the morality plays broadened into secular dramas of political life, the tradition carried over to political villains. From them, it went on to the nonpolitical villain.[7] As such the tradition is directly connected to medieval scholasticism, which taught that God has given all creatures "a 'nature' or 'form' in virtue of which they are necessitated both to be what they are, and to seek that which is proper to them." [8] We find the point restated by Richard Hooker, the leading English theologian of Shakespeare's day. "Things natural," he writes, "do so necessarily observe their certain laws that as long as they keep those forms which give them their being they cannot possibly be apt or inclinable to do otherwise then they do; seeing the kinds of their operations are both constantly and exactly framed according to the several ends for which they serve." [9] The whole structure of natural law, of the teleological universe, indeed, of life itself was bound up in the concept of the interrelation of appearance and nature. For a thing — or a person — to "be" other than what his "form" dictated was purely and simply unnatural. What shows either was or should be a true reflection of what is. In the Restoration things were different.

"But, good God!" wrote Pepys, "what an age is this, and what a world is this! that a man cannot live without playing the knave and dissimulation." [10] Pepys was troubled by the Restoration habit of pretense, but other, less earnest members of his society reveled in it. "At this time," writes Bishop Burnet, recalling 1668,

> the court fell into much extravagance in masquerading; both king and queen and all the court went about masked, and came into houses unknown, and danced there, with a good deal of wild frolic. People were so disguised that, without being in the secret, none could distinguish them. They were carried about in hackney chairs. Once the queen's chairmen, not knowing who she was, went from her; so she was alone, and was much disturbed, and came to Whitehall in a hackney-coach; some say in a cart.[11]

The Duchess of Cleveland, who became Wycherley's mistress after making his acquaintance in the novel way we have seen, is said to have gone to his chambers in the Temple, "dressed like a country maid, in a straw hat, with pattens on, and a box or basket in her hand." [12] A letter of 1670 tells how,

Last week, there being a faire neare Audley-end, the queen, the Dutchess of Richmond, and the Dutchess of Buckingham, had a frolick to disguise themselves like country lasses, in red petticoats, wastcotes, &c, and so goe see the faire. Sir Bernard Gascoign, on a cart jade, rode before the queen; another stranger before the Dutchess of Buckingham; and Mr. Roper before Richmond. They had all so overdone it in their disguise, and looked so much more like antiques than country volk, that, as soon as they came to the faire, the people began to goe after them; but the queen going to a booth, to buy a pair of yellow stockins for her sweet hart, and Sir Bernard asking for a pair of gloves sticht with blew, for his sweet hart, they were soon, by their gebrish, found to be strangers, which drew a bigger flock about them. One amongst them had seen the queen at dinner, knew her, and was proud of her knowledge. This soon brought all the faire into a crowd to stare at the queen. Being thus discovered, they, as soon as they could, got to their horses; but as many of the faire as had horses got up, with their wives, children, sweet harts, or neighbours behind them, to get as much gape as they could, till they brought them to the court gate. Thus, by ill conduct, was a merry frolick turned into a penance.[13]

Burnet says that the notorious Earl of Rochester "gave himself up to all sorts of extravagance, and to the wildest frolics that a wanton wit could devise. He would have gone about the streets as a beggar, and made love as a porter." [14] Once, when Rochester had been exiled briefly from the court, he disguised himself as a merchant to enjoy the luxury of the city merchants. "His first design was only to be initiated into the mysteries of those fortunate and happy inhabitants; that is to say, by changing his name and dress, to gain admittance to their feasts and entertainments; and, as occasion offered, to those of their loving spouses." [15] By railing at the profligacy of the court, Rochester became so popular that he "grew sick of their cramming and endless invitations," and changed his plans. "He disguised himself so, that his nearest friends could not have known him, and set up in Tower Street for an Italian mountebank, where he practised physic for some weeks, not without success." [16] Under the name Alexander Bendo, his advertisement announced:

However, gentlemen, in a world like this, where virtue is so exactly counterfeited, and hypocrisy so generally taken notice of, that every one, armed with suspicion, stands upon his guard against it, it will be very hard, for a stranger, especially to escape censure. All I shall say for myself on this score is this: — if I appear to any one like a counterfeit, even for the sake of that, chiefly, ought I to be construed a true man. Who is the counterfeit's example? His original; and that, which he employs his industry and pains to imitate and copy. Is it therefore my fault, if the cheat by his wits and endeavours makes himself so like me, that consequently I cannot avoid resembling him? [17]

While so toying with appearance and nature, Rochester was visited by two maids of honor (Miss Jennings and Miss Price) who in turn disguised themselves as orange-girls to consult the new astrologer. *The Memoirs of Count Grammont,* that inimitable western Genji, recounts their misadventures in the playhouse and the street with some of the more lecherous and less observant members of the court. "Such as these tricks being ordinary, and worse among them," said Pepys about such goings-on among maids of honor, "thereby few will venture upon them for wives." [18] We have seen in the plays the custom of the mask behind which a woman could carry on her private affairs. We have seen, too, the speculations to which the mask gave rise: whether the lady when masked was more or less "herself." Masquerades were evidently a popular form of amusement at the court.[19]

Disguise, of course, was nothing new. In 1635 Queen Henrietta Maria had been pleased "to grace the entertaynment by putting of[f] majesty to putt on a citizens habitt, and to sett upon the scaffold on the right hande amongst her subjects." [20] In pre-Revolutionary times it was a charming gesture on the part of the queen to express her sense of participation in the amusements of her subjects. With the Merry Monarch, however, the purpose and frequency of disguise were somewhat different, and "Old Rowley" came to symbolize the monarch's pleasure in throwing off kingship with his clothes, for example, on the occasion when Charles II met Nell Gwyn:

Before her acquaintance with the king she is by some said to have been mistress to a brother of Lady Castlemaine, who studiously concealed her from Charles. One day, however, in spite of his caution, his Majesty saw her, and that very night possessed her. Her lover carried her to the play, at a time when he had not the least suspicion of his Majesty's being there; but as that monarch had an aversion to his robes of royalty, and was incumbered with the dignity of his state, he chose frequently to throw off the load of kingship, and consider himself as a private gentleman. Upon this occasion he came to the play *incog.*, and sat in the next box to Nelly and her lover. As soon as the play was finished, his Majesty, with the Duke of York, the young nobleman, and Nell retired to a tavern together, where they regaled themselves over a bottle; and the king shewed such civilities to Nell, that she began to understand the meaning of his gallantry. The tavern keeper was entirely ignorant of the quality of the company; and it was remarkable, that when the reckoning came to be paid, his Majesty, upon searching his pockets, found that he had not money enough about him to discharge it, and asked the sum of his brother, who was in the same situation: upon which Nell observed, that she had got into the poorest company that she was ever in at a tavern. The reckoning was paid by the young nobleman, who that night lost both his money and his mistress.[21]

One of Charles's biographers describes him in more serious, political circumstances as "full of *Dissimulation* and very *adroit* at it"; another says, "He had so ill an opinion of mankind, that he thought the great art of living and governing was to manage all things and all persons with a depth of craft and dissimulation."[22] What had been a Machiavellian anathema to Shakespeare's audiences (although probably not to those who actually played Elizabeth's politics) became to the Restoration an openly avowed political reality. "The People judge by out sides," wrote an early eighteenth-century theorist, "and if you avoid the external Resemblance, by condemning the Form, you may have the Essence espoused by 'em."[23] The Marquess of Halifax, shortly after Charles's death in 1680, adopted an equally cynical point of view:

> Dissimulation is like most other Qualities, it hath two Sides; it is necessary, and yet it is dangerous too. To have none at all layeth a Man open to Contempt, to have too much exposeth him to Suspicion, which is only the less dishonourable Inconvenience. If a Man does not take very great Precautions, he is never so much shewed as when he endeavoureth to hide himself. One Man cannot take more pains to hide himself, than another will do to see into him.[24]

While the court's behavior is enough to explain the dramatists' interest in and use of disguise, we ought not to let the limited outlook of laundry-list scholarship rule out the possibility suggested by these political quotations, that both court and dramatists were responding to a larger trend. Attitudes toward disguise, dissimulation, and affectation had changed across the century. First, there was an increasing belief that the personality is hard to know under the appearances it puts on; second, affectation (semi-conscious pretense) was uniformly condemned; third, dissimulation (conscious pretense) tended increasingly to be accepted as a necessity. The total attitude toward human conduct that these three views represent is nothing more nor less than that of the early plays of Etherege and Wycherley: dissimulation is the rake-hero's way to success; affectation is a folly because one becomes unable to stop acting. Of course, there is nothing new in recognizing a difference between appearance and nature in human conduct. Man has always thought and joked about the difference between what is and what shows. The crucial change is that formerly men had felt that what shows either was or *should be* a true reflection of what is; now, at the end of the seventeenth century, men came increasingly to feel that what shows not only was not but often *ought not to be* a true reflection of what is.

Human conduct, politics, and comedies, moreover, were not the only areas in which such a difference was accepted. The same notion of an outside and an inside applied also, for example, to language. Language itself was regarded as an outside — clothing, ornament, or, in general, a shell of accidents — within which the real substance, thought, lay hidden. The image of clothing for language occurs again and again in Dryden's essays.[25] In one long passage, for example, he compared poetry to painting and to feminine beauty: expression is to the fable of a poem as colors are to the design of a painting or as clothes and cosmetics are to a woman. "The words, the expressions, the tropes and figures, the versification, and all the other elegancies of sound, as cadences, turns of words upon the thought, and many other things, which are all parts of expression" are like colors to a lady's maid, in that "she clothes, she dresses her up, she paints her, she makes her appear more lovely than naturally she is." [26] Addison, in *The Spectator*, referred continually to words as clothing thoughts. For example, he described the simplicity of the writings of the ancients as the "Strength of Genius to make a Thought shine in its own natural Beauties." According to one of his famous definitions, "*True Wit* consists in the Resemblance of Ideas, and *false Wit* in the Resemblance of Words." Thus, in an extended allegory of "The Region of False Wit," "There was nothing in the Fields, the Woods, and the Rivers, that appeared natural," but when the goddess of Falsehood was defeated, "The whole Face of Nature [recovered] its true and genuine Appearance." [27]

The idea of language clothing thought was hardly new. On the contrary, it was at least as old as Horace, and in medieval times, it had already become a commonplace.[28] Sidney, writing in 1580, had said of Plato that "who so ever well considereth, shall finde that in the body of his worke though the inside & strength were Philosophie, the skin as it were and beautie depended most of Poetrie." [29] Edmund Bolton in 1618 had called "Language and Style, the Coat and Apparel of matter," and the Earl of Stirling in the thirties also said, "Language is but the Apparel of Poesy, which may give Beauty, but not Strength." [30] This is simply that neo-classical theory of poetry which someone has described as the belief that "a poem should not be but mean." Literature, said Thomas Nashe, is "sower pils of reprehension wrapt up in sweete words." [31]

As the seventeenth century wore on, however, this idea came to be more and more frequently expressed and to have more and more effect on literary style. Montaigne became a model for later essayists (Congreve, for example, owned four copies of the *Essais*),[32] because, Savile wrote, "He scorned affected Periods to please the mistaken Reader with an empty *Chime* of *Words*. He hath no *Affectation* to set himself out, and dependeth wholly upon the *Natural Force* of what is his own." [33] "Tho' Invention be the Mother of Poetry," wrote Sir William Temple, Swift's employer, "yet this Child is like all others born naked, and must be . . . Cloathed with Exactness and Elegance." The metaphysical style, Temple said, had "Conceit as well as Rhyme in every Two Lines." "This was just as if a Building should be nothing but Ornament, or Cloaths nothing but Trimming; as if a Face should be covered over with black Patches, or a Gown with Spangles." [34]

What was special about the later seventeenth century's reaction to metaphor was (1) treating the discrepancy between thought and language as a discrepancy between plain prose and ornament, and therefore (2) relegating figures of speech to the passions and poetry and dismissing them in reason and prose as "affectation." Thus, the Earl of Mulgrave divided poetic composition in two:

> Fancy is but the Feather of the Pen;
> Reason is that substantial, useful part,
> Which gains the Head, while t'other wins the Heart.

It is quite logical in such a frame of reference to compare imagery to cosmetics:

> *Figures* of *Speech*, which Poets think so fine,
> Art's needless Varnish to make Nature shine,
> Are all but Paint upon a beauteous Face,
> And in Descriptions only claim a place.[35]

"Men apprehend or suspect a Trick," wrote William Wotton in 1694, "in every Thing that is said to move the Passions of the Auditory in Courts of Judicature or in the *Parliament-House*. . . . And therefore, when Men have spoken to the Point, in as few Words as the Matter will bear, it is expected they should hold their Tongues." [36] The proper place for metaphor is in poetry. "A poet," wrote Thomas Shadwell, the playwright, "ought to do all that he can decently to please that so he may instruct: To adorn his Images of *Vertue* so delightfully to affect people with a secret veneration of it." [37] "Rhetorick, or Oratory, Poesie, and the like," wrote one critic in 1654, "serve for adornation, and are as it were the outward dress, and attire of more solid sciences . . . they might tollerably pass, if there were not too much affectation towards them." [38]

This use of the word "solid" suggests what lies behind the limitations on metaphor. "Solid," in the later seventeenth century, became very much of a "plus" word, as, for example, in Richard Flecknoe's description of the advent of scenery in the public theaters: "Now, for the difference betwixt our Theaters and those of former times," he wrote, "That which makes our Stage the better makes our Playes the worse perhaps, they striving now to make them more for sight then hearing, whence that solid joy of the interior is lost."[39] John Bunyan apologized for his allegorical method with the same idiom:

> Be not too forward therefore to conclude,
> That I want solidness; that I am rude:
> All things solid in Shew, not solid be . . .
> My dark and cloudy words, they do but hold
> The truth, as Cabinets inclose the Gold.[40]

To be "a solid and honest" preacher, wrote Glanvill in 1678, "you must avoid such odd and foolish affectations" as the use of conceits and involved expressions.[41] *The Tatler* contrasted "the most solid philosophers" with "the most charming poets," and Mr. Spectator complained, "People are got into . . . a manner of overlooking the most solid Virtues, and admiring the most trivial Excellencies."[42]

"Solid" became a "plus" word because it suggested realness, the mass and volume the new physics could measure, as opposed to other illusory and immeasurable qualities such as color, taste, or smell. In effect, the new physics established a scientific basis for the operation of figures of speech. "The Ornaments of speaking," wrote Bishop Sprat in telling of the Royal Society's program for improving the English language, "were at first, no doubt, an admirable Instrument in the hands of *Wise Men* . . . to represent *Truth,* cloth'd with Bodies; and to bring *Knowledg* back again to our very senses, from whence it was at first deriv'd to our understandings." In other words, an image or metaphor appeals to the senses, as nature does; it makes things "real" to us. But sensory appeal is not an end in itself. The real end is "Knowledg," that is, understanding sensory experience in the mind, truth no longer "cloth'd with Bodies." "Ornaments," Sprat complained, had become ends in themselves, and therefore the Royal Society took it upon themselves to try to correct prose style: "to return back to the primitive purity and shortness, when men deliver'd so many *things* almost in an equal number of *words*"; "a close, naked, natural way of speaking, positive expressions, clear senses, a native easiness, bringing all things as near to the Mathematical plainness as they can."[43]

Oddly enough, it was probably through this scientific source that the dramatists were influenced. There were, of course, other bases for linguistic reform, the Puritan interest in a "plain style" for sermons, for example; but the Puritans had little influence on the playwrights. There can be little doubt that the playwrights acquired their distrust of metaphor through literary connections with the scientific Royal Society.[44] Dryden, for example, who wrote heroics, and George Villiers, Duke of

Buckingham, who spoofed them, the belle-lettrist John Evelyn, and the poets Waller and Cowley were all associated with the Society's committee "for improving the English language."

Through the Royal Society, literary men and even Charles's court had been brought face to face with the ultimate disguise, the disguise of reality itself that the new science had revealed. "We must allow that corporeal things exist," Descartes had written;

> However, they are perhaps not exactly what we perceive by the senses, since this comprehension by the senses is in many instances very obscure and confused; but we must at least admit that all things which I conceive in them clearly and distinctly, that is to say, all things which, speaking generally, are comprehended in the object of pure mathematics, are truly to be recognized as external objects.
>
> As to other things, however, which are either particular only, as, for example, that the sun is of such and such a figure, etc., or which are less clearly and distinctly conceived, such as light, sound, pain, and the like, it is certain that . . . they are very dubious and uncertain.[45]

Cartesian science linked the separation of appearance and nature to the tradition of sensory skepticism.

Of course, the idea that nature consisted of a solid core of substance and an overlying shell of attributes was not new. "Every substantial form," Dante had written, following St. Thomas, "that is distinct from matter, or that is united with it, has a specific virtue collected in itself which is not perceived unless in operation, nor does it show itself save by its effect, as by green leaves the life in a plant."[46] Moreover, in 1551, the separation of appearance from nature had even been made dogma by the Council of Trent:

> If any one . . . shall deny that wonderful and singular conversion of the whole substance of the bread into the Body, and of the whole substance of the wine into the Blood, the species only of the bread and wine remaining, which conversion indeed the Catholic Church most aptly calls Transubstantiation; let him be anathema.[47]

Neither was sensory skepticism new. There had been Pyrrho and his disciple Sextus Empiricus in the second century, Averroes in the twelfth, Pomponazzi and Agrippa in the fifteenth, Fulke Greville, Raleigh, and Montaigne in the sixteenth. But to all of these earlier skeptics, seventeenth-century writers and thinkers turned with increasing frequency.[48]

There were two new factors in the seventeenth century that made these two traditional ideas most powerfully reinforce each other. First, there was the Cartesian emphasis on method, particularly mathematical method, in studying natural events. Certain phenomena — those that lent themselves to mathematical description — came to be thought of as "truer" than others. Mass and volume became part of "nature"; color or odor became part of mere "appearance." "Solid," as we have seen, became a "plus" word. Second, there were the optical devices that struck at man's most useful sense. Sextus Empiricus could point to the fact that a straight stick looks bent in water, but that is not likely to trouble anyone very much. A Restoration man, however, was confronted with an oceanic jungle in a clear drop of water and heavens about which two millennia had been mistaken. "Our faculties," wrote Locke, "are not fitted to penetrate into the internal fabric and real essences of bodies."

> Had we senses acute enough to discern the minute particles of bodies, and the real constitution on which their sensible qualities depend, I doubt not but they would produce quite different ideas in us. . . . This microscopes plainly discover to us; for what to our naked eyes produces a certain colour, is, by thus augmenting the acuteness of our senses, discovered to be quite a different thing.[49]

Scientific discoveries had shown that truths which not so long before had seemed blatantly obvious were in fact purely and simply not so. Men's senses were not to be trusted, and it was science that had shown their falsity. As I sit at my desk, I cannot say it is hard and green, for the "true" description is that it is billions of colorless atoms, themselves only bundles of differential equations. So for the seventeenth-century man, only those things, as Descartes said, "which, speaking generally, are comprehended in the object of pure mathematics, are truly to be recognized as external objects." "Your True Philosopher," wrote the popularizer Fontenelle in 1686, "will not believe what he doth see, and is alwaies conjecturing at what he doth not."[50] Thus, that scientifically minded believer in witchcraft, Joseph Glanvill, wrote in 1664:

> What shews only the outside, and sensible structure of Nature; is not likely to help us in finding out the *Magnalia*. 'Twere next to impossible for one, who never saw the inward wheels and motions, to make a watch upon the bare view of the *Circle* of *hours,* and *Index:* And 'tis as difficult to trace natural operations to any practical advantage, by the sight of the Cortex of sensible Appearances. He were a poor *Physitian,* that had no more *Anatomy,* then were to be gather'd from the *Physnomy.*[51]

The unreliability of the senses and the separation of appearance from nature became axia to the great seventeenth-century philosophers. Locke we have already heard from. Hobbes wrote earlier — early enough to have influenced the dramatists directly. He knew, moreover, the court and the Merry Monarch himself. "This seeming or fancy," he wrote,

> is that which men call Sense; and consisteth, as to the eye, in a light, or colour figured; to the ear, in a sound; to the nostril, in an odour; to the tongue and palate, in a savour; and to the rest of the body, in heat, cold, hardness, softness,

and such other qualities, as we discern by feeling. All which qualities called sensible, are in the object which causeth them but so many several motions of the matter, by which it presseth our organs diversely.

And from hence also it followeth, that whatsoever accidents or qualities our senses make us think there be in the world, they be not there, but are seeming and apparitions only; the things that really are in the world without us, are those motions by which these seemings are caused. And this is the great deception of sense.[52]

Paradoxically, seeing had become a problem precisely because science saw so well.

To the medieval man, "that which was real about objects was that which could be immediately perceived about them by human senses," notes Professor Burtt. "Things that appeared different *were* different substances, such as ice, water, and steam." But as the "century of genius" grew, there grew with it "the doctrine of primary and secondary qualities," "the clear distinction between that in the world which is absolute, objective, immutable, and mathematical; and that which is relative, subjective, fluctuating, and sensible. The former is the realm of knowledge, divine and human; the latter is the realm of opinion and illusion." [53]

Alfred North Whitehead calls this theory of primary and secondary qualities, "the state of physical science at the close of the seventeenth century." "Nature," he says, became the orderliness of "spatio-temporal relationships." The mind, however, in apprehending, clothes bodies with sensations which in fact are purely the offspring of the mind itself. Nature became "a dull affair, soundless, scentless, colourless; merely the hurrying of material, endlessly, meaninglessly." [54] Perhaps this is the reason the gaiety of Restoration comedy sometimes seems forced: the hero is imprisoned in a set of thoroughly unreliable senses, locked, in effect, in his own hedonism. "What else [but pleasure] has meaning?" asks one of Congreve's rakes. Certainly not the orderliness of spatio-temporal relationships.

Instead of assuming that the dramatists simply took their material from the court, we should recognize that court and dramatists alike were responding to a common stimulus. The court, for all its frivolity, was not divorced from the intellectual life of its day. On the contrary, Hobbes, by virtue of his lively wit, became an honored member of that charmingly irresponsible body. "Order was given," Aubrey notes, "that he should have free accesse to his majesty, who was always much delighted in his witt and smart repartees." [55] Similarly, we find the Duke of Buckingham, than whom history offers few more light-headed individuals, discussing rather learnedly the relation of appearance and nature to an idea expressed in Burnet's *Theory of the Earth* and the doctrine of transubstantiation:

Those who maintain the Eternity of the World, are forc'd to say, that the Matter of it is not changed, but the Accidents only, tho' this be a sort of Argument, which they will not allow of in others, for when it is by Papists urg'd in Defense of Transubstantiation in the Sacrament, that the Accidents of the Wafer remain, though the Substance of it be changed, they reject that, as a ridiculous Notion; and yet it is not one Jot more absurd to say, that the Accidents remain when the Matter is changed; than that the Matter remains when the Accidents are changed.[56]

We have come some distance from Rochester's disguising himself as an Italian mountebank, but, in a sense, we have come back where we started. In so doing, we have seen that the separation of appearance from nature was a central concept in Restoration manners, morals, pranks, politics, science, and literary and linguistic theory. Clothing, cosmetics, manners, social rules, similitudes, disguise, deception, affectation, dissimulation, reputation (the stuff of Restoration comedies) all acquired special meaning in the Restoration, just as clockwork devices did in the eighteenth century, growing things in the nineteenth, or myths and symbols in our own. It is highly unlikely that the court was insulated from the philosophy of its day. On the contrary, those rootless ladies and gentlemen doubtless found a charming piquancy in the philosophical implications of their antics.

The drama, too, was not unaffected by the new philosophy. Most obviously, of course, its language was changed. No longer did the playwright use the thick ragout of metaphor that had gratified pre-Restoration audiences. On the contrary, language became thin and spare; "similitudes" replaced metaphors — and not many of those. Professor Dale Underwood in his book on Etherege shows that his early plays developed a very special kind of comic language which later dramatists followed. First, the language is built primarily out of nouns. Second, these nouns tend to play down sensory experience in favor of "generalized classes and categories." Third, the language is primarily engaged in setting up logical and schematic relations among these categories. It is almost as though "easie *Etheridge*" were trying for Bishop Sprat's "Mathematical plainness." These similitudes, however, are not as rigid and schematic as Sprat's mathematical talk would have been. On the contrary, in the hands of a skilled writer, they become a trope of surprising subtlety and flexibility. Professor Underwood quotes from *The Man of Mode:* "Women then [when they are ugly] ought to be no more fond of dressing than fools should be of talking." Explicitly, the sentence is a simple proportion: ugly women/dressing = fools/talking. But, as in any proportion, the terms can be transposed: ugly women/fools = dressing/talking. "The dressing," Professor Underwood notes, "becomes a kind of talking, the talking a kind of dressing; and the fools and women are brought together in a way which enlarges and particularizes the general relationship explicitly asserted."[57]

Though the change is less obvious than that in language, the subject matter of drama changed, too. Professor Andrews Wanning has pointed out that the prototype of the change was the development of the novel. Sixteenth-century romances seem to us, not novels, but mere successions of events. The real novel (Congreve, by the way, wrote one of the first) comes as writers begin to have a Lockean interest in psychological laws that parallel other scientific laws. "The history of the novel," he suggests, "might almost be written as a changing balance in the interest in outward action for its own sake, or for the inward conflict it symbolizes." The drama, he points out, reached this interest earlier partly "from the almost inevitably symbolic value the stage gives to any action upon it, and partly from the sometimes prophetic genius of Shakespeare."[58] Even so, the lines of choice and conflict in Restoration plays are far more clearly drawn than in Shakespeare (though the plays are not the better for that); also, characters do far more reasoning about their own states of mind than Elizabethan characters do (unless the Elizabethans are disordered). Moreover, the Restoration character is much more clearly divided into a nucleus of inner self or nature and a peripheral shell of appearances which may be the product of that inner self or may be a product of dissimulation, affectation, or disguise. The central problem in each of our eleven comedies is how the nucleus of personality shows itself through the shell of appearances and how it gets to know other nuclei through their shells. Clearly, these Restoration comedies, no matter how frivolous they seem to us, are probing some of the most basic assumptions of their century — and our own.

The mere fact that these assumptions are abstract, philosophical, or even scientific ought not to make us overlook their dramatic potential or make us think them unlikely to have affected such light-hearted *types* as our three playwrights. It was common in the seventeenth century for gentlemen to interest themselves, even if only in a dilettante way, in philosophical problems. We have already seen how the rakish "Duke of Bucks" could discuss fairly learnedly the doctrine of transubstantiation and its relation to the problem of substances and attributes. Furthermore, seventeenth-century writers almost habitually put abstract thought, practically unchanged, into their artistic works. *Paradise Lost* is the most obvious example, but there are many, many others. Dryden, in his operatic version of Milton's epic, shifted from the theology of his original toward the increasingly popular Cartesian philosophy. Thus, in the most wonderfully naïve way, Dryden has his Adam wake for the first time, saying:

> What am I? or from whence? For that I am
> I know, because I think.[59]

Cogito ergo sum, in a somewhat undigested form.

Etherege, Wycherley, and Congreve were all gentlemen and, though frivolous, they were both well educated and well read. Congreve's library of some 620 titles, known to us through Professor Hodges' discovery of his book list,[60] contained some twenty books of a strictly philosophical nature, among them Plato's works with Dacier's commentary and, by the three leading philosophers of his own century (to whom I have referred in this chapter), Locke's *Essay Concerning Human Understanding,* Hobbes' *Leviathan,* and a commentary on Descartes' system. In addition, Congreve owned a quite surprising number of the minor works quoted in this chapter, Gilbert Burnet's *History of His Own Time, The Memoirs of Count Grammont,* the literary criticism of Sir William Temple, Thomas Shadwell, and John Dryden; most surprising of all, he owned *The Canons and Decrees of the Council of Trent.* His library contained (besides some twenty-two works on medicine and pharmacology) eleven books on mathematics and the physical sciences, among them Newton's *Opticks* and a commentary on Newton's system as a whole and Fontenelle's *A Plurality of Worlds.* If Congreve's interests can be taken as typical, then all three of the writers of these comedies must have been influenced by the Restoration climate of opinion, certainly by such an intrinsically "stagy" idea as disguise.

In any case, Etherege's, Wycherley's, and Congreve's nondramatic writings show, as one would expect, a preoccupation with the contrast between appearance and nature. Of the three, Etherege is the least explicit, but even he in the few letters and poems he left behind speaks of human nature as obscured by a shell of accidents (as it is in *The Comical Revenge*). Thus, in congratulating two friends on new titles, he writes:

> The favours which fortune bestows move the weak to admire and the false to flatter; I look upon them as fine clothes which are ornaments to such as nature has been kind to, and never fail to make them more loathsome who have no merit. Such as are immediately distinguished from other men by heaven, will ever be preferred by me to such who only wear the marks [of] a Prince's kindness.
>
> You had no need of a title to make you great. . . . Nevertheless the glittering favours of fortune are necessary to entertain those who, without examining any deeper, worship appearances.[61]

We have already seen in his plays his concern with the problem of letting appearances intrude in relationships where they do not belong, a habit exemplified by Lady Cockwood, for example. In the same terms, he tells how, in Ratisbon,

> The plague of ceremony infects,
> Ev'n in love, the softer sex;
> Who an essential will neglect
> Rather than lose the least respect.
> In regular approach we storm,
> And never visit but in form,
> That is, sending to know before
> At what o'clock she'll play the whore.[62]

Wycherley was much more explicit. He left behind a large body of nondramatic works, including an immense number of woefully bad poems that should be reserved only for the most hardy students of the Restoration. In these nondramatic works, the theme of inside and outside recurs constantly. In particular, large books have bad insides, words belie actions, and wit and virtue are best shown by hiding them. Thus, his poem on the theme of "all the world's a stage" contrasts the overt pretense of the actor with the covert pretenses of society:

> Why are harsh Statutes 'gainst poor Players made,
> When Acting is the Universal Trade?
> The World's but one wide Scene, our Life the Play
> And ev'ry Man an Actor in his Way:
> In which he, who can act his ill Part well,
> Does him, who acts a good one ill, excell.
> Since it is not so much his Praise, whose Part
> Is best, but His, who acts it with most Art.
>
> . . . .
>
> Thus in the World, as on the Stage, we see
> Men act, unlike themselves, in each Degree.
> But 'twixt the World and Stage this Diff'rence lies,
> Play'rs to reform us wear a known Disguise;
> We no such warrantable End can boast,
> But still are Hypocrites at others' Cost.[63]

One of his letters translates the separation of appearance and nature into terms of sensory perception. Wycherley writes to Pope urging him to take care of those famous eyes:

> Pray look to your Eyes, because the[y] usd to look so kindly on me; and do not loose your sight in reading, to mend your inward decerning at the expence of your outward, since you may spoyl your Eye Sight and make it become weak or dark but you can hardly emprove your reasons insight which can never fail you; wherefore you may better bear the weakness of your owtward sight, since it is recompenc'd by the strength of your imagination and inward penitration, as your Poetic Forefathers were down from Homer to Milton.[64]

Congreve, too, shows an awareness of the problem of inside and outside in writings other than his comedies. One of his poems, for example, says of a lady:

> O she was heav'nly fair, in Face and Mind!
> Never in Nature were such Beauties join'd:
> Without, all shining; and within, all white;
> Pure to the Sense, and pleasing to the Sight.[65]

Congreve, however, is unique in that he has left behind a critical essay on the contrast between appearance and nature. It links the scientific doctrine of primary and secondary qualities to the dramatists' sense of affectation and dissimulation. In this essay, "Concerning Humour in Comedy," Congreve gives the following definition: "*Affectation,* shews what we would be, under a Voluntary Disguise. Thô here I would observe by the way, that a continued Affectation, may in time become a Habit." [66] Congreve goes on to define "humour" as something roughly equivalent to what we mean by "character."

> Humour is neither Wit, nor Folly, nor Personal defect; nor Affectation, nor Habit. . . . Our *Humour* has relation to us, and to what proceeds from us, as the Accidents have to a Substance; it is a Colour, Taste, and Smell, Diffused through all; thô our Actions are never so many, and different in Form, they are all Splinters of the same Wood, and have Naturally one Complexion, which thô it may be disguised by Art, yet cannot be wholly changed: We may Paint it with other Colours, but we cannot change the Grain. So the Natural sound of an Instrument will be distinguish'd, tho the Notes expressed by it, are never so various, and the Divisions never so many. Dissimulation may, by Degrees, become more easy to our practice; but it can never absolutely Transubstantiate us into what we would seem: It will always be in some proportion a Violence upon Nature.
>
> A man may change his Opinion, but I believe he will find it a Difficulty, to part with his *Humour,* and there is nothing more provoking, than the being made sensible of that Difficulty. . . . Nature abhors to be forced.[67]

In other words, "Wood" represents "us," the "Grain" being "our *Humour.*" Both "us" and "our *Humour*" Congreve includes under "Substance"; they correspond to the "primary qualities" of seventeenth-century science which I have been calling "nature." These things Congreve puts on one side as what we "naturally" are. On the other, he sets appearances created by affectation, dissimulation, or art. Those appearances are no less real than the paint on furniture, but they are "Accidents," secondary qualities, not what *we* are. To make our real selves over into appearance requires a "transubstantiation" (and we recall the Duke of Buckingham's remarks). The rake-hero is reformed in the fifth act when he puts aside his affectations. The affected, precise ladies, the hypocritical merchants, and the rest of the "victims" of Restoration comedy refuse to learn that people cannot make themselves over into what they would like to seem.

In a very real sense, therefore, these comedies represent a brilliant synthesis of abstract thought about primary and secondary qualities with the disguises and affectations of Restoration court life. Only too rarely do dramatists find intrinsically dramatic abstractions with which to inform their plays. Shakespeare did: he used the intensely dramatic interplay between the private and the public aspects of political leaders. (The problem in its abstract form was central to such Renaissance political theorists as Gentillet or, on the other side of the fence, Machiavelli.) We can watch the concept grow in Shakespeare's mind from the soliloquies of Richard III, where the Machiavellian villain contrasts his secret thoughts with his public actions, to the personal inadequacies of Richard II which become public errors. The concept achieves its great positive form in *Henry V*, where the personal exploits of the riotous prince grow into his famous victories; the stage of history referred to by the Chorus becomes the dominant image of the play. Shakespeare's concept of public versus private man achieves its great tragic form in *Macbeth* where the personal destiny of the man meshes with the political destiny of Scotland.

Shakespeare was working with the Renaissance version of the theme of "inside" and "outside." For the Restoration playwright, appearance and nature are normally different; for Shakespeare, private and public roles are matched by the end of the play. Where the Restoration writer of comedies treats the theme in social and personal terms, Shakespeare, like the writer of heroic drama, treats the theme in political terms — the "outer" man being identified with the historical figure whose actions have enormous consequences for great numbers of people, and the inner man being identified with the private person whose actions affect only himself. For Shakespeare, the political scientist's abstract differentiation became an informing principle for drama.

Shaw, too, based his plays consciously or unconsciously on an abstract idea which was intrinsically "stagy": the Hegelian or Marxist dialectic. The pattern of thesis, antithesis, and synthesis provided Shaw with both dramatic conflict and resolution. We can see it, for example, in *Man and Superman:* the conventions of Ramsden and Tavy (thesis) opposed by the New Man, Tanner (antithesis), the conflict being resolved by Tanner's engagement to Ann (synthesis). In *Arms and the Man,* the old lover Sergius, the old military order, and the old-style romantic play all represent the thesis; the new lover Bluntschli, the new military style, and the new style of play all represent the antithesis. The conventional boy-gets-girl ending makes a synthesis at all three levels — between the persons of the play, between the social orders they represent, and between Shaw's antiromantic play and the romantic wishes of his audience. One could go on, in virtually all of Shaw's plays, to find this underlying dialectical pattern of thesis, antithesis, and synthesis, derived from the most abstruse of abstruse philosophies.

The dramatist is indeed fortunate whose age presents him with such an abstraction, one that has a built-in dramatic potential, and Etherege, Wycherley, and Congreve are among the lucky ones. Seventeenth-century metaphysics separated appearance from nature; seventeenth-century political theorists separated the "natural" man from the social man; and the Restoration writers of comedy cashed in. Both these ideas have enormous dramatic possibilities, and Etherege, Wycherley, and Congreve realized them. Disguise, affectation, dissimulation, pretense, and hypocrisy on their stage grow from a sense of cosmic disguise. Their seventeenth-century metaphysic gave them a stage beyond their stage. And if Restoration comedy is merely "a passionate dance-figure, or an arabesque of words and repartees," as some critics say, the pattern of the dance is the metaphysic of modern science.

7 • *The Gentleman Dancing-Master*

Wycherley's second play was produced at the new theater, Dorset Garden, apparently in the fall of 1672. It was indifferently received then—and has been since. No one revives this play; critics rarely give it more than passing mention. Frankly, I find this hard to understand, because *The Gentleman Dancing-Master* stands out as perhaps the most ingenuous and innocuous comedy of the period. Restoration audiences received it coolly, possibly because it is less smutty than most Restoration comedies, but more probably because it was too simple for their tastes: the intrigue is not very complicated and the humor is more slapstick than verbal. But the qualities that made the Restoration dislike it are precisely the things that should make a modern critic or audience prefer it, for it is intrigue and verbal wit that make most Restoration plays hard to follow. This, therefore, should be an ideal play for revival. On its own merits, *The Gentleman Dancing-Master* has a pretty charm that contrasts with and overshadows the small amount of Restoration vulgarity that remains in it.

By Restoration standards, its plot, based on Calderón's *El Maestro de Danzar*, is almost unbelievably simple. Sir James Formal has adopted Spanish clothes, manners, oaths, even the name Don Diego. He has therefore confined his daughter Hippolita to the care of a duenna, her aunt, Mrs. Caution, until her forthcoming marriage to Monsieur de Paris, an English fop who returned from France just as French as Don Diego is Spanish. Hippolita, who is only fourteen, but wonderfully clever, tricks Paris into bringing her a wit of some repute, Gerrard, whom she decides to marry instead of Paris. When her father finds them together, she passes Gerrard off as a dancing-master, although he cannot dance, and although Mrs. Caution warns Don Diego. While Paris intrigues with two prostitutes and Don Diego tries forcibly to translate his prospective son-in-law's French ways into Spanish ones, Gerrard and Hippolita plan to elope. After two false starts, they are married by the parson Paris had brought and the pseudo-Frenchman is left to make a settlement on the prostitute Flirt, and the pseudo-Spaniard to cover his humiliation by pretending he knew their plan all along.

The play makes its point simply, directly, and amusingly. In the title lies the theme: the contrast between the dancing-master (one of "those tripping outsides of Gentlemen" — 179)[1] and the true gentleman, form alone as opposed to form plus substance. Dancing itself in the play serves as one half of a sustained *double-entendre* (194, 231): dancing is an outward form that cloaks the real dance of marriage (220) — "*Adam* and *Eves* dance, or the beginning of the World," or at least of its populating (197). The lovers who concentrate on the substance of their relation are surrounded by absurd people who devote all their attentions to appearances: Paris, of whom, when Hippolita asks, "Is he no man?" her maid replies, "He's but a *Monsieur*" (157–158); Don Diego Formal — the name is significant — whom Paris calls a "capricious, jealous Fop" (188) and Gerrard calls "old Formality" (198); Mrs. Caution, who consistently attaches more importance to the fact of chastity than to the state of mind that gives rise to it. In the first scene, Mrs. Caution and Hippolita discuss the contrast that dominates and shapes the play:

Mrs. Caution. I know you hate me, because I have been the Guardian of your Reputation. But your Husband may thank me one day.

Hippolita. If he be not a Fool, he would rather be oblig'd to me for my vertue than to you, since, at long run, he must whether he will or no. . . .
I have done no ill, but I have paid it with thinking. . . .

Mrs. Caut. O that's no hurt; to think is no hurt. . . .

Hipp. I am for going into the Throng of Temptations. . . . And making my self so familiar with them, that I wou'd not be concern'd for 'em a whit . . . And would take all the innocent liberty of the Town, to tattle to your men under a Vizard in the Play-houses, and meet 'em at night in Masquerade.

Mrs. Caut. There I do believe you again; I know you wou'd be masquerading . . . O, the fatal Liberty of this masquerading Age[!] when I was a young woman.

Hipp. Come, come, do not blaspheme this masquerading Age, like an ill-bred City-Dame . . . by what I've heard 'tis a pleasant-well-bred-complacent-free-frolick-good-natur'd-pretty-Age; and if you do not like it, leave it to us that do. (162–163)

Don Diego also reverses the proper roles of social forms and state of mind, in a broader sense, of appearance and nature. Thus, he congratulates Mrs. Caution on keeping even priests away from Hippolita:

We are bold enough in trusting them with our Souls, I'le never trust 'em with the body of my Daughter, look you *Guarda,* you see what comes of trusting Church-men here in *England;* and 'tis because the Women govern with Families, that Chaplains are so much in fashion. Trust a Church-man — trust a Coward with your honour, a Fool, with your secret, a Gamester with your Purse, as soon as a Priest with your Wife or Daughter, look you, *Guarda,* I am no Fool, look you. (173)

This is Wycherley's peculiarly caustic sense of humor: the ability to laugh at the whole "masquerading Age," that has given the soul the value of the body and the body the value of the soul, the ability to laugh on one side at the chaplains and the ladies who engage them and on the other at Don Diego who complains for a wrong reason.

Mrs. Caution's hypocrisy is only a more subtle version of the attention to forms that constitutes the humors of Diego and Paris. "Ha — is dere any ting in de Universe so jenti as de *Pantalloons*?" cries Paris, "any ting so *ravisaunt* as de *Pantalloons*." "I must live and dye for de *Pantaloon* against de *Spanish* hose" (189). Marriage, compared to clothing, is a mere nothing: "Dere is not the least Ribbon of my Garniture, but is as dear to me as your Daughter, Jernie" (191). Paris believes — almost logically — that since the French have them, the way to achieve good manners is to imitate the French, to speak one's native English with a French accent, and the like. Anything English, such as Gerrard, is *ipso facto* objectionable (160): "I wou'd not be judg'd by an *English* Looking-glass, Jarnie" (190). He thus debases "Civility and good Breeding more then a City Dancing-Master" (158). He is the real dancing-master (the outside of a gentleman), and Gerrard is the real gentleman. Fittingly, then, Monsieur is duped into bringing Hippolita her lover, standing watch for them, bringing a parson, and guarding them while they are married.

Don Diego, too, though his pretense is a little subtler than Paris', values clothing more than his daughter: "He that marry's my Daughter shall at least look like a wise Man, for he shall wear the *Spanish* Habit" (190). Whereas Paris seeks only good manners, Don Diego seeks wisdom itself. His only mistake is to assume that by putting on Spanish clothes, beard, and oaths, one achieves "*Spanish* Care, Circumspection, and Prudence" (198). But Don Diego is at least a shade wiser than his French counterpart. He can see Paris is "so much disguis'd" (188); he can see Gerrard is "a very honest man, though a Dancing master" (192) — even if Gerrard is deceiving him as he speaks. He can at least say: "The Hood does not make the Monk, the Ass was an Ass still, though he had the Lyons Skin on; this will be a light *French* Fool, in spight of the grave *Spanish* Habit, look you" (202). Most important, Don Diego can make a turnabout pretense at the end, to fill out the happy ending for the story (230).

In contrast to these absurd people who pretend almost unconsciously, stand the witty lovers who know what they are doing, even if they are impelled by the disturbing influence of love: "Love, indeed," says Gerrard, "has made a grave Gouty Statesman fight Duels; the Souldier flye from his Colours, a Pedant a fine Gentleman; nay, and the very Lawyer a Poet, and therefore may make me a Dancing-Master" (183). It is an error to assume that the satire deals only with "nationalities." On the contrary, the satire, both in language and action, contrasts two kinds of pretense: we might call them clever and foolish, conscious and unconscious, pretense as a means as opposed to pretense as an end in itself, or more accurately, pretending in order to achieve a proper appearance with which to express one's nature as opposed to pretending in order to substitute appearances for the emptiness of one's nature.

Wycherley even uses the play as a play to flesh out this contrast: the actor in a part as opposed to the foolish character he plays makes up a perfect instance of dissimulation as opposed to affectation. To call attention to the play as a play, Wycherley uses a number of asides to be delivered directly to the audience. He also puts in two amusing little bits, Pirandello-like in the way they break down the dramatic illusion. Paris, a fictional fool, played by James Nokes, debates with Hippolita the relative merits of two stage-fools — Edward Angel (who probably played Don Diego) and James Nokes. (Needless to say, Nokes prefers Nokes.) At a later point, Hippolita remarks to the audience:

> I am thinking if some little filching inquisitive Poet shou'd get my story, and represent it on the Stage; what those Ladies, who are never precise but at a Play, wou'd say of me now, that I were a confident coming piece, I warrant, and they wou'd damn the poor Poet for libelling the Sex; but sure though I give myself and fortune away frankly, without the consent of my Friends, my confidence is less than theirs, who stand off only for separate maintenance. (221)

Paris and Hippolita in these two situations call the audience's attention to the whole joke: appearance assumed to belie inner nature, the difference between the conscious pretense of the actor and the unconscious pretense of the foolish characters. This concentration on the play becomes in *The Plain-Dealer* an even more important device. Here, it serves to highlight the comedy of pretense.

Women, to Wycherley, are like plays and reality: they deceive. Each of the women in this play, Mrs. Caution, Hippolita, Prue her maid, even Flirt, the prostitute, is wiser than any of the men, including Gerrard. "Let an old Woman make discoveries," cries Mrs. Caution, "the young Fellows cannot cheat us in any thing. . . . Set your old Woman still to grope out an Intrigue" (180). Men are no more than pets to women, albeit an adult taste, "for after the Shock-dog and the Babies [i.e., dolls], 'tis the mans turn to be belov'd" (176). Gerrard very quickly learns that what he thought was "the Innocency of an Angel" (174) is a rather terrifying amount of cleverness (178). "The mask of simplicity and innocency," remarks the fourteen-year-old Hippolita, "is as useful to an intriguing Woman, as the mask of Religion to a States-man" (174). Women are as deceiving as the Devil (214): "Fortune we sooner may than Woman trust" (215). Even the foolish Monsieur can see it: "Women are made on purpose to fool men; when they are Children, they fool their Fathers; and when they have taken their leaves of their Hanging-sleeves, they fool their Gallants or Dancing-masters" (217).

Hippolita, it is true, uses pretense, but she uses it to fill out a social form, not, as her father or Paris use it, to replace substance with an empty form. Hippolita creates a marriage of love, by a growth from within, whereas the real pretenders try to impose an empty marriage from without. She uses pretense to manipulate Gerrard, to bring him to her and correct his attitudes. Their relation grows from their random desires at the opening of the play, Hippolita's for "any man, any man, though he were but a little handsomer than the Devil, so that he were a Gentleman" (158), and Gerrard's desire for "a new City-Mistress" (169). At their first meeting, their relation grows to a frank sexuality; they talk about money matters (II.ii). They come to admire one another's wit when Gerrard sees Hippolita devise the dancing-master scheme. Finally, when Hippolita pretends she is penniless, she causes a real meeting of selves, free of social criteria.

On the other hand, Paris' relations with his prostitute Flirt lead from aggression on Flirt's part (like Hippolita's initiative) to a quasi-marriage, "keeping" with all the forms of marriage, settlements, maintenance, house, coach, and the rest, but without affection or cohabitation (228ff.). The scene in the last act between Monsieur and Flirt adds to the general contrast in the play. Paris is blackmailed into "keeping"— explicitly contrasted to marriage — at almost exactly the same moment that Gerrard and Hippolita are being married in fact.

Not only is there this contrast between Hippolita's more or less genteel pursuit and the pursuing prostitutes: "Bailiffs, Pursevants" (167), a press-gang to a "hot Service" (168); there is also a continued discussion and contrast of right and wrong kinds of marriage. In addition to Gerrard and Hippolita's marriage based on love, and Monsieur's quasi-marriage, there is the Don's idea that "as soon as she's marry'd, she'd be sure to hate him; that's the reason we wise *Spaniards* are jealous" (201). Whereas in the world around the lovers money can change a woman's very nature ("O money, powerful money! how the ugly, old, crooked, straight, handsom young Women are beholding to thee"— 177), Gerrard cannot part with his love, even when he thinks she is penniless (211). There are the marriages in which "Cuckolds by their Jealousie are made" (198), and wives are confined to that absolute evil, the country (183, 196), marriages in which the husband takes his privileges in the dark — and the wives by day (158). Opposed to them is Hippolita's simple announcement and Gerrard's agreement that she will have none of it: jealousy is "arrant sawciness, cowardise, and ill breeding" (220). Some marriages are forced by parents (185) and these, even Prue the maid can see, are bad (158): Gerrard and Hippolita's marriage is anything but forced. It becomes, in effect, a symbol for the harmonious marriage of appearance and nature, just as the various kinds of false marriage become symbols for false relationships between appearance and nature, the affectations of Monsieur and the Don, for example.

The general movement of the comedy parallels these contrasts: the action works through barriers of pretense toward an underlying situation. At the opening of the play, Don Diego's house constitutes a prison of folly and affectation in which Hippolita is confined like a sleeping beauty. "Around the castle," the story goes, "a hedge of thorns began to grow, which became taller every year, and finally shut off the whole estate." [2] Before Hippolita is irrevocably fenced in (by her forthcoming marriage to a foolish fop) Gerrard comes, though he has to break through the gallery window to get to her (174). The action moves further inward when Gerrard secures his entrance by the dancing-master fiction and when the lovers go into a closet to be married (225); the final inward movement would be the consummation after the curtain. "Together they came down the stairs and the king awoke and the queen and the entire courtly estate, and all looked at each other with big eyes." But neither Don Diego (the king?) nor Mrs. Caution (the queen?) is awakened out of pretense to a true perception of reality. The Don resolves instead on a further pretense. He makes believe he was never deceived and acts the part of the pleased father with blessings and gifts:

> Rob'd of my Honour, my Daughter, and my Revenge too! Oh my dear Honour! nothing vexes me but that the World should say, I had not *Spanish* Policy enough to keep my Daughter from being debauch'd from me; but methinks my *Spanish* Policy might help me yet. . . . I am resolv'd to turn the Cheat upon themselves, and give them my Consent and Estate. (230)

Wycherley has turned the opening situation around. Instead of being able to force the form of marriage on a loveless relationship as he had planned, Don Diego himself is forced to shape his own formal pretense to fit the inner reality given outward form in Hippolita and Gerrard's marriage. "Nature" grown into appearance scores a complete victory over appearance forced on nature.

The Gentleman Dancing-Master pictures two decent people surrounded by a world of folly. Decency means simply two things: the ability to see through to reality and the ability to make the forms one puts on reflect one's private life or "nature." Folly, on the other hand, means the substitution of appearance for one's nature, Spanish clothes for wisdom, a French accent for good breeding, or the form of marriage for the emotional basis of marriage. This kind of folly blinds its fools so they see into others no better than they see into themselves. To Etherege, folly was the confusion of private life with public front. Wycherley saw that much and more: folly represented a commitment to a life of pretense. The unconscious pretenders, Don Diego, Monsieur, and Mrs. Caution, are foolish, even to some extent evil, but without exception less happy than Hippolita and Gerrard, who pretend for a limited purpose, binding themselves temporarily to pretense to gain a permanent freedom from it. Such a contrast shapes a comic action based almost entirely on intrigue. Comedy becomes a chain of results set off by an initial discrepancy between appearance and nature or form and inner reality; for example, the loveless marriage a foolish parent tries to impose. Wycherley's unique contribution to Restoration comedy was a sense that folly, evil, and limitations to happiness were all related, that there is a right way and a wrong way.

Wycherley's awareness of alternatives creates for itself a characteristic kind of ironic simile: Paris, for example, remarks: "Love, dam Love, it make the man more redicule, than Poverty, Poetry, or a new Title of Honeur, Jernie" (199). "Redicule" is the word that energizes the comparison. One could say that love, like poverty, poetry, or a new title of honor makes a man aspiring, absent-minded, careless, or even (that *bête noire* of Restoration writers like Hobbes) "enthusiastick." The comparison reminds us that love and poverty and poetry and a new title are alike in certain ways. Monsieur, however, adds another element — himself. By saying they all "make the man redicule," Monsieur emphasizes one possible connection at the expense of the more obvious ones. We, his audience, contrast in our minds the connections important to Monsieur with other connections. From Monsieur's description of himself and others who laugh at love, we infer a condition in which reactions are appropriate, in which people do not laugh at love, poverty, poetry, or a new title. The simile does not simply compare *A* to *B*; it also compares *ways of comparing* *A* to *B*. That is, the oddity of the stated connection between *A* and *B* (in this case, "redicule") leads us to infer other connections, and we compare the *stated* connection of *A* to *B* with the *inferred* connections. Usually, the stated connection tends to be a "wrong" way of relating *A* to *B*, and the inferred connections tend to be "right." Thus, the real comparisons in these similes are between the stated wrong way of comparing *A* to *B* and the inferred right way. Monsieur's simile talks not so much about love, poverty, poetry, and titles as about Monsieur himself and people like him. The simile represents in itself a kind of dramatic irony.

At another point, Monsieur remarks, "There's little difference betwixt keeping a Wench, and Marriage," and the connection between them seems obvious enough, though we might infer a larger difference than Monsieur. Monsieur, however, goes on to say, "Only Marriage is a little the cheaper; but the other is the more honourable now" (228). From Monsieur's statement, we infer its opposite — a way of life in which one spends more on a wife than on a mistress and in which marriage is more honorable. The simile becomes a comparison of the way of life implicit in the word "now" and a more normal way. This right-way–wrong-way simile is not limited to the absurd characters. Hippolita, for example, compares a lover to a pet (176), but this simile only clothes the real comparison, that between the fondling kind of love one has for a pet and the mature kind of love one ought to have for a lover. The simile itself has an inside and an outside, just as the pretenses and affectations of the characters do.

"Right" and "wrong" in these similes can range widely in meaning. At one end of the scale, "right" can mean merely "socially correct," "modish," as in Monsieur's remark about "Poverty, Poetry, or a new Title of Honeur." At other times, "right" and "wrong" can refer to better and worse ways of modishness, as in Monsieur's comparison of marriage and "keeping." The "right" way can also mean simply the "successful" way. It can even be the morally right way, though "morally" cannot be thought of in Sunday-school terms — Restoration society was far too loose for that. Nevertheless, within even that loose ethical framework, some things were clearly "wrong," for a gentleman to kiss and tell, for example, to cuckold a friend, or to steal money, or for a lady to take love outside marriage — before she is married. In other words, a right-way–wrong-way simile can be based on ways which are more and less modish, more and less successful, or more and less moral; most often, all three apply at once. In particular, the ideas of rightness as success and as ethical rightness tend to overlap — a comic version of the poetic justice of the "serious" plays.

The right-way–wrong-way simile is, moreover, not just a figure of speech, but a basic frame for the entire action. Etherege's *The Comical Revenge* and *She wou'd if she cou'd* and Wycherley's *Love in a Wood* all contrast right ways of behaving (in all three senses) with wrong ways. As Etherege and Wycherley develop, however, this basic pattern becomes more complex; the right and wrong ways in their second plays tend to be hidden under a shell of appearances. Thus, in *She wou'd if she cou'd,* both the heroes and the fools pretend; both get lured into the confinements of marriage and the country; both drink, wench, and otherwise carouse. One must look beneath the surface to see the difference. Just as the heroes show up the fools, so the fools stand as ironic comments on the heroes. In *The Gentleman Dancing-Master,* both the lovers and the fools pretend, but from the wrong way represented by Diego, Paris, and Mrs. Caution, we infer the rightness of the way represented by Gerrard and Hippolita. The difference between Etherege's use of this strategy and Wycherley's is simply that Wycherley puts the right way on the stage, while Etherege either leaves it to inference or, if he does put it on stage, ironically undercuts it (Freeman as opposed to Courtall; Dufoy as opposed to Sir Frederick). With both dramatists, however, this sense of right and wrong way creates the apparently cynical and satirical tone, because they make the texture of the play the wrong way. Our reaction to the play, however, consists of contrasting the situation embodied in the language and action on the stage and an opposite state of affairs that we infer (or infer the rightness of). The very immorality of these plays implies an ethic, but an ethic of wisdom. The hero does what the villain does, and one must look inside to see the difference.

8 · *The Country Wife*

With his third play, Wycherley hit the jackpot. The King's company produced at Drury Lane in January 1675 *The Country Wife,* the first of the great Restoration comedies. Many critics think it *the* best; certainly it is one of the great comedies of all time. With it, Restoration comedy came of age. The play is often criticized, often adapted (i.e., expurgated), and is probably the most often revived of all the Restoration comedies. Too often, however, critics and directors fail to realize that *The Country Wife,* like *The Gentleman Dancing-Master,* is a right-way–wrong-way play. That is, the significance of the play lies in the contrast and interaction of three closely woven lines of intrigue. Two of these intrigues define a "wrong way," a limited, half-successful way of life. The third intrigue defines a "right way" that contrasts with the limitations of the other two.

The intrigue of the title makes up one of the wrong ways. Pinchwife, an aging, conceited rake, has married a naïve, simple country girl in hopes that her ignorance (and hence, he says, her innocence) will keep her faithful to him, but things don't work out that way. Pinchwife's constant references to cuckolding plant the idea in his rakish friends' minds. Moreover, every step that Pinchwife takes to prevent being cuckolded seems to bring him closer to it — with a little help from Margery, his wife, and Horner, the rake he is most worried about. Pinchwife disguises Margery as a boy; this makes Horner think he is concealing a wench, i.e., fair game, and he flirts with her and kisses her. Pinchwife forces Margery to write a letter rebuffing Horner; she cleverly substitutes a love letter. Finally, Pinchwife decides to use his sister Alithea to bribe Horner into leaving his wife alone; Margery disguises herself as Alithea, and Pinchwife literally puts his wife in Horner's arms. Margery, of course, is the most delightful character of the play. "*Mrs. Margery Pinchwife,*" wrote Hazlitt, "is a character that will last for ever, I should hope; and even when the original is no more, if that should ever be, while self-will, curiosity, art, and ignorance are to be found in the same person, it will be just as good and just as intelligible as ever in the description." [1]

Pinchwife is not by any means as charming, and most critics say so.

Though one finds the seduction of Margery "grim tragedy,"[2] most feel that Pinchwife, for the sake of social justice, ought to be cuckolded.[3] Even Steele, probably the most insistently moral of Wycherley's early critics, dismisses Pinchwife as "one of those debauchees who run through the vices of the town, and believe, when they think fit, they can marry and settle at their ease."[4] Other critics find in the Pinchwife plot a narrow, tidy little moral. "*The Country Wife*," writes Henry Ten Eyck Perry, "is built around the idea that jealousy is petty, mean, absurd, and ultimately fatal to its own ends."[5] "*The Country Wife*," says L. J. Potts, "has a moral, and a sound one: that the husband who mistrusts his wife and tries to keep her from other men will merely stimulate her desires and teach her to deceive him, however ill-equipped she is with natural cunning. This is in accord with the rationalism of the period."[6] It is true, of course, that each step Pinchwife takes to prevent his being cuckolded brings him closer to it, but Wycherley, I think, is dealing with matters much more basic.

Pinchwife boasts constantly, "I understand the town, Sir" (20ff.),[7] but he actually knows only enough to hate and fear the liberty the Town offers a woman. His speech is riddled with quasi-heroic images of hostility. For example:

> Good Wives, and private Souldiers shou'd be Ignorant. (19)
>
> There is no being too hard for Women at their own weapon, lying, therefore I'll quit the Field. (29)
>
> Damn'd Love —— Well —— I must strangle that little Monster, whilest I can deal with him. (55)
>
> If we do not cheat women, they'll cheat us; and fraud may be justly used with secret enemies, of which a Wife is the most dangerous; and he that has a handsome one to keep, and a Frontier Town, must provide against treachery, rather than open Force. (59)

Pinchwife threatens with his sword twice in the play (66, 84); he threatens Margery in the famous letter-writing scene (IV.ii): "Write as I bid you, or I will write Whore with this Penknife in your Face" (56). Wycherley, of course, had not read Freud: we cannot expect that he was aware of the overtones of swords and knives. Nevertheless, his insight here is brilliant. Pinchwife — his name is significant — fears and distrusts women; these fears create a hostility that tends to make him an inadequate lover: unconsciously, he satisfies his aggressive instincts by frustrating and disappointing women he makes love to.[8] Disappointing women, in turn, creates further situations that increase his fears. Thus he falls into the typical self-defeating spiral of neurosis. As Pinchwife himself puts it, free of the cumbersome jargon of psychology,

"The Jades wou'd jilt me, I cou'd never keep a Whore to my self" (20).

Set off against the defeat of Pinchwife are the successes of Horner, successes achieved by a fabulous device that Wycherley probably took from Terence's *Eunuchus*. Horner has announced to the town that he is a eunuch, that, after a recent visit to France, the pox emasculated him. His strategy is to find out by their abhorrence the ladies "that love the sport" and then, by letting them in on the secret, to guarantee the safety of their reputations. His ruse brings Sir Jaspar Fidget, delighted to have found a safe "playfellow" for his wife. That lady, delighted that she can keep her "honour" (i.e., reputation) intact, promptly and joyfully becomes the first victim. Later, however, when she shares the secret with her girl friends, she learns, much to her annoyance, that Horner has also shared "the dear secret" with them. In the final scene, Sir Jaspar and Pinchwife begin to worry when they find their wives in Horner's apartment, but all turns out well: the ladies force Margery to lie and say Horner is impotent, and the husbands go away satisfied.

At least some critics see Horner as a villain: Mr. Bonamy Dobrée compares him to Tartuffe and calls them both "grim, nightmare figures, dominating the helpless, hopeless apes who call themselves civilized men." [9] Is he a villain, though? He is undeniably a bad man who does bad things, but he is not a villain in the sense that, say, Iago is, for he does not prey on innocents. The people Horner victimizes, his cuckolds and mistresses, are either far worse than he, or, like Margery, do not feel that they have been harmed. Horner is meaningful in other ways. His pretense that he is a eunuch, for example, is nicely symbolic — one might call it an anti-phallic symbol. Insofar as it is a pretense, it satirizes the importance of pretense in the town, particularly the conventional and convenient pretense on society's part that sexual desires do not exist. Horner is simply carrying into actuality the conventions of *Reader's Digest* morality. Insofar as his ruse is a maiming, it suggests the psychological and moral impotency of Sir Jaspar, Lady Fidget, her entourage, and Pinchwife; it parallels also the stultifying effects on Margery of her confinement to the country. Most important, it suggests Horner's own maiming; part of him has died. There are few things in his world above the belt-line, none higher than eye-level. His world never rises above the natural, and for him, the natural never rises above the animal: "A Quack is as fit for a Pimp, as a Midwife for a Bawd; they are still but in their way, both helpers of Nature" (11), he says as the curtain rises; and his metaphors never get much higher.

These two lines of intrigue, the Horner plot and the Pinchwife plot, define the play's "wrong way" — deception. It may be Horner's deceiving others or Pinchwife's deceiving himself, but the generic idea is that of forcing an appearance on a contrary nature. Insofar as the two plots contrast with each other, they set off town against country. Thus, Pinchwife's emphasis on appearance leads him to believe a country wife will be different. "I have marry'd no *London* wife," he says proudly. "We are a little surer of the breed there [in the country], know what her keeping has been, whether foyl'd or unsound," to which Horner drily replies, "Come, come, I have known a clap gotten in *Wales*" (19). Town and country are, of course, different; their difference is the contrast between Lady Fidget on one hand, and Margery on the other. "The Country is as terrible," laughs a ladies' maid, "to our young English Ladies, as a Monastery to those abroad" (52). "A Country Gentlewomans pleasure," says Alithea of walking, "is the drudgery of a foot-post" (22). The country is a place of bad manners (27) and restrictions. "The Town," however, is a place of pleasures, "Plays, Visits, fine Coaches, fine Cloaths, Fiddles, Balls, Treats"; it is no wonder that Margery, who begins by preferring the country, soon learns to like the town (23). It can be a place of "innocent liberty" (22), or "free education" (72): to poor, silly Margery a "*London* woman" is the very standard of cleverness (58).

But these are superficial differences — real, but appearances nevertheless. Underneath, human nature is the same in town or country. "I'm sure if you and I were in the Countrey at Cards together," writes Margery to Horner, "I cou'd not help treading on your Toe under the Table" (58). When Pinchwife brags how different women in the country are, Horner comments simply, "There are Cozens, Justices Clerks, and Chaplains in the Country, I won't say Coachmen" (19). This, then, is the irony of Pinchwife's repeated assertions, "I understand the Town, Sir" (20ff.) He understands the town only enough to know that he might be cuckolded — not enough to know that the human nature underneath the social appearance is what matters, that a woman's state of mind is the index to the physical fact of her chastity, not *vice versa*. Even Sparkish, the fop of the play, can call Pinchwife "a silly wise Rogue" that "wou'd make one laugh more than a stark Fool" (26). "If her constitution incline her to't, she'll have it sooner or latter" (70).

The only underlying difference between town and country is the amount of pretense each involves. It is worth noting, for example, that while Horner's ruse is necessary for his seduction of Lady Fidget, it plays no part whatsoever in his seduction of Margery Pinchwife. The Country Wife knows what she wants — Horner. And says so: "Don't I see every day at *London* here, Women leave their first Husbands, and go, and live with other Men as their Wives?" she asks Horner. "You shall be my Husband now" (82). The town wife, on the other hand,

Lady Fidget, goes through elaborate subterfuges and pretenses. She pretends to hate the pretended eunuch, she rants about her "honour," and she speaks in the most elaborate periphrases, for example, the famous "china scene" (61–63).

Lady Fidget is interrupted in Horner's closet and enters the room apologizing: "I have been toyling and moyling, for the pretty'st piece of China, my Dear." The lady who interrupted (and who is in on "the dear secret") asks if she can have some china, too, and Horner replies: "This lady had the last there," and so on. The word "china" is used six times in the scene and much of the sardonic, Swift-like force of the episode, as Professor Bateson points out,[10] derives from these insistent repetitions. The *double-entendre* is funny itself, but, at the same time, a simile of extraordinary complexity. "China," as a vessel for food, makes one more of the many conversions of love (or sex) down to mere appetite. China, furthermore, is an object of surface aspects. Originally mere clay, it has become worked and decorated to the point where its appearance now completely hides its earthy origin. So sex for Horner and Lady Fidget and their kind has become almost fantastic and allegorical, it is so separated from any of its original emotional or biological purposes. Moreover, as Wycherley handles the dialogue, not only is Horner's virility compared to china; also relatively right and wrong ways of relating them are contrasted. At first, the comparison of Horner's sexual energy to china simply conceals his relation with Lady Fidget; china stands for virility by way of appetite and fancy earthiness. As the conversation continues, that more or less reasonable relation is contrasted with the idea of Horner as a universal donor of china — and virility. "I cannot make China for you all," he tells Lady Fidget's friend, "but I will have a Rol-waggon for you too, another time" (63). The comparison of china to virility ultimately compares a monogamous appetite with a promiscuous one. Horner, as Professor Bateson puts it, becomes "a Grotesque or mere mechanism."[11]

Contrasted both to the concealed, elaborated earthiness of the town wife and the direct earthiness of the Country Wife, there is the "right way" of the lovers, Harcourt and Alithea. In this, the third line of intrigue, Alithea, an intelligent and sophisticated girl, is about to marry the fop Sparkish, whom she has accepted only because he shows no jealousy, even when Harcourt, the lover-hero, and Horner's friend, declares his love and urges her to drop Sparkish and marry him. Actually, of course, Sparkish can afford to be indifferent because he only wants to marry her estate. In the complications coming from Margery's disguise as Alithea, Sparkish accuses her of having given herself to Horner, so that Alithea drops the fop and marries Harcourt who still believes in her. The action of this third line of intrigue is the education of Alithea. She has to learn two things. First, she must learn not to substitute a mere appearance (Sparkish's lack of jealousy) for inner nature (Harcourt's merits), as she does when she says of Sparkish: "I own he wants the wit of *Harcourt*, which I will dispense withal, for another want he has, which is want of jealousie, which men of wit seldom want. . . . 'Tis *Sparkish's* confidence in my truth that obliges me to be so faithful to him" (51). In effect, she must learn not to let her knowledge of the deceptions of the town make her "over-wise"; thus, in her moment of revelation, she cries:

I wish, that if there be any over-wise woman of the Town, who like me would marry a Fool, for fortune, liberty, or title; first, that her husband may love Play, and be a Cully to all the Town, but her, and suffer none but fortune to be mistress of his purse; then if for liberty, that he may send her into the Country, under the conduct of some housewifely mother-in-law; and if for title, may the World give 'em none but that of Cuckold. (77)

Second, she must learn a wisdom of ends, a faith in love, a willingness to prefer love as an end to "fortune, liberty, or title."

Alithea and Harcourt reflect this concern with ultimate ends in their speech, which is starred with conversions upward, celestial, even religious images. Harcourt loves Alithea, the "Divine, Heavenly Creature," the "Seraphick Lady" (53), "the most estimable and most glorious Creature in the World" (42); he loves her "with the best, and truest love in the world" (44) "above the World or the most Glorious part of it, her whole Sex" (25), a love that "can no more be equall'd in the world, than that Heavenly form of yours" (44), and so on. It is symbolic that Harcourt disguises himself as a priest to court her. Alithea herself talks the same way. She twits her admirer: "You look upon a Friend married, as one gone into a Monastery, that is dead to the World." " 'Tis indeed, because you marry him," replies Harcourt (25). So, too, Alithea converts Pinchwife's "greasie" comparison of a masked woman to a covered dish to: "A Beauty mask'd, like the Sun in Eclipse, gathers together more gazers, than if it shin'd out" (37).

The persons of the wrong way, like Lady Fidget, cannot grasp this kind of simile:

Lady Fidget. But first, my dear Sir, you must promise to have a care of my dear Honour.

Horner. If you talk a word more of your Honour, you'll make me incapable to wrong it; to talk of Honour in the mysteries of Love, is like talking of Heaven, or the Deity in an operation of Witchcraft, just when you are employing the Devil, it makes the charm impotent.

La. F. Nay, fie, let us not be smooty; but you talk of mysteries, and bewitching to me, I don't understand you. (60)

And Horner dutifully converts the image to one of money: "I tell you, Madam, the word money in a Mistresses mouth, at such a nick of time, is not a more disheartening sound to a younger Brother, than that of Honour to an eager Lover like my self." "They fear the eye of the world, more than the eye of Heaven" (59).

Practical reality dominates the metaphors of all but Harcourt and Alithea. Thus, to Pinchwife, as to the pompous Sir Jaspar, a woman is a possession, like money. "Our Sisters and Daughters," says Pinchwife, "like Usurers money, are safest, when put out; but our Wives, like their Writings, never safe, but in our Closets under Lock and Key" (75). "To squire women about for other folks," sneers Sir Jaspar, "is as ungrateful an employment as to tell money for other folks" (61). Both these gentlemen look down on what they suppose to be the frivolities of Horner and his friends. "Business," counsels Sir Jaspar, "must be preferr'd always before Love and Ceremony with the wise Mr. *Horner*." "And the impotent Sir *Jaspar*," laughs the supposed eunuch (13). "I have business, Sir, and must mind it," says Pinchwife, "your business is pleasure, therefore you and I must go different ways" (45). Pinchwife's and Sir Jaspar's concern with a supposedly practical reality contrasts with and highlights Harcourt and Alithea's achievement of an impractical reality, romantic love.

In the pretenses of the "low" plots, love, honor, and all abstractions are converted downward to physical facts. Thus, honor is a collateral or security (34), or, to Alithea's maid, "a disease in the head, like the Megrim, or Falling-sickness" (51). Love is something one can be cheated of, just as money is "the common Mistriss" (38). Marriage, Pinchwife describes as giving "Sparkish to morrow five thousand pound to lye with my Sister" (19). Love is most often compared to food (45): thus the town offers "such variety of dainties" rather than the "course, constant, swinging stomachs in the Country" (19). Lady Fidget, for example, is puzzled to know why gallants prefer to eat in an ordinary, "where every man is snatching for the best bit" rather than "be the only guest at a good Table" (80). "A woman mask'd," says Pinchwife, "like a cover'd Dish, gives a Man curiosity, and appetite, when, it may be, uncover'd, 'twou'd turn his stomach" (37). "A Rival," says Sparkish, is "as good sawce for a married Man to a Wife, as an Orange to Veale" (68). Even Mrs. Margery, walking about London, cries with outrageous innocence, "I han't half my belly full of sights yet" (41). Disease, too, is a word for love: "the *London* disease" (68). "Wife and Sister," complains Pinchwife, "are names which make us expect Love and Duty, Pleasure and Comfort, but we find 'em plagues and torments" (72–73). Horner's supposed maiming impliedly contrasts the old heroic idea of the "wound of love" with the venereal diseases or "that worse Distemper, love" (11), just as Dufoy's disease in *The Comical Revenge* did.

These two last conversions downward suggest the other important kind of metaphor: what we have called in *The Gentleman Dancing-Master,* the right-way–wrong-way simile. Wife and sister can mean love and duty or plagues and torments. One can have Horner's "wound of love" or Harcourt's. Thus, Lady Fidget says, "Our Virtue is like the State-man's Religion, the Quaker's Word, the Gamester's Oath, and the Great Man's Honour," and so far the comparison is more or less innocuous, "but to cheat those that trust us" (80). The hearer is left to compare in his mind the society Lady Fidget describes in which these things are related by their falsity to a better society in which they would be related by their truth. The "given" of the play raises the same kind of question. Horner's pretending to be a eunuch not only compares—rather graphically—love as an ideal to love as a venereal fact; it also contrasts the ways in which society will react to him. As long as he is thought a eunuch, he is received with joy by the husbands and contempt by the ladies; once they know his secret, however, the ladies receive him with delight. In a different society, he might as a supposedly real eunuch be received with sympathy; as a pretended eunuch—one simply marvels at Restoration mores. The opening scene of the comedy develops exactly these right and wrong ways, thereby setting the tone. Horner's doctor puzzles at the effect of the ruse; Sir Jaspar crows over the eunuch; Horner affects to be surprised the ladies have not more sympathy for him (11–15).

Not just the language, but the whole action of the play and all of its characters develop this right-way–wrong-way comparison. The wrong way is symbolized by Horner, the maimed man. In his way of life, limited to the world, the flesh, and the devil, things are never what they seem to be. Two kinds of deception, deceiving others and deceiving oneself, shape the absurdities of human life. One deceives others by pretending to a character one does not have. "A Pox on . . . all that force Nature, and wou'd be still what she forbids 'em," cries Horner. "Affectation is her greatest Monster" (16). He is himself, of course, his own worst offender. He pretends to be a "shadow" (15), a "sign of a Man" (17) to hide his sexual intrigues. Knowing that no one would believe he had reformed, he pretends to virtue by assuring the town he has been forced into it. Lady Fidget affects more obviously; she pretends to honor "as criticks to wit, only by censuring others" (31). "Your Virtue is your greatest Affectation, Madam," Horner calmly assures her (13). Lady Fidget adopts the outward appearance of a precise woman of honor, to hide her inner, lecherous nature. Sparkish also pretends—

he is a remarkably complex instance of the type-character of the fop. He pretends to conversational wit: that is his foppishness. But his foppishness is itself a pretense to cover up his small, scheming nature. Under both these pretenses, Sparkish seems rather well endowed with a self-serving wit. Just as Horner uses his well-known lechery to create an appearance of virtue, so Sparkish rather cleverly uses his own disinterest in Alithea. It enables him to be unjealous, and that lack of jealousy persuades Alithea he has a real faith in her and very nearly enables him to marry her estate.

As with Etherege, pretending to a nature one does not have brings two results. First, by long usage, it corrupts both one's pretended outer appearance and also one's inner nature. The pretense and the self become so ludicrously confused that the pretense can never really be put away. Thus, Lady Fidget, even at the moment she is about to give herself to Horner, is saying: "You must have a great care of your conduct; for my acquaintances are so censorious, (oh, 'tis a wicked censorious world, Mr. *Horner,*) I say, are so censorious, and detracting, that perhaps they'll talk to the prejudice of my Honour, though you shou'd not let them know the dear secret" (60). Secondarily, however, continued pretense also gives the deceiver a certain cynical wisdom about human nature: an awareness that since one's own appearance does not reveal one's own nature, the same thing is probably true of the rest of mankind. "Most men," says Harcourt, who knows his way about the town, "are the contraries to that they wou'd seem" (17). Horner bases his whole plot on this kind of shrewd knowledge of social pretense:

> I can be sure, she that shews an aversion to me loves the sport. . . . And then the next thing, is your Women of Honour, as you call 'em, are only chary of their reputations, not their Persons, and 'tis scandal they wou'd avoid, not Men: Now may I have, by the reputation of an Eunuch, the Privileges of One; and be seen in a Ladies Chamber in a morning as early as her Husband. (14)

Even Sparkish is clever in this way: to Pinchwife, he says, "Let me tell you Brother, we men of wit have amongst us a saying, that Cuckolding like the small Pox comes with a fear, and you may keep your Wife as much as you will out of danger of infection, but if her constitution inclines her to't, she'll have it sooner or latter" (70).

At the same time, however, one can be overwise, as Alithea is at the beginning of the play. One can deceive oneself by substituting appearances for a real satisfaction of "natural" desires. Sir Jaspar, for example, wants his wife to have the appearance of having a gallant, he forces Horner on her — and is cuckolded. All of Pinchwife's ruses, disguises, and other pretenses represent appearances designed to frustrate Margery's innocently lecherous desires and they end only in Pinchwife's cuckolding. Similarly, Alithea substitutes (at first) Sparkish's lack of jealousy for Harcourt's naturalness. All of these people are "overwise," in that they substitute appearances for nature.

Opposed to the wise and overwise is Harcourt, who seems by contrast bumbling and ineffective. His schemes consistently misfire. He is ridiculed by the fools of the play, Sparkish and Pinchwife. Sincerity is the essence of his apparent folly. Everyone laughs at his sincere declarations of love, and they get him nowhere until Alithea finally learns the difference between the superficial appearance of faith and real faith. Harcourt's pretending to be a parson is symbolic enough, but only accidentally useful in the plot. The real key with which he unlocks the situation is his offer to marry Alithea even when she has apparently given herself to Horner. He succeeds only when he shows he is willing to make a fool of himself for her. In the end, though, his is the greater achievement. He brings about a real union with the woman he loves; Horner settles for fleeting affairs. Harcourt wins reality; Horner wins pretense.

Wycherley contrasts the women, too. Margery, the naïvely direct country wife, is set off against Alithea, the sophisticated London girl. Here, sophistication wins. Whereas in Harcourt's case, a bumbling sincerity succeeded, Alithea's strength comes from her knowledge of town ways. Wycherley is not being inconsistent. He is comparing two kinds of wisdom, a wisdom of means and a wisdom of ends. To select one's ends rightly is a matter of faith, and this wisdom sets Harcourt and Alithea off from the rest of the people. To achieve these ends, however, one must have the wisdom of means, the "free education" of the town. Even Lady Fidget's silly friends know "women are least mask'd, when they have the Velvet Vizard on" (80). Margery, however, while she can by flashes of ingenuity cut through the social barriers Pinchwife puts up, cannot sustain her effort and, ultimately, fails. Margery knows she wants love, and though her aim is the same as Alithea's, she cannot get it. Margery's intuitions are right, but she lacks the social acumen to carry them out. In other words, she has an intuitional wisdom about ends, but intuition will not give her a knowledge of means. She cannot translate her love for Horner into an enduring social form.

This, then, is the measure of success in the play — the extent to which the characters can free themselves from pretense by *openly* translating their "natural" desires into visible, enduring social forms. Horner's world, for example, is closed, defined by his pretense. It initiates the action, and, in the end, the husbands can be persuaded of their wives' fidelity only when Margery is forced to lie and keep up the pretense of Horner's impotency. Margery's love for Horner is open and honest, but she cannot translate it into the outward fact of marriage, even though she calls Horner her "husband." Lady Fidget openly reveals her relationship with Horner (V.iv) to her girl friends; her openness leads only to them have been pretending and must continue to do so. Another open act is Horner's sympathy for Harcourt's love: "Thy wedding!" he says to Sparkish. "I'm sorry for't. . . . 'Tis for her sake, not yours, and another man's sake that might have hoped, I thought — (*Aside*) Poor *Harcourt*, I am sorry thou hast mist her" (67). Yet Horner's sympathy must remain untranslated into action. When Harcourt demands that Horner clear Alithea's honor by assuring the company he has not slept with her, he cannot comply. Despite his willingness, he has become so enmeshed in his own pretenses that he cannot help his friend (83–84). Sir Jaspar and Pinchwife, at the end, resign themselves to further pretense, taking a cold, epistemological comfort: "For my own sake fain I wou'd all believe./ Cuckolds like Lovers shou'd themselves deceive" (87). The only open, unpretended impulse that can be translated into permanent social form is Harcourt's love for Alithea. Only these two are completely successful, first, because they know how to achieve their aims in the social framework of pretense and, second, because they each realize the importance of an aim that goes beyond the merely social and answers one's inner nature. Each of the others is confined to the social box he has helped make, forced to continue a pretense that must finally corrupt the concealed inner nature. Only Horner is corrupt enough and wise enough to use social pretenses for his own purposes, to master them instead of being mastered. He, however, wins only a limited success. He is, in effect, maimed, cut off from the real and permanent happiness represented by the exuberant union of Harcourt and Alithea, and for which Horner expresses a half-regretful longing: "I alas, can't be [a husband]" (87). This is Wycherley's sense of the two ways: one accepts limited social aims; the other transcends them.

The play, however, does not deal simply with one right way *versus* one wrong way; it deals complexly with a gradation of "ways." The basic division is between Harcourt and Alithea on the one hand and all the rest of the characters on the other. Harcourt and Alithea are the most successful and the most right ethically; they seem foolish but turn out to be wiser than all the rest. Among the other characters, there is another right way, Horner's, more limited than Harcourt's and hardly ethical, but successful in a narrow sense on its own terms. We could diagram the action of the play as in the accompanying chart (using the semanticists' trick of subscripts to denote the two senses of "right" involved, $right_1$ meaning successful and $right_2$ meaning ethically right).

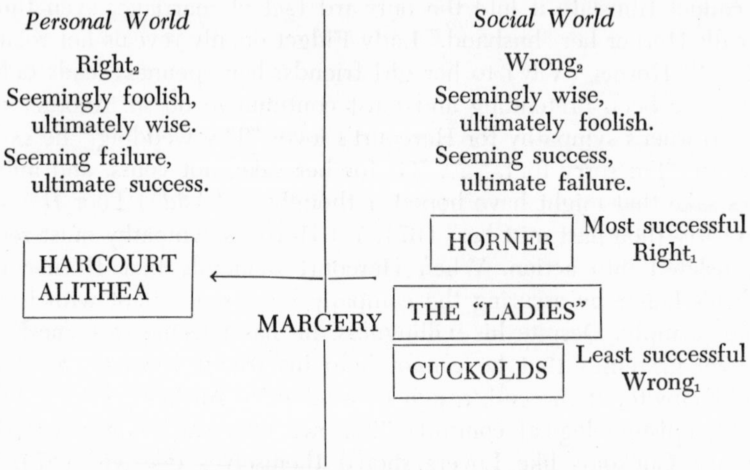

Margery, and perhaps this is why she is the title character, stands at the center: her country naïveté links her to the sincerity of Harcourt and Alithea, but she lacks the social acumen they have to make her sincere aims survive. The action of the play brings Harcourt and Alithea out of the social whirl into a private world. The happy ending, as so often in comedy, affirms the idea of poetic justice: right$_2$ equals right$_1$; the good succeed, and the bad fail — unless they are Horner. For it is he and the complexity associated with him that keep *The Country Wife* from having simply a "happy ending."

Nevertheless, we can see that the right-way–wrong-way structure has undergone a change in Wycherley's mind. *The Country Wife* represents a development beyond *The Gentleman Dancing-Master* toward the final, magnificent *The Plain-Dealer*. *The Gentleman Dancing-Master* was also a right-way–wrong-way play, but most of the dramatic interest was concentrated in the wrong way, the antics of Don Diego and Monsieur. The right way, moreover, was thoroughly realistic: Gerrard was a typical Restoration gallant and Hippolita a flirtatious Restoration coquette. In *The Country Wife*, the dramatic interest is still focused on the wrong way, the doings of Horner, Margery, and Lady Fidget; but the right way has become more idealized in the person of Harcourt whose ineffectual schemes are definitely not typical of the hero of a Restoration comedy. *The Plain-Dealer* will carry the trend even further — the dramatic interest in that play centers on the misanthrope of the title who represents an almost supernatural, totally unreal "right way." The Plain Dealer, moreover, is perfectly opposite to the typical Restoration hero, and so is the girl he finally becomes engaged to. The right way of *The Country Wife* represented by Harcourt and Alithea, becomes in *The Plain-Dealer,* a colorless, half-successful center position.

The chronology of this trend in Wycherley's work is deceptive. Restoration comedy is, so far as the three major writers are concerned, nearing its apex. The antiheroic phase has ended, and the first of their five great comedies has appeared. Yet what is usually thought the first full-fledged "comedy of manners," *The Man of Mode,* has not yet been produced. And even in that supposedly heartless play this double sense of Wycherley's appears, though Etherege portrays the ideal far more ironically than Wycherley does in Harcourt. These later plays — including *The Country Wife* — constitute a second phase after the purely antiheroic comedies like *The Comical Revenge.* Though the heroics have dwindled to a faint overtone (Horner's castration can be thought of as a heroic "wound of love" like Dufoy's venereal disease), the dual structure persists. The two alternatives, however, are not heroic and antiheroic, but right way and wrong way, in the sense of successful and unsuccessful, but also in the sense of good and evil.

These comedies have far more meaning than the term "comedy of manners" suggests. The presence in one play both of an ideal and of activities like Horner's creates a very complex meaning indeed. The ideal developed by this pattern is not all the imposing of a code of manners on the self; it is just the opposite — adapting social forms to the expression of "natural" desires. But the ideal is nonetheless an ideal, and the presence of an ideal in a realistic situation signals the beginning of what we think of as eighteenth-century sentimentalism. The dreary "weeping comedy" of the "reformed" eighteenth-century stage was simply that — the presentation of an ideal in a realistic setting. The strength, then, of this second phase of plays (which includes all five of the "great" Restoration comedies) stems from a trace of that sentimentalism which literary historians almost unanimously relegate to the eighteenth century. *The Country Wife,* by showing an ideal in a realistic context, shows both the beginning of the great period of Restoration comedy and its decay.

9 · *The Man of Mode; or, Sir Fopling Flutter*

There have been few audiences in history as lucky as the one that in 1676 braved the March weather of London and the crowding at Dorset Garden to see Etherege's new play, destined to be his last. *The Man of Mode* was a tremendous success; its easy, witty dialogue was the finest yet to appear, and its hard, brilliant portrait of the Restoration rake was never to be equaled. Etherege, however, had not taken over the sense of good and evil that Wycherley had begun to develop in *The Country Wife*. *The Man of Mode* still treats cleverness as the ultimate virtue.

The play develops its theme and humor from the contrast between two parallel lines of intrigue, one "high" and one "low." The high intrigue involves Harriet, Young Bellair, and Emilia. The low involves Mrs. Loveit, Dorimant, and Bellinda. In each, a young man is involved with two women, one he wants and one he does not want but who pursues him: Dorimant wants Bellinda, but is pursued by Mrs. Loveit; Young Bellair wants Emilia, but is pursued by Harriet, or, more properly, she is forced on him by their families who wish the match. In each line, the young man uses another young man to decoy the extra woman away: Dorimant uses Sir Fopling for Mrs. Loveit, and Bellair helps Dorimant's relationship with Harriet along. Dorimant thus occupies a pivotal position in both lines of intrigue: he is the decoy for the "high" line and he is the man pursued in the "low."

In more detail, Dorimant, at the beginning of the play, has begun the exchange of an old mistress, Mrs. Loveit, for a new and younger one, Bellinda. To do the business Bellinda uses Dorimant's attention to a masked lady (actually Bellinda herself) to work Mrs. Loveit into a jealous rage, while Dorimant accuses her of flirting with Sir Fopling Flutter, the "man of mode." In the second intrigue, young Bellair, one of Dorimant's friends, is in love with Emilia, but his father is forcing him to marry Harriet. Dorimant falls in love with Harriet, but she pretends to be in love with Young Bellair just long enough to let him fool his father and marry Emilia, and, unknown to her, long enough to let

Dorimant consummate his affair with Bellinda. Finally, however, Dorimant succumbs to Harriet's charms and agrees to go off to the country (no less!) to court her.

Etherege contrasts the characters as he does the two plot lines. Most critics agree that the play sets off the sleek competence of Dorimant against the strained effects of Sir Fopling. Actually, however, not just these two, but all the principal characters are ranged on a scale. For the men, affectation is the negative value and the worst offender is, of course, Sir Fopling, who absurdly and magnificently incarnates the idea. He has no inner personality, only externals — clothes, attendants, and mannerisms. For example, he criticizes Dorimant for not having a mirror in his drawing room, for "In a glass a man may entertain himself." "The shadow of himself," remarks Dorimant. Medley, Dorimant's gossipy friend, ironically adds: "I find, Sir *Fopling*, in your Solitude, you remember the saying of the wise man, and study your self" (260–261).[1] Sir Fopling's self is totally outside: there is neither inner man nor inner desires.

Medley, Dorimant's confidant, slightly older than the other young men of the play, is almost as bad. He too remains always a spectator of the action, never a participant (255). For his natural self, he has substituted the gossip the ladies enjoy, so much so that Emilia calls him "a living Libel, a breathing Lampoon" (225), and Dorimant, "the very Spirit of Scandal" (226). Medley is also rather effeminate, the only character who indulges in "the filthy trick these men have got of kissing one another," or who calls Dorimant, "my Life, my Joy, my darling-Sin" (191). Young Bellair is next to Medley in the scale of affectation. "By much the most tolerable of all the young men that do not abound in wit," "ever well dress'd, always complaisant, and seldom impertinent," are the judgments of his peers (201–202). Harriet, more subtle, says of him: "The man indeed wears his Cloaths fashionably, and has a pretty negligent way with him, very Courtly, and much affected; he bows, and talks, and smiles so agreeably, as he thinks. Varnish'd over with good breeding, many a blockhead makes a tolerable show" (220). He is to Dorimant what the heroic people of *The Comical Revenge* were to Sir Frederick Frolick, but Etherege has developed: the contrast is much subtler.

The cynical, witty Dorimant is far more "wild" and "bewitching" (213) than earnest Young Bellair, but even he, as Harriet sets him out, has some affectation. His reputation as a lover is as important to him as clothing is to Sir Fopling. Thus, Dorimant speaks of his long affair with Loveit as old clothes (194) and compares his own person to a bauble or a fashion (229). This play has not just one "man of mode," but two:

Dorimant, as well as Sir Fopling, both occupying similar places in the structure. Etherege is laughing at the hero as well as the fop.

There is, then, a second pattern on which the men are ranked: sexual success, an alternative kind of affectation. Thus, the ladies laugh at Sir Fopling; Medley achieves some popularity, but no particular successes; Young Bellair reaches consummation, but only within the framework of marriage, while Dorimant has two successful illicit affairs and one matrimonial courtship. This scale parallels the other; modishness is a sublimation of sexuality, or replaces it. Sir Fopling thus sees men and women simply as clothes, equipage, or the like (230); he treats his own gown as a person (253). In short, he is one of "the young Men of this Age" who are "only dull admirers of themselves, and make their Court to nothing but their Perriwigs and their Crevats, and would be more concern'd for the disordering of 'em, tho' on a good occasion, than a young Maid would be for the tumbling of her head or Handkercher" (245). Sir Fopling's importance is not so much that he is affected about clothes and "manners," but that his affectation supplants his sexuality, indeed, his very self.

Etherege sets up this relation between Sir Fopling and Dorimant in his brilliant post-seduction scene (IV.ii); the dialogue contains some appalling insights into the ways of womankind. Critics have complained of the frank stage direction calling for Dorimant's manservant "*tying up Linnen.*" His inconspicuous, useful presence, however, is a meaningful realistic note, an ironic comment on the fancy speeches of Dorimant and Bellinda downstage. She escapes just as Sir Fopling enters. He, by way of contrast to Dorimant's sexual affectation, immediately starts to dance by himself and to talk of mirrors and clothes. The juxtaposition of the fop's affectations with the hero's, like the juxtaposition of the false courtship of Bellinda and the "real" courtship of Harriet, reveals Dorimant's Don Juanism for what it is, simply another kind of affectation.

Etherege puts the ladies of the play into a pattern based on the opposite of affectation: "Wildness," which shows itself mostly as sexual promiscuity. Just as Dorimant displays a permissible, or at least curable, kind of affectation, so a woman must be only "as wild as you wou'd wish her," and should have "a demureness in her looks that makes it so surprising" (193). Mrs. Loveit is far from this ideal. Her affair with Dorimant is the common gossip of London. At the slightest provocation she tears a passion to tatters with a welter of invective (out of Restoration tragedy): "Insupportable! insulting Devil! this from you, the only Author of my Shame!" and so on. Her inner self is always on the surface. She has virtually no concern with appearances, no "affectation," as that word applies to the men. Bellinda is next in the scale. Although she conceals her affair with Dorimant, she lets her passionate, private self burst the outer restraint of reputation. She cannot control herself, even though she sees how Dorimant used Loveit (274). Emilia does not hide her affectations so adeptly as Bellinda, but she is considerably more chaste. Yet even her virtue is not above suspicion: Dorimant cynically hints that once she is married he might have better luck with her (202). Harriet alone is so completely in control of her passions as to confine her wildness to the dressing table (219). She is outraged that anyone should think her "easy" to marry, let alone to be seduced (279). Yet to Dorimant she can say: "My Eyes are wild and wandring like my passions, / And cannot yet be ty'd to Rules of charming" (248). She is hardly passionless: she simply does not allow her wildness any unfitting expression.

The comedy opens with two brilliantly drawn characters who appear only once: Foggy (i.e., puffy) Nan the orange-woman and Swearing Tom the shoemaker who call on Dorimant at his levée. They introduce, the critics say, a touch of low life and suggest vices among the lower classes like those of the aristocracy. While they certainly do these things, they occupy a good deal of valuable space at the beginning of the play for purely gratuitous bits of local color. One must, I think, find some sort of keynote they represent, or else conclude that Etherege erred seriously in starting with two irrelevancies instead of exposition. Actually, they serve as "sign-post characters." They establish the two scales along which the other characters are ranged. Nan's business is fruit, something appropriate to one's natural self as opposed to one's social front. (The rest of the ladies in the play face chiefly this problem, expressing their "natural" desires within the limits of society.) Thus, fruit is used later in the play (267) as a *double-entendre* for Bellinda's misbehavior: "She has eaten too much fruit, I warrant you." " 'Tis that lyes heavy on her Stomach." "I was a strange devourer of Fruit when I was young, so ravenous—" says Mrs. Loveit's ingenuous maid. Harriet's mother criticizes the appetite of the age for "green Fruit," instead of ladies like herself, "kindly ripen'd" (246). Swearing Tom, on the other hand, deals in shoes, and the men in the play are ranked by clothing or other factors of appearance. Secondarily, he is concerned with his own inner vices "too gentile for a Shoomaker." "There's never a man i' the town," he says, "lives more like a Gentleman, with his Wife, than I do" (198). Just as Medley and Dorimant are called atheists by Bellair, the orange-woman calls Tom an atheist, religious devotion being a continued metaphor in the play for love (278ff.). Tom's chief attribute, swearing, reflects Dorimant's pretended loves and broken vows.

Besides the main characters and these "sign-post" characters, there are three older people. Harriet's mother and Old Bellair (who falls in love with Emilia) make themselves ridiculous by their flirtatious efforts to impose their outmoded selves on the young. Lady Townley, however, Young Bellair's aunt, is urbane and sophisticated, wise enough to accept her role as elder stateswoman, a charming instance of the wisdom "the Town" offers: how to express one's inner nature in outward forms that will withstand time.

To the satirical contrasts between the two plots and the characters associated with them, Etherege adds further contrasts; for example, the differing treatments of love in the two plots. To Loveit, in the low plot, love is subject to disease and death (217), for which jealousy is the best medicine (239). Dorimant, before Harriet brings him from the low plot to the high, calls love a sickness (242), a disease, a "settled Ague" or "irregular fitts" (249), for which intercourse is the cure (260); an appetite, though one can very quickly get one's "belly full" (257). It is a deception: "Love gilds us over," says Dorimant, "and makes us show fine things to one another for a time, but soon the Gold wears off, and then again the native brass appears" (216). To the people in the low plot, love seems a kind of adversary proceeding, a duel (201), no different for people than for "game-Cocks" (224), for an affair is "a thing no less necessary to confirm the reputation of your Wit, than a Duel will be to satisfie the Town of your Courage" (231). Love affairs are lawsuits (208), carried on with ladies who are "practising Lawyers" (228). Love is a game, in which a woman ought to lose her reputation fairly (269): "The deep play is now in private Houses" (228). Sex, in the low plot, is thoroughly animal: poaching (190), hunting (207, 217), or fishing (242). Only while Dorimant is still in the low plot can he think of Harriet as a business enterprise, requiring "Church security," or speak of their relation as gambling (235). In the high plot, however, the loves of Harriet, Emilia, and Young Bellair are described in half-serious religious images, "Faith" as opposed to "sence" or "reason" (198–199).

Etherege contrasts the two plots further by their use of acting and dissembling. In the Bellinda-Loveit intrigue, all the affairs are illicit and must be concealed. The whole atmosphere is one of dissimulation. In the Emilia-Harriet plot, acting is a mere *jeu d'esprit.* The orange-woman sets the tone when she describes Harriet's playful imitation of Dorimant (191), for Harriet does indeed enjoy "the dear pleasure of dissembling" (222), as do Emilia and Lady Townley when they mimic Old Bellair (233). They and Harriet and Young Bellair, however, play-act only to "deceive the grave people" outside the threesome. In the Bellinda-Loveit intrigue, the pretenses are to deceive the people within the threesome:

Bellinda and Dorimant conceal their affair; Mrs. Loveit feigns an interest in Sir Fopling. In the low plot, Loveit can say: "There's nothing but falsehood and impertinence in this world! all men are Villains or Fools" (286); "Women, as well as men, are all false, or all are so to me at least" (265). Dorimant sees "an inbred falshood in Women" (269). Acting is not sport but deadly earnest, to hurt, as when Dorimant imitates Sir Fopling (267) or pretends indifference to Loveit (238), or to deceive and manipulate — Bellinda's pretenses (V.i) or Loveit's feigned indifference to Dorimant (242).

Etherege provides still a third contrast. In the low plot, everyone — Loveit, Bellinda, even Medley — is a "Devil" (193, 208, 210, 214, 218, 270), though Dorimant "has something of the Angel yet undefac'd in him" (210), and is charming enough to "tempt the Angels to a second fall" (237), as indeed he does. True love and the high plot, on the other hand, represent Heaven, at least linguistically. Dorimant establishes the metaphor in the opening speech of the play when he compares his being forced to write a billet-doux "after the heat of the business is over," to a "Fanatick" paying tithes. Medley and Young Bellair also discuss in the first scene the contrast between the "Heaven," "Faith," and "Salvation" of true love and the "doubts and scruples" of the rakes (199). But in the end, the most cavalier of Cavaliers gives up his skepticism for "repentance" and "the prospect of . . . Heav'n" (278).

In this, as in most Restoration comedies, the action involves a cure or therapy for one of the characters, and the important therapy of this play is to tame Dorimant. He must be brought out of the "hell" of the low plot where pretense is the normal order of business, "good nature and good manners" (216); where it is laughable when one's emotions show (as Mrs. Loveit's or Young Bellair's do); and where sex comes not from love, but from hostility. "There has been such a calm in my affairs of late," says Dorimant, summing up this stormy way of life, "I have not had the pleasure of making a Woman so much as break her Fan, to be sullen, or forswear her self these three days" (195). He must be brought into the "heaven" of the high plot in which the emotional, natural desire can be made a social fact. The critics' sympathies for Loveit and Bellinda in this situation are simply wasted words. By Restoration, or for that matter Victorian, standards these ladies are irretrievably lost, condemned to an endless series of pretenses. The fault in the situation is not that Dorimant gives up his mistresses in favor of a wife, but that the ladies wrongfully succumbed to his blandishments. Neither of them expects Dorimant to marry her; all they ask is that he continue his illicit relationships. Surely Dorimant is more to be praised than censured for preferring the honorable course of matrimony.

It is, of course, Harriet who performs the cure. She very quickly realizes what is wrong with Dorimant: affectation in a much broader sense than the other characters conceive it — for example, Young Bellair in the dialogue quoted above. She knows that Dorimant concerns himself too much with superficial sexual affairs that answer only his vanity: "begging . . . the Ladies Good liking, with a sly softness in your looks, and a gentle slowness in your bows, as you pass by 'em — as thus, Sir — [*Acts him*] Is not this like you?" (236). She realizes that Dorimant is used to a group that keeps appearance from revealing the private self, to whom dissembling is the normal condition. She therefore refuses to have anything to do with the oaths that Bellinda and Loveit had regarded as such important tokens, and that Dorimant had broken so lightly (216, 227, 259): "Do not speak it, if you would have me believe it; your Tongue is so fam'd for falsehood 'twill do the truth an injury" (278). Before she will let him come over to the way of life she shares with Young Bellair and Emilia, she puts him through a sort of initiation:

Harriet. I was inform'd you used to laugh at Love, and not make it.
Dorimant. The time has been, but now I must speak —
Har. If it be on that Idle subject, I will put on my serious look, turn my head carelessly from you, drop my lip, let my Eyelids fall and hang half o're my Eyes — Thus — while you buz a speech of an hour long in my ear, and I answer never a word!

This is, of course, exactly the same kind of play-acting she fell into so naturally with Bellair. But while that was to "deceive the grave people," this is to achieve a catharsis in Dorimant. Dorimant, however, resists.

Har. . . . why do you not begin?
Dor. That the company may take notice how passionately I make advances of Love! and how disdainfully you receive 'em.
Har. When your Love's grown strong enough to make you bear being laugh'd at, I'll give you leave to trouble me with it. Till when pray forbear, Sir. (249–250)

Submitting to being laughed at is only the beginning.

Dorimant's final submission or "initiation" comes in Act V. It is marked by the transition from Act V, scene i, at Mrs. Loveit's, where all the characters of the low plot are treacherously deceiving each other, to Act V, scene ii, Lady Townley's house, where all the pretenses are broken down and all is camaraderie and good fellowship. (In both scenes, three women work on Dorimant, in each case, two ladies and a maid. Not much is made of the parallel in the text; it is more in the director's realm, to be brought out in the grouping of the players.) Whereas the earlier scene is a study in continued deception, Dorimant having betrayed both the ladies, the initiation scene moves from deception to truth. At first, Harriet quite consciously plays Dorimant's game to make him play hers; she makes herself appear indifferent to force him to commit himself;

Har. [*Aside turning from* Dorimant.] My love springs with my blood into my Face, I dare not look upon him yet.
Dor. What have we here, the picture of a celebrated Beauty, giving audience in publick to a declar'd Lover?
Har. Play the dying Fop, and make the piece compleat, Sir.
Dor. What think you if the Hint were well improv'd? The whole mystery of making love pleasantly design'd and wrought in a suit of Hangings?
Har. 'Twere needless to execute fools in Effigie who suffer daily in their own persons. (277)

Half-serious religious imagery marks Dorimant's progress toward the "heaven" of the high plot:

Har. In men who have been long harden'd in Sin, we have reason to mistrust the first signs of repentance.
Dor. The prospect of such a Heav'n will make me persevere, and give you marks that are infallible.
Har. What are those?
Dor. I will renounce all the joys I have in friendship and in Wine, sacrifice to you all the interest I have in other Women —
Har. Hold — Though I wish you devout, I would not have you turn Fanatick — (278–279)

Because she knows Dorimant is in the habit of hiding or suppressing his emotions, Harriet insists now, in effect, that he train himself into the habit of letting his actions reflect his state of mind. If Dorimant is to love Harriet, she laughingly insists, not only must he submit to being mocked, he must pursue her into the country: "To a great rambling lone house, that looks as it were not inhabited, the family's so small; there you'l find my Mother, an old lame Aunt, and my self, Sir, perch'd up on Chairs at a distance in a large parlour; sitting moping like three or four Melancholy Birds in a spacious vollary — Does this not stagger your Resolution?" (287). As in Etherege's earlier plays, the country was to be understood by his audience as a place highly unpleasant because close observation forces the inner self to conform to visible mores; it is therefore a suitable House of Holiness for Dorimant's penance:

Har. What e're you say, I know all beyond *High-Park's* a desart to you, and that no gallantry can draw you farther.
Dor. That has been the utmost limit of my Love — but now my passion knows no bounds, and there's no measure to be taken of what I'll do for you from any thing I ever did before.
Har. When I hear you talk thus in Hampshire, I shall begin to think there may be some little truth inlarg'd upon. (279)

Dorimant, Professor Underwood points out, is undergoing the conflict between reason and passion which is traditional for comic heroes, though in this case the "reason" is that of the libertine and Machiavellian school of naturalism.[2] The passion, moreover, is antirational and fideistic.

Harriet has forced Dorimant from the finite loves of the low plot to a love nominally, at least, infinite. Appropriately enough, she can now sneer at Mrs. Loveit, "Mr. *Dorimant* has been your God Almighty long enough, 'tis time to think of another — " and suggest a nunnery as the fashionable place for her retreat. Harriet has made it quite clear she does not want Dorimant to abandon his naturalistic desires, but to translate them into marriage: "Though I wish you devout, I would not have you turn Fanatick." In the play's terms, she does not want a permanent residence in the country which would stifle Dorimant's energy and competence. What she does want is to teach him to bring his natural desires to the social framework of marriage. Only "this dear Town," as Harriet calls it, admits the full expression of self.

This, then, is the action of the comedy and its sense of humor: to bring Dorimant — and through him the audience — from the low plot where the private self fights social restrictions by deception to the high plot where one can realize his private life in viable social forms. Old Bellair, in these last few lines of the play, hails Sir Fopling indignantly, "What does this man of mode do here agen?" as though Etherege wanted to underline his point: that Dorimant has left that status in favor of a richer kind of "modishness."

In other words, the play is nothing more nor less than the old sentimental story of the rake reformed, indeed redeemed, by the love of a good woman. At least that *would* be the basic form of the action, were it not so variously undercut by irony. One very basic irony is the fact that Harriet (the good woman) occupies a position in the plot structure that corresponds to Mrs. Loveit's; similarly Dorimant functions as a decoy like Sir Fopling. Harriet's making Dorimant court her in the country, in fact, her whole "holding out" for marriage is nothing but a more elaborate and safer form of the oaths and conditions Bellinda required from Dorimant. The entire first scene of the play makes Dorimant look arrogant and arbitrary by showing him as he berates and badgers his servants in his slovenly, helter-skelter household. In general, the opening scene provides a variety of episodes running the gamut of love from the poor whore's trade to Young Bellair's neoplatonic adoration; all these episodes serve to strip the conventions and formalities from life and lay bare the naturalistic substratum at the core of every social pretense. There is still more ironic crossfire in the final scene: at the very moment when Dorimant is agreeing to go off to the country to court Harriet, he is deftly assuring Loveit (out of one side of his mouth, as it were) that he is only marrying Harriet for her money and (out of the other side) trying to make another assignation with Belinda.[3] The play bristles with so many ironies, all undercutting one another, that it is difficult to say what, if anything, Etherege wants us to take seriously. Virtually every action of every character becomes a gambit in a great and meaningless social game.

One thing is clear, however. The comedy does not simply laugh at those who do not have "manners." There are two absurdities. One lies in substituting arbitrary formalism for the inner self, as Sir Fopling does. He lists some French rules of courtship and Medley drily comments, "For all this smattering of the Mathematicks, you may be out in your Judgment at Tennis" (251). The opposite kind of absurdity is Loveit's ranting, an attempt to impose her unformalized inner self on others: "Horrour and distraction seize you, Sorrow and Remorse gnaw your Soul," and so on (215). "Ill customs," wrote Etherege from his diplomatic post at Ratisbon, "affront my very senses, and I have been so used to affectation that without the help of the air of the court what is natural cannot touch me. You see what we get by being polished, as we call it."[4] Precisely this kind of "affectation" is the value the comedy half-seriously puts forward: to express the private self in a social form which is decorous, natural, and even redeeming, or, as Old Bellair somewhat crudely puts it (280): "To Commission a young Couple to go to Bed together a Gods name."

10 · *The Plain-Dealer*

No self-respecting commentator on Restoration comedy passes by Wycherley's last play without leaving behind a purple passage of tribute. This is the one play that everyone calls moral and Wycherley is the one Restoration dramatist who all the commentators think shows an earnest and proper disgust with his age. This play is more discussed than any other Restoration comedy except *The Way of the World,* yet no play is more commonly misunderstood. *The Plain-Dealer,* first produced in December 1676, is supposed to be an unequivocal damnation of Restoration society, including — or even, perhaps, especially — the graceful Harriets and Dorimants.

The confusing factor is the title character, the nominal hero Manly. Wycherley describes him in the *Dramatis Personae* as "of an honest, surly, nice humour . . . and chusing a Sea-life, only to avoid the World" (104).[1] Most critics, despite this ambiguous description, assume that Manly speaks for Wycherley. As a result, the play has had its critical ups and downs. The critic John Dennis recorded its reception when it was first produced; "The Town, as the Authour has often told me, appeard Doubtfull what Judgment to Form of it," and it took all the efforts of the court wits to get it accepted.[2] Dryden called it "one of the most bold, most general, and most useful satires which has ever been presented on the English theatre." [3] Hazlitt praised the play for his Romantic readers with only a little more precision: "It penetrates to the core; it shows the immorality and hateful effects of duplicity, by shewing it fixing its harpy fangs in the heart of an honest and worthy man." [4] Leigh Hunt, however, described Manly as having a "gusto of desecrated animal passion, fit only for some ferocious sensualist who believed himself as great a rascal as he thought everybody else." [5] Macaulay, of course, damned it, and Meredith called it a "coarse prose adaptation of the *Misanthrope,* stuffed with lumps of realism." [6] Finally, however, *The Cambridge History of English Literature,* Volume VIII, appeared. "Here at last," notes Heldt, "it is openly and distinctly said that Wycherley was a moralist." "The savage blasphemer in the halls of beauty and of art," declared *The Cambridge History,* "is, after all, at heart a moralist, indignantly flagellating vice as well as gloating over her deformities." [7]

The decision that Wycherley is a moralist "makes the character of the Plain Dealer, despite everything," a standard literary history says, "a strong and personal creation; the symbol of a furious, incoherent, powerless anger of the traditional English temperament, against the treachery of a refined corruption which captures it through the senses, dominates its intellect, and leaves nothing save the fitful straining of its will." [8] Wycherley's attitude toward the Restoration comes to be understood, by Joseph Wood Krutch, for example, as a "genuine and savage disgust at its baseness." [9] The decision that Wycherley is a moralist leads also to a comparison, invariably invidious, to Molière, for, as one author says, "The boldness of Wycherley's satire need not be disputed, but the hypocrisy which he lashed was not that of vicious passion." [10] "Compare Molière's Alceste in *Le Misanthrope*," said William Archer, "with the foul-mouthed brute into whom Wycherley converted him in *The Plain Dealer*, and you have the measure of the difference between the French and English comedy of the period. It is in very truth Hyperion to a satyr." [11]

The comparison to Molière led only to further confusion, for Rousseau had decided that Alceste was "un homme droit, sincère, estimable, un véritable homme de bien," and that Molière had treated him very shabbily indeed.[12] Alceste's comic nature, however, became re-established, but Manly's comic nature has not been — even for the very writers who see that Alceste is comic.[13] Oddly enough, it is assumed that Wycherley's attitude is the same as Rousseau's, that "the social folly ridiculed in Molière becomes the virtue praised in Wycherley." [14] *The Plain-Dealer* is interpreted as a ridicule directed "not at society, at foibles, or vanity, but at mankind itself," and even the leading authority on Restoration comedy assumes that Manly equals Wycherley: "Wycherley threw himself into the character, and with his rage for the absolute came to an extreme of furious passion, imagining himself in the worst conceivable situations, so that every event would prove him right in his indignation." [15] The problem becomes further confused by the introduction of biographical evidence, for Wycherley was nicknamed "Manly" and the "Plain Dealer." [16] Wycherley's dedication of the play to Mother Bennett, a notorious procuress, in words that parallel some of Manly's speeches in the play, tends to support this interpretation.

There are, however, some two or three commentators who question, as I do, this identification and its relevance. Professor Fujimura reexamines the biographical evidence and concludes, quite correctly I think, that what we know about the actual Wycherley — his affair with Barbara Villiers, for example — suggests that he was not like Manly at all. Thus, Granville wrote: "*Congreve* is your familiar Acquaintance, you may judge of *Wycherley* by him: They have the same manly way of Thinking and Writing, the same Candour, Modesty, Humanity, and Integrity of Manners." [17] We should remember, too, that Dryden said of Wycherley, he "sometimes . . . says more than he needs . . . but never more than pleases." [18] Professor Fujimura goes on to point out that the motto of the play prefers ridicule to severity, that the prologue is ironic and urbane rather than savage, and that Captain Manly throughout the play acts ridiculously when compared to his sophisticated lieutenant, Freeman.[19] Miss Kathleen Lynch points out that Manly acts throughout like a madman.[20] Professor Chorney, from a consideration of seventeenth-century "characters," literary vignettes of personality types, concludes: "The real character of Manly is, of course, neither serious, philosophic, nor misanthropic: Wycherley's contemporaries would have recognized him as a 'humours' character and an object of satire." [21] Congreve, at least, felt this way when he re-drew the character as Heartwell in *The Old Batchelor.*

In fact, we would have to assume Wycherley was a fool to identify him with Manly, for Manly is actually not heroic at all, but blundering, blustering, and self-deceived. A sea-captain, Manly returns from fighting the Dutch to find the one woman he believed in, his fiancée Olivia, surrounded by foppish admirers, married, and refusing to give him back the money with which he entrusted her. When he sees that Olivia has conceived a sudden desire for his cabin-boy, Manly has this person keep an assignation with her, intending to substitute himself and sleep with her out of revenge. In the dark, Olivia meets her new lover (and the concealed Manly), but her husband arrives. In the resulting confusion, the money is returned, and Olivia's unlucky husband turns out to be Vernish, Manly's one supposedly true friend. The cabin-boy, however, turns out to be Fidelia, a girl who disguised herself to follow Manly's merit. Manly rewards her with the somewhat doubtful benefit of his love.

Manly is a dupe, not a hero. His railing only blinds himself. Neither is he a moralist. What he objects to in society is not wrongdoing, but the unwillingness to admit it — pretense and affectation. He carries his demands for sincerity to absurd lengths, holding that "a true heart admits but of one friendship, as of one love" (109). His ideal of sincerity makes him unfit for civilized living: "I rather choose to go where honest, downright Barbarity is profest, where men devour one another like generous hungry Lyons and Tygers, not like Crocodiles; where they think the Devil white, of our complexion, and I am already so far an *Indian*" (118). Ironically, Olivia deceives him by the very kind of play-acting he despises: "I knew he loved his own singular moroseness so well, as to dote upon any Copy of it; wherefore I feign'd an hatred to the World too, that he might love me in earnest" (171). Manly's virtue is his failing: he cannot — or is unwilling to — tell the copy from the real.

He boasts of his knowledge of human falsity, then rejects his one true friend, his easy-going lieutenant, Freeman, and embraces Vernish, saying, "Nay, here is a Friend indeed" (182). Even his sailors realize the absurdity of his foibles: "Dost thou remember after we had tug'd hard the old leaky Long-boat, to save his life, when I welcom'd him ashore, he gave me a box on the ear, and call'd me fawning Water-dog" (108). Manly is hardly virtuous himself; he prefers his affairs with prostitutes whom he respects (as Wycherley in the prologue does Mother Bennett) to normal social intercourse because, he says, there is no hypocrisy in the paid relationships. The fact that he has virtually cut himself off from other people makes him all the easier to deceive, as Olivia is shrewd enough to discover: "He that distrusts most the World, trusts most to himself, and is but the more easily deceiv'd, because he thinks he can't be deceiv'd: his cunning is like the Coward's Sword, by which he is oftner worsted, than defended" (171). He says of Olivia and Vernish, "I have such proofs of their faith, as cannot deceive me" (118), but never says what those proofs are or, indeed, could be. The attitude of the other people in the play proves conclusively that Manly is not to be taken seriously. If he were, the other people would respect him but hate him; actually, they like him and laugh at him.

The one thing that makes us think of Manly as heroic is his raging, furious honesty. Because his own exterior is a true reflection of his inner self, he expects the same of others and is enraged when he does not find it. That rage is the only large, heroic thing about him, and even though it expends itself on absurdities, it is in some sense praiseworthy. A psychologist, I think, would say that Manly felt too guilty about his own failings. His guilt makes him aggressive and hostile and makes him punish himself by attacking insincerity or "adjustment" in others. By these attacks he not only punishes himself by tempting others to dislike him, but at the same time he persuades himself that he is better than they are because he judges them. His concept of plain dealing is simply raw hostility. One thinks of a tolerant, relaxed attitude as plain-dealing (see 121), but Manly thinks it should be to "tell my promising Friend, the Courtier, he has a bad memory"; "tell the great Lawyer . . . that he takes oftner Fees to hold his tongue, than to speak"; "tell the new Officer, who bought his Employment lately, that he is a Coward"; "tell the Scribler of Honour, that Heraldry were a prettier and fitter Study, for so fine a Gentleman, than Poetry"; and "tell the holy Lady too, she lies with her Chaplain" (110). Manly's faith that these insults will reform people (111) is a touching measure of his naïveté.

In any case, all the *brouhaha* about Manly's rages at pretense has obscured three rather more striking features of the play. After all, there is nothing very novel in the plot of the perfidious woman or in the contrast between Manly's passion for sincerity and his lieutenant Freeman's complaisance at pretense. Far more evocative are three strange unrealities: the odd ending, the character of Fidelia, and the presence of Eliza, Olivia's cousin.

Eliza is highly significant, even though she scarcely appears except to defend *The Country Wife* against Olivia. Their argument, in which Olivia hypocritically attacks the morals of the play and Eliza tolerantly defends them, is a rather striking feature in the play. This English version of the *Critique de l'Ecole des femmes* seems at first glance an outrageously irrelevant digression. Actually, it is an organic part of the action — and not a new trick with Wycherley. In *The Gentleman Dancing-Master,* two characters in the play discuss the merits of two of the actors in the play (see above, p. 67). There, as in *The Plain-Dealer,* the effect is to emphasize the "playness" of the play, to break the dramatic illusion and remind the audience that the actors are really just play-acting. As such, this episode keynotes the theme in *The Plain-Dealer* — pretense.

Eliza is by no means "principally a mouthpiece for the author, without any real part in the dramatic action." [22] She serves as a reflector for Fidelia just as Freeman does for Manly. Though she does not play any causal part in the plot, her presence develops a tension. There is a natural relation between her and Freeman. They are much alike and ideally suited to each other, and the fact that this relationship is conspicuously and completely undeveloped constitutes an important part of the meaning of the play as a whole. Like Freeman, she knows "the Town." She contrasts with Olivia, and their dialogue about *The Country Wife* reveals the exact nature of Olivia's villainy to anyone, like Freeman and Eliza, wiser than Manly. She knows "A Woman betrays her want of modesty, by shewing it publickly in a Play-house, as much as a Man does his want of courage by a quarrel there; for the trully modest and stout say least" (128) and because "we ought to leave off dissembling since 'tis grown of no use to us; for all wise observers understand us now a-dayes, as they do Dreams, Almanacks, and *Dutch Gazetes,* by the contrary" (121). "Grimaces of honour, and artificial modesty, disparage a Woman's real Virtue, as much as the use of white and red does the natural complexion; and you must use very, very little, if you wou'd have it thought your own" (127). In other words, Eliza knows that in society a person's appearance and nature are normally not the same and that all intelligent people realize this.

Fidelia, like Eliza, is another odd and highly significant factor in the play. The most important thing about her is that she is unreal, scarcely more than a literary convention — the girl who, disguised as a boy, follows and serves the indifferent object of her affections. It is almost as though Wycherley had borrowed her from heroic drama. Bonamy Dobrée calls her a "curious evocation from Fletcherian romance. . . . flitting through the play as an angel might flit through purgatory if conjured up in the imagination of a tortured soul." [23] She is Illyrian, the highly unlikely embodiment of all of Manly's unreal demands, completely out of place in the realistic London the rest of the characters inhabit. Her unreality makes her in some sense an ideal of sincerity and devotion: "There is nothing certain in the World, Sir," she tells Manly, "but my Truth, and your Courage" (161). Her presence, putting an unreal, ideal goodness in a realistic situation is, by the way, an important step toward eighteenth-century sentimental comedy, but typical of sentimental comedy, she cannot really be considered an ideal, not, at least, by any sensible standard. "The north" that bred this superhuman fidelity is, to the London of the play, an Erewhon like "the West Indies" where Manly hopes to find barbarity outrightly professed or the sea where he could vent his rage with honor. Significantly, Fidelia was willing to follow him to both these places. Her love for Manly, like Manly's love of sincerity, overrides any realistic sense of limit or decorum she might have and ultimately degrades her. Not even a twentieth-century father would care to have his daughter disguise herself and join the Navy to pursue a man like Manly. Neither is she the kind of contained heroine (like Harriet) that the Restoration liked; on the contrary, she is guilty of a deplorable degree of "wildness." Eliza is the admired heroine, just as Freeman is socially more desirable than Manly. Fidelia is ideal only in supernatural, nonrealistic terms; from a realistic point of view, she is degraded and sordid. Her name, Grey, embodies the ambiguity of her nature.

But surely the most striking feature of *The Plain-Dealer* is neither Manly's rage for sincerity nor even the unreal Fidelia nor the unnecessary Eliza: it is the utterly artificial part of the ending in which we learn on the last page that Fidelia is an heiress who left behind two thousand pounds a year and multitudes of admirers to disguise herself as Manly's cabin-boy and so adore his merits. Outrageous! But it makes the final statement about the basic theme of the play, pretense.

In this, as in the other Restoration comedies we have considered, one of the basic themes is the contrast between appearance and nature. It is developed in part by talk. Manly, of course, rails constantly at pretense, as does Olivia; Freeman and Eliza (Olivia's tolerant cousin) both discuss the problem. Less explicitly, but more effectively, the imagery of the play develops the contrast or conflict between appearance and nature. On the side of appearance are the references to clothes and customs; on the "natural" side are Manly's (and others') furious images of animals, sex, and money. Indeed, the whole action takes place within the convention that love and money are the two things that motivate human conduct, the two universal mainsprings. "Those two grateful businesses," Olivia calls them, "which all prudent Women do together, [secure] money and pleasure" (170). This equalizing of love and money is a kind of simile, the conversion downward we have seen before in Restoration comic diction; it suggests, too, the prostitution Manly sees everywhere (196). Yet even Manly feels he must give with his love, those "certain Appurtenances to a Lover's heart, call'd Jewels, which alwayes go along with it" (134); he gives his money first to Olivia and then to Fidelia (195).

The minor characters must be understood, in this as in other Restoration comedies, in terms of their attitude toward the difference between appearance and nature. Novel and Plausible, Olivia's admirers, are typical Restoration fools in that they concentrate all their attentions on externals. Plausible insists on forms and ceremonies, Novel on clothes, gossip and false wit, insisting, "A man by his dress, as much as by any thing, shews his wit and judgment, nay, and his courage too" (131). The things they find in themselves that a lady might like are revealing: the title Viscount — the name Novel; "the softness, and respectfulness of my behaviour" — "the briskness of my Raillery"; "the sleepiness of my Eyes" — "the fierceness of mine"; "the gentleness of my smile" — "the subtilty of my leer"; "the whiteness of my teeth" — "my janty way of picking them" (167–168). They are, in short, all outside, no inside: as Manly calls them, "these two Pulvillio Boxes, these Essence Bottles" (130), "Parrots of the Town, Apes and Ecchoes of Men only" (117, 129). What Manly fails to see is that their affectations and hypocrisies oil the social wheels and allow hostilities to become smoothed over under pretenses. Novel and Plausible get along reasonably well together, even though they detest each other (125).

The subplot, too, is based on pretense. It traces the efforts of Freeman, Manly's complaisant, and therefore much criticized, lieutenant, to marry the rich, litigious Widow Blackacre. He succeeds finally in discovering that her son is really over twenty-one and is being defrauded by his mother, and he uses this information to force her to settle an annuity on himself.

Major Oldfox, Freeman's rival for the hand of the Widow Blackacre, concentrates his attentions on appearances, his "parts," literary and intellectual pretensions pasted on a corrupt and senescent Roundhead (154). The widow herself by her litigiousness concentrates on externals, for law is, as manners are, "the Arts and Rules, the prudent of the World walk by" (105). Lawyers, we are told, substitute form for substance; as one of them says: "I will, as I see cause, extenuate, or examplifie Matter of Fact; baffle Truth with Impudence; answer Exceptions with Questions, tho' never so impertinent; for Reasons give 'em words; for Law and Equity, Tropes and Figures: and so relax and enervate the sinews of their Argument, with the oyl of my Eloquence" (144). The widow has tried to make her son over into a lawyer by forcing him to wear "the modest seemly Garb of Gown and Cap," and giving him an "inns of Chancery breeding" (164), though in his real nature he is simply a dull country squire. The widow herself has become "this Volume of shrivel'd blur'd Parchments and Law, this Attornies Desk" (150).

The major characters must also be understood in terms of their relationship to the conflict between appearances and nature. Thus, though Freeman is the one true friend Manly has, Manly constantly vituperates him because he is willing to admit and accept a difference between social, outward appearance and inner nature. Freeman, like Molière's Philinte, contrasts in this respect with the misanthrope — and that contrast is central to the significance of the play as a whole. Thus, in the hunt for love and money in which all the characters — even Manly and Fidelia — are engaged, Freeman succeeds by pretending and by knowing about pretense. He can, for example, see through someone like Olivia who is opaque to everyone else in the play (but Eliza): "She stands in the Drawing-room, like the Glass, ready for all Comers, to set their gallantry by her: and like the Glass too, lets no man go from her, unsatisfi'd with himself" (169). Freeman can reach inside the widow's pretenses, catch the natural fact she is concealing (that her "minor" has come into his majority), and manipulate that reality to achieve his ends. More important than his success, he has a tolerance that compares most favorably with Manly's fanaticism:

Manly. Why, thou art a *Latitudinarian* in Friendship, that is no Friend; thou dost side with all Mankind, but wilt suffer for none. Thou art indeed . . . the Pink of Courtesie, therefore hast no Friendship; for Ceremony and great Professing, renders Friendship as much suspected, as it does Religion.

Freeman. And no Professing, no Ceremony at all in Friendship, were as unnatural and as undecent as in Religion. (109)

Freeman is far more sophisticated than Manly, simply because he knows appearance does not normally reflect nature.

Olivia, on the other hand, wants society to believe that appearance reveals or even is nature. She, like the Widow Blackacre, uses her concentration on externals to ruin others by forged evidence. They are natural mates: when Olivia is trapped at the end, the widow cries, "I'll follow the Law for you," and Olivia snarls, "And I my Revenge" (195). For Olivia's own pretenses and affectations to deceive others, people in general must believe that appearance is all of reality. Though she knows appearances do not necessarily represent a true state of affairs, she insists that they be treated as though they did. That is the essential difference between Eliza's and Olivia's reactions to *The Country Wife:*

Olivia. I say, the lewdest, filthiest thing, is his *China;* nay, I will never forget the beastly Author his *China:* he has quite taken away the reputation of poor *China* it self, and sully'd the most innocent and pretty Furniture of a Ladies Chamber, insomuch that I was fain to break all my defil'd Vessels. You see I have none left; nor you, I hope.

Eliza. You'll pardon me, I cannot think the worse of my *China,* for that of the Play-house. (128)

Eliza realizes that the play-action is only a kind of pretense; Olivia insists that it — like her own pretenses — be treated as an objective reality.

Manly's virtue is like Olivia's villainy: he, too, demands that appearance be thought of as reflecting real, inner nature, though for a different reason. Because his own outward appearance reveals his real nature, he expects the appearances of others to do the same. His rhetoric of honesty and hers of hypocrisy are almost indistinguishable:

I cou'd not laugh at a Quibble, tho' it were a fat Privy Counsellor's; nor praise a Lord's ill Verses, tho' I were my self the Subject; nor an old Lady's young looks, tho' I were her Woman; nor sit to a vain young *Simile-maker,* tho' he flatter'd me; in short, I cou'd not glote upon a man when he comes into a Room, and laugh at him when he goes out; I cannot rail at the absent, to flatter the standers by, I —— (120)

One must look underneath the linguistic surface to tell if the speaker speaks truth, but Manly is unwilling to admit that he must.

As in Wycherley's other plays, the intrigue is tailored to bring out the difference between two heroes. In *The Country Wife* they were a rake-hero and a lover-hero. In this play, they are two kinds of plain dealers, a misanthrope and a "Complier with the Age." At the outset, Manly knows only that most people use appearance to hide their real feelings.

This is only superficial wisdom, only the beginning of knowledge. Armed with only this one insight. Manly has no idea of underlying realities. He is easily deceived by Olivia's hypocritical railing as Freeman would not be or as Eliza in fact is not. For Freeman knows what Manly does plus the fact that despite inconsistency between appearance and nature, the inner nature may be good (as Fidelia's turns out to be) or bad (like Olivia's).

As in *Love in a Wood,* Wycherley uses darkness to reveal the truth. "Kind darkness," Olivia calls it, "that frees us Lovers from scandal and bashfulness, from the censure of our Gallants, and the World" (192), "for young Lovers, like game Cocks, are made bolder, by being kept without light" (169). Darkness, in other words, by rendering appearances invisible, brings inner nature out. "Wuh!" says Manly at Olivia's behavior in the dark, "she makes Love like a Devil in a Play; and in this darkness, which conceals her Angel's face; if I were apt to be afraid, I shou'd think her a Devil" (171). The first scene of darkness, Olivia's first meeting with her lover, creates confusion, but, as in Wycherley's first play, the second resolves it when Manly and Vernish make themselves known.

The action of *The Plain-Dealer* is to educate the two idealists, Manly and Fidelia, by dragging them through the very mire they despise. Fidelia tries to escape the deceptive world, but she cannot and is forced into the worldly requirement of pretense. She has to disguise herself to follow Manly — "Love has chang'd your outside," Vernish tells her (175). She is wise enough not to tell Manly of her pretense or her love until she can do

> Under this habit, such convincing Acts
> Of loving Friendship for him, that through it
> He first might find out both my Sex and Love. (117)

But the first such act is to pimp for him, and she is naïve enough to think that Olivia's contempt will cool Manly's love (172). She is forced to learn, as Manly is, that Olivia's pretenses of love and virtue will convince sooner than her own proofs — that reality itself is part pretense and deception is a condition of existence.

Manly too has to learn. The widow drags him off to the law courts, where he is forced to witness in quantity the very hypocrisy he hates. At first, he tries to fend off the hypocritical lawyers with force and ends up with three quarrels and two law suits (152). Then he learns that a better way is to pretend that he needs a lawyer to do charity work *in forma pauperis,* and Freeman comments, "So, you have now found a way to be rid of people without quarrelling" (155). In the larger action,

Manly is forced to use deception to free himself of Olivia, just as in this miniature action, he deceives to rid himself of the lawyer. He confesses:

Manly. I dissembled last night.
Fidelia. Heavens! (143)

He begins to win his revenge only when he gets behind Olivia's pretenses and uses Fidelia to manipulate her lust (just as Freeman uses Squire Jerry to manipulate the widow's law lust). Manly even lies to his friend Vernish (when he supposes him still true) in saying that he has slept with Olivia (183). This lie, and his use of Fidelia to mask his access to Olivia, are the rather sordid and dishonest means of his final revenge. Compared to Manly, Freeman is far more honest. His proposals to the widow are frank offers to gratify her sexual desires if she will satisfy his monetary ones. Though he blackmails her at the end, the widow is a villainess, and Freeman asserts her son's rights as well as his own. Moreover, in the process, two of the widow's professional perjurers are arrested.

Though Manly dissembles even more than Freeman, and admits it, he never acquires Freeman's skill:

How hard it is to be an Hypocrite!
At least to me, who am but newly so.
I thought it once a kind of Knavery,
Nay, Cowardice, to hide ones faults; but now
The common frailty, Love, becomes my shame. (141)

The fact that this speech is in verse is significant. Fidelia and Manly speak the only verse in the play (except the tag ends of scenes), and they each speak it only when they admit their own pretenses. Their love-speeches at the end when they have stopped pretending are in prose. It is as though verse were the only medium adequate to the stress felt by an idealist forced to accede to the way of the world.

Fidelia sums up their problem:

O Heavens! is there not punishment enough
In loving well, if you will have't a Crime;
But you must add fresh Torments daily to't,
And punish us like peevish rivals still,
Because we fain would find a Heaven here? (173)

Manly and Fidelia must be taught their own mortality; they must realize, despite their attacks on pretense, that it is a condition of existence to deceive and be deceived by the contradictions between appearance and nature. There is no Heaven here. Manly's reformation in the finale consists of acquiring exactly the knowledge that Freeman had at the beginning:

> I will believe there are now in the World
> Good natur'd Friends, who are not Prostitutes,
> And handsome Women worthy to be Friends.

Manly must learn, in other words, that though dissimulation may be an evil, there are more basic goods and evils concealed beneath its surface.

But surely no feature of this play, not even the character of Manly, shouts for attention more than the complete artificiality of the ending. Just as there are two plots and two heroes, Freeman and Manly, there are really two endings, one plausible and realistic, and one out of some romantic Never-Never-land. In the realistic ending, the villains, Olivia and Vernish, are punished by the appearances they have misused. Vernish is left believing that Olivia has deceived him with Manly, Olivia's reputation is ruined by appearances, and Freeman forces the Widow Blackacre to give him an annuity. But Wycherley carefully omits what would have been a real "happy ending" for Freeman. The obvious, natural ending would have Eliza and Freeman meet and fall in love and Manly go off to his self-inflicted exile. This is substantially what Molière does. Wycherley, however, gives Freeman only the annuity he sought and rewards Manly beyond his wildest dreams and by the most outrageous kind of improbability.

Freeman's final realistic simile, "I think most of our quarrels to the World, are just such as we have to a handsome Women [*sic*]: only because we cannot enjoy her, as we wou'd do," matches Eliza's earlier statement, "The World is but a constant Keeping Gallant, whom we fail not to quarrel with, when any thing crosses us, yet cannot part with't for our hearts" (119). The tension of the uncompleted, even unbegun, match between these two natural mates suggests how they are confined to the social world of their own making.

A director would make the point by the grouping in the finale — the only scene where Freeman and Eliza appear together on the stage. The minor characters would be placed upstage, Manly brought downstage off-center by Fidelia (195). She stands on one side of him and Freeman somewhat further off on the other side. Eliza would stand downstage next to Freeman, closer to him than he is to Manly, but not so close as Fidelia to Manly. Eliza has no lines and her position in the foreground would raise the very question the play asks: how can the blundering, blustering Manly marry an heiress, when the sleek, competent Freeman fails even to meet the girl he is obviously so well suited to?

For Manly is given a blatantly unlikely "happy ending": he is rewarded with the utter and abject devotion of a lovely, virtuous heiress, herself the highly unlikely embodiment of all of Manly's idealistic demands. Fidelia is a pastoral heroine, who simply does not belong in the realistic London of the rest of the play. She is, like the ending as a whole, a trick. The artificiality of her character and of the ending, like the defense of *The Country Wife,* remind us of the "playness" of the play. The play becomes not a realistic representation of life, but a comment on it. We are, in *The Plain-Dealer,* to remember what the prologue said:

> And where else, but on Stages do we see
> Truth pleasing, or rewarded Honesty?

On the stage, the realists, Freeman and Eliza, are confined to the real world: no Fidelias or other miracles come their way. Manly, on the other hand, is rewarded artificially and unrealistically. Freeman achieves only his limited social objective; Manly, however, is rewarded as though he were touched by God.

Indeed, what Kierkegaard said of Abraham applies to Manly: "There was one who was great by reason of his power, and one who was great by reason of his wisdom, and one who was great by reason of his hope, and one who was great by reason of his love; but Abraham was greater than all, great by reason of his power whose strength is impotence, great by reason of his wisdom whose secret is foolishness, great by reason of his hope whose form is madness, great by reason of the love which is hatred of oneself." [24] Freeman also offers a parallel to Kierkegaard's thought: he is the ordinary hero, whose achievement is confined to a wordly plane and who must be judged by ordinary ethical criteria. Manly, however, is the "knight of faith" who has enlarged his desires (his love of honesty) to his whole being, resigned them (when disappointed in Olivia), and then turned around and achieved them through his union with Fidelia. He and his achievement cannot be understood except in terms of a half-rational absolute: through him we get a glimpse of a supernatural quality beyond good and evil. The artificiality of virtue's triumph hints at another world where such miraculous absurdities can be.

The Plain-Dealer, then, does not simply make a statement about the baseness of the Restoration. In a uniquely comic way it asks a question: Can an idealist find his ideal in this imperfect world in which appearances can never really be consistent with nature? Wycherley offers only a hint at a supernatural answer, and that laughingly. It is in this sense that the play is as Dryden said, "one of the most bold, most general, and most useful satires"; it is, indeed, a satire on all the world. The wise man like Freeman accepts the contradiction between appearance and nature and deals with the inner, important attributes; the fools like Novel and Plausible are unaware of it and pursue vain outward appearances;

the villains (Olivia and Vernish) make use of the contradiction to defraud others. But finally, there is a special kind of folly, the idealist's, touched with godliness, that tries to escape the paradox, to run away to sea or the West Indies: this is Manly's folly and Fidelia's. In this sense, *The Plain-Dealer* is, like all great comic art, *encomium moriae*,[25] the praise of Manly's folly in fighting the contradictions of society and Freeman's in accepting them. The play becomes an almost cosmic right-way–wrong-way simile: by showing us two wrong ways of this world, the ending implies a right way — improbable, unreal, in short, supernatural.

Having understood this, we can understand Wycherley's relation to Manly. The playwright who devised intrigues to work out the exact limits of Manly's and Freeman's virtues can hardly be said to share in Manly's blind rage or his inability to find any merit in Freeman's position. On the contrary, Wycherley's identification with Manly is not savage, but, if it exists at all, jocular, self-deprecating, as though he were saying, "This is the kind of fool I am." As he wrote in his *Epigrams:*

> Every Man is a Player on the Stage of the World, and acts a different Part from his own natural Character, more to please the World, as more he cheats it.
>
> The wise Man, who lives in the World, must move and do as a Man in a Crowd, that is rather carried than goes his own Pace; for if he thinks to advance in spight of the Opposition, he will be spurned, elbowed, squeez'd, and trodden down, or else heaved from the Ground, and born up upon others Shoulders, whether he will or no.[26]

Both things happened to Manly, to Wycherley — and to Alceste.

After all the opprobrium that has been heaped on this play by American and English critics and all their praise for *Le Misanthrope*, I would hesitate to say that Wycherley had outdone Molière, but I do not hesitate to say that, among the world's great plays, *The Plain-Dealer* ranks beside its French source. The long-held belief that *The Plain-Dealer* is simply a diatribe on its age obscures its merits. Actually, both playwrights are dealing with the same subtle problem: whether an idealist can live in this real world. Molière deals with it tragically; Wycherley deals with it comically. When Alceste leaves the stage we are not laughing; he is defeated like a tragic protagonist, pinned down to the contradictions of reality. Wycherley's Manly, like every comic protagonist from Dionysus to Chaplin, improbably, indeed supernaturally, transcends those contradictions. The ending in this sense is not unreal at all — if we are willing to look at it from another world.

Mr. Empson suggests, in his brief analysis of this play,[27] that the complex word that describes it is "honest"; I submit that a better word is "world." It is the word most repeated in the play and acquires an extraordinary complexity, whereas the two concepts of "plain dealing" serve only to set off Freeman and Eliza from Manly and Fidelia. There is, for example, the land-world as opposed to the sea-world set out by Manly's use of the epithet "Sea," as in "Sea Pimp" (108). In the seventeenth century people believed quite literally that the sea was a world of its own with a type in the sea to correspond to each type on land. The sea, however, is only one of a series of such "worlds." There is the world of the play and the world of the audience, set off from each other by the artificiality of Fidelia and the ending. The pastoral desire to escape defines the difference between the natural, real world and the supernatural, ideal world, the "enchanted island" represented in this play by the West Indies or "the North," as opposed to "the practice of the whole World" where

> they seem to rehearse *Bay*'s grand Dance: here you see a *Bishop* bowing low to a gaudy *Atheist;* a Judge to a Doorkeeper: a great Lord, to a Fishmonger, or a Scrivener with a Jack-chain about his neck; a Lawyer, to a Sergeant at Arms; a velvet Physician, to a thred-bare *Chymist:* and a supple Gentleman Usher, to a surly Beef-eater; and so tread round in a preposterous huddle of Ceremony to each other, they can hardly hold their solemn false Countenances. (111)

There is the world of talk and the world of action, set apart by all the incidents in the play — repeated almost to the point of tedium — in which people profess one thing and immediately do its opposite. Olivia, for example, rails against vanity in dress and then scolds her maid for not arranging her tower of hair properly. These several worlds are linked linguistically and dramatically in the play. Just as Manly's sea voyage is an attempt to escape toward an ideal, his invectives and diatribes are verbal voyages through every corruption in real society: "Ay, ay," says Manly to the disguised Fidelia:

> thou art a hopeful Youth for the shore only; here thou wilt live to be cherish'd by Fortune, and the great ones; for thou may'st easily come to out-flatter a dull Poet, out-lie a Coffee-house, or Gazet-writer, out-swear a Knight of the Post, out-watch a Pimp, out-fawn a Rook, out-promise a Lover, out-rail a Wit, and out-brag a Sea-Captain: All this thou canst do, because thou'rt a Coward, a thing I hate, therefore thou'lt do better with the World than with me, and these are the good courses you must take in the World. (113)

By a variant of the right-way–wrong-way simile, Manly, like Piers Plowman, implies what these people ought to be by describing what they are.

The most important use of "world" is that in the passage just quoted: the contrast between "the World" and "I." By every kind of device the play creates the impression of an all-engulfing world of universal corruption — by the sailors' speeches in the first scene, by the realistic and corrupt atmosphere of Westminster Hall, and most important, by the fact that every character assumes that all the rest of the world tries to deceive him. Whether, like Manly, a character seeks to dissociate himself from that world, or, like Olivia, to participate in it, the relation of that individual to the world finds linguistic expression in the device we noted in *She wou'd if she cou'd* and that Professor Wanning terms "the language of split-man observation." [28]

Professor Wanning's dissertation discusses this linguistic effect with reference to Congreve's dialogue, making clear, however, that all Restoration dramatists use it to some extent, although Congreve is undeniably the master. As Leigh Hunt remarked with charming naïveté, "Everything seemed to be of value, only inasmuch as it could be likened or opposed to something else." [29] I have chosen to defer my own illustrations of the practice to this play where it keynotes the whole theme of the relation of the individual to the world.

Manly's speeches with few exceptions set up a felt antagonism between himself and the principles governing the rest of the world:

> . . . this thou canst do, because thou'rt a Coward, a thing I hate, therefore thou'lt do better with the World than with me. (113)

Freeman. You use a Lord with very little Ceremony, it seems.
Manly. A Lord! What, thou art one of those who esteem men only by the marks and value Fortune has set upon 'em, and never consider intrinsick worth; but counterfeit Honour will not be current with me. (109)

> Tell not me . . . of your *Decorums,* supercilious Forms, and slavish Ceremonies; your little Tricks, which you the Spaniels of the World do daily over and over, for, and to one another; not out of love or duty, but your servile fear. . . . I'll have no Leading-strings, I can walk alone; I hate a Harness, and will not tug on in a Faction. (105)

Olivia's speeches set up the same sense of antagonisms — when she is hypocritically pretending to virtue. But in her unguarded moments of passion, she sounds like this:

> So, I have at once now brought about those two grateful businesses, which all prudent Women do together, secured money and pleasure; and now all interruptions of the last are remov'd. Go, Husband, and come up, Friend; just [like] the Buckets in the Well; the absence of one brings the other; but I hope, like them too, they will not meet in the way, justle, and clash together. (170)

> Come hither, come; yet stay, till I have lock'd a door in the other Room, that may chance to let us in some interruption; which reciting Poets, or losing Gamsters fear not more than I at this time do. (172)

She reveals a felt alliance with the way the world goes, with "all prudent Women," the physical behavior of buckets in a well, with the vanity of the reciting poet, and the urgency of the losing gamester.

The point is that, whether the character feels antagonism or kinship to the general principles of the world, he feels he must establish some kind of relation to them. He seeks out quasi-scientific laws to apply deductively to his own behavior. By so doing, Professor Wanning points out, the speaker escapes the prison of his own illusory sensations and attaches his action to a larger system of generalization, giving it the authority of science. At the same time, the actor becomes a split man: his reason comments rationally on the irrational actions his passions force on him.[30] William Oldys, the early eighteenth-century antiquary, gives a curious illustration of Professor Wanning's point. He attributes to Jonson and Shakespeare a pair of couplets on the theme, *Totus mundus agit histrionem:*

> *Jonson.* If, but stage actors, all the world displays,
> Where shall we find *spectators* of their plays?
> *Shakespeare.* Little, or much, of what we see, we do;
> We're all both *actors* and *spectators* too.[31]

Oldys' Shakespeare (surely a very eighteenth-centuryish Shakespeare) states exactly what "the language of split-man observation" implies.

As Professor Wanning's dissertation suggests as a whole, these are the assumptions of Restoration comedy itself, not just its language. There are two basic characteristics of Restoration comedy: first, the plays are based on the assumption that society is corrupt in that it runs on principles of self-interest; second, the plays are focused on the relation of the individual to those principles. Thus, by the title of this play, Manly the individual is related to the general type or principle — proverbial in this case: "Plain-dealing is a jewel." In its title, but more important, in its fundamental assumptions, *The Plain-Dealer* does not differ from *She wou'd if she cou'd* or *The Man of Mode.*

Yet Wycherley's last play marks a basic change in the values behind Restoration comedies. In the earlier plays, the dramatic tension pulled between two kinds of people, the competent rake-heroes with complete command of both appearance and nature, and the fools who confused the two or devoted their attention entirely to appearances: Sir Frederick Frolick was opposed to Sir Nicholas Cully, Dorimant contrasted with Sir Fopling. This kind of comedy reaches its peak with *The Man of Mode,* generally considered the first comedy of manners, but actually coming at the peak of the form. Manly is a new kind of hero, compounded of Harcourt's goodness and incompetence and Pinchwife's self-deception ("I know the Town") and hostility. Freeman, like Horner, is a typical rake-hero. While Horner overshadowed Harcourt, Manly is now the center of interest, not Freeman. There are three kinds of people in *The Plain-Dealer:* fools devoted to outward things, a competent rake-hero who plays the social game of disguise and pretense, and, at the top of the scale, a man who is innately good and who is a deviant from his society. This is the new hero and structure that Congreve took and built upon to bring Restoration comedy to its peak, but at the same time Wycherley's innovation is the seed of sentimentalism.

The two hallmarks of the sentimental "weeping comedy" that replaced the so-called "comedy of manners" on the reformed eighteenth-century stage are, first, the presence of ideal goodness in a realistic situation, and second, the sense of natural goodness inherent in every man.[32] Fidelia, Professor Bernbaum points out, is a "romantic or sentimental heroine,"[33] and even Manly, if the play did not treat him as less clever than Freeman, would be a sentimental hero. In the first of our eleven plays, folly was allied with evil and cleverness was goodness. In this last play of Wycherley's, cleverness represented by Eliza and Freeman becomes separated from goodness represented by Manly and Fidelia. The trend becomes even stronger in Congreve's plays; though his and Wycherley's are the most brilliant plays of the Restoration, they are the direct forerunners of "weeping comedy." In short, the sense of good and evil that was Wycherley's great contribution to Restoration comedy became its tragic flaw, the seed both of greatness and decay.

11 • *A Sense of Schism*

In the first three plays we considered, we saw the theme of the comedies grow from a mere spoofing of heroic conventions to the more general notion of a separation of appearance and nature. Chapter 6 suggested that behind this theme in the comedies lay a larger climate of opinion; in politics, in linguistics, metaphysics, criticism, court pranks, in virtually every phase of Restoration thought, secondary qualities were felt to be separated from primary. Appearance and nature were — and *ought* to be — different.

In the next four plays, we saw a second theme or style emerge: a schism between "right" and "wrong" ways of life. That is, the plays tend to set off plots or characters which succeed or are ethically or socially correct (the "right" way) against plots or characters which fail or win only a limited success or are ethically or socially incorrect (the "wrong" way). This sense of alternatives finds a characteristic metaphor, the right-way–wrong-way simile, which, in comparing two things, actually compares right and wrong ways of comparing them. This chapter is an attempt to do for this second theme what I hope Chapter 6 did for the first, that is, set out its context.

Part of that context is the Restoration theory of literature. Virtually all Restoration writers seem to have taken it for granted that literature, including drama, should in some sense teach. We have seen already the blithe assumption that heroic drama taught by means of exaggerated examples. Realistic comedy, however, was said to teach in a much more complicated way — by laughter. In Hobbes's famous definition:

> The passion of laughter is nothing else but *sudden glory* arising from some sudden *conception* of some *eminency* in ourselves, by *comparison* with the *infirmity* of others, or with our own formerly.[1]

Dryden applied Hobbes's theory to drama, showing how the comic dramatist used this sense of "sudden glory" for cathartic purposes:

> If he works a cure on folly, and the small imperfections in mankind, by exposing them to public view, that cure is not performed by an immediate operation. For it works first on the ill-nature of the audience; they are moved to laugh

by the representation of deformity; and the shame of that laughter teaches us to amend what is ridiculous in our manners.[2]

Vanbrugh, in answering the charge that the comedies were immoral, wrote:

If therefore I have shewed . . . upon the stage, what generally the Thing call'd a Fine Gentleman is off on't, I think I have done what I shou'd do. I have laid open his Vices as well as his Virtues: 'Tis the Business of the Audience to observe where his Flaws lessen his Value; and by considering the Deformity of his Blemishes, become sensible how much a Finer Thing he wou'd be without 'em.[3]

Dryden and Vanbrugh have detailed in these passages the right-way–wrong-way technique of the comedies. The playwright puts onstage the wrong way or, in Dryden's phrase, "the representation of deformity." The audience laughs at it, and from their own laughter, they infer a right way "to amend what is ridiculous." Similarly, Vanbrugh shows the flaws and blemishes of a gentleman so the audience can infer a right way, "how much a Finer Thing he wou'd be without 'em." Vanbrugh, however, introduces still another element, the stage itself.

The stage (in comedy at least) was to be a mirror of life. "*Comedy*," said Rapin, the fearsome theorist, "is as it should be when the spectator believes himself really in the company of such persons as he has represented [to him], and takes himself to be in a family whilst he is at the *theatre*." [4] Thus, Congreve, speaking in a poem about his retiring from the stage, says of his Muse:

> No more in mean Disguise she shall appear,
> And Shapes she wou'd reform be forc'd to wear:
> While Ignorance and Malice join to blame,
> And break the Mirror that reflects their Shame.[5]

Vanbrugh describes his method as comparing a gentleman offstage and on; he is actually comparing, in other words, the stage and the world or what is actually shown on the stage (a mirror of the world) and what might be shown on the stage if the world were better than it is:

The Business of Comedy is to shew people what they shou'd do, by representing them upon the Stage, doing what they shou'd not. . . . The Stage is a Glass for the World to view itself in; People ought therefore to see themselves as they are; if it makes their Faces too Fair, they won't know they are Dirty, and by consequence will neglect to wash 'em.[6]

Almost all the prologues and epilogues of Restoration comedy throw the play as play back at the audience, saying, "It is a picture of you," as, for example, this prologue of Tom D'Urfey's:

He who comes hither with design to hiss
And with a bum revers'd, to whisper Miss,
To comb a Perriwig, or to show gay Cloathes,
Or to vent Antique non-sense with new oaths;
Our Poet welcomes as the Muses Friend;
For he'll by irony each Play commend.[7]

Thus comedy was thought to achieve its reform of morals and manners by exactly the same kind of right-way–wrong-way comparison we have seen in the language and structure of the last four plays: (1) the stage is the mirror of life; (2) it reveals the wrong ways of society; (3) the audience infers a right way and so is reformed. Not just individual jokes and characters, but the didactic effect of a play, indeed the institution of the stage itself become elements in this larger right-way–wrong-way comparison.

This conception of the stage as a mirror underlies the use of the stage or the play itself as a symbol. In *The Gentleman Dancing-Master,* Monsieur (played by James Nokes) praised the merits of James Nokes as a comedian. In the middle of *The Plain-Dealer* two characters justify Wycherley's last play, *The Country Wife.* Over and over again in Restoration comedies, the playwright picks up the play and, in effect, drops it in his audience's laps by such remarks as Witwoud's magnificent entrance in the final scene of *The Way of the World:* "What are you all got together, like Players at the End of the last Act?" By calling attention to the play as play, the dramatist says the play, the mirror of society, is a pretense and so exposes society itself as a pretense.

In the comedies we have considered so far, the right-way–wrong-way structure tends to identify society as the wrong (or at least limited) way and personal emotion as the right way. The wrong way tends to be identified with disguise and the separation of appearance and nature; the right way becomes identified with naturalness and complete candor. Increasingly, we find a tendency to present an idealized right way in a realistic situation: Alithea, for example, or Fidelia. The wrong way converts everything downward; love, in particular, is expressed in terms of a lowest physical denominator, as in Pinchwife's or Medley's "greasie" similes. The right way converts everything upward; love, in particular, is converted into neoplatonic religious images, as in Young Bellair's or Harcourt's talk. The right way thus becomes associated with an escape to a place where one can be candid, to Manly's West Indies, for example; even Dorimant takes a trip to the country. All these tendencies will become even stronger in Congreve's plays.

Behind this sense of right and wrong ways lies a whole pattern of separations. Mr. Eliot has taught us to call it "a dissociation of sensibility," a cleavage of thought from feeling that made each cruder.[8] One can equally well, as Professor Bush does, stress the separation of faith from reason. He describes the balance of reason and Christian faith which was the humanistic tradition of the Renaissance, slipping into one or the other of two extreme positions: a Cavalier rationalism, skeptical, naturalistic, scientific and anti-Christian or a Puritan, antirational fideism.[9] Other formulas could be found, but the important thing is the sense of schism. Many things which to the Renaissance man had seemed divinely unified, cohesive, and coherent, in the intellectual climate of the Restoration seemed split apart.

In one sense all these separations were old ideas. Even Aquinas had separated faith from reason, and Professor Lovejoy has shown the common ancestry of eighteenth-century deists and fideists to lie in such figures as Tertullian who relied on the test of individual reason at the same time that they emphasized the anti-rational and the paradoxical in divinity.[10] Both the rationalistic Cavalier and the fideistic Puritan represented traditional and orthodox points of view; but they felt the differences between their points of view more strongly than ever before; and there was no common authority over them which encompassed both. The seventeenth century's sense of schism represented few new ideas; it did represent a far more intense feeling for certain old ideas. What was new, what was causing men to stress old fideistic and skeptical ideas, was science.

Professor Basil Willey introduces his admirable study in intellectual history, *The Seventeenth Century Background,* by pointing out that ideas of "truth" or "explanation" are relative: at different times and different places, people demand different kinds of explanation. In the later seventeenth century, there was a general demand for a new kind of explanation. Such a demand does not, of course, imply that the old explanation is "false." The two explanations, old and new, may coexist quite comfortably.

> For example, the spots on the moon's surface might be due, theologically, to the fact that it was God's will they should be there; scientifically they might be "explained" as the craters of extinct volcanoes. The newer explanation may be said, not so much to contain "more" truth than the older, as to supply the *kind* of truth which was now demanded. An event was "explained" — and this, of course, may be said as much of our own time as of the seventeenth century — when its history had been traced and described. . . .
>
> Scientific explanation was received as the revelation of truth. Not immediately received by everybody. . . . But there is a deepening chorus of approval as the century wears on, and after the Restoration the unanimity is wonderful.[11]

In sum, men came to prefer an explanation of reality that told "how" things took place to one that told "why" in terms of ultimate purposes and final causes. The description of "why," however, had, for earlier ages, not only "explained"; it had related everyday life to cosmic, spiritual events. Each could be understood in terms of the other teleologically. In general, then, as phenomenological explanations replaced explanations on the basis of final ends and values, spiritual reality was, in effect, separated more and more from everyday life. The separation of appearance from nature discussed in Chapter 6 was only one aspect of a general separation of spiritual from physical reality, of the fact from the value formerly associated with the fact.

In essence, the change was simply in the meaning of the word "Providence." In the earlier tradition, and to the Puritans of the seventeenth century, writes Professor Miller,

> the visible world was not the final or the true world; it was a creation of God and it was sustained by Him from moment to moment. Deeper than their belief in the more obvious articles of their creed lay their sense of the world as a created fabric, held together by a continuous emanation of divine power, apt to be dissolved into nothing should the divine energy be withheld. . . . It was not enough to imagine that God organized a mechanical world and merely set the first wheel in motion: "As he *predetermines* Second Causes, so he *concurres* with them in their operations. And this *Praedetermination,* and *Concurse* is so necessary; that there can be no real Effect produced by the Creature without it." [12]

"Providence" meant *concursus dei,* the continuous participation of God in the ordinary affairs of the world. "What is called Providence," wrote Calvin, "describes God, not as idly beholding from Heaven the transactions which happen in the world, but as holding the helm of the universe, and regulating all events." [13] From written history an Elizabethan historian like Raleigh could understand "How Kings and Kingdomes have flourished and fallen; and for what vertue and piety God made prosperous and for what vice and deformity he made wretched, both the one and the other. . . . In a word, wee may gather out of History a policy no lesse wise than eternal." [14] Causality was impregnated with divine immanence.

The analogy that explained the universe to the Renaissance, Miss Nicolson suggests, was that of an organism: "It lived and flourished as did man, and like man was susceptible of decay, even of death." [15] Moreover, that organism was directly and immediately responsive to God through the doctrine of Providence. "During the seventeenth century this conception gave way to the idea of the world as *mechanism* — a world-machine, no longer animate, but mechanically responsive to the 'laws of Nature.'"[16] Thus, the great organism had become to Glanvill in 1664 "the great Automaton," and Locke spoke of matter as "all these curious machines," as "the great parts and wheels, as I may so say, of this stupendous structure of the universe."[17] "The life of an Animal," Burnet wrote, "is a piece of Nature's clockwork." He compared the human body to "a Mill, where the Water may represent the nourishment and humours in our Body, and the frame of Wood and Stone, the solid parts."[18] In the later tradition, and to the Cavaliers, both scientific and dramatic, of the Restoration, "Providence" meant simply that God had ordained a great over-all clockwork system which functioned through natural laws. "They will have the World to be in great," wrote Fontenelle in 1686, "what a watch is in little; which is very regular and depends only upon the just disposing of the several parts of the movement."[19] God in effect had been promoted: no longer a continuously present Operator, He became a sporadically appearing Maintenance Man. We can see in a work like Pope's *Essay on Man* the Enlightenment's version of Providence. God could no longer be said to take a direct interest in ordinary events. A version of Providence, however, could be salvaged, because man's science could be said to be inadequate to fathom the total plan, the "Ends of Providence," the "universal Good." But the sense of God's workings becomes a sense only of a final end. God drops out of the space and time of the real world. He ceases to be immanent and becomes transcendent.

The Restoration man, in Professor Willey's terms, tended to describe this "doctrine felt as fact" as indeed a fact. "The infinite distance," wrote Pascal, "from the body to the spirit symbolizes the infinitely more infinite distance from the spirit to love, for love is supernatural."[20] And symbol slipped into perception: "There is," wrote Burnet in 1684, "an infinite distance and interval betwixt us and God Almighty."[21] In "Natures Next of boxes," as Donne described the cozy correspondences the Renaissance found between the different spheres of being, the outermost box, the macrocosm, had expanded infinitely, leaving neither space nor time for God. Man had fallen another infinity below Him. "The whole cosmic movement," writes Professor Willey, "In the heavens and on the earth, must now be ascribed, no longer to a divine pressure acting through the *primum mobile,* and to angelic intelligences controlling the spheres, but to a gravitational pull which could be mathematically calculated. . . . Since every effect in nature had a physical cause, no room or need was left for supernatural agencies, whether divine or diabolical."[22] Over and over again in the century, we read of the "physical" separation of the spiritual from the "real," i.e., material. It is, again, not a new idea, but one felt with special force because of the appeal of the "new philosophy." Indeed, the separation of spiritual from physical is the assumption *sine qua non* of modern science.

Faith and reason, attached to these two separated planes of experience, also separated and became — ultimately — irrelevant to each other. "And this I think," wrote Sir Thomas Browne, "is no small part of Faith, to believe a thing not only above, but contrary to Reason, and against the Arguments of our proper Senses." [23] Here again the idea was old, as old as Tertullian's *credo quia absurdum*. But the seventeenth century felt the idea more strongly, as it did the infinite distance of God and the unreliability of the senses. The success of scientific explanations, ostensibly not based on faith, gave the idea a tremendous impetus.

The infinite separation of God from man — and, to some extent, from reason — made Him finally unknowable. Fundamental to Renaissance optimism, writes Professor Baker, was a God "whose attributes could be inferred from the universe which He created in time and sustains by His providence, even though His essence be unknowable." These attributes, men "at least partially shared and thus could comprehend. In God such attributes were projected on an infinite plane, and they all focused in His perfection, but they did humanize the concept of deity and brought Him, as it were, down to earth, where He could be handled in familiar fashion." [24] As the universe became less anthropocentric, God became less anthropomorphic. A mechanistic universe presented only the most abstract evidence of His nature. Partly as a result of God's removal beyond space and time and partly as a result of the general distrust of attributes as evidence of nature, God came to be less knowable. The crowded state of ignorance brought together such strange bedfellows as Hobbes and Bunyan. "Christ," wrote the fideistic author of *Pilgrim's Progress*, "is so hid in God from the natural apprehensions of the flesh, that he cannot by any man be savingly known, unless God the Father reveals him to them." Hobbes rationalistically argued that it was improper to say one had an idea of God in his mind, for that rendered Him finite. "Reason dictates one name alone which doth signify the *nature* of God, that is, *existent*, or simply, *that he is*." [25] Beyond this lies only the abstraction worshiped in eighteenth-century deism.

God's removal from the real world inevitably made it less valuable. "Had you not formerly a more sublime Idea of the Universe?" asked Fontenelle of his charming interlocutor in a popularized account of the new science. "Do you not think you did then honour it more than it deserv'd? For most have the less esteem of it since they have pretended to know it." [26] Similarly, the fact that men could no longer seriously believe that society was divinely ordered made society seem less than it had been before the Revolution. It was hard, after all, to believe in the divine right of a rake. Moreover, society, like the universe, could be explained in secular terms, and "an explained thing," Professor Willey points out," except for very resolute thinkers, is almost inevitably 'explained away.' "[27]

The average Elizabethan felt, though his surroundings were by no means perfect, that the principles on which they were arranged were divinely ordained: there was the evidence of the entire cosmos to prove it. In an Elizabethan play supernatural and natural events stood side by side:

> There's such divinity doth hedge a king,
> That treason can but peep to what it would.[28]

Shakespeare's Richard II could say, and his audience nod in agreement:

> Not all the water in the rough rude sea
> Can wash the balm off from an anointed king.[29]

The sea and the symbolic value of the balm coexisted at the same level, and because they did, they held together in the natural order a divine and natural union of the visible and invisible attributes of royalty. Even an Elizabethan politician, writing of Elizabeth's conduct during the Essex rebellion, could say: "I then beheld her Majesty with most princely fortitude and matchless magnanimity, to stand up like the Lord's anointed, and offer in person to face the boldest traitor in the field, relying on God's almighty providence, which had heretofore maintained her." [30] For the Elizabethan, the natural and supernatural attributes of royalty were united in the appearance and nature of the monarch.

One could hardly attach the same cosmic significance to the Merry Monarch, particularly in view of the nocturnal activities of "Old Rowley," the monarch in mufti. In a sense, one could say that the Elizabethan looked at reality as a Roman Catholic looks at his church: it is not perfect, but it imitates a perfection beyond reality. One could say that the Restoration man looked at reality as a Protestant looks at the Catholic Church: it is not perfect; therefore one looks directly to Heaven for a perfection beyond reality.

The Elizabethan by a simple ethic of duty was able in some sense to take part in the order of perfection. "In this one thing," wrote George Chapman sometime before 1613,

> all the discipline
> Of manners, and of manhood is contain'd;
> A man to ioyne himselfe with th' Vniuerse,
> In his maine sway, and make (in all things fit)
> One with that all, and goe on, round as it;
> Not plucking from the whole his wretched part.[31]

The Restoration man felt no such intimacy with the divine order of the universe or his society: he had become merely a spectator of "natural laws." Both the universe and society lacked any kinship with perfection; even his own spectatorship, his understanding of "natural laws," was imperfect and fragmentary.

It is in this sense that such diverse writings as our eleven "immorality plays" and *Paradise Lost* "belong" in the Restoration. They all look away from "the Town" toward a Paradise, and a Paradise seen specifically in terms of knowledge. The rake-hero found perfect knowledge in the candor of love, but most seventeenth-century writing showed it in a religious heaven. "The knowledge of the greatest wise men and philosophers of the world," wrote the mellifluous Taylor,

> even in things natural, is full of ignorance and deceit; because they know not the substances of things, but through the shell of accidents: so as the most simple peasant, arriving at the height of glory, shall be replenished with a knowledge, in respect of which the wisdom of Solomon and Aristotle were but ignorance and barbarism.[32]

The idea of Paradise as perfect knowledge was not new. Dante had said of the Eternal Light, "I saw that in its depth is enclosed, bound up with love in one volume, that which is dispersed in leaves [pages] through the universe; substance and accidents and their modes, fused together, as it were, in such wise, that that of which I speak is one simple Light." [33] In other words, man, when he sees the Creator in Paradise, understands through Him all things created. In the seventeenth century, however, the idea acquired a different emotional value, for "new Philosophy" had proved how sadly lacking knowledge was in this world. In particular, Paradise acquired the connotation of perfect secular knowledge, and that secular knowledge was thought of as collateral to the knowledge of God, not simply an aspect of it. "The Painter cannot transcribe a face upon a Transient view; it requires the information of a fixt and observant Eye," wrote Glanvill in one of those splendid passages that unite an Elizabethan sense of the flow of time with the Restoration concept of the separation of appearance and nature,

> And before we can reach an exact sight of Truth's uniform perfections, this *fleeting Transitory* our *Life*, is gone. Thus we see the face of Truth, but as we do one anothers, when we walk the streets, in a careless *Pass-by*: And the most diligent observers, view but the backside o' th' *Hangings;* the right one is o' th' other side the *Grave:* so that our Knowledge is but like those *broken ends,* at best a most confused adumbration. Nature, that was veiled to *Aristotle,* hath not yet uncover'd, in almost two thousand years.[34]

In his *Theory of the Earth,* Thomas Burnet asked what the chief employment of people in the millennium would be: "To this one might answer in short, by another question, *How* would they have entertain'd themselves in Paradise, if man had continued in Innocency?" He answered himself — they would have contemplated God and speculated on many things, among them, the "*Theory of humane Nature,*" which "will be carried on to perfection in that state." "It will not be hard to discover the springs of actions and passion: how the thoughts of our mind, and the motions of our body act in dependence upon one another." [35] By contrast, in this world, "We neither know what our neighbors are nor what they really suffer. Man is too finite," John Dennis wrote, "too shallow, and too empty a Creature to know another Man thoroughly, to know the Creature of an infinite Creator." [36] Henry Vaughan contrasted man's perfect knowledge in Paradise and the half-successful methods of "new Philosophy" — in this case, the telescope:

> O Father of eternal life . . .
> Either disperse these mists, which blot and fill
> My perspective (still) as they pass,
> Or else remove me hence unto that hill,
> Where I shall need no glass.[37]

No perfect knowledge of "things natural" was to be found in this life where the substances of things are covered over by a shell of accidents. No perfect knowledge of "humane Nature" was to be found in "the Town" where people's real selves are obscured by pretense, affectation, and hypocrisy. Men looked to a Paradise, hereafter or before the Fall, for a world in which people did not affect or dissemble.

"Our Reason was given us to judge of Things," wrote an anonymous critic in 1702, "and our Tongues, to declare that judgment: Art and Dissimulation came into the World when it began to be sinful, and they're now become so familiar to us, we hardly know 'em to be Vices." [38] *The Tatler* praised a lady: "Methinks, I now see her walking in her garden like our first parent, with unaffected charms, before beauty had spectators, and bearing celestial conscious virtue in her aspect. Her countenance is the lively picture of her mind, which is the seat of honour, truth, compassion, knowledge, and innocence." [39] Thus, Milton described the relations of Adam and Eve in the Garden:

> Then was not guilty shame: dishonest shame
> Of nature's works, honour dishonorable,
> Sin-bred, how have ye troubl'd all mankind
> With shows instead, mere shows of seeming pure,
> And banisht from man's life his happiest life,
> Simplicity and spotless innocence.

Into their inmost bower
Handed they went; and eas'd the putting off
These troublesome disguises which wee wear.

. . . [Love]
Reigns here and revels; not in the bought smile
Of Harlots, loveless, joyless, unindear'd,
Casual fruition, nor in Court Amours,
Mixt Dance, or wanton Mask, or Midnight Ball. . . .[40]

Milton here looked back from the "simplicity" and "spotless innocence" of Paradise to make an invidious comparison to the "shows" and "disguises" of the Restoration London he knew. In the same way, though admittedly with a different tone, the rake-hero of Restoration comedy, when he turned toward his "Heaven," turned away from the "Art and Dissimulation" of his former ways.

This, then, is the climate of opinion behind Restoration comedy. At the risk of overschematizing, one can set down the several cleavages as in the accompanying table, in which the ambiguous position of appearances

Why		How
Faith		Reason
Providence		Natural laws
Man as a soul		Man as an animal
Moral judgments	(Appearances)	Scientific statements
Paradise with perfect knowledge, candor, and love		Society with dissimulation, deception, and sex
Perfection		Imperfection
Value		Fact

shows what makes the comedies intellectually provocative. All these separations can be formulated as one in a variety of ways: I prefer the formula of separating facts from values. To the Renaissance man, values had been mixed directly in with facts; each was implicit in the other. The Restoration man saw two worlds, the world of solid, scientific facts, and another world, elusive, and uncertain, of values. He was, in short, "modern."

While I have spoken only of a general *malaise,* a sense of schism, historians have isolated specific factors. Tawney emphasizes the "abdication of the Christian Churches from departments of economic conduct and social theory long claimed as their province" with the resulting attitude (so fundamental to modern political thought) that the secular and religious aspects of life are not "successive stages within a larger unity" (as they were for the Renaissance), but "parallel and independent provinces governed by different laws, judged by different standards, and amenable to different authorities." [41] Professors Burtt and Whitehead emphasize the separation of appearance from nature: the feeling that man's ordinary experience lies, that only the abstract perceptions of scientific reason are "true." [42] Their analysis explains the naturalistic, non-ethical attitude toward society in the comedies, and the interest in all forms of disguise. Professors Willey and Baker point to the separation of supernatural from natural reality and of faith from reason as the results of scientific discoveries.[43] This sense of separation underlies the dramatic search for realistic, reachable ideals. Professor Underwood finds that the comedies are based on the opposition of two traditions: "on the one hand Christianity and Christian humanism, the 'heroic' tradition, the honest-man tradition, and the tradition of courtly love; on the other, philosophic and moral libertinism, Machiavellian and Hobbesian concepts as to the nature of man, and Machiavellian ethics." Thus it is the hero becomes a master at Machiavellian maneuvering and thinks of himself in Hobbesian terms; thus, too, it is that the dupes are often Christian hypocrites or ladies given to courtly love and "heroic" vocabulary (Mrs. Loveit, for example). Thus, too, particular words shift in meaning: "honor," for example, comes to mean mere "reputation" or sometimes even "virility"; "kind" becomes "seduceable"; and so on.[44] These subtle *double-entendres* focus in themselves this "sense of schism."

The Restoration man, as exemplified in the heroes of our eleven comedies, felt both loss and freedom in his "new philosophy." He felt a loss in that he felt cut off from any reality save the imperfect one of this world; he was, in effect, locked in the prison of his own hedonism. At the same time, he was freed from the moral restrictions of an earlier day. His freedom fitted the revolt against Puritan morality after the Commonwealth period; his loss blended with the post-Revolutionary disillusionment of the Restoration. "On the one hand," writes Miss Nicolson of the seventeenth century, "man is shrinking back from an unknown gulf of immensity, in which he feels himself swallowed up; on the other, he is, like Bruno, 'rising on wings sublime' to a spaciousness of thought he had not known before." [45] The hero of the greatest of Restoration comedies expressed this ambivalence, regret for the past and welcome for maturity, as follows:

> O goodness infinite, goodness immense!
> That all this good of evil shall produce,
> And evil turn to good; more wonderful
> Than that which by creation first brought forth
> Light out of darkness! full of doubt I stand,
> Whether I should repent me now of sin

By mee done and occasion'd, or rejoice
Much more, that much more good thereof shall spring,
To God more glory, more good will to Men
From God, and over wrath grace shall abound.[46]

Milton's Adam was thinking of the Fall, not the increase in scientific knowledge, but in wondering whether to repent the passing of the old or to rejoice in the new he was supremely typical of the Restoration.

This ambiguous reaction shaped what Professor Sypher calls the "governing law of dynamics" in baroque art, "which is, in brief, a technique of, first, closure, then expansion or expulsion into space. Without this preliminary closure baroque cannot gain its special illusion of distance, release, and triumph," which, by overstating the world below, substitutes for the world above.[47] In *Paradise Lost*, the initial movement of closure (Book I) that corresponds to the Fall itself is followed by expansion through redemption on the earthly level. *O felix culpa, quae talem ac tantum meruit habere redemptorem.* The same principle underlies the movement of the average Restoration comedy, *The Man of Mode*, for example. The hero accepts enclosure in the limitations of his own senses for four acts; in the fifth, he is redeemed and released by love. With his usual sporadic omniscience, Milton's Adam has in mind the Pauline question, "Shall we continue in sin, that grace may abound? God forbid." [48] The hero of the ordinary Restoration comedy, I am afraid, was apt to forget the "God forbid." His creators made him revel in his naturalistic efforts to make his final conversion to true love more spectacular, perhaps because "where sin abounded, grace did much more abound." [49] In any case, the final conversion of the hero almost without exception comes in theological terms, "deifications," *The Tatler* called them, "pure flames, constant love, eternal raptures, and a thousand other phrases drawn from the images we have of heaven, which all men use for the service of hell, when run over with uncommon vehemence." [50] It was in religious terms that Dryden answered the charges of immorality leveled at Restoration comedy: "We make not vicious persons happy, but only as Heaven makes sinners so; that is, by reclaiming them first from vice. For so it is to be supposed they are, when they resolve to marry; for then, enjoying what they desire in one, they cease to pursue the love of many." [51] Milton's Adam and the rake-hero of Restoration comedy were each in their different ways trying to find in a postlapsarian world, "a paradise within thee, happier far." [52]

The ending of a right-way–wrong-way Restoration comedy reaches up to a Paradise, but the texture of the play, the wrong way, reaches down. The right-way–wrong-way structure embodies the sense of separation between secular, scientific knowledge and spiritual knowledge; so also the trope we have called "conversion down" confines perception to the physical world of sensations. Comparing love to eating or fighting or poaching simply leaves the invisible values out in favor of the visible physical qualities. Science, in the seventeenth as in later centuries, laid the way for literary naturalism. That is, science took its first steps by separating moral and theological values from the quantitative facts of stars or falling bodies or chemical reactions. The Restoration playwright, no less than Zola or Dreiser, imitated his scientific contemporaries. He, too, separated moral values from hard facts, but in human conduct — a far more significant form of separating fact from value than the scientists'!

In an Elizabethan or Jacobean play, whether tragedy or comedy, the language expands the action outward through the analogical correspondences of the Renaissance world-picture to a cosmic implication. The action on the stage is projected onto a supernatural "stage behind the stage." This linguistic resource is not open to the Restoration playwright. In Restoration tragedy the action is reflected back into the individual psyche. Dramatic action becomes a dialogue of the mind with itself. In Restoration comedy the action is translated into terms of physical reality; appearances are stripped off and only the "solid" facts are left, because in a scientific sense, there is no other reality.

Any reality other than the mere physical facts or appearances had to be relegated to the invisible, uncertain realm of value. A far cry it was from the Elizabethan sense of the coexistence of fact and value. To the Elizabethans, the character who announced his freedom from connection with the supernatural or from his "natural" obligations to king or family or community was a villain. "This is the excellent foppery of the world," said Edmund,

> that, when we are sick in fortune, — often the surfeits of our own behaviour, — we make guilty of our disasters the sun, the moon, and stars, as if we were villains on necessity, fools by heavenly compulsion, knaves, thieves, and treachers by spherical predominance, drunkards, liars, and adulterers by an enforc'd obedience of planetary influence, and all that we are evil in, by a divine thrusting on.

"Virtue! a fig! 'tis in ourselves that we are thus or thus," cried Iago, "Our bodies are our gardens, to the which our wills are gardeners." [53] In the Restoration, however, it is the hero who stands in splendid isolation. "Few historical lines of development for 17th-century comedy of manners," notes Professor Underwood, "are clearer in fact than the one by which the Renaissance 'villain' and his 'world' ('Thou, Nature, art my goddess') became the Restoration comedy of manners 'hero' and his 'world.'" [54] Dryden's Almanzor, for example, proudly proclaimed:

But know, that I alone am king of me.
I am as free as nature first made man,
Ere the base laws of servitude began,
When wild in woods the noble savage ran.[55]

In almost all our eleven comedies, the hero first appears alone, or with menials; his first words establish his isolation from others and his dedication to irresponsibility. Thus, Sir Frederick said to his bruised and beaten servant, "Set me down a Crown for a Plaister; but forbear your rebukes." We first see Dorimant when he is preparing to abandon a mistress; Horner in his opening lines commits himself to "nature," nature being at the level of quack, pimp, and bawd. These characters have the same sense of experimenting with their new maturity that college freshmen have when first away from home. They have, too, a sense of the special quality of their age, of the newness of their isolation. It is this sense, I think, that underlies the contemptuous laughter at older people who tried to apply older standards, like Mrs. Caution or Major Oldfox. It is the basis, too, for the continual local jokes, as though playwrights and characters alike wanted to insist, "I am of this age. I am of this age." And "this masquerading Age," said pert Hippolita, "'tis a pleasant-well-bred-complaisant-free-frolick-good-natur'd-pretty Age; and if you do not like it, leave it to us that do."

It is this sense of schism, then, that by making up the intellectual climate of the Restoration engenders the tone, the language, the incidents, the action, and the structure of Restoration comedy. As one seventeenth-century writer, Sir Thomas Browne, put it, "Thus is Man that great and true Amphibium whose nature is disposed to live, not only like other creatures in divers elements, but in divided and distinguished worlds."[56] Out of this "pluralistic multiverse," as Robert Oppenheimer has recently called it, comes the first "modern" drama, insisting on its own modernity with a welter of local jokes and satire on old-fashioned ways. Out of the sense of appearance divorced from nature, in scholastic terms, form severed from being, or in the terms of the new science, secondary qualities separated from primary, comes the interest in dissimulation and the idealization of candor. From an attempt to see physical reality stripped of any dressing-up comes the "conversion down." Thus, Etherege, whose plays deal primarily with the conversion downward of heroic conventions to physical realities, in his letters shows a tendency to convert the heroic conventions of the "wound of love" downward to the sexual duel itself; as, for example, in a letter congratulating the Earl of Arran on his marriage:

I have had the honour of your confidence and you have told me of mighty deeds you have performed. I should be glad to be satisfied whether you are as great a hero now you fight in a good cause as when you drew your sword in a querelle d'allemande; the truth is that sort of courage is a little too violent for the present purpose. The business you have now on your hands is to be spun out in length and not to be ended at once.[57]

He uses the same conversion downward in the delicately pornographic "Imperfect Enjoyment," both too long and too ribald to be reprinted here.[58]

Out of the division of experience into the rational, natural order of facts and the supernatural order of value comes the sense of alternatives, the right-way–wrong-way simile and structure. Thus, Wycherley in his nondramatic writings refers constantly to the belief that there is a complex of ideas, love, poetry, and religion, all forms of the irrational, which should be kept separate from ordinary reason. One of his poems is "A Song, against Reason in Love":

Since Love's a Passion, Sense in Love
 Were senseless, dull Impertinence,
For Love, no more than Faith, we prove
 By pedant Reason, babling Sense;
Faith in Love, as Religion too,
By Good-Works, not Good-Sense, we show.

In busie Life's most base Concerns,
 Of Honour, Pow'r, or Interest,
That Reason something more discerns,
 Than Blind Faith can, it is confest;
But in the great Affair of Love,
Reason, shou'd Reas'ning, disapprove.[59]

"A Man must renounce his Reason to prove his Faith," says one of his *Epigrams*. "Mystery, Silence, and Secrecy," says another, "are Aids to Politicks as well as pious Frauds; since the not being understood creates Reverence and Respect, as sacred Truth demands our Faith, chiefly for being past humane Understanding."[60] We sense the perspective from which such characters as Harcourt and Manly are drawn, and sense, too, Wycherley's feeling that there is a romantic haven removed from the hustle and bustle of ordinary worldly concerns seemingly based on reason. Thus, one poem on the seventeenth-century commonplace, "For Solitude and Retirement against the Publick, Active Life," hints that one's real nature can be expressed only by escape (as Manly tries to do):

Thus as his prudent Privacy is more,
He's most Himself, and least in Fortune's Pow'r.[61]

Etherege, though far less explicit than Wycherley, reveals in one of his personal letters from Ratisbon the same sense as Wycherley that religion is subjective, intuitional, and irrational: "I have ever enjoyed a liberty of opinion in matters of religion; 'tis indifferent to me whether there be any other in the world who thinks as I do; this makes me have no temptation to talk of the business, but quietly following the light within me [*sic!*] I leave that to them who were born with the ambition of becoming prophets or legislators." [62] Congreve, though he does not use the language of Quakerism as Etherege did, shows the same sense of schism. Thus, in his *Mourning Bride* he has his hero, Osmyn, muse about Heaven's "Eternal Justice," setting it beyond

Reason, the Power
To guess at Right and Wrong; the twinkling Lamp
Of wand'ring Life, that winks and wakes by turns,
Fooling the Follower, betwixt Shade and Shining.[63]

Similarly, a passage I quoted in Chapter 6 to show Congreve's interest in "inside and outside" shows also his assumption (at least for purposes of hyperbole) that they cannot match in nature:

O she was heav'nly fair, in Face and Mind!
Never in Nature were such Beauties join'd:
Without, all shining; and within, all white;
Pure to the Sense, and pleasing to the Sight.[64]

Also, the book list of Congreve's library shows that Congreve owned and presumably read a number of the books quoted in this chapter as showing the belief that faith is inconsistent with reason: Thomas Burnet's *Theory of the Earth,* both the English and Latin versions, *Paradise Lost,* Locke's *Essay Concerning Human Understanding,* Fontenelle's *A Plurality of Worlds,* and Sir Thomas Browne's *Religio Medici.*

It should not surprise us, then, that all these comedies carry out in their structure this sense of schism, this separation of how from why, reason from faith, thought from feeling, or fact from value. That is, the comedy deals with "the Town" rationally and naturalistically for four acts; then the hero escapes into fideistic love in the fifth act — a love idealized, converted upward, in religious imagery. Hence, as time goes on, the comedies acquire more and more improbable happy endings, as with such writers as Cibber and Vanbrugh. The hero, in effect, escapes into his ideal in this world, not the next. Personal emotion substitutes for what had once been a personal relation with an immanent God. Thus, Congreve in "A Satyr against Love," says,

So our first Parent was of Heav'n bereft,
And Love [the] only comfort he had left.[66]

Paradise was to be found in irrational emotions; the "natural" had fallen out of "supernatural," and from the schism sprang modern drama.

12 · *The Old Batchelor*

Perhaps because he is unquestionably the most brilliant of all the Restoration dramatists, William Congreve's plays are those most often dismissed as frothy, empty collections of polished dialogue. Yet, the supposedly rawer, cruder Wycherley was the writer to whom Congreve turned for a model. Wycherley's plays appeared in 1671, 1672, 1675, and 1676; Congreve's appeared in 1693, 1695, 1697, and 1700. In the nearly twenty years between these two major writers, the stage was filled by a host of rather minor ones, Edward Ravenscroft, for example, Mrs. Aphra Behn (the rather smutty "Incomparable Astraea"), and the not-so-minor Thomas Shadwell. Congreve, who had been just a small boy when the last plays of Etherege and Wycherley were produced, nevertheless turned back to the earlier style of, in particular, Wycherley. Their contemporary, George Granville, Lord Lansdowne — one of Pope's early patrons — found them alike not only in personality but in art.[1] Congreve was even more precocious than Wycherley. He wrote his first play at twenty, his third at twenty-five, and his dramatic career was over at thirty. "Among all the efforts of early genius which literary history records," writes Dr. Johnson, "I doubt whether any one can be produced that more surpasses the common limits of nature than the plays of Congreve."[2]

Congreve's life was marked by his two long romances, the first with the beautiful Ann Bracegirdle, that blushing brunette for whom he created four of the most brilliant feminine roles in drama. Whether there was consummation even his contemporaries did not know, for Mrs. Bracegirdle was one of the very few chaste ladies on the Restoration stage.[3] His second affair was with Lady Henrietta Godolphin, later Duchess of Marlborough, and was less inconclusive; literary historians have decided that the Earl of Godolphin was blessed with an extra daughter.[4] Congreve's plays brought him immediate fame; they gave him also minor government posts that survived even changes of party. Years later, after promotions, these appointments made him a wealthy man, though there were long, lean years. By 1700, the tastes of the audience had changed so that his masterpiece, *The Way of the World,* failed. After its failure, Congreve gave up playwriting and became a somewhat retiring elder statesman of the stage. In his last years, as he told the celebrity-hunting Voltaire, he wished to be visited "upon no other footing than that of a gentleman, who led a life of plainness and simplicity."[5] Legend has it — and *se non è vero è ben trovato* — that after his death the Duchess memorialized him in a life-size wax automaton that she seated beside her at the dinner table. It held a glass in its hand and bowed and nodded when she spoke to it; she had it fed and treated for the gout, an ailment to which Congreve had been particularly susceptible.[6]

His first comedy, *The Old Batchelor,* proved a brilliant success when it was first produced at Drury Lane in March of 1693. There are several plots, each complex and each a comment on the others. The three principal characters are: Bellmour, a conventional Restoration gallant; Vainlove, a gallant whose humor it is to woo ladies, but if they consent, to abandon the actual "Drudgery in the Mine" to Bellmour; and Heartwell, the title character, a surly old misanthropic bachelor who has fallen in love with Silvia. He supposes her innocent, but she has in fact been through the Vainlove-Bellmour double play. All of the plots in *The Old Batchelor,* in one way or another, are concerned with the problem of marrying an unchaste woman. Congreve dramatizes in this form the constant Restoration theme of inconsistency between nature (the hidden fact of infidelity and the state of mind that accompanied it) and outward appearances (the lady's pretense of chastity). The play treats different ways of coping with this inconsistency.

Like earlier playwrights, Congreve makes his fools people who consist only of appearances and who are aware only of appearances. There are two fools in *The Old Batchelor,* Sir Joseph Wittoll and the *miles gloriosus* Captain Bluffe. They drift somewhat inconclusively through the plot, cheated by the confidence man Sharper, and in the finale they marry the leftover mistresses of the gallants. Sir Joseph Wittoll is described as a suit of clothes, "a tawdry Outside" "and a very beggarly Lining" (35),[7] and Captain Bluffe, "the Image of Valour" (36), "that Sign of a Man," "that Pot-Gun charged with Wind" (61) who is, like a drum, "full of blustring Noise and Emptiness" (36). These people are nothing but appearances and they believe anything anyone tells them. Sir Joseph, for example, believes Sharper when he says he was the one that saved the knight from marauders and lost £100 (II.i); Bluffe, after Sharper has abused, cuffed, and kicked him, simply denies that these blows ever took place: "'Tis false — he sucks not vital Air who dares affirm it to this Face." Sir Joseph recognizes the importance of the face: "To that Face I grant you Captain — No, no, I grant you — Not to that Face by the Lord *Harry* — If you had put on your fighting Face before, you had done his Business" (62). Both fools believe Setter (a pimp) when he says one of the high plot ladies loves them; they have no idea of the real nature of the lady or of themselves. Similarly, they marry masked women on Setter's say-so (106). Appropriately, they are punished in the denouement by having their wives' real nature carefully pointed out to them (107). Their answer, in short, to the Restoration problem of perception is that of all the fools in the comedies: "Ignore it; concentrate your attention on appearances alone."

The comedy concerned with Fondlewife presents a more sophisticated answer to the problem of appearance and nature involved in marrying an unchaste woman. Fondlewife, an elderly hypocritical Puritan, has a young and beautiful wife Laetitia, who is no fonder of him than one would expect. At a party, Vainlove has made an assignation with her, but in his usual way he turns the lady over to Bellmour. Bellmour disguises himself as a parson and makes his entrance; Fondlewife returns, is assured his wife mistook Bellmour for a real parson, and, more or less consciously, allows himself to be deceived.

Fondlewife is aware (as the fools are not) of the difference between appearance and nature: "But does not thy Wife love thee, nay doat upon thee? — Yes — Why then! — Ay, but to say truth, she's fonder of me, than she has reason to be; and in the way of Trade, we still suspect the smoothest Dealers of the deepest Designs" (69). He adds, furthermore, a new coloration to the problem: what a man wants he sees as the appearance (a loving, doting wife) but what he gets is hidden nature (infidelity). Like Heartwell, Fondlewife goes through a laughable reason-passion soliloquy, trying to resolve the difference. He tries to reason his wife into living up to his expectations (68–69). Reason, however, is not enough to overcome either his own passionate desire for his wife, or hers for satisfaction. Reason, though it tells him to avoid the trap of reality with its basic inconsistency, cannot keep him free of its appearances. When he returns and is confronted with a highly suspicious situation and a doubtful explanation, Fondlewife accepts the choice of self-deception. Belief has the power to persuade him of the existence of a nature that lives up to his desires ("As long as I believe it, 'tis well enough"), even though his belief is inconsistent with even the appearances of the situation, let alone the hidden reality: "I won't believe my own Eyes," he finally says (90). Bellmour commends him ironically: "See the great Blessing of an easie Faith; Opinion cannot err" (and, of course, Fondlewife as a Puritan fanatic is the ideal choice to develop this aspect of the theme):

> No Husband, by his Wife, can be deceiv'd:
> She still is vertuous, if she's so believ'd. (90)

We recognize the coldly epistemological comfort allotted to the cuckolds in *The Country Wife.*

Heartwell, like Fondlewife, knows the general inconsistency between appearance and nature and hates and fears it. Unlike Fondlewife, however, he cannot accept the solution of self-deception; instead, he rails at the dilemma: "My Talent is chiefly that of speaking Truth, which I don't expect should ever recommend me to People of Quality" (34). His highest social ideal is not the hope that people will improve, but that the inconsistency will be resolved: "I am for having every body be what they pretend to be; a Whoremaster be a Whoremaster" (33). Because he sees the trap, he does not rush into temptation, but tries to remain aloof: "'Tis true indeed, I don't force Appetite, but wait the natural Call of my Lust" (32).

Heartwell, though both misanthrope and misogynist, has fallen in love with Silvia, formerly Bellmour's mistress, who pretends chastity to induce Heartwell to marry her. In a soliloquy he debates with his reason against his passion, trying to escape Silvia (54), but cannot resist, and almost takes Fondlewife's way out: "I'll run into the Danger to lose the Apprehension." Heartwell is tempted and deluded, both by Silvia's "dissembl[ing] the very want of Dissimulation" (53) and by his own tendency to see what he wants to see, her supposed innocence that at once torments and pleases him (65). Silvia very cleverly pretends to be the one thing dearest to the old bachelor's heart, a girl whose outward appearance and nature are the same, both "honest." Yet even so, Heartwell fears that she must have the same double aspect as the rest of reality: "dear Angel, Devil, Saint, Witch," "thou beauteous Changeling" (64). He tries to buy her, but she refuses. Then, he cannot resist and consciously asks for "One Kiss more to confirm me mad," willingly deluding himself as Fondlewife does, but only so long as he believes she is true to his ideal.

Finally, of course, the gallants teach him again what he has known all along, that Silvia is, as all reality is, an illusion, a wish-fulfillment — that her appearance was his hope; her nature, his disappointment. He learns, in short, that

> We hope to find
> That Help which Nature meant in Woman-kind,
> To Man that Supplemental Self design'd;
> But proves a burning Caustick when apply'd. (103)

Like Manly, Heartwell is saved from the trap of reality by an improbable *deus ex machina.* Once he has decided to marry, he luckily fails to find his brother's chaplain. Instead, he happens to pick a Puritan fanatic to perform the ceremony. But the fanatic, *mirabile dictu,* is actually Bellmour disguised as a parson, returning from the seduction of Laetitia Fondlewife. The gallant decides to release the old bachelor from his predicament and persuades Silvia and her maid to go along with the joke. The three factors that make up Heartwell's improbable rescue are luck, the friendship of a gallant he contemns for his fawning on the ladies, and disguise, the very division between appearance and nature he despises. Heartwell's rescue is, like Manly's, improbable, but Manly's was so idealized and so unlikely that it made us think him a man with one foot in eternity. Heartwell's is less so and hence we do not feel as with Manly that there is no escape from the deception of reality but the supernatural. Instead, we feel that Heartwell trapped himself but was saved by the charity that a pretending person like Bellmour may actually have. (The gallant's disguise as a minister, while a common device, is in this case meaningful.)

The chief weakness of the play, of course, is the improbability of this episode, Heartwell's rescue. It is this incident that makes the play look like "a hodge-podge of characters and incidents,"[8] as though it were trying to suggest the amount of sheer improvisation required simply to get along in the London Heartwell faces. Heartwell himself is unwilling to improvise, and his solution — or lack of one — to the problem of appearance and nature embodied in marrying an unchaste woman is a fruitless railing at it.

Bellmore offers as a solution the same kind of tolerant acceptance of the dilemma that Freeman offered Manly. Bellmour, moreover, is the only one in the play who in the finale enters into a real marriage (with the witty and charming Belinda). He accepts with a vengeance the contradictions of existence: "What else [but pleasure] has meaning" (25). "Then I must be disguised — With all my Heart — It adds a Gusto to an Amour" (27). A Socratic in believing that wisdom is the ability to distinguish accidents from substance, Bellmour is hedonistic and skeptical in his doubt that such knowledge is possible or even necessary if one devotes oneself to pleasure. "Ay, ay, Wisdom's nothing but a pretending to know and believe more than we really do. You read of but one wise Man, and all that he knew was, that he knew nothing. Come, come, leave Business to Idlers, and Wisdom to Fools: they have need of 'em: Wit, be my Faculty; and Pleasure, my Occupation; and let Father Time shake his Glass" (25–26). Bellmour accepts disguise, infidelity, and self-contradiction, and is even willing — up to a point — to be a victim: "Why faith I think it will do well enough — If the Husband be out of the way, for the Wife to shew her Fondness and Impatience of his Absence, by chusing a Lover as like him as she can, and what is unlike, she may help out with her own Fancy. . . . The Abuse is to the Lover, not the Husband: For 'tis an Argument of her great Zeal towards him, that she will enjoy him in Effigie" (26–27). The fact that Bellmour is willing to carry on affairs with women who love Vainlove shows he is concerned with externals as the fools in the play are; it stresses again the kinship of rake and dupe in this respect (like Olivia and the Widow Blackacre or Dorimant and Sir Fopling).

Dissembling comes as naturally to Bellmour as to Silvia and the other women of the play: "I confess, I could be well enough pleas'd to drive on a Love-Bargain in [silence] — 'twould save a Man a world of Lying and Swearing at the Years end" (51). Belinda describes their marriage as a banquet that "when we come to feed, 'tis all Froth, and poor, but in show"; he describes it as a play, i.e., a continued pretense or disguise (102); finally, they both describe it as a prison, a "lasting Durance" to that reality which Heartwell calls a "Snare" (108, 107). Only Bellmour and the fools are married at the end. If he is the hero, it is with a qualification.

Vainlove offers the opposite solution, the possibility that qualifies Bellmour's answer. Like his peers Bellmour and Sharper and his servant Setter, Vainlove is a master of the arts of conversation and social pretense. Confronted with the problem of a note of assignation supposedly from his beloved Araminta, he comments, "Now must I pretend Ignorance equal to hers, of what she knows as well as I" (80). Very quickly he and Araminta unravel Silvia's simple forgery.

Unlike his friend Bellmour, however, Vainlove voyages on and on, refusing to come to rest and accept a lesser aim, a permanent compromise, such as marriage, wenching, or money. He refuses to marry his sweetheart Araminta at the end, just as, in his random gallantries, he enjoys the courtship but leaves the consummation to Bellmour. He insists on "the Pleasure of a Chase." By being always in pursuit, he sees only the idealized appearance; as soon as a woman consents, he becomes aware of the inferior inner self, becomes disgusted, and turns away. He pursues Araminta because she continually eludes his success, "is a kind of floating Island; sometimes seems in reach, then vanishes and keeps him busied in the search" (31). "Could'st thou be content to marry *Araminta*?" asks Bellmour. "Could you be content to go to Heav'n?" he replies (55). He flirts with the trap of reality, but refuses to commit himself, holding off for an ideal. In Heartwell's terms, "*Vainlove* plays the Fool with Discretion" (31).

The comedy, then, leaves us with a dilemma represented by Vainlove and Heartwell on one side and Bellmour on the other. As Shaw says: "There are two tragedies in life. One is not to get your heart's desire.

The other is to get it." Bellmour gets his heart's desire; Vainlove refuses to. In the finale, Bellmour calls his impending marriage imprisonment, while Vainlove can still speak of "hope." The trick of reality is, as the epilogue applies it to the way an audience treats a play:

> Just as the Devil does a Sinner . . .
> You gain your End, and damn 'em when you've done.

Coming to rest means the acceptance of something less than ideal, a thing that Heartwell and Vainlove refuse to do. Reason tells you to avoid the trap. Passion draws you into it. Only a discretion like Bellmour's can make the best bargain the limitations of the world permit; only in Vainlove's "Heaven" is what men hope for, what they get, or appearance nature. The play does not resolve the question it raises: Which is better, Bellmour's reality or Vainlove's unrealized ideal?

The women of the play are differentiated along much the same lines, although Congreve drew them in less detailed strokes. They, too, are grouped about the basic problem of appearance and nature. Whereas the men are ranked by their ability to deal with the problem, the women rate according to their ability to create it. As Silvia puts it: "I find dissembling to our Sex is as natural as swimming to a *Negro*" (66). It is "natural" because sexual desire is part of their nature, but must not openly appear. Error and absurdity lie (as in earlier plays like *She wou'd if she cou'd*) in wrongful satisfaction of that desire, in letting that satisfaction appear openly, or in letting dissimulation creep in where it does not belong. Silvia is the worst offender. She does not conceal her desires, nor can she maintain for long the reputation of not satisfying them. Her deceptions are not clever. The trick of forging a note from Araminta had become very stale indeed by 1693. Appropriately, Silvia at the end is reduced to the level of her maid, who marries Captain Bluffe; Silvia marries the other fool, Sir Joseph Wittoll. Laetitia, with Bellmour's help, manages to hide her *faux pas,* though she erred earlier and lost Vainlove by letting him know he could have her. Her future, moreover, bodes no good for her: her estimable husband will probably be even more reluctant to leave her alone. As tokens of their lesser stature, both she and Silvia are forced to accept the disguised Bellmour in lieu of Vainlove.

Araminta and Belinda are in another class entirely, at the top of the scale. Belinda, however, carries her dissimulation too far in pretending to her friend that she does not love. "Fie, this is gross Affectation," says Araminta (45), and the *dramatis personae* so describes Belinda: an "affected Lady." Araminta is the mistress of this delicate sort of dissimulation, as indeed she has to be to please Vainlove. She keeps an equilibrium between desire and admitting to it that corresponds to his discretion in refusing to commit himself to what might be a disappointment.

Dr. Johnson calls this play, "one of those comedies which may be made by a mind vigorous and acute, and furnished with comick characters by the perusal of other poets, without much actual commerce with mankind. . . . The characters, both of men and women, are either fictitious and artificial . . . or easy and common." [9] He is right — the characters are artificially created, but for once, I think Steele is correct when he says, "In [this] comedy there is a necessary circumstance observed by the author, which most other poets either overlook or do not understand, that is to say, the distinction of characters. . . . This writer knows men; which makes his plays reasonable entertainments, while the scenes of most others are like the tunes between the acts." [10] Each character is created from a single factor, his reaction to the central problem of appearance contradicting nature. While this method does not make for very lifelike characters, it does give the play a beautiful unity: every detail of character, action, and language becomes linked to the focal concept of disguise.

"The dialogue," says Johnson, "is one constant reciprocation of conceits, or clash of wit, in which nothing flows necessarily from the occasion, or is dictated by nature," [11] and there he was right. The "polish" of Congreve's prose is proverbial, but there seems to be no very clear idea of what that "polish" consists. Professor Dobrée has analyzed Congreve's prose rhythms in some detail and shows that he closed satiric passages with a spondee or iambic, strong endings, but used a trochee for the close of delicate passages requiring sympathy, a "dying fall" like Fletcher's feminine double ending. Congreve used contrasts in vocal sounds to set off the antithetical parts of a sentence, and in a succession of repetitions varied the last one to stress it.[12]

Sentence structure, of course, plays an important part in creating this impression of polish. Constructed always with an element of paradox and antithesis, Congreve's sentences suggest a dialectic between general principles of human behavior and the particular occasion of speech — Vainlove's description of Fondlewife, for instance:

Vainlove. A kind of Mongrel Zealot,
[1] sometimes very precise and peevish:
But I have seen him pleasant enough in his way;
[2] much addicted to Jealousie,
but more to Fondness:
[3] So that as he is often Jealous without a Cause,
he's as often satisfied without Reason.
[3a] *Bellmour.* A very even Temper,
[3b] and fit for my purpose. (28)

Vainlove announces his topic, Fondlewife, then [1] finds a contradiction in it, [2] explores the contradiction, and [3] resolves it in a general rule about Fondlewife's behavior. Bellmour indicates [3a] his awareness of the principle (that Fondlewife believes what he wants to believe) and [3b] relates that general principle to the particular occasion of the speech. Despite the prodigious number of subordinate clauses, Congreve keeps his prose moving by this dialectic between particular case and general rule, which is the matter as well as the style of his discourse. So too, leaving an antithesis open or unresolved tends to push the dialogue forward; closing it suggests a half-stop or full stop depending on the degree of epigrammatic or paradoxical quality in the final clause.

Even more important is the sheer number of figures of speech. Judging simply from a count of the slips on which I note such things, I would guess that there are 30 per cent more figures of speech in *The Old Batchelor* than in *The Man of Mode*. There are approximately the same number in *The Country Wife* as in this play, but *The Country Wife* is between 35 and 40 per cent longer than *The Old Batchelor*. The metaphorical density of Congreve's prose is enough greater than any we have encountered so far as to create a distinctly new impression. Like a jewel with more facets, his prose sparkles more. One would expect, however, from this density not the "polish" we do find, but the busyness and energy we associate with Jacobean writing. The key to Congreve's style is not so much the number of metaphors but the way he handles them. While Wycherley and Etherege most often make use of what we have called the right-way–wrong-way simile, Congreve is the master of "the language of split-man observation," which sets up the question of the extent of the speaker's involvement with the action described. Because the speaker comments dispassionately on his own actions, the "split-man observation" divides him into actor and observer and hides in the apparent indifference created by this separation the metaphorical energy of the play. The language does not add to the intensity of the action; rather action and language each cast a comic perspective on the other. The language covers over the action much the way appearance covers nature.

The speech of Bellmour's which opens the play is a good example:

> *Vainlove*, and abroad so early! good Morrow; I thought a Contemplative Lover could no more have parted with his Bed in a Morning, than he could have slept in't.

The action involved in the speech is simply one young man's greeting another and expressing interest in his current love affair. The exposition carries the information that Vainlove is in love and is a "Contemplative

Lover." Bellmour shows his interest and involvement in Vainlove's love affair by his opening exclamation. He establishes a perspective on his interest in the second sentence by assuming the role of an observer trying rather dispassionately to relate Vainlove's appearance on the street to a general principle of human nature: that lovers sleep poorly. The metaphorical energy of Bellmour's speech is all concentrated in the general principle — the faint paradox of "Contemplative Lover"; the implicit comparison of the bed to the person contemplated through the use of the verb "parted" with its association of two persons parting; the contrast between thinking in bed and sleeping in bed; the image of the lover confined to his bed, yet unable to sleep in it. The language applies its force to the general principle, not the action. The forces of language and action subtract, rather than add. They pull apart, creating an outward appearance of lassitude that masks a hidden internal tension between involvement and noninvolvement. This, of course, is Congreve's sense of the comic: the felt conflict between a decorous appearance and a passionate nature. Johnson was right: practically none of Congreve's figures of speech "flows necessarily from the occasion, or is dictated by nature," but that is Congreve's joke, and, in that sense, they do flow from the occasion.

Within the larger scheme of split-man observation, Congreve uses the tropes his predecessors prepared for him; for example, the conversion downward of abstractions or emotions to things, as when Belinda says of love: " 'Tis in the Head, the Heart, the Blood, the — All over" (45). For the most part, however, this figure is confined to the low characters and to Heartwell, who says, "chinking" his purse after an entertainment at Silvia's:

> Why 'twas I sung and danc'd; I gave Musick to the Voice, and Life to their Measures — Look you here *Silvia,* here are Songs and Dances, Poetry and Musick — hark! how sweetly one Guinea rhymes to another — and how they dance to the Musick of their own Chink. This buys all the t'other. (63)

Of his affections he says: "No reflux of vigorous Blood: But milky Love, supplies the empty Channels; and prompts me to the Softness of a Child — A meer Infant and would suck" (63). It is not surprising, then, that for the most certain sign of his love for Silvia, he gives her his money (64). Fondlewife, in a similar comparison, speaks of his wife's body as "her separate Maintenance," i.e., her trust fund, that "she'll carry . . . about her" (89). Captain Bluffe, in one of Congreve's rare puns, converts "mettle" down to "metal" (41); he substitutes his sword for wit or logic: "This Sword I'll maintain to be the best Divine, Anatomist, Lawyer or Casuist in *Europe;* it shall decide a Controversie or split a Cause — " (43–44). "I'll pink his Soul," he threatens Sharper (59). The gentle Sir Joseph can say to Sharper, "I'm very sorry . . . with all my Heart, Blood, and Guts, Sir" (38). Lucy, Silvia's maid, exemplifies the figure, by thinking of her mistress's reputation as a physical thing that Vainlove and Bellmour have made a "gap" in, "And can you blame her if she make it up with a Husband?" (92). Setter gives the clew to the antiheroic basis of this kind of metaphor when he, the servant, uses heroic language: "Why, how now! prithee who art? . . . Thou art some forsaken Abigail, we have dallied with heretofore" (57).

This conversion downward of love is paralleled in physical terms by images of weight, such as Fondlewife's amusing description of adultery as "a very weighty Sin; and although it may lie heavy upon thee, yet thy Husband must also bear his Part" (69), i.e., his horns. Bellmour, with mock sorrow, describes his promiscuity as "too heavy" a load: "I must take up, or I shall never hold out; Flesh and Blood cannot bear it always" (29). Thus, Heartwell describes the gallants as "Womens Asses bear[ing] greater Burdens; Are forc'd to undergo Dressing, Dancing, Singing, Sighing, Whining, Rhyming, Flattering, Lying, Grinning, Cringing, and the drudgery of Loving to boot" (33). He feels the "Load of Life" (103) and finds women no help in carrying it; rather man becomes a beast "and with what anxious Strife,/ What Pain we tug that galling Load, a Wife" (108).

Balancing these conversions downward are comparisons that tend to point the action up toward a supernatural level; for example, Vainlove's statement that to marry Araminta would be like going to Heaven (55). Bellmour puts himself at a more earthy level when he replies that he would rather not go immediately: "I'd do a little more good in my generation first, in order to deserve it." Vainlove, as the highest character in the scale, is the one most given to this kind of neoplatonic imagery: the favors of a much-petitioned lady are "due Rewards to indefatigable Devotion — For as Love is a Deity, he must be serv'd by Prayer" (48–49). Belinda, too, can talk this way: "A Lover in the State of Separation from his Mistress, is like a Body without a Soul" (79–80); more often she laughs at a lover with "Darts, and Flames, and Altars, and all that in his Breast" (45). Rather, she says, "I would be ador'd in Silence" (50).

Most often these images appear ironically, as when Bellmour assures his helper he will "confess" Laetitia (55), when he tells her eternity was in the moment of her kiss (75), or when he speaks of adultery as "Zeal" (27). Sharper kindly explains to Heartwell, who thinks he is married to Vainlove's ex-mistress, "Few Women, but have their Year of Probation, before they are cloister'd in the narrow Joys of Wedlock" (99–100). Setter, Vainlove's servant, describes Bellmour's plan to seduce Laetitia as going well, "As all lewd projects do, Sir, where the Devil prevents our Endeavours with Success" (55). Even Bluffe and Wittoll come in for a bit of religion: Bluffe "is ador'd by that Biggot Sir *Joseph Wittoll*, as the Image of Valour" (36).

Araminta sums up the tension expressed by these faintly supernatural conversions upward and bestial conversions downward when she replies to Belinda's raillery: "Love a Man! yes, you would not love a Beast" (45). Naturally, most human relations take place neither at the exalted level of neoplatonic love imagery nor at some subhuman depth, but on a realistic plane. At this level, love is an adversary proceeding, a lawsuit to Vainlove's servant (58) or, to Sir Joseph, a military attack (78). For his major characters, however, Congreve sets up a more subtle kind of adversary relationship.

To the men, love is something that affects the inner man. From the neoplatonic convention comes the notion that love is a wound: "By those Eyes, those killing Eyes; by those healing Lips" (75). To Heartwell, love is a disease, a folly, a madness (64) for which "if whoring be purging (as you call it) then . . . Marriage, is entering into a Course of Physick" (34). In another sense love is something one puts inside oneself, for Laetitia is a "delicious Morsel" (27) and even Araminta, after Vainlove has received her supposed note, is "a delicious Mellon pure and consenting ripe, and only waits thy cutting up" (72). Bellmour, when he and Belinda have resolved to marry, say to the equilibrists, "May be it may get you an Appetite to see us fall to before ye" (108). Thus a man (as in Etherege's plays) is a hunter. Vainlove is "continually starting of Hares for [Bellmour] to course" (27). It is not true that Vainlove cannot digest love; he can,

> But I hate to be cramm'd — By Heav'n there's not a Woman, will give a Man the Pleasure of a Chase: My Sport is always balkt or cut short — I stumble over the Game I would pursue — 'Tis dull and unnatural to have a Hare run full in the Hounds Mouth; and would distaste the keenest Hunter — I would have overtaken, not have met my Game. (72)

Man's appetite for love means that he can be baited and trapped. Thus, Silvia's maid encourages her to "Strike *Heartwell* home, before the Bait's worn off the Hook. Age will come. He nibbled fairly yesterday, and no doubt will be eager enough to Day, to swallow the Temptation" (52), for a man's passion is "that very Hook your selves have baited" (32).

While man engulfs woman, woman engulfs man, consuming him almost as Thurber's famous cartoon suggests. Over and over again, woman is (à la Freud) a house, to Fondlewife a "Tabernacle" (68), and to Vainlove "the Temples of Love" (49). Heartwell thinks of his supposed wife as "that Corner-house — that hot Brothel" (100). For a man to have a handsome wife, says Fondlewife's servant, "[if] the Man is an insufficient Husband. 'Tis then indeed, like the Vanity of taking a fine House, and yet be forced to let Lodgings, to help pay the Rent" (68). Setter calls Silvia's maid "the Wicket to thy Mistresses Gate, to be opened for all Comers" (57), and even Belinda finds a country girl she meets "like the Front of her Father's Hall; her Eyes were the two Jut-Windows, and her Mouth the great Door, most hospitably kept open for the Entertainment of travelling Flies" (77). A house can easily become a prison. Vainlove thus can consider himself an "Offender" who "must plead to his Araignment, though he has his Pardon in his Pocket" (80), and Bellmour says, when he and Belinda decide to get married, he has become a "Prisoner," committed "to a lasting Durance" and "Fetters" (108). Quite literally thinking of woman as surrounding man, Heartwell calls falling in love "to put on the envenom'd Shirt, to run into the Embraces of a Fever, and in some raving Fit, be led to plunge my self into that more consuming Fire, a Womans Arms" (54). He hesitates, but "her Kiss is sweeter than Liberty" (66), and he suffers the "Execution" of marriage (91, 105). His wife becomes absorbed into him so that he would have to be maimed to be divorced (105).

The paradox of man ingesting love and woman surrounding man matches on a human, realistic plane the tension between upward conversions toward Heaven, and downward conversions toward physical animality. It matches, too, the central paradox of the play — the contradiction between appearance and nature. Just as men and women consume each other, so they deceive each other. As Heartwell with great solemnity counsels the supposedly innocent Silvia: "Lying, Child, is indeed the Art of Love; and Men are generally Masters in it: But I'm so newly entred, you cannot distrust me of any Skill in the treacherous Mystery" (64). The women are the real experts, however, for as Lucy says, "Man, was by Nature Womans Cully made" (53). Setter, Vainlove's servant, when he sees Lucy in a mask tells her: "Lay by that worldly Face and produce your natural Vizor," while she accuses him of being "made up of the Shreds and Pairings of [thy Master's] superfluous Fopperies" (57).

Just as one is composed of appearances and a nature underneath them, so one is moved by these tensions but at the same time is a spectator of one's own motion. Thus, the crotchety Heartwell debates with himself before Silvia's house:

> Why whither in the Devil's Name am I a going now? Hum — let me think — Is not this *Silvia*'s House? . . . . Ha! well recollected, I will recover my Reason, and be gone. . . . Well, why do you not move? Feet do your Office — not one Inch; no, foregad I'm caught — There stands my North, and thither my Needle points — Now could I curse my self, yet cannot repent.

> . . . Death, I can't think on't — I'll run into the danger to lose the Apprehension. (53–54)

So, too, Belinda warns Araminta: "But you play the Game, and consequently can't see the Miscarriages obvious to every stander by" (45). Bellmour tries to persuade his beloved that "Courtship to Marriage, is but as the Musick in the Play-House, 'till the Curtain's drawn; but that once up, then opens the Scene of Pleasure," though she insists, "Rather, Courtship to Marriage, as a very witty Prologue to a very dull Play" (102). To Congreve, each of us plays both actor and spectator and our two roles interact. In a sense, watching can change actuality, as Bellmour says, "[A Wife] still is vertuous, if she's so believ'd" (90). Understandably, this further paradox leads one quite naturally to Bellmour's hedonistic skepticism, where only pleasure has meaning and wisdom is only a pretending to know. The conflict between actor and spectator represents still another tension.

A third dimension is added to the picture of man created by Congreve's metaphors. There is the sense of time as an irreversible process. We roll our lives like bowling a ball, says Bellmour (25) in what is almost the opening image of the play. Bellmour closes the play with a related image: "Now set we forward on a Journey for life." Heartwell sums it up:

> With gaudy Plumes and gingling Bells made proud,
> The youthful Beast sets forth, and neighs aloud.
> A Morning-Sun his Tinsell'd Harness gilds,
> And the first Stage a Down-Hill Green-sword yields.
> But, Oh —
> What rugged Ways attend the Noon of Life!
> (Our Sun declines,) and with what anxious Strife,
> What Pain we tug that galling Load, a Wife;
> All Coursers the first Heat with Vigour run;
> But 'tis with Whip and Spur the Race is won. (108)

Passion is what drives human conduct: as Heartwell says, "Yet I must on — 'Tis a bearded Arrow, and will more easily be thrust forward than drawn back" (64). Reason, he knows, is what holds us back: "I will recover my reason and be gone" (54).

In short, Congreve's metaphorical structure creates an impression of that most characteristic of seventeenth-century inventions — the co-ordinate system. We have seen how the individuals in the play present themselves as in tension — between conversion up and conversion down, between consuming and being consumed in love, and between reason and passion in the forward progress through time. We could picture it as in the accompanying diagram. The "journey of life" idea presents itself

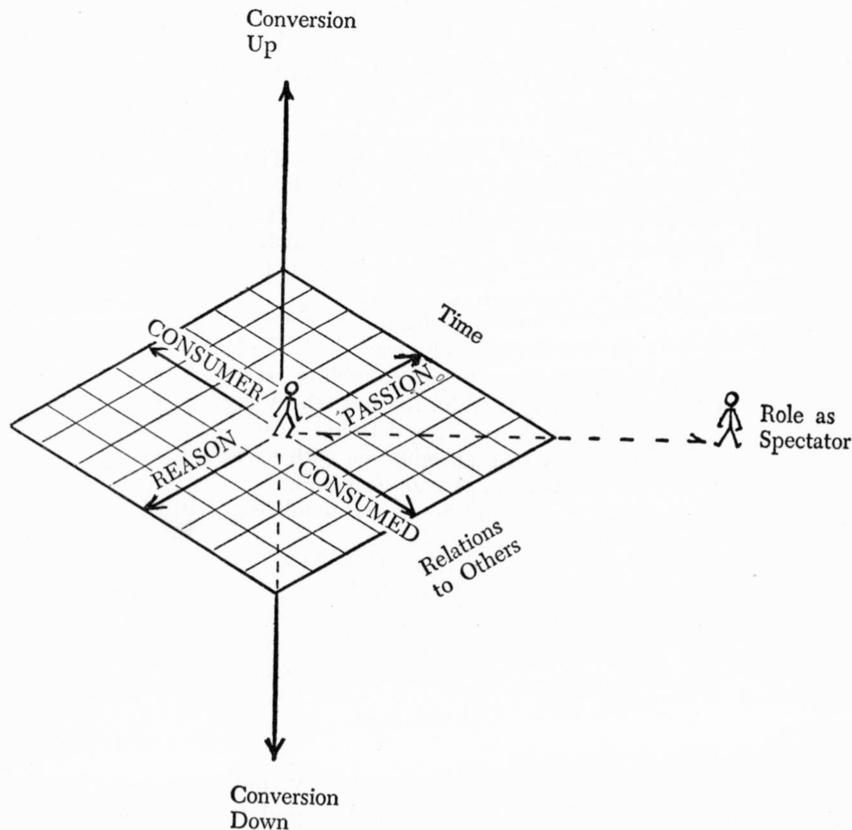

as forward or backward; the relation to ideals as up or down; the love-relationship as from side to side. At the same time that the individual stands in the center of these tensions, he stands outside them as a spectator of himself.

I would be much more reluctant to admit this rather schematic idea were it not that it conveys exactly what many critics have said about Congreve's characters: "They are without a background, without roots," writes Professor Bateson. "We do not know how old [Mirabell] is, whether he has been at the University, whether he is in Parliament, or whether he has a post. We do not know *anything* about him. It is to be presumed that we were not meant to."[13] We are to sense them as isolated individuals surrounded by choices. *The Way of the World* is organized about a similar kind of co-ordinate system. Furthermore, we find in Congreve's noncomic poetry the same sense of tensions surrounding the individual. For example, the passage from *The Mourning Bride* that Dr. Johnson called "the most poetical paragraph" in "the whole mass of English poetry":

> No, all is hush'd, and still as Death — 'Tis dreadful!
> How reverend is the Face of this tall Pile,
> Whose ancient Pillars rear their Marble Heads,
> To bear aloft its arch'd and pond'rous Roof,
> By its own Weight made stedfast and immoveable,
> Looking Tranquility. It striks an Awe
> And Terror on my aking Sight; the Tombs
> And Monumental Caves of Death look Cold,
> And shoot a Chilness to my trembling Heart.
> Give me thy Hand, and let me hear thy Voice;
> Nay, quickly speak to me, and let me hear
> Thy Voice — my own affrights me with its Echo's. . . .
> No, I will on; shew me *Anselmo*'s Tomb,
> Lead me o'er Bones and Skulls and mould'ring Earth
> Of Human Bodies. . . .
> That Thought
> Exerts my Spirits; and my present Fears
> Are lost in dread of greater Ill. Then shew me
> Lead me, for I am bolder grown: Lead on
> Where I may kneel and pay my Vows again
> To him, to Heav'n, and my *Alphonso*'s Soul.[14] (II.iii)

One of the reasons the passage is so effective is a similar use of directions. Three physical dimensions image the psychological tensions surrounding the speaker. The rise of the pillars and the arch of the roof balancing its own "pond'rous" weight parallel in the up-and-down direction the conflict between the speaker's heavenly and earthly obligations set out in the last three lines. The picture of ruins and death shows the passage of time; "I will on" suggests a parallel forward movement with fears pulling back and greater fears pushing forward. "Give me thy Hand" parallels the reciprocation of the speaker's voice, "its Echo's," and her tensions with the other people in the play. This somewhat abstruse connection between a more or less heroic drama and the comic action of *The Old Batchelor* is the same kind of link Professor Sypher finds as the transition between mannerist and baroque art and literature: the baroque resolution of mannerist tensions.[15] We could say that Congreve's three-dimensional conception is mannerist in having unresolved tensions and a shifting point of view (spectator's and actor's), but baroque in that these tensions are seen along orthogonal, clearly defined directions.

I would, however, still regard this analysis as far too schematic, were it not that Congreve uses to reinforce this picture two rather curious image clusters, each related to movement in three dimensions. As in Etherege's comedies, man is regarded as "that filthy, awkward, two-leg'd Creature" (44) and compared to birds. The gallants are hawks (26), or "young, termagant flashy Sinners" (32). Bellmour calls himself "a Cormorant in Love" (29), while Sharper compares Sir Joseph and Captain Bluffe to "Owls" (79). They, in turn, think of Sharper as a "Cock" (41). Belinda, when she encounters two country girls, thinks of them as "fat as Barn-door Fowl: But so bedeck'd, you wou'd have taken 'em for *Friezland* Hens, with their Feathers growing the wrong way" (76).

A much more unusual image depicts travel over water: the possibility of sinking supplies the third direction. Thus, Vainlove is described as "ever embarking in Adventures, yet never comes to Harbour," "because he always sets out in foul Weather, loves to buffet with the Winds, meet the Tide, and fail in the Teeth of Opposition." He has "not dropt Anchor at *Araminta*" though "she fits his Temper best, is a kind of floating Island; sometimes seems in reach, then vanishes and keeps him busied in the search" (31). Sharper says to Bellmour: "You steer another Course, are bound,/ For Love's Island: I, for the golden Coast" (36). When Bellmour returns from Laetitia, Vainlove's servant asks him:

Setter. Joy of your Return, Sir. Have you made a good Voyage? or have you brought your own Lading back?

Bellmour. No, I have brought nothing but Ballast back — made a delicious Voyage, *Setter;* and might have rode at Anchor in the Port 'till this time, but the Enemy surpriz'd us. — I would unrig. (90–91)

This same servant describes Araminta, whom he is supposedly to bring to Vainlove, as "a noble Prize," "A goodly Pinnace, richly laden, and to launch forth under my auspicious Convoy. Twelve thousand Pounds, and all her Rigging; besides what lies conceal'd under Hatches" (97). Heartwell, in his relation with Silvia, looks on himself as a kind of Odysseus going to "*Silvia*'s House, the Cave of that Enchantress," yet he cannot navigate away for "There stands my North, and thither my Needle points" (53–54). She finds "dissembling to our Sex is as natural as swimming to a *Negro;* we may depend upon our skill to save us at a plunge, tho' till then we never make the experiment" (66). Sir Joseph apologizes for having forgotten that Sharper rescued him from some seventeenth-century delinquents ("Canibals" — 37): "My intire Dependance, Sir, [is] upon the superfluity of your Goodness, which, like an Inundation will, I hope, totally immerge the recollection of my Error, and leave me floating in your Sight, upon the full blown Bladders of Repentance — by the help of which, I shall once more hope to swim into your Favour" (38).

Both these images — man as a bird or man as a swimmer or sailor — show the individual isolated in space. He is surrounded by choices. He can choose high aspirations or low sensuality, progression or regression, love or hostility, and the over-all system of metaphors puts choices in terms of directions. This three-dimensional system is simply the character grouping we noted at the beginning of the discussion, turned inside out. The characters are grouped around the central problem of appearance and nature, differing only in their involvement or non-involvement with it. The language inverts the situation: it puts the individual composed of an appearance and a nature at the center of tensions representing his choices. The action and language pull against each other, giving different, even inconsistent, points of view on the things a particular individual does. The "language of split-man observation" covers over the turbulent action by metaphors that constantly evaluate it. These continual evaluations create the effect of a smooth, polished appearance laid over a harshly physical nature. This contrast between language and action is Congreve's special sense of humor, his version of the continuing theme of appearance versus nature, and his unique, indeed triumphant, contribution to Restoration comedy.

13 · *The Double-Dealer*

Congreve's second play represents a sophomore slump. His first carried on themes Wycherley had developed. It treated folly and vice as kindred failings in which people pay too much attention to externals. *The Old Batchelor,* moreover, introduced a new technique, the tension between language and action, and a new theme: the play identified appearances with the ideals people seek and "nature" with the disappointments they find. Congreve had pushed *The Plain-Dealer* to the next logical step in *The Old Batchelor,* but after that first brilliant success, *The Double-Dealer,* when produced at Drury Lane in October 1693, was a comparative failure. Dryden wrote his friend Walsh:

> His Double Dealer is much censured by the greater part of the Town; and is defended onely by the best judges, who, you know, are commonly the fewest. Yet it gets ground daily, and has already been acted Eight Times. The women thinke he has exposed their Bitchery too much; & the Gentlemen are offended with him; for the discovery of their follyes: & the way of their Intrigues, under the notion of Friendship to their Ladyes Husbands.[1]

While Dryden's solicitude is touching, it is more likely that the combination of realistic tragedy and realistic comedy in the same play annoyed Congreve's audiences, as it was to do again in *The Way of the World.* "Indeed," writes Macaulay, "there is something strangely revolting in the way in which a group that seems to belong to the house of Laius or of Pelops is introduced into the midst of the Brisks, Froths, Carelesses, and Plyants."[2]

The Double-Dealer does combine a "serious" plot with an unusually airy comic action, but the play uses each to look at the other. The comic plot satirizes folly in the usual Restoration way; the serious plot, however, attacks villainy in a manner quite unusual for a Restoration comedy. Nevertheless, both plots develop in terms of appearance and nature, and the combination of the two suggests relationships between folly and villainy. For example, both the folly and the villainy take the same two characteristic forms: suppressing the real self or overexpressing it.

The comic plot works out the several follies of Lord and Lady Froth and Sir Paul and Lady Plyant. The husbands are deceived, of course;

Froth by Brisk, a pseudo-wit, and Sir Paul by Careless, a friend of the hero, Mellefont. The Froths overexpress themselves, fawning on each other in public, showing off their pretentious affections. The Plyants show the folly of suppressing nature. Sir Paul Plyant, the father of Cynthia, the heroine, is henpecked by his second wife, who is so "nice" that she keeps him tied up in bed to prevent any normal marital relations. Lady Plyant has suppressed Sir Paul's "natural" desires, indeed, she has to some extent suppressed her own (163),[3] and when Careless woos her, he has to suppress his own natural response of laughter to be able to say the absurd things he must to win her (172). This kind of foolishness is given its best exposition by Lord Froth: "There is nothing more unbecoming a Man of Quality, than to Laugh; 'tis such a Vulgar Expression of the Passion! every Body can Laugh. . . . To be pleased with what pleases the Croud! Now when I laugh, I always laugh alone" (129). He never laughs at comedies, "to distinguish my self from the Commonalty, and mortifie the Poets. . . . I swear, — he, he, he, I have often constrain'd my Inclinations to laugh, — he, he, he, to avoid giving them Encouragement" (130). He and Brisk conclude the scene:

Lord *Froth.* Oh, for the Universe, not a Drop more I beseech you. Oh Intemperate! I have a Flushing in my Face already.
[*Takes out a Pocket-Glass, and looks in it.*]
Brisk. Let me see, let me see, my Lord, I broke my Glass that was in the Lid of my Snuff-Box. Hm! Duce take me, I have encourag'd a pimple here too.
[*Takes the Glass and looks.*]
Ld. *Froth.* Then you must mortifie him with a Patch; my Wife shall supply you. (131–132)

Not a very pretty image, but it is magnificently appropriate to the idea of stifling one's inner nature.

Opposed to suppression is the other form of indecorum: overexpression — akin to "wildness" in the earlier comedies. It is shown here by the cuckolding intrigues, by the wives who dominate their husbands, and by the frequent and effusive expressions of love all the spouses make. Overexpression here, like Mrs. Loveit's in *The Man of Mode,* is the failure to control and direct one's inner nature into socially acceptable channels; it is represented in the intrigue by the false, strained wit of Brisk and Lady Froth, particularly their forcedly laughing courtship (179–180):

Brisk. Yet, ha, ha, ha. The Deuce take me, I can't help laughing my self, ha, ha, ha; yet by Heav'ns, I have a violent Passion for your Ladyship, seriously.
Lady *Froth.* Seriously? Ha, ha, ha.
Brisk. Seriously, ha, ha, ha. Gad I have, for all I laugh.
L. *Froth.* Ha, ha, ha! What d'ye think I laugh at? Ha, ha, ha.

Brisk. Me, I'gad, ha, ha.
L. *Froth.* No the Deuce take me if I don't laugh at my self; for hang me if I have not a violent Passion for Mr. *Brisk,* ha, ha, ha.
Brisk. Seriously?
L. *Froth.* Seriously, ha, ha, ha.
Brisk. That's well enough; let me perish, ha, ha, ha. O miraculous, what a happy Discovery. Ah my dear charming Lady *Froth!*
L. *Froth.* Oh my adored Mr. *Brisk!* [*Embrace*]

Sir Paul's advice to his daughter on marrying is another form of effusiveness: she is to think of her father on her wedding-night,

For I would fain have some Resemblance of my self in my Posterity, he *Thy*? Can't you contrive that affair Girl? Do Gadsbud, think on thy old Father; heh? Make the young Rogue as like as you can. . . . I'll give thee 500£ for every Inch of him that resembles me; ah this Eye, this Left Eye! A thousand Pound for this left Eye. . . . — Let it be transmitted to the young Rogue by the help of Imagination. . . . — Ah! when I was of your Age Hussey, I would have held fifty to one, I could have drawn my own Picture. . . . Don't learn after your Mother-in-Law my Lady here. . . . If you should take a Vagarie and make a rash Resolution on your Wedding Night, to die a Maid, as she did; all were ruin'd, all my Hopes lost! . . . I hope you are a better Christian than to think of living a Nun; he? (176)

Instead of satisfying his desire to express himself through progeny in the normal marital way, he tries to extend his wishes through the family triangle to his grandchildren. He tries by overexpression through Cynthia to compensate for his suppression by Lady Plyant. As both these quotations show, Congreve embodies this effusiveness in its own special logorrhea.

Indeed, Lady Froth gives overexpression its own special literary form in her "Songs, Elegies, Satires, Encomiums, Panegyricks, Lampoons, Plays, or Heroick Poems" with which she gives vent to her "Whimsies and Vapours" (136). Her major effort is an "Essay toward an Heroick Poem," the subject being "my Lord's Love to me" (139). This epic is called *The Sillabub* (i.e., a wine and cream frappé, the seventeenth-century version of an ice cream soda) "because my Lord's Title's *Froth,* I'gad, ha, ha, ha" (139). The most trivial transactions of Lady Froth's trivial life must be blown up to heroic size: "That *Episode* between *Susan,* the Dairy-Maid, and our Coach-Man is not amiss" (165). The maid is called "*Thetis,*" and the coachman is to be compared to the sun and called "*Heav'ns Charioteer.*" The fragment of this epic that Congreve gives us is one of the most delightful things in the play:

For as the Sun shines ev'ry Day,
So, of our Coach-man I may say,
He shows his drunken fiery Face,
Just as the Sun does, more or less.

And when at Night his Labour's done,
Then too, like Heav'ns Charioteer the Sun:
Into the Dairy he descends,
And there his Whipping and his Driving ends;
There he's secure from Danger of a Bilk,
His Fare is paid him, and he sets in Milk. (165–166)

It even has footnotes, as Brisk very wisely advises, to forestall the criticism that "*Bilk* and *Fare*" are "too like a Hackney Coach-man":

I'm answer'd, if *Jehu* was a Hackney Coach-man. — You may put that in the marginal Notes tho', to prevent Criticism — only mark it with a small Asterism, and say, — *Jehu* was formerly a Hackney Coach-man.

Lady Froth's literary pretensions also serve as a mask:

Brisk. I hope you'll make me happy in communicating the Poem.
Lady *Froth*. Oh, you must be my Confident, I must ask your Advice.
Brisk. I'm your humble Servant, let me perish, — I presume your Ladyship has read *Bossu*?
L. *Froth*. Oh yes, and *Rapine*, and *Dacier* upon *Aristotle* and *Horace*. — My Lord, you must not be jealous, I'm communicating all to Mr. *Brisk*.
Lord *Froth*. No, no, I'll allow Mr. *Brisk;* have you nothing about you to shew him, my Dear?
L. *Froth*. Yes, I believe I have. — Mr. *Brisk*, come will you go into the next Room? and there I'll shew you what I have. (139–140)

Brisk's substitution of neo-classic rules for literary intelligence is only one instance of his general principle: "Why should I disparage my Parts by thinking what to say? None but dull Rogues *think;* witty Men, like rich Fellows, are always ready for all Expences; while your Blockheads, like poor needy Scoundrels, are forced to examine their Stock, and forecast the Charges of the Day" (178). Wit is not a faculty, but a possession, money or a "Diamond" (130).

As in *The Old Batchelor,* language and action tend to pull apart. In the comic plot, figures of speech enlarge the most trivial actions to epic proportions. We have already seen Lord Froth's way of refusing a drink: "Oh, for the Universe, not a Drop more I beseech you." Sir Paul finds he must draw on religious and political imagery adequately to describe his prodigious marriage: "Have I approach'd the Marriage Bed with Reverence as to a sacred Shrine, and deny'd myself the Enjoyment of lawful Domestick Pleasures to preserve its Purity, and must I now find it polluted by foreign Iniquity?" (182). The fact that Careless is using him to gain access to Lady Plyant is "the very traiterous Position of taking up Arms by my Authority, against my Person!" and Careless ought to "be damn'd for a *Judas Maccabeus*, and *Iscariot* both" (182). Mellefont describes Plyant as "like a gull'd Bassa that has marry'd a relation of the *Grand Signior*" (158) and indeed when Sir Paul ventures to object to his cuckolding, Lady Plyant shrieks at him: "Heathen," "Turk, Sarazen," "Jew" (183). Lord Froth, on the other hand, finds his marriage "happy Slavery" (138).

In the Brisk-Froth plot, the very cosmos must be pressed into service to describe the important events. For example, when Mellefont asks Brisk to return to the after-dinner company, the would-be wit replies: "Gad you shall command me from the *Zenith* to the *Nadir*" (125). Lady Froth says of her idiotic husband: "I think I may say he wants nothing, but a blue Ribbon and a Star to make him shine, the very Phosphorus of our Hemisphere" (136). Later, Lady Froth's astronomy, like her literary efforts, serves as a mask to cover her doings with Brisk:

Lady *Froth.* My Dear, Mr. *Brisk* and I have been Star-gazing, I don't know how long.
Sir *Paul.* Does it not tire your Ladyship? are you not weary with looking up?
L. *Froth.* Oh, no, I love it violently. . . . Well, I swear, Mr. *Brisk,* you understood Astronomy like an old *Egyptian.*
Brisk. Not comparably to your Ladyship; you are the very *Cynthia* of the Skies, and Queen of Stars.
L. *Froth.* That's because I have no Light, but what's by Reflection from you, who are the Sun.
Brisk. Madam, you have Eclips'd me quite, let me perish. (209)

In one of the few brilliant touches in this play, after the real villainy and tragedy have been revealed, Lady Froth comments simply: "You know I told you *Saturn* look'd a little more angry than usual" (210). I wish Congreve had put in a stage direction: *Giggle.* "Nothing had really happened," writes Professor Dobrée. "It is like an icy douche, everything is brought to a standstill, and we are once more in the realm of that comedy where none of the emotions are important." [4] But something has happened: we realize with a sudden and violent revulsion how appallingly trivial Lady Froth and her kind are, how she levels everything, and how the magnitude of an action depends on the perceiver as well as its intrinsic importance.

To the fools, everything is the same size. Mellefont's leaving the room becomes, to Brisk, "thy Amputation from the Body of our Society. —He, I think that's pretty and Metaphorical enough" (124). Nothing is more important than anything else. The event and its metaphor are made equal and reality becomes a smooth surface polished by Brisk's false wit. For the fools, the forms of life equal the substance.

By way of contrast, the serious plot has few figures of speech and no literary effusions. Instead there is real play-acting, and what few metaphors there are create the impression, not of a polished surface that reflects all things equally, but of layers of complexity through which there is inward and outward movement. The main plot concerns the marriage of Mellefont and Cynthia, and particularly the villainous obstructions set up by Lady Touchwood, Mellefont's lusty aunt, who has conceived a desire for him. She selects for her ally and lover Maskwell, Mellefont's supposed friend who he thinks is helping him to bring off his marriage. Just as Maskwell is about to trick everyone and achieve his ambition to marry the wealthy Cynthia himself, Mellefont's uncle, Lord Touchwood, discovers the plot and sends his unfaithful wife and Maskwell off to punishment.

Both in language and action everything goes in and out. The images of penetration or nonpenetration parallel on a linguistic level the actions of the wives who refuse their husbands intercourse so they can sleep with other men. Thus, when the crimes of Lady Touchwood are finally revealed, Lord Touchwood cries out in a metaphor of inward movement: "Where will this end?" (205) "Heavens, what a long Track of dark Deceit has this discover'd! I am confounded when I look back, and want a Clue to guide me through the various Mazes of unheard of Treachery" (207). Earlier, Maskwell describes Lady Touchwood as having a "dam'd penetrating Head" (155) and she herself speaks of his knowing "the very inmost Windings and Recesses of my Soul" (135). Sir Paul's description of his wife is exactly the opposite: he calls her "impenetrable" and she speaks of her honor as "white" and "unsully'd" like a fair Sheet of Paper" (143). One is reminded also of Brisk's presumably unpimpled face.

In short, the fools' similes show that, to them, perception is no problem: everything is alike — a smooth surface. The language of the "serious" plot, however, reflects a self-conscious awareness of the difficulty of perception itself. Thus, Cynthia says of Mellefont's concentration on getting his uncle's consent rather than on the marriage itself: "You have look'd through the wrong End of the Perspective [i.e., telescope] all this while" (170). The wise people see into things rather than perceive superficial similarities:

> *Careless.* I find women are not the same bare-faced and in Masks, — and a Vizor disguises their Inclinations as much as their Faces.
>
> *Mellefont.* 'Tis a Mistake, for Women may most properly be said to be unmask'd when they wear Vizors; for that secures them from Blushing and being out of Countenance, and next to being in the Dark, or alone, they are most truly themselves in a Vizor Mask. (159)

Mellefont can tell Careless not to "wear" sense (125), and Maskwell says, "*Cynthia*, let thy Beauty gild my Crimes; and whatsoever I commit of Treachery or Deceit, shall be imputed to me as a Merit" (149).

Each of the two characteristic types of folly, suppression and overexpression, has its corresponding kind of villainy: Lady Touchwood is effusive and Maskwell hides his real nature. Both their names are indicative, of course. His expresses his hypocrisy. Hers, Touchwood, refers to old, decayed wood used for tinder; her name thus reveals both her age and the easy inflammability of her passions. Mellefont continually compares her to a witch or devil who has stirred up a destructive storm or fire (125, 126, 127, 157, 169). She, in turn, whose every passion bubbles Loveit-like to the surface, contrasts her fiery effusiveness with Maskwell's cold hypocrisy:

Calm Villain! How unconcern'd he stands, confessing Treachery, and Ingratitude! Is there a Vice more black! — O I have Excuses, thousands for my Faults; Fire in my Temper, Passions in my Soul, apt to ev'ry Provocation, oppressed at once with Love, and with Despair. But a sedate, a thinking Villain, whose black Blood runs temperately bad, what Excuse can clear? (132–133)

Maskwell's complete suppression of self in various pretenses presented Congreve with a problem of dramatizing such a character and drove him to that use of soliloquies that he said in his dedication his contemporaries so much deplored. Maskwell pretends even to his own desires: "Pox I have lost all Appetite to her . . . Therefore I must dissemble Ardour and Ecstasie; that's resolv'd: How easily and pleasantly is that dissembled before Fruition!" (155) He has substituted deception for plain-dealing in the old proverb: "Well, this Double-Dealing is a Jewel" (155). He has substituted deceit for his own real self even to the point of confusing his own appearance and nature: "Why, let me see, I have the same Face, the same Words and Accents, when I speak what I do think; and when I speak what I do not think — the very same — and dear Dissimulation is the only Art, not to be known from Nature" (149–150).

The villainy in the play involves dissimulation and discovery which form important parts of the in-out imagery. That is, discovery, as we have seen, is a penetration, an inward movement, while dissimulation has the special sense of inwardly inventing a mask and projecting it outward. Lord Touchwood describes it as a birth when he summarizes the revelations in the finale:

Like Vipers in the Womb, base Treachery lies,
Still gnawing that, whence first it did arise;
No sooner born, but the Vile Parent dies. (211)

Lady Touchwood threatens Maskwell: "You want but Leisure to invent fresh Falshood, and sooth me to a fond Belief of all your Fictions; but I will stab the Lie that's forming in your Heart" (204), or "Ten thousand Meanings lurk in each Corner of that various Face. O! That they were written in thy Heart, That I, with this, might lay thee open to my Sight!" (205). Indeed, dissimulation in this special sense is to be associated with sight and vision rather than darkness. Thus, Mellefont describes Lady Touchwood: "She has endeavour'd to do me all ill Offices with my Uncle; yet has managed 'em with that Subtilty, that to him they have born the Face of Kindness; while her Malice, like a dark Lanthorn [a seventeenth-century flashlight] only shone upon me, where it was directed" (126). Just as knaves bring their villainy to the surface, so fools bring their folly. Cynthia describes some: "They have all Jests in their Persons, though they have none in their Conversation" (164). As Maskwell says:

> No Mask like open Truth to cover Lies,
> As to go naked is the best disguise. (195)

References to mirrors have a particular appropriateness in this context. In the stage version of the play, between the discovery of Brisk's pimple (132) and Lord Froth's self-love in looking-glasses (138), Lady Touchwood denounces Maskwell as "one, who is no more moved with the reflection of his Crimes, than of his Face; but walks unstartled from the Mirrour, and straight forgets the hideous form." Lady Touchwood, when she pretends repentance, cries, "I was surprised to see a Monster in the Glass, and now I find 'tis my self" (189). The fact that she is pretending creates a double perspective on her remark. The question of what we see in the mirror — the self or its skin — is the question of the play.

As opposed to the mirror images, the high plot abounds in animal images that bring out hidden aspects of human nature. "Oh, 'tis such a Pleasure," says Maskwell, "to angle for fair fac'd Fools! Then that hungry Gudgeon Credulity, will bite at any thing" (149). Mellefont tells Lady Touchwood, "I have you on the Hook; you will but flounder your-self a weary" (189). He calls her an animal with "no more Holes to your Burrough" (188). She calls herself a "Vulture" (188), and Lord Touchwood calls the villains "Vipers" (211).

There are some parallels in the low plot. Lady Plyant says, "I am as red as a Turky-Cock" (146), and Sir Paul says of Mellefont, "Snakes are in his Peruke, and the Crocodile of *Nilus* is in his Belly, he will eat thee up alive" (143). But these images refer always to superficies: the false appearance of Mellefont's supposed attempt to seduce Lady Plyant, or that estimable gentlewoman's skin. Thus, Brisk describes one old lady as "chewing the Cud like an old *Ewe*," another without teeth as looking, when she laughs, "Like an Oyster at low Ebb, I'gad" (167). He says to Sir Paul, "You're always brooding over [your daughter] like an old Hen, as if she were not well hatch'd" (177). But his similes deal with appearances; those in the high plot reach toward a hidden self.

While other people are described as animals, Mellefont is associated with vegetables. Lord Touchwood describes him as "the alone remaining Branch of all our ancient Family" (194). Careless describes him as having cultivated Maskwell's interest like a plant (128), and Mellefont describes himself as a kind of farmer whose misfortune it is "to have a sudden Whirlwind come, tear up Tree and all, and bear away the very Root and Foundation of his Hopes" (192). Mellefont is given neither to affectation nor to pretense, and except for Cynthia (who remains a witty nonentity) he is the most "natural" of the troop.

He stands alone, expressing his isolation in the same image we saw used in *The Old Batchelor,* when he says to Maskwell, "Thy Presence is a view of Land, appearing to my shipwrack'd Hopes: The Witch has rais'd the Storm and her Ministers have done their Work. . . . There's Comfort in a Hand stretch'd out, to one that's sinking; tho' ne'er so far off" (147). While he is — to some extent — an actor in the situation, his most important role is that of spectator. Through the language of split-man observation he evaluates the relation of Maskwell and Lady Touchwood to him as "Like any two Guardians to an Orphan Heiress" (156). He can stand outside himself and see he is essentially alone, an orphan, in a corrupt world. He is even a spectator in his relationship with Cynthia. Both of them keep a perspective on their situation by pretending that their courtship and the machinations it entails are a race or a hunt or a contract in which Mellefont must give "a very evident Demonstration of his Wit" as "Consideration" (170). They treat their situation as a game and debate whether it is more like cards or bowling (140). Cynthia agrees to allow for "irresistible Odds" if Mellefont fails against Lady Touchwood. He, when he is actually scheming, describes his operations in terms of military strategy (147, 187, 188), as does Careless (127).

Ultimately, of course, the play fails because Mellefont is so woefully inadequate as a hero. He is like the passive heroes of contemporary tragedies, such as Osmyn in Congreve's own *The Mourning Bride* (1697). (Heroic plays in this, their later phase, strove for an emotional effect of pathos, not of admiration.) Mellefont represents in some sense an ideal of spectatorship, but in so doing, he is guilty of the same kind of self-suppression as the fools: he replaces himself as actor by Maskwell, his "better *Genius*" (157). All the derring-do that is admirable or endearing in a Dorimant or a Freeman is completely lacking. Mellefont lamentably fails to live up to Cynthia's challenge that he prove his wit by forcing Lady Touchwood to give her consent (170). In the denouement, it is Cynthia and Lord Touchwood — and chance — who uncover the villainy. In effect, if we apply to this play the co-ordinate diagram suggested by *The Old Batchelor* (page 145), the division of the individual into actor and spectator has resulted in dividing the play between a hero-spectator and a villain-doer. The excuse for Mellefont's failure, that Maskwell is a "Miracle of Ingratitude" (210), is utterly unconvincing. The conception of the play is flawed.

The public reaction to Mellefont's incompetence was precisely what we would expect. Congreve attempted to justify himself in the dedication:

> Another very wrong Objection has been made by some who have not taken Leisure to distinguish the Characters. The Hero of the Play, as they are pleas'd to call him, (meaning *Mellefont*) is a Gull, and made a Fool, and cheated. Is every man a Gull and a Fool that is deceiv'd? At that rate I'm afraid the two Classes of Men will be reduc'd to one, and the Knaves themselves be at a loss to justifie their Title: But if an Open-hearted honest Man, who has an entire Confidence in one whom he takes to be his Friend, and whom he has oblig'd to be so; and who (to confirm him in his Opinion) in all Appearance and upon several Trials has been so: If this Man be deceiv'd by the Treachery of the other; must he of necessity commence Fool immediately, only because the other has prov'd a Villain? Ay, but there was Caution given to *Mellefont* in the first Act by his Friend *Careless*. Of what Nature was that Caution? Only to give the Audience some light into the Character of *Maskwell* before his appearance; and not to convince *Mellefont* of his Treachery; for that was more than *Careless* was then able to do: He never knew *Maskwell* guilty of any Villany; he was only a sort of Man which he did not like. As for his suspecting his Familiarity with my Lady *Touchwood:* Let 'em examine the Answer that *Mellefont* makes him, and compare it with the Conduct of *Maskwell's* Character through the Play.
>
> I would beg 'em again to look into the Character of *Maskwell* before they accuse *Mellefont* of weakness for being deceiv'd by him. For upon summing up the Enquiry into this Objection, it may be found they have mistaken Cunning in one Character, for Folly in another. (115–116)

Congreve's justification cannot save his hero from a Catoesque passivity, nor the play itself from being a hodge-podge of tragedy and comedy. The motto says that "sometimes even comedy lifts her voice"; unfortunately, in this play, it quavered off into a falsetto.

Mellefont's passivity, however, does serve one useful purpose: it allows full scope for the development of Maskwell, who is the active principle in the drama, and in that sense the real "hero." It is Maskwell for whom the intrigue was designed, and Maskwell who understands and makes use of the inconsistency between appearance and nature on which intrigue is based. It is Maskwell who is worldly wise, who realizes more than any other character the difficulty of seeing things clearly or acting them out directly: "Is there not such a Thing as Honesty? Yes, and whosoever has it about him, bears an Enemy in his Breast: For your honest Man, as I take it, is that nice scrupulous, conscientious Person, who will cheat no Body but himself; such another Coxcomb, as your wise Man, who is too hard for all the World, and will be made a Fool of by no Body but himself." . . .

> Why will Mankind be Fools, and be deceiv'd?
> And why are Friends and Lovers Oaths believ'd?
> When, each, who searches strictly his own Mind,
> May so much Fraud and Power of Baseness find? (149–150)

We should remember that Brisk and Careless in the comic plot are double-dealers, too.

Mellefont, like Manly, has to learn that Maskwell's cynical wisdom has at least one or two grains of truth in it. He must learn, as even the preposterous Lady Plyant can tell him: "Alas! Humanity is feeble, Heav'n knows" (145). He learns it by his own feebleness in love, for, as Maskwell says, "Love [is] like Death an universal Leveller of Mankind" (149). Here again, as in *The Old Batchelor,* the influence of *The Plain-Dealer* is strong — though somewhat less obvious. The relation between Mellefont, Maskwell, and Careless is much like that between Manly, Vernish, and Freeman. But while Freeman carried enough weight to establish a norm of common sense, Careless does not; he sees mostly surface as Mellefont does: "I am a little superstitious in Physiognomy," he says (127). Mellefont, of course, hasn't the idiosyncracies of Manly; still, he is like Manly in that he would prefer to remain aloof both from the follies of the low plot and villainies of the high. He cannot; he is drawn into them by his own involvement with Cynthia and his aunt's desire for him, just as Manly was drawn back into reality by his love, first for Olivia, then for Fidelia. As in *The Plain-Dealer,* the problem is to educate the hero to his own fallibility.

Were Mellefont not in the play, we would have a fairly ordinary Restoration comedy; there have been melodramatic villains in comedies before. With Mellefont in the play, however, the comedy is no longer a conflict between those who see only the surface and those who see beneath it, the contrast between the wits and the fools of *The Old Batchelor.* With Mellefont in the play, the tension is between one who intrigues and is evil and one who, though he may know both appearance and nature, is good and does not intrigue. Congreve's denials in the dedication cannot change the parallel stressed in the play between Mellefont's goodness and his credulity.

The axis of Congreve's comedy has shifted. Wisdom is no longer prized: "There are Times," says Mellefont, "when Sense may be unseasonable, as well as Truth" (125). Cynthia's soliloquy sums it up:

> If Happiness in Self-content is plac'd
> The Wise are Wretched, and Fools only Bless'd. (169)

Her ironic tone hints that happiness is not merely self-content, that the world is not merely sex and money (which even Wycherley seemed to accept); something beyond folly or wisdom is real happiness. No longer is the dramatic tension between wise men and fools, but between fools and villains on the one hand, and Mellefont, who is "all goodness" (207), on the other. In short, the comic axis is no longer wisdom and folly, but good and evil. Congreve has added to the tendency to present an ideal in a realistic context still another symptom of eighteenth-century sentimentality: a faith in the "natural goodness" of people which social forms only interfere with, as here the social context serves to obscure Mellefont's noble impulses. This was Congreve's development beyond Wycherley, a failure in *The Double-Dealer,* but supremely successful in *The Way of the World,* where he pitted an evil clever man against a good clever man. It is to Congreve's credit that he never again carried the trend to the extreme he showed in this play. Nevertheless, the development of his plays does show a pattern. In these first two plays, as in the other Restoration comedies we have considered, intrigue defines an ethic based on intelligence. In Congreve's last plays, the final brilliant sparkle of Restoration comedy, intelligence is overshadowed by morality. Behind this pattern hides the unwritten assumption that cleverness and morality are inconsistent, and therein lurks an awful solemnity.

14 · *Love for Love*

Congreve's third comedy, *Love for Love,* surely his most neatly conceived and executed, was a *succès fou* when it was first produced on April 30, 1695, at the new theater Lincoln's Inn Fields, and it has been a favorite of critics and audiences ever since. Almost as though Congreve were testing his own innovations, he wrote his third play about three different kinds of knowledge, three different ways of life — we might call them presocial, social, suprasocial.

The high or "suprasocial" plot deals with Valentine Legend's courtship of the lovely Angelica. Already at the opening of the play, he has run heavily into debt in his efforts to win her, while she, in a manner not entirely becoming, has kept up an appearance of complete indifference. Even when Valentine gets into more and more trouble, she ignores his declarations of love. Sir Sampson Legend, Valentine's father, tries to disinherit him in favor of his younger brother, the sailor Ben, and even tries to marry Angelica himself. Tattle, an indiscreet beau, also tries to marry Angelica, and Mrs. Frail, a none too virtuous lady, tries to marry Valentine, who is at this point reduced to feigning madness. Mad or not, he and his servant Jeremy dupe Mrs. Frail and Tattle into marrying each other; but still none of his schemes to win Angelica, even his feigned madness, succeeds until he finally agrees to renounce his estate and consent to his father's marrying her. Then, she says his love is true and accepts him.

Valentine in this high plot progresses from lover to poet to madman to martyr, almost as though Congreve were remembering:

> The Lunaticke, the Louer, and the Poet
> Are of imagination all compact. . . .
> And all their minds transfigur'd so together,
> More witnesseth than fancies images,
> And growes to something of great constancie,
> But howsoever, strange, and admirable.[1]

His progress is through three confinements. In Act I, he is forced to remain in his house to elude his creditors, having run heavily into arrears in his pursuit of Angelica. At this stage, he contemplates becoming a poet to support himself. In the second confinement (Act IV), he agrees to relinquish his estate to get his father to pay his creditors, and, to avoid signing the final papers and to get Angelica's sympathy, he feigns madness, confining himself to his house again. In his third confinement (Act V) — this one metaphorical — he actually relinquishes his estate and Angelica, but she rescues him and accepts him. "I yield my Body as your Prisoner," he says (330).[2] His progress involves the familiar neoclassic coupling of religion, love, and the *furor poeticus,* as aspects of the irrational. "The divine Part of me, my Mind," he says to Angelica, "has worn this Masque of Madness, and this motly Livery, only as the Slave of Love and menial Creature of your Beauty" (308). Thus Valentine's friend, Scandal, can comment drily on his wish to write satire: "Who would die a Martyr to Sense in a Country where the Religion is Folly?" (223). In the context, it is completely appropriate that Valentine's final effort to win Angelica is to feign lunacy, for "He that was so near turning Poet yesterday Morning, can't be much to seek in playing the Madman to Day" (286).

Valentine's progress through confinements relates to knowledge as well as to madness. When Scandal suggests to Anglica that her indifference to Valentine is an affectation of ill nature, Valentine ruefully makes a remark which is a key not only to this play but to all of Restoration comedy: "I know no effectual Difference between continued Affectation and Reality" (262). His failure to realize that outside society there is a difference and his related failure to seek Angelica through something other than a show or "affectation" are what keep him from winning her. *Love for Love,* like most of the comedies we have considered, is based on the idea of an education or therapy, and this is the point at which Valentine needs education: that there is a reality which is higher and larger than "continued Affectation."

In all his schemes to win Angelica, Valentine neglects the one method that finally succeeds — directness. He pretends to poetry, to madness, and to devotion; not until the finale does he resort to a simple direct proposal with obvious evidence of his sincerity. When he plans to turn poet, he tells his servant Jeremy:

> Now I am poor, I have an Opportunity to be reveng'd on 'em all; I'll pursue *Angelica* with more Love than ever, and appear more notoriously her Admirer in this Restraint, than when I openly rival'd the rich Fops, that made Court to her; so shall my Poverty be a Mortification to her Pride, and perhaps make her compassionate the Love, which has principally reduc'd me to this Lowness of Fortune. (220)

Despite his protestations, though, he is keeping a barrier between himself and Angelica, trying to create a "Mortification to her Pride," rather than a direct bond between them. His feigning madness is another ruse.

Angelica quickly realizes it is and resolves to "play Trick for Trick" (288). She refuses to recognize that he is feigning, even when he says:

> You see what Disguises Love makes us put on; Gods have been in counterfeited Shapes for the same Reason; . . . . Nay Faith, now let us understand one another, Hypocrisie apart, — The Comedy draws toward an end, and let us think of leaving acting, and be our selves; and since you have lov'd me, you must own, I have at length deserv'd you shou'd confess it. (308)

In effect, Valentine still keeps a distance between them, revealed by his speaking of "acting." He has soiled his relationship with Angelica as she promptly makes him confess:

> *Valentine.* My seeming Madness has deceiv'd my Father, and procur'd me time to think of Means to reconcile me to him; and preserve the right of my Inheritance to his Estate; which otherwise by Articles, I must this Morning have resign'd: And this I had inform'd you of to Day, but you were gone, before I knew you had been here.
>
> *Angelica.* How! I thought your Love of me had caus'd this Transport in your Soul; which it seems you only counterfeited; for mercenary Ends, and sordid Interest. (308–309)

She meets his social show with an answer in social terms and demands instead that he show real madness: "I'll tell you two things before I leave you; I am not the Fool you take me for; and you are mad, and don't know it" (311). Thus, too, Angelica replies to Tattle's proposal: "O fie for shame, hold your Tongue, A passionate Lover, and five Senses in perfection! when you are as mad as *Valentine,* I'll believe you love me, and the maddest shall take me" (304).

In this "mad" scene with its echoes of *Hamlet* and *The Plain-Dealer,* Valentine takes on some of the character of the playwright. Valentine's statement about his "Comedy" certainly supports this view, as do the frequent references to art and artifice. But, as in *The Way of the World,* drama is tested and found wanting. Valentine has in no sense achieved completeness by becoming inspired and literary. On the contrary, Valentine has yet to learn what Angelica's trial of his constancy has to teach him — "real" madness.

He must prove to her that the underlying reality, "the naked Hook" that one gets when the bait (appearances and disguises) is thrown off (268), is worth the loss of liberty and the chase. He must, in other words, prove that Vainlove in *The Old Batchelor* is wrong, that indeed Angelica herself is wrong when she says: "Uncertainty and Expectation are the Joys of Life. Security is an insipid thing, and the overtaking and possessing of a Wish, discovers the Folly of the Chase. Never let us know one another better; for the Pleasure of a Masquerade is done, when we come to shew our Faces" (310–311). To prove her statement wrong, when the other characters show it is clearly right for the ordinary social world, Valentine must show a "real" madness, that lifts him above ordinary social realities. That "real" madness comes when Valentine consents to ruin himself simply, as he believes, to please her. He has come, in effect, to the knowledge that the final reality is not affectation, but expectation: "He that loses Hope may part with any thing" (328).

When he resigns both his love and his money, Angelica accepts him. He sees her then as a kind of religious fulfillment. The idea is implicit, of course, in her name. Valentine had commented on it in the mad scene: "You're a Woman,—One to whom Heav'n gave Beauty, when it grafted Roses on a Briar. You are the Reflection of Heav'n in a Pond, and he that leaps at you is sunk" (306). The religious or neoplatonic imagery gets particularly strong in the finale. "*Tattle,*" says Valentine to the foppish rival whom he has tricked into marrying Mrs. Frail, "You would have interposed between me and Heav'n; but Providence laid Purgatory [i.e., Mrs. Frail] in your way—You have but Justice" (330). Even the cynical Scandal is converted; he says to Angelica:

Scandal. There is a third good Work, which I, in particular, must thank you for; I was an Infidel to your Sex, and you have converted me. . . .

Angelica. . . . Men are generally Hypocrites and Infidels, they pretend to Worship, but have neither Zeal nor Faith: How few, like *Valentine,* would persevere even to Martyrdom, and sacrifice their Interest to their Constancy! In admiring me, you misplace the Novelty.

> The Miracle to Day is, that we find
> A Lover true: Not that a Woman's kind. (331)

In other words, the end of Valentine's education is to bring him to a higher kind of reality, a Providence or God's justice, that transcends the chance and show of ordinary social reality. Valentine here shows, like Manly, overtones of the Kierkegaardian hero: he makes the final act of resignation in giving up all he hopes for, his love and his estate, and then achieves what he had given up.

In spite of the neoplatonic religious imagery, much of the material of *Love for Love* is concerned with Locke's conception of man, published five years before the play. Thus, Valentine demands of his father: "If you don't mean to provide for me, I desire you would leave me as you found me."

Sir *Sampson.* With all my Heart: Come, uncase, strip, and go naked out of the World, as you came into't.

Valentine. My Cloaths are soon put off:—But you must also deprive me of Reason, Thought, Passions, Inclinations, Affections, Appetites, Senses, and the huge Train of Attendants that you begot along with me. . . . I am of myself a plain easie simple Creature; and to be kept at small Expence; but the Retinue that you gave me are craving and invincible. (251)

Part of Valentine's education in the play is to realize that his social desires are not part of his intrinsic nature. When he came naked into the world, he was a *tabula rasa.* Indeed, he says to Angelica, "You are all white, a Sheet of lovely spotless Paper, when you first are born; but you are to be scrawl'd and blotted by every Goose's Quill" (306) — a quite accurate statement of Locke's idea that we come into the world as clean slates, and our minds are made up of the accumulated scribblings on the slates by all our experiences. The play is so Lockean that there are two actual *tabulae rasae,* the presocial "naturals," Ben and Prue.

Ben is Valentine's younger brother, a boorish but likable sailor. He has come home to see his father, Sir Sampson Legend, who is trying to force Valentine to sign over his estate to his younger brother. Prue is the boorish, countrified daughter of the silly astrologer Foresight. Foresight and Sir Sampson plan a match between the "Sea-Beast" and the "land-Monster," but their plans fail when the couple fall out and when Valentine manages to avoid signing the document dispossessing him.

Whereas Valentine and Angelica in the course of the play come *through* the obstacles of society to their neoplatonic, suprasocial status at the end of the play, Ben and Prue are *pre*social, barely beyond the *tabula rasa* stage. Shortly after *Love for Love* appeared, Congreve wrote to Dennis, describing among other things this type of character:

> Under this Head may be ranged all Country-Clowns, Sailers, Tradesmen, Jockeys, Gamesters and such like, who make use of *Cants,* or peculiar *Dialects* in their several Arts and Vocations. One may almost give a Receipt for the Composition of such a Character: For the Poet has nothing to do, but to collect a few proper Phrases and terms of Art, and to make the Person apply them by ridiculous Metaphors in his Conversation, with Characters of different Natures. Some late Characters of this kind have been very successful; but in my mind they may be Painted without much Art or Labour; since they require little more, than a good Memory and Superficial Observation.[3]

Dr. Jonson said of Ben, with admirable simplicity, "The Sailor is not accounted very natural, but he is very pleasant,"[4] and Coleridge remarked of Congreve's characters generally, "There is no growth from within."[5] In the case of Ben, at least, this character structure is exactly what is called for. Ben is unnatural because Congreve was drawing a "natural man," an intellectual construct. By making Ben less lifelike, Congreve makes us more aware of the character as symbol.

Ben's sea-jargon sets him off from the other people in the play, and his seaworthiness suggests his association with nature and sincerity: "Flesh, you don't think I'm false-hearted, like a Land-Man. A Sailor will be honest, tho'f may-hap he has never a Penny of Mony in his Pocket — May-hap I may not have so fair a Face, as a Citizen or a Courtier; but for all that, I've as good Blood in my Veins, and a Heart as sound as a Bisket" (283). When Sir Sampson tries to coerce Ben into marriage, he is fighting nature itself: "If so be, that I ben't minded to be steer'd by him; 'tis as tho'f he should strive against Wind and Tide" (283).

Ben and Prue, being presocial, have "natural" sexual desires that they do not conceal, as when Prue, in a manner reminiscent of Hippolita, says: "Now my Mind is set upon a Man, I will have a Man some way or other. Oh! methinks I'm sick when I think of a Man; and if I can't have one, I wou'd go to sleep all my Life: For when I'm awake, it makes me wish and long, and I don't know for what — And I'd rather be always asleep, than sick with thinking" (321).

While Ben is of the sea, Prue is of the land and hence more naturally inclined toward the social pretenses to which the foppish beau Tattle introduces her: "All well-bred Persons Lie — Besides, you are a Woman, you must never speak what you think: Your Words must contradict your Thoughts; but your Actions may contradict your Words." "O Lord," cries Prue delightedly, "I swear this is pure, — I like it better then our old fashion'd Country way of speaking one's Mind" (259–260). Ben, however, finds social pretense unnatural; he tells her, "It's but a Folly to lie: For to speak one thing, and to think just the contrary Way; is as it were, to look one way, and to row another" (272). Neither Ben nor Prue has the proper social habit of concealing what one thinks, and as a result they can quickly see their natural mismatch and quarrel over it (272–273).

There is a curious kinship between Ben and Prue, the presocial people, and Valentine and Angelica, the suprasocial people. Throughout the play, both Ben and Angelica are free of the pretenses of society; Valentine becomes free at the end, and Prue is free at the beginning (though she learns pretense from Tattle). It is as though Congreve were saying the highest social wisdom is the naturalness of those who never saw society. Thus, Angelica establishes a naturalness like Ben's when she says: "Passions are unreasonable and involuntary; if he loves, he can't help it; and if I don't love, I can't help it; no more than he can help his being a Man, or I my being a Woman" (289). Prue uses a neoplatonic image such as we would expect from Valentine or Angelica, when she asks about making love, "Is it like the Catechism?" (259). (The connection between presocial and suprasocial is made even stronger by the fact that one of the first things Prue learns is that love in society is *not* like the catechism: one must say the opposite of what one believes.) Valentine calls himself and his brother "Twin-Stars, and cannot shine in one Sphere; when he rises I must Set" (267), like opposed "suns."

The presocial and suprasocial characters share as one form of naturalness the fondness for perpetually seeking that was Vainlove's humor in *The Old Batchelor.* Angelica shows it in her speech, "Uncertainty and Expectation are the Joys of Life" (310–311). Ben shows it when he says, "I love to roam about from Port to Port, and from Land to Land: I could never abide to be Port-bound, as we call it: Now a Man that is marry'd, has as it were, d'ye see, his Feet in the Bilboes, and may-hap mayn't get 'em out again when he wou'd" (270). Valentine, however, differs from Ben precisely at this point when in the closing scene he yields himself to Angelica as her "Prisoner" (330). Prue also differs from Ben in the matter of perpetual seeking: Ben seeks freedom; Prue just wants to get into the social swim.

Thus, society lies between the "naturalness" of the presocial people on the one hand and on the other the "naturalness" of the suprasocial people. The social group is composed of a younger generation (Tattle, Scandal, Mrs. Frail, and Mrs. Foresight) and an older generation (Sir Sampson and Foresight). Tattle, after a flirtation with Prue, tries to dupe Angelica into marrying him. Mrs. Frail, after a flirtation with Ben, tries to dupe the supposedly mad Valentine into marrying her. Tattle disguises himself as a friar for the purpose, Mrs. Frail as a nun, and suddenly by the deft doings of Valentine's servant Jeremy, they find themselves married to each other. Tattle mangles reputations by pretending to mend them; his friend Scandal mangles reputations by direct attack. Even Scandal is impressed, though, by Mrs. Foresight's *sang-froid* — he seduces her, and she pretends not even to know him the next day. Congreve may have had a real person in mind when he drew Mrs. Foresight, for one of his poems, "To Doris," says:

But who o'er-night obtain'd her Grace,
She can next Day disown,
And stare upon the Strange-Man's Face,
As one she ne'er had known.
So well she can the Truth disguise,
Such artful Wonder frame,
The Lover or distrusts his Eyes,
Or thinks 'twas all a Dream.[6]

Finally, there is some comedy of humors associated with the old astrologer Foresight and Sir Sampson, Valentine's tyrannical father who is trying to marry Angelica himself. Together, these two represent the older generation in society.

The essence of society in this as in other Restoration plays is the separation of appearances from nature. Most of the material in the somewhat slow first act serves to set the tone of the social world; for example, the amusing episode — otherwise irrelevant — of Trapland. He comes to collect £1500 from Valentine, who in turn tries to divert him from his purpose by plying him with several glasses of sherry and talk of a widow Trapland admires. Unfortunately, however, the moneylender returns to business and Scandal says, "I'll rip up his Stomach, and go the shortest way to his Conscience" (228). "He begs Pardon like a Hangman at an Execution" (229). The impression we get is of a dog-eat-dog world. Everyone in it, debtor or creditor, is equal in appetite, whether for drink, sex, or money. Everyone masks his motives of self-interest as Valentine does in fawning on Trapland or as the moneylender himself does: "Sincerely, I am loth to be thus pressing, but my Necessity—" (229). We get the impression, too, of the whirligig of improvisation and intrigue that goes into living in such a world when one of Trapland's tipstaffs says, "We have half a dozen Gentlemen to arrest in *Pall-mall* and *Covent-Garden;* and if we don't make haste the Chairmen will be abroad, and block up the Chocolate-Houses, and then our Labour's lost" (228). This is a world in which critics are dogs and poets hunters, and "If you can't be fairly run down by the Hounds, you will be treacherously shot by the Huntsmen" (223). This is the world of which Valentine says, "I know no effectual Difference between continued Affectation and Reality" (262).

Living in this social world calls for the ability to see through appearances, which means knowledge—and several different kinds and levels of knowledge occur among the social people. Foresight, the old astrologer, holds what had become in Congreve's day an outmoded Renaissance and medieval belief in direct supernatural influence on the physical world. He believes that certain appearances—stars, moles on the face, and the like—show the hidden aspects of the present and future. His belief is based on the facile assumption that all these events are controlled equally by supernatural influence. I "Can judge of Motions Direct and Retrograde," he says, "of *Sextiles, Quadrates, Trines* and *Oppositions*, Fiery *Trigons* and Aquatical *Trigons.* Know whether Life shall be long or short, Happy or Unhappy, whether Diseases are Curable or Incurable. If Journeys shall be prosperous, Undertakings successful; or Goods stoll'n recover'd" (247). Foresight judges people by physiognomies and events by his crackbrained astrological predictions. His knowledge of both persons and events is utterly false, and as if to prove the point he is cuckolded.

Sir Sampson uses another kind of outmoded knowledge. He believes in a kind of Elizabethan "nature" in which a father's authority is like a king's—absolute, divinely ordained: "I warrant my Son thought nothing belong'd to a Father, but Forgiveness and Affection; no Authority, no Correction, no Arbitrary Power; nothing to be done, but for him to offend, and me to pardon" (246). For him, therefore, personal experience — particularly travel and family relations — is the core of reality: "I . . . know the World, and Men and Manners," he says (295):

There's no time but the time present, there's no more to be said of what's past, and all that is to come will happen. If the Sun shine by Day, and the Stars by Night, why, we shall know one another's Faces without the help of a Candle, and that's all the Stars are good for. . . . I know the length of the Emperor of *China's* Foot; have kissed the *Great Mogul's* Slipper, and rid a Hunting upon an Elephant with the Cham of *Tartary,* — Body o' me, I have made a Cuckold of a King, and the present Majesty of *Bantam* is the Issue of these Loyns. (246–247)

His fatherhood, he believes, gives him absolute rights over Valentine (250) and anything other than complete submission on his son's part is "unnatural." Yet, as if to give him the lie, his son Ben, the "Hopes of my Family" (267) shows a lamentable lack of such "nature":

Ben. Well Father, and how do all at home? How does Brother *Dick,* and Brother *Val?*

Sir *Sampson. Dick,* body o' me, *Dick* has been dead these two Years; I writ you word, when you were at *Legorne.*

Ben. Mess, that's true; Marry I had forgot. *Dick's* dead as you say — Well. (269–270)

Later, Ben says, "It seems Brother *Val.* is gone mad, . . . but . . . what's that to me?" (298). Furthermore, despite his protestations in favor of the "natural," Sir Sampson's words and actions are most remarkably unnatural. His only actions in the play are to try and reverse the natural positions of older and younger brother and to attempt to marry a woman thirty-odd years younger than himself. Over and over, he makes exclamations like, "Body o' me, why was not I a Bear? that my Cubs might have liv'd upon sucking their Paws." "What, wouldst thou have me turn Pelican, and feed thee out my my own Vitals?" (252–253). Valentine turns the tables on this walking *Pseudodoxia Epidemica* by counterfeiting a disorder in nature, madness: "Indeed, I thought, Sir, when the Father endeavoured to undo the Son, it was a reasonable return of Nature" (328). It is fitting that the lesson Sir Sampson learns in the play is, "Learn to be a good Father, or you'll never get a second Wife" (329).

Valentine's servant Jeremy and Scandal use another kind of knowledge, a skeptical naturalism representative of the younger people in the social group. They reject philosophy, poetry, love, and other intangibles in favor of belly-knowledge (I.i and ii), and they are the most successful characters within the ostensibly rational social framework. This fact, typical in restoration comedy, hints that for the social people this is the best answer. Thus, Jeremy says of his master's reading philosophy: "Does your *Epictetus,* or your *Seneca* here, or any of these poor, rich Rogues, teach you how to pay your Debts without Mony? Will they shut up the Mouths of your Creditors? Will *Plato* be Bail for you? Or *Diogenes,* because he understands Confinement, and liv'd in a Tub, go to Prison for you?" (220) Wits, to him, are only a poor substitute for money (287).

To Mrs. Foresight, family relations are not real at all. "By my Soul," she cries, when Prue speaks to her, "I shall fancy my self old indeed, to have this great Girl call me Mother" (256). If parenthood can be concealed, it ceases to exist. For her, as for Mrs. Frail and Tattle, reputation is reality. "How can any Body be happy, while they're in perpetual Fear of being seen and censur'd" (254). Thus, Scandal, meeting Mrs. Foresight the morning after he has slept with her, is finally reduced by her denials to commenting, "This I have heard of before, but never believ'd. I have been told, she had that admirable Quality of forgetting to a Man's Face in the morning, that she had lain with him all Night, and denying that she had done Favours with more Impudence, than she cou'd grant 'em" (297). In effect, the previous night becomes unreal. So too, for Mrs. Frail and Tattle, only the realization that their marriage will be published makes it real to them (326).

Among the social people, Tattle and Scandal are contrasted throughout the play. Though both base most of their actions on reputation, Tattle pretends secrecy and openly undercuts his pretense. Scandal cries down the vices of the age and secretly undercuts his railing. "The Liberty I take in talking, is purely affected for the Service of your Sex," he tells Mrs. Foresight, "He that first cries out stop Thief, is often he that has stol'n the Treasure" (282). Low in social acumen, Tattle is finally duped, because he thinks the "real" thing is not what people say, but what they do, as he explains to Prue (259). Scandal is more acute. He realizes as Valentine does that in society there is "no effectual difference between continued Affectation and Reality" (262). He realizes what a playwright like Etherege was laughing at; namely, the confusion of the pretended self with "real" self that results from continued pretense. Scandal cannot go beyond this knowledge and remain in the social framework. For a reality that is not "continued Affectation," he must be converted to the religion of love in the final scene. He is, at the end of the play, almost ready to cross the boundary between the social and suprasocial people.

Thus, plot, character, humors, language, in short, all the elements of the play are tailored to bring out in terms of different kinds of knowledge the distinctions among the presocial, social, and suprasocial people. The accompanying diagram shows the relations among the three groups:

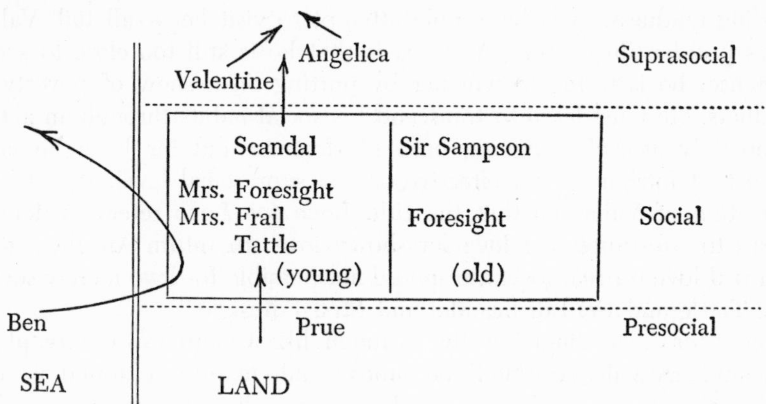

The knowledge necessary for living in the social whirl separates Ben and Prue, who do not have it yet, from the social people who do and from Valentine and Angelica who are rising above it. Ben, Valentine, and Angelica are all seeking something outside the ordinary social framework. Ben, separated from the others by being a "Sea-Beast," is beyond social distinctions. He refuses to come to rest, but Valentine and Angelica, by the end of the play, have gone beyond society as they wanted to. One critic notes that Ben "seems out of place";[7] that is Congreve's point — Ben is a "natural" man in this highly unnatural society. Prue, on the other hand, seeks only social status. Scandal, who has it, is converted at the end to seeking what Valentine and Angelica have found, while the rest of the purely social people are confined to a box of their own making. As if to make the point, Congreve contrasts the tricked marriage of Tattle and Mrs. Frail with the real betrothal of Valentine and Angelica: the hero and heroine speak of their marriage as heavenly, a kind of true religion; Tattle and Mrs. Frail were disguised as a friar and a nun to wed.

The diagram looks as though Congreve had taken one of Etherege's plots and framed around it the actions of Ben, Valentine, and Angelica, thus giving his play a theme that rises above the purely social world. Within that world, people confine themselves to purely social aims, trying to see through the shell of appearances, pretenses, affectations, and dissimulations to real nature. In a sense that is just what the author has done: the action of the play is to make Valentine bring his real nature out from under the shell of pretenses he has drawn round himself. In so doing, Valentine grows out of the limited social world into something larger. He has, like any Restoration hero, plenty of social acumen; he marries off Tattle and Mrs. Frail as if with a dexterous flick of the hand. Yet all his intrigues to win Angelica — spending his money, pretending madness, even his simple attempt to visit her — all fail. Valentine's problem in winning Angelica is that he is still too close to social pretense; he is trying to win her by putting on a show of poverty or madness. He must learn to transcend his social habits through an action completely asocial, resigning both his fortune and his love; he must learn that intrigue is not effective on the suprasocial level. It is to the education of Valentine that the title *Love for Love* refers: Valentine learns to substitute real love for showy love. In return Angelica gives him real love for real love, a response not possible for love merely social; viz., Tattle and Frail or Scandal and Mrs. Foresight.

Love for Love, linguistically, is much like Congreve's earlier plays. The imagery still has the three-dimensional quality we found in *The Old Batchelor.* Ben's voyaging is keyed into the passage of time, and both suggest a forward movement. There is the conversion upward in the somewhat hackneyed neoplatonism of Valentine and Angelica and the conversions downward in the speeches of the social people. The confusion of appearance and nature and social and sexual intercourse among the social people generally suggest the same transverse motion as the consuming-consumed metaphors of *The Old Batchelor.* Increasingly, however, Congreve gives the usual tropes of Restoration comedy only to the people confined in the social whirligig. Thus, Scandal dismisses dreaming in favor of "willing, waking Love" (286), a conversion downward. He attacks honor and conscience: "Honour is a publick Enemy, and Conscience a Domestick Thief; and he that wou'd secure his Pleasure, must pay a Tribute to one, and go halves with t'other" (281). In the same way Tattle converts Valentine and Angelica's love to weight: "You will pardon me, if from a just weight of his Merit, with your Ladiship's good Judgment, I form'd the Ballance of a reciprocal Affection" (263). The right-way–wrong-way simile is a resource of description only for the social people. Tattle decides that the universities are all right for servants, "But the Education is a little too pedantick for a Gentleman" (317), a remark that tells us more about Tattle's idea of a gentleman than about the nature of a seventeenth-century university education. Mrs. Foresight says, as she is offering Prue up to Tattle, "They're all so, Sister, these Men — they love to have the spoiling of a young thing, they are as fond of it, as of being first in the Fashion, or of seeing a new Play the first Day" (257). Mrs. Frail, when she is trying to trick Ben into marrying her, says: "You know, marrying without an Estate, is like Sailing in a Ship without Ballast. . . . And tho' I have a good Portion; you know one wou'd not venture all in one Bottom" (283). The contrast is between right and wrong ways of comparing marriage to a vessel: marriage being like a vessel because it requires steadiness represented by ballast (a conversion downward of emotional solidity) and marriage being like a vessel because it is a commercial venture. By contrast, the suprasocial people, Valentine and Angelica, speak a language fraught with cosmological implications — almost in the Elizabethan manner.

The imagery, as well as the figures of speech, is no longer as loose as in *The Old Batchelor*. There is less reliance on isolated image clusters than in Congreve's earlier plays. Imagery is largely controlled by character: astrological images for Foresight, for example, or nautical images for Ben. Each character has a specific area of experience to which he belongs. He is, in effect, placed at a point along one of the three axes of page 145 rather than at their intersection. His choices, represented by his similes, are more limited. Ben is confined to the continual forward movement of perpetual seeking. The social people are limited to their transverse relations. Valentine, though the most free, moves only upward. Language does not pull apart from action; rather, it constantly tests knowledge, establishing the character's position and the choices open to him. This parallel motion of language and action is what makes us think this the most "stageable" of Congreve's plays. The inside-out quality we saw in the relation of language and action in *The Old Batchelor* is retained in the form of a central paradox: Valentine and Angelica escape the social world by finding a liberating confinement within it.

In another sense, *Love for Love* marks a distinctly new stage in Congreve's development as a comic dramatist. In this epistemological comedy, he contrasts two worlds and two kinds of knowledge: the realistic social world, apparently rational, and the intuitional and unrealistic suprasocial world of aims and seeking. The heart of the irony — it is, of course, the same as that of *The Plain-Dealer* — is that the realities of society are deceptive and social aims limited. The relation among Valentine, Scandal, and Tattle is still faintly like that among Manly, Freeman, and Vernish; the thematic contrast is still between the two worlds of Manly-Valentine and Freeman-Scandal. "Real" reality and success, the fusion of "real" natures, are lodged in the intuitional. Intrigue, with its specious logic of plots and pretenses, is left a role subordinate to naturalness, "generous," irrational, and ingenuous action.

There is a corresponding change in the position of the isolated individual. I come increasingly to the conclusion that *The Plain-Dealer* is the single most important influence on Congreve, and if we consider that play as a kind of first stage in his development, we see a slow growth. At first the deviant individual is a central figure — Manly. As Congreve develops from Heartwell to Ben to Sir Wilfull Witwoud in *The Way of the World,* the solitary one moves further and further out toward the periphery of the action, though still retaining his original function of casting a comic perspective on it. In the last two plays, this figure becomes alien, one coming from elsewhere and going elsewhere, one "passing through" the social whirl. Ben goes through society in a spatial voyage in much the way that Valentine "passes through" in a psychological voyage. Valentine grows up to be able to make his way in society and then rises above it. Although Ben's voyage is analogous to Valentine's voyage of life, they travel at right angles to each other; they are "Twin-Stars and cannot shine in one Sphere."

By juxtaposing the two brothers, one foolish but essentially good, and the other both clever and good, Congreve continues the shift in the comic axis we noted in *The Double-Dealer*. Goodness and cleverness are no longer to be equated; the ethic of Etherege is gone. Knowledge to Congreve serves a different function. No longer does it simply enable the hero to succeed in a corrupt and foolish society. In this play it becomes a means to a larger freedom, and that freedom is not necessarily denied to the ignorant man — Ben. But while Ben's freedom means a physical escape from society, Valentine's freedom is a greater thing, a spiritual freedom. The action of *Love for Love* perfectly exemplifies the last phase of Restoration comedy. The hero retreats from the social world of deception and illusion to a personal haven of psychological truth and emotional sincerity. He discovers the heart behind the mask.

15 · *The Way of the World*

The one play that generations of readers, actors, audiences, and even critics have singled out as the triumphant quintessence of Restoration comedy is Congreve's *The Way of the World.* Lytton Strachey is guilty of no exaggeration when he ranks it "among the most wonderful and glorious creations of the human mind." [1] Nevertheless, or perhaps naturally, it started with a flop. It seems to have gone right over the heads of the audience that first saw it in March 1700 at Lincoln's Inn Fields. One spectator said it had no plot; another called it satire.[2] Congreve wrote somewhat snidely in the dedication, "Little of it was prepar'd for that general Taste which seems now to be predominant in the Pallats of our Audience" (336).[3]

Possibly the audience had been influenced by Jeremy Collier's foolish tract, which appeared in 1698. Collier made a vicious and stupid attack on the supposed immorality of the stage. He stirred up a good deal of controversy, and apparently his pamphlet had a considerable effect on audiences, creating a real taste for sentimental and moralistic comedies. In any case, *The Way of the World,* though it is without any question one of the world's great plays, failed before its post-Collier audience. Fortunately, later audiences with better "Pallats" have agreed with Congreve, not with Collier, and the play has had a long and happy series of revivals.

What strikes us most is the language. If Shakespeare's diction, as one of Keats's sonnets suggests, is "the voice of waters," then surely Congreve's is the sound of champagne, with all the virtues and limitations of that singular beverage. You cannot help moving your lips as you read *The Way of the World,* savoring the speech of it, imagining the intonations and hesitations with which an actor would realize it. Professor Bateson points out that the characters are "without roots"; they exist only in the moment of their appearance on the stage and they grow only from the style and rhythms of the language.[4] While this is not strictly so — we know a good deal of the past histories of the Witwoud clan, of Lady Wishfort and her maid and her daughter — the characters do stem from their speech in the sense that each character's language establishes his position in a certain area of experience. The style and diction allotted to each of the characters is so brilliantly and thoroughly conceived that we literally see the speaker sketched in his words. Even the three maids in the play speak differently. Given two lines from any person in the play, one can tell who the speaker is — with one possible exception, and that exception is the key to the achievement of the play. I do not think you can easily tell the hero from the villain.

A number of critics think this play a witty but unstageable closet drama, largely because the plot is so intricate. Of course, this is a difficult play to stage, like most plays worth doing, but it is not unstageable. In fact, the play is almost inconceivable apart from a stage — its speech demands a speaker. The supposed complexity of the plot, as we shall see, is intended to be confusing; the confusion is an essential part of the dramatic impact. In part the complication comes from the standard Restoration convention about intrigue. That is, as long as there is an inconsistency between appearances and emotions, power is given to the person who knows this inconsistency. The power ceases if the inconsistency ceases, if there are no secrets left to be discovered. More important, the plot becomes complex because Congreve deals out the secrets of the play so slowly, so gradually, that they assume an intricacy far beyond that of the actual situation.

Within this complicating convention, Congreve (I hope to show) makes four points: (1) he compares and contrasts two kinds of reality, emotional and dynastic; (2) he builds two actions, unraveling and emancipating; (3) he develops and evaluates his characters in terms of their relation to these two actions and these two kinds of reality; (4) finally, he unifies his material around a single Romantic idea.

The Way of the World deals with a typical family situation — a fight for the control of an estate. Presiding over the family at the beginning of the play is the absurd Lady Wishfort who holds in a "Cabal," a gossip club, her daughter Mrs. Fainall and her niece Millamant. She controls all of Mrs. Fainall's estate and part of Millamant's as well. As the plot thickens, a contest develops as to who shall get these estates from Lady Wishfort: Mr. Fainall or Millamant's lover, Mirabell.

So far, so simple. But Congreve seems to complicate these fairly straightforward family relations by such statements as this by Fainall, "[Sir Wilfull Witwoud] is half Brother to this *Witwoud* by a former Wife, who was Sister to my Lady *Wishfort,* my Wife's Mother. If you [Mirabell] marry *Millamant,* you must call Cousins too" (349). Congreve has added (and one wonders why) the confusing brothers Witwoud. Anthony, a town fop, is one of Lady Wishfort's cabal; his half-brother and Lady Wishfort's nephew, Sir Wilfull, comes to town from the country (where he has been a bumpkin these many years) on his way abroad. Lady Wishfort forces him into a half-hearted courtship of Millamant. This terribly complicated family tree can be diagramed (as in the accompanying figure, where the characters in the play are itali-

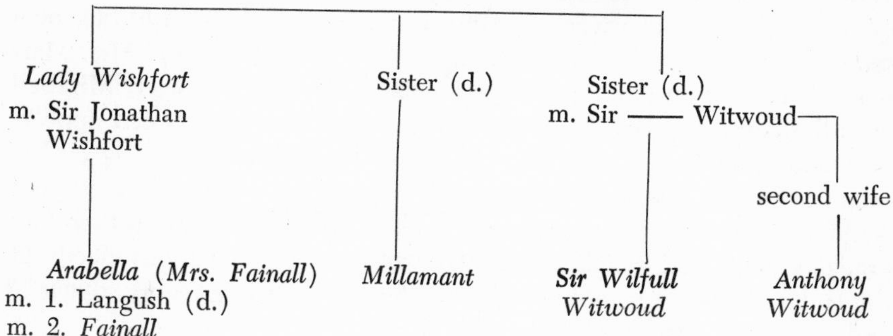

cized). To an audience, however, only two facts emerge: that Mrs. Fainall is Lady Wishfort's daughter and that Lady Wishfort has control over Millamant's estate. The other relationships, particularly the confusion of Witwouds, serve only to create the impression of a welter of consanguinity. Congreve is confusing his audience gratuitously, and we must infer he has some reason for doing so.

He does the same thing with the emotional relations that he does with the family structure. Behind the already complicated dynastic relations lie even more complicated emotional affairs. In Act I we learn that Mirabell has made advances to Lady Wishfort to cover his wooing of Millamant. Mrs. Marwood, another member of the cabal, betrayed him to the old lady, who, naturally enough, despises him now. Act II tells us that Mirabell had been Mrs. Fainall's lover when she was a widow, and, when she seemed pregnant, he married her off to Fainall. We learn, too, that Mrs. Marwood is now Fainall's mistress, but yearns for Mirabell.

The discrepancy between the family structure and the emotional structure plays into the Restoration convention about intrigue: a discrepancy between appearances (the overt family relations) and "nature" (the hidden emotional facts) gives power to the man who knows the discrepancy. At the beginning of the play, Mirabell is trying to set up such a situation. He has married his servant Waitwell to Lady Wishfort's maid Foible and plans to have Waitwell disguise himself as a nobleman, court, *and marry* Lady Wishfort. Then Mirabell plans to reveal the disguise, show Lady Wishfort that she has married a servant, and offer to release her if she will let him marry Millamant *cum* estate. Unfortunately, Mrs. Marwood (who for at least two reasons wants to spike Mirabell's courtship of Millamant) discovers the plan and tells Lady Wishfort. Mrs. Marwood also tells Fainall of his wife's former affair with Mirabell; he threatens to publish it to the world unless Lady Wishfort signs over to him not only his wife's but also Millamant's estate and even the reversion after her life of Lady Wishfort's own estate. Mrs. Fainall then ineffectually reveals that she knows Mrs. Marwood is having an affair with her husband. Finally, however, Mirabell wins the contest by knowing the ultimate discrepancy between appearance and nature. He produces a deed by Mrs. Fainall conveying all her estate to him as her trustee; she made it when she was a widow (and could execute a valid conveyance of her property), and it therefore predates any deed Fainall could now obtain. These various deeds at the end of the play combine and fuse the two kinds of reality, dynastic and emotional, from which the play is built.

Congreve, even though the plot is complicated enough, makes it seem even more complicated. There are certain hidden facts — we could call them quanta of knowledge — and a large part of the so-called complexity simply involves revealing these facts, slowly unraveling the appearances which cover them over. There are only four such quanta in the play: Marwood's desire for Mirabell, Marwood's relationship with Fainall, Mirabell's past affair with Mrs. Fainall, and Mirabell's plot with his disguised servant. But Congreve gives the impression of far greater complexity by measuring out each secret slowly, person by person, until the final complete revelation. He adds even more complexity by having each of these underlying motives and relationships refer back into the group instead of expanding to include outsiders; he makes it seem as though these five people knew only these five people.

An example of the way Congreve uses these quanta of knowledge is his treatment of Mrs. Marwood's and Fainall's liaison. In the first act, there are only a few hints: Fainall reveals he doesn't know his wife's doings (344); Mirabell describes Marwood ironically to Fainall as "your Friend, or your Wife's Friend" (345); he remarks to Fainall, who is suggesting Marwood is overfond of Mirabell, "You are conscious of a Concern for which the Lady is more indebted to you, than is your Wife" (346). Act II, scene iii, fully reveals the affair to the audience in the dialogue between Fainall and Marwood. Act III contains only a hint by Mrs. Marwood that Foible, the maid, knows the secret: "Why this Wench is the *Pass-par-toute*, a very Master-Key to every Body's strong Box" (384). Nothing further is done with this knowledge until Act V, when Foible tells Mrs. Fainall, who tells Mirabell, who tells all. At the last, the revelation, the complete knowledge, contributes virtually nothing to the denouement, because Fainall plays his trump — the threat of scandal — immediately after it.

It is in revealing these hidden facts that Congreve deals with the basic Restoration theme of the contrast between appearance and nature. The first act serves to define the outer, obvious social framework of family relationships, admitted loves, and professed friendships. It is, however, riddled with hints of the underlying currents of emotion, unrevealed until the second act, which is primarily devoted to unmasking — to the audience only — the emotional involvements of Mirabell, the Fainalls, and Mrs. Marwood. In Act III, the characters gain partial awareness of the undercurrents: Marwood and Fainall learn of Mirabell's plan and of his past affair with Mrs. Fainall. The fourth act does not appreciably change the quanta of knowledge the several characters have, but contrasts the decorous, moderated honesty of Mirabell and Millamant with the indecorous openness of Sir Wilfull and the deceptions and pretenses of Lady Wishfort and the other characters. In Act V, all pretenses are destroyed with Fainall's and Mirabell's revelations and the bringing out from a black box of the deed that renders Fainall powerless. The pattern is that the difference between visible and invisible factors gives power to him who knows it; breaking down the difference, i.e., revealing the hidden facts, destroys that power.

Congreve has unduly complicated both kinds of relationship, dynastic and emotional, and in both cases some of the complications are not essential to the plot. We must look for the reason. The confusion which is the prevailing atmosphere of the play becomes almost a kind of symbol for one of the points Congreve wants to make. That is, the confusion asks the question that underlies almost every facet of the play: What is the true interaction between these two kinds of relationships? To some extent, I think, we are meant to be aware simply of the idea "family" and the idea "emotion," without necessarily following through the involved details. The technique is much the same as that in T. S. Eliot's *The Confidential Clerk*, where emotional and dynastic relations proliferate in the same way to define two kinds of reality and test their relative "realness." As it develops, *The Way of the World* does just exactly that; act after act tests the relative realness of dynastic and emotional relations. In Act I, only the family relations and Mirabell's love for Millamant are particularly evident, and they artificially overshadow the implicitly more "real" relations developed in Act II. As the play develops, however, the undercurrents of emotion assume greater and greater force. In Act III, Marwood's role becomes increasingly important. She has no family connection to the central group, but is related instead by her affair with Fainall and resentment of Mirabell, emotional connections. Her overhearing Mirabell's plan and learning of his past affair with Mrs. Fainall are crucial to the plot development. The entrance at this point of Sir Wilfull Witwoud as a country bumpkin ridiculed by the fops reveals the ultimate irrelevance of the dynastic tie that brings him there, compared to the importance of Marwood's emotional tie. Linguistically, there is the contrast between the superficial banter on Sir Wilfull's entrance and the urgent plotting by Marwood and Fainall immediately after. Act IV continues to set off Sir Wilfull's blunt openness against the duplicity of the social situation. His entrance, which was like a breath of fresh air from the country, becomes, when he is drunk, a "Breath like a Bagpipe" (415). His stillborn courtship of Millamant, with only the family tie for a basis, contrasts with Mirabell's supremely urbane wooing, derived from an emotional attachment. Mirabell, in turn, establishes a mean between the knight's willfulness and the social pretenders. In the last scene, the emotional undercurrents seem to have established final dominance over the family relations. Marwood and Fainall have complete control, and are manipulating the family relations as a lever to gain their ends. Lady Wishfort's plaintive remark, "Ah! her first Husband, my Son *Languish,* wou'd not have carry'd it thus" (431), seems to mark the nadir of dynastic strength. Sir Wilfull's sword, though on the side of family and good-nature, is powerless; it is Mirabell's deed that saves the day.

The unraveling with its final clue, the deed, suggests the relation between the two complex realities of family and emotional ties: that the "real" reality is the inward, emotional nature; this reality is a changing flux that gives birth to a more stable framework of overt social facts (dynastic relations); when, for whatever reason, these social facts are not true reflections of the underlying emotional relations (Mrs. Fainall's marriage, the projected "marriage" of Lady Wishfort to Mirabell's servant, and the like) a situation of power results in favor of one who knows the inconsistency; the antidote to such situations is to create an overt, social situation which will truly reflect the underlying realities. This interplay between two kinds of reality leads, naturally enough, to two kinds of action in the play. The first — I will call it the *unraveling* — peels off bit by bit the surface appearances to get at the real facts of emotion underneath. The second, which I will call the *emancipating,* sets up a new social structure based on those underlying emotional realities.

In the unraveling action, the final deed is the final fact, the heart of the whole situation hidden in a mysterious black box. Just as Mirabell's contract with Millamant suggests an ideal of balance between the social and personal aspects of marriage, so this deed represents a fusion of the social and personal aspects of the entire dramatic situation. The deed is effective in law as a result of Mrs. Fainall's social and dynastic status: only as a widow could she make a valid conveyance of her property. Yet the deed formalized a hidden emotional situation. The deed is effective because it destroys the very *res* of Fainall's actions; his motive is brought out into the open and dealt with directly as motive. In all these respects, this deed contrasts with the deed Fainall attempts to get from Lady Wishfort, which is based on an opposition of social and emotional situations. "Ironically," Paul and Miriam Mueschke point out, "the double-dealer whose life has been a sham meets shattering defeat through overconfidence in a spurious document."[5] Fainall's deed is an abortive attempt to make social pressure permanently dislocate emotions, to create a retrograde movement in which the fear of scandal separates Mirabell and Millamant. In the nature of things it fails. There is a third deed to which both the others are contrasted, the one Mirabell's disguised servant Waitwell promises to bring to "prove" his identity to Lady Wishfort (420). Its connection with the others is established by Waitwell's remark, when he brings the real deed, "I have brought the Black-Box at last, Madam" (437), referring to his earlier promise when he pretended to have a deed. The illusory deed symbolizes the weakness of Mirabell's scheme. It would have created a focus of power by the disparity between the appearances of the situation, Lady Wishfort's marriage to a gentleman, and Waitwell's nature as a servant, but the scheme is defeated by the breakdown of the difference in knowledge when Marwood discovers the plan. Sir Wilfull's sword-play contrasts with all the deeds. "S'heart an you talk of an Instrument, Sir," says the redoubtable country knight. "I have an old Fox by my Thigh shall hack your Instrument of *Ram Vellam* to Shreds, Sir" (434). His attempt to maintain the social *status quo* is inadequate because it does not take into account either the concealed motives or the outward realities of the situation. It is subsocial, even subhuman ("an old Fox," "a *Bear-garden* Flourish"). The final deed is more powerful than either Wilfull's coercive sword or Fainall's or Mirabell's attempts to use disparities between appearances and nature, because this deed harmonizes the social and emotional situations. Because it is a crystallization of an earlier emotional situation into a valid social form, because it moves with the emotional realities rather than against them, the deed can even create a new social order. "It may be a Means, well manag'd, to make you live easily together," says Mirabell to Mrs. Fainall (441).

The deed is thus not only the most hidden secret in the unraveling action; it is also one of the foundation posts for the new social structure evolved in the emancipating action. In that slow emancipation, by the end of the play, all of the characters who are dependent on Lady Wishfort are freed. The most important, of course, is Millamant. She is won away from her aunt's cabal where she is emotionally imprisoned like a sleeping beauty under the control of witchlike Lady Wishfort; she is drawn into a marriage in which she is at least an equal partner. Mrs. Fainall, Lady Wishfort's daughter, establishes control over her own marriage, and Sir Wilfull is free of Lady Wishfort's matchmaking to "prosecute his Travels." He even plans to take Witwoud and Petulant, members of her cabal, away with him. The last remaining member of the cabal, Mrs. Marwood, has on her own passed beyond the pale. Even Lady Wishfort's maid, Foible, will after the closing curtain retire to the farm she and her new husband, Waitwell, are to receive from Mirabell.

Appropriately enough for the action dealing with the breakdown and build-up of social structures, a dance symbolizes the emancipation. It is held at the end of the play, "that we who are not Lovers," says Sir Wilfull, "may have some other Employment, besides looking on." This particular dance should be an exception to the general rule of omitting the numerous dances and masques with which Restoration comedies are larded. Neither should this dance be the motions Martha Graham-like of improbable young ladies in leotards who so often turn up in productions of old plays calling for dances. Nor do I mean a quick hop-skip-and-jump that suggests only the general embarrassment of actors and director at the whole idea. This dance is worth some time, for it is an important part of the symbolism. For example, some seven speeches before it, the dim-witted Witwoud says, "I'm in a Maze yet, like a Dog in a Dancing-School" (440), and, of course, that is just what Witwoud is when compared to the clever Mirabell and Fainall. The dance suggests the pattern of building up and breaking down social structures that is the stuff of the play. It raises a visible image of rules evolved by people, then imposed restrictively on themselves — Yeats's phrase, "How can we know the dancer from the dance," applies. Though it has become fashionable these days to cry down ritual interpretations, nevertheless this dance quite obviously resembles the *komos* or wedding procession which closed the archetypal fertility drama. Indeed, this very sophisticated play is quite close to the archetypal, primeval pattern of comedy: one can easily think of Lady Wishfort as the "Old King" or winter or death imprisoning the maiden Millamant and of Mirabell as the spring or "New King" who wishes to release her.

The musicians should come in slowly and the dancers arrange themselves in a leisurely manner. The dance itself should be a *bourgée* or "country dance" (*contredanse*), in any case, something like a slow Virginia reel,[6] that involves the building up and breaking down of patterns.

Mirabell and Millamant should probably not enter in, but stand upstage of the dancers talking to each other and watching. Sir Wilfull at first should hold back from entering the figure, adopting the role of enthusiastic spectator, but finally, allowing himself to be drawn in, take one of the maids, fumble through a few steps, and leave the dance on the opposite side of the stage. (I have in mind the diagram of *Love for Love* on p. 171 which is more or less equally applicable here.) The tempo of the dance accelerates, Lady Wishfort drops out, exclaiming, "As I am a Person, I can hold out no longer," the musicians stop, and the other dancers disperse toward Millamant. Mirabell comes downstage to answer Lady Wishfort and deliver his curtain lines.

The dance as a whole should suggest Mirabell's having taken over control of the social situation from Lady Wishfort. At the end of the dance, as Miss Elizabeth Mignon points out, Lady Wishfort "is a worn-out old woman; more important, she recognizes her own physical bankruptcy."[7] There is a tendency, in casting Lady Wishfort, to make her little, fidgety, and farcical. That is not necessary: she is funny enough as is. The characterization should tend rather toward the stentorian. Lady Wishfort must appear at her first entrance, ridiculous, affected, and absurd, but imposing enough to constitute a real obstacle in the action. At the end, she should appear deflated and awry, and for that effect, she must first have a substantial, authoritarian personality to deteriorate.

One scene in *The Way of the World* fuses both the unraveling action and the emancipating, the "contract scene." Mirabell and Millamant finally drop their elaborate façades and get down to business; they contract for their marriage which will ultimately form one half of the new social structure at the end of the play. Lady Wishfort sets the jolly bumpkin Sir Wilfull to courting Millamant. She laughs him away, and as a contrast, Mirabell comes in. Trapped by a locked door, Millamant finally agrees to negotiate about marrying him. This dialogue, the most brilliant in the play, indeed the most brilliant in all Restoration comedy, is worth quoting in full:

Millamant. . . . Ah! I'll never marry, unless I am first made sure of my Will and Pleasure.

Mira. Would you have 'em both before Marriage? Or will you be contented with the first now, and stay for the other 'till after Grace?

Milla. Ah don't be impertinent — My dear Liberty, shall I leave thee? My faithful Solitude, my darling Contemplation, must I bid you then Adieu? Ay-h adieu — My Morning Thoughts, agreeable Wakings, indolent Slumbers, all ye *douceurs, ye Someils du Matin,* adieu. — I can't do't, 'tis more than impossible — Positively *Mirabell* I'll lye a-bed in a Morning as long as I please.

Mira. Then I'll get up in a Morning as early as I please.

Milla. Ah! Idle Creature, get up when you will —— And d'ye hear, I won't be call'd Names after I'm marry'd; positively I won't be call'd Names.

Mira. Names!

Milla. Ay, as Wife, Spouse, my Dear, Joy, Jewel, Love, Sweet-heart, and the rest of that nauseous Cant, in which Men and their Wives are so fulsomly familiar —— I shall never bear that —— Good *Mirabell* don't let us be familiar or fond, nor kiss before folks, like my Lady *Fadler* and Sir *Francis*: Nor go to *Hide-Park* together the first *Sunday* in a new Chariot, to provoke Eyes and Whispers; And then never be seen there together again; as if we were proud of one another the first Week, and asham'd of one another ever after. Let us never Visit together, nor go to a Play together; but let us be very strange and well bred: Let us be as strange as if we had been marry'd a great while; and as well bred as if we were not marry'd at all.

Mira. Have you any more Conditions to offer? Hitherto your Demands are pretty reasonable.

Milla. Trifles, —— As Liberty to pay and receive Visits to and from whom I please; to write and receive Letters, without Interrogatories or wry Faces on your part; to wear what I please; and chuse Conversation with regard only to my own Taste; to have no Obligation upon me to converse with Wits that I don't like, because they are your Acquaintance; or to be intimate with Fools, because they may be your Relations. Come to Dinner when I please, dine in my Dressing-Room when I'm out of Humour, without giving a Reason. To have my Closet inviolate; to be sole Empress of my Tea-Table, which you must never presume to approach without first asking leave. And, lastly, where-ever I am, you shall always knock at the Door before you come in. These Articles subscrib'd, if I continue to endure you a little longer, I may by degrees dwindle into a Wife.

Mira. Your Bill of Fare is something advanc'd in this latter Account. Well, have I Liberty to offer Conditions —— That when you are dwindled into a Wife, I may not be beyond measure enlarg'd into a Husband.

Milla. You have free leave; propose your utmost, speak and spare not.

Mira. I thank you. *Inprimis* then, I covenant that your Acquaintance be general; that you admit no sworn Confident, or Intimate of your own Sex; no she Friend to skreen her Affairs under your Countenance, and tempt you to make trial of a mutual Secresie. No Decoy-Duck to wheadle you a *fop-scrambling* to the Play in a Mask —— Then bring you home in a pretended Fright, when you think you shall be found out — And rail at me for missing the Play, and disappointing the Frolick which you had to pick me up and prove my Constancy.

Milla. Detestable *Inprimis!* I go to the Play in a Mask!

Mira. Item, I Article that you continue to like your own Face, as long as I shall: And while it passes currant with me, that you endeavour not to new Coin it. To which end, together with all Vizards for the Day, I prohibit all Masks for the Night, made of Oil'd-skins, and I know not what — Hog's Bones, Hare's Gall, Pig Water, and the Marrow of a roasted Cat. In short, I forbid all Commerce with the Gentlewoman in *what-d'ye-call-it* Court. *Item,* I shut my Doors against all Bauds with Baskets, and pennyworths of *Muslin, China, Fans, Atlasses,* &c. —— *Item,* when you shall be Breeding ——

Milla. Ah! Name it not.

Mira. Which may be presum'd, with a Blessing on our Endeavours ——

Milla. Odious Endeavours!

Mira. I denounce against all strait Lacing, squeezing for a Shape, 'till you mould my Boy's Head like a Sugar-loaf; and instead of a Man-child, make me Father to a Crooked-billet. Lastly, to the Dominion of the *Tea-Table* I submit. —— But with *proviso,* that you exceed not in your Province; but restrain yourself to native and simple *Tea-Table* Drinks, as *Tea, Chocolate,* and *Coffee.* As likewise to Genuine and Authoriz'd *Tea-Table Talk* —— Such as mending of Fashions, spoiling Reputations, railing at absent Friends, and so forth —— But that on no Account you encroach upon the Mens Prerogative, and presume to drink Healths, or toast Fellows; for prevention of which I banish all *Foreign Forces,* all Auxiliaries to the *Tea-Table,* as *Orange-Brandy,* all *Anniseed, Cinamon, Citron* and *Barbado's-Waters,* together with *Ratafia,* and the most noble Spirit of *Clary.* —— But for *Couslip-Wine, Poppy-Water,* and all *Dormitives,* those I allow. —— These *Proviso's* admitted, in other things I may prove a tractable and complying Husband.

Milla. O horrid *Proviso's!* filthy Strong waters! I toast Fellows, Odious Men! I hate your odious *Proviso's.*

Mira. Then we're agreed. Shall I kiss your Hand upon the Contract? (406–409)

The contract scene, like proviso scenes in earlier plays, shows how social forms can balance and preserve an emotional reality, but this contract scene goes farther: it shows the enchanting Millamant brought from girlhood to maturity. Before the contract scene, Millamant insists on treating love lightly and distantly. She uses her love letters to pin up her hair and, with elaborate casualness, informs her admirers of the fact (371). She loves to give suitors pain (371), and looks down on Marwood (388) who has let herself become emotionally involved. It is only *after* the contract scene that Millamant can make a mature statement about love: "Well, if *Mirabell* shou'd not make a good Husband, I am a lost Thing; — for I find I love him violently" (410). The locked door that forces the showdown not only constrains Sir Wilfull to a social courtship for which he is neither suited nor willing; it suggests also, as Mirabell points out, "That here the Chace must end, and my Pursuit be crown'd" (405). The lovers have found a social edge to what we have called in Congreve's earlier plays the "cult of chase." Millamant, however, insists that she will never be deprived of "the agreeable Fatigues of Solicitation" (406), a girlish reaction belied by her own words in the finale: "Why does not the Man take me? Wou'd you have me give my self to you over again?" (440).

None of her charming but almost feminist provisos deals with the personal aspects of marriage. They all, the Mueschkes point out, "are the result of her desire to prolong and increase the prenuptial glamour." [8] They are developed, with the one exception of her exclamation, "My dear Liberty," in a typically feminine way: by the enumeration of a number of specific things from which one could evolve a general principle, though, of course, Millamant doesn't. Her first proviso in a general sense is that she be able to keep the integrity of her individuality; specifically, it is: "I'll lye a-bed in a Morning as long as I please" (406), in her case, a particularly significant expression of her narcissistic girlishness. Her second is that they will continue to present a decorous appearance in public; the third is that she have free communication with others — both these ideas being represented only by specific instances.

Mirabell's conditions are quite different; they are frankly sexual in content, directed to his not being cuckolded or to her bedroom manners. Just as Millamant's are developed femininely, Mirabell's are developed in a typically masculine way. "The wit of Mirabell," the Mueschkes note, "is predominantly judicial, that of Millamant is fanciful." [9] Each of Mirabell's provisos begins with its *inprimis* or *item:* first, the general principle ("that your Acquaintance be general"), then specific instructions ("no she Friend") and an illustration of the forbidden behavior ("to wheadle you a *fop-scrambling* to the Play in a Mask"). One specific instance leads him to the next general principle: the mask to leaving her face alone, beauticians to bawds, bawds to breeding, the foetus' sugar-loaf head to the tea-table. (The way in which each party in this scene presents conditions is certainly the most brilliant of all of Congreve's dramaturgic strokes.) Whereas Mirabell receives Millamant's asexual requirements with equanimity ("Your Demands are pretty reasonable"), she meets his sexual ones with at least pretended disgust: "Detestable *Inprimis!*" "Ah! name it not," "Odious Endeavours!" or "O horrid *Proviso's!*" Mirabell has drawn her out of herself toward maturity.

Just as the contract scene serves both to unravel and to emancipate, so these two actions are fused in the one person who towers over the play. Although she is technically only a supporting character and does not appear until Act III, Lady Wishfort is talked about all through the first two acts, and in the finale she becomes a kind of tribunal before whom the opposed forces in the play plead their causes. She says of herself, "I look like an old peel'd Wall" (382), a metaphor that operates in a number of ways. She is a wall in that she tries to enforce a separation between appearance and nature, not only for herself but for those under her influence. She is a wall, too, in that she stands as an obstacle to the natural progress of passions. The peeling suggests not just the failure of her cosmetics, but that such a wall is bound to decay and crumble. Thus, Lady Wishfort acts as a wall with respect to both the major actions of the play, the unraveling of appearances from nature and the emancipating of the younger group.

With respect to the first action, Lady Wishfort tries to maintain a grandly absurd bundle of pretenses. She is preoccupied with cosmetics to cover her age. Her library features Collier's moralistic *Short View,* while she herself is familiar with D'Urfey's ribald *Don Quixote.* Sometimes she uses an affected sesquipedelian speech and sometimes her justly famous "boudoir Billingsgate." Congreve gives her his most magnificent invective, and, revealingly enough, most of her images are taken from lower-class occupations. Her "way of the world," in short, is symbolized by her coachmen perfumed to serve as footmen.

Specifically, Lady Wishfort pretends by substituting art for nature. As Foible, her maid, says: "A little Art once made your Picture like you; and now a little of the same Art must make you like your Picture. Your Picture must sit for you, Madam" (382). When she meets Sir Rowland, her posture is artistically contrived (401), just as her fifth-act *Weltschmertz* is expressed in the absurdities of literary pastoral: "I would retire to Desarts and Solitudes; and feed harmless Sheep by Groves and purling Streams. Dear *Marwood,* let us leave the World, and retire by our selves and be Shepherdesses" (425). Part of her substitution of art for nature is suggested by her speech-tag, "As I am a person," which is, in turn, belied by her continually calling others by subhuman epithets: "Puppet, thou wooden thing upon wires," "Borachio," "Caterpillar," "viper," "serpent," and the like. In a sense, the whole question is whether she really has any personality left at all.

With respect to the first action, Lady Wishfort reverses appearance and nature; she tries to prevent the unraveling. With respect to the second action, emancipation, she stands as a block to the natural growth and development of emotions. She boasts, for example, of her daughter's repressive education: "To impress upon her tender Years a young Odium and Aversion to the very sight of Men, — ay Friend, she would have shriek'd if she had but seen a Man, 'till she was in her Teens" (427). This education, of course, is the real cause of Mrs. Fainall's adult maladjustments. Lady Wishfort, despite her age, blocks the affairs of the younger generation by intruding herself as one of them, and assuming that Mirabell should really be attached to her rather than to Millamant. Her description of Mirabell, like the image of the wall, suggests her age: "He is as terrible to me as a *Gorgon;* if I see him I fear I shall turn to Stone, petrifie incessantly" (432). In the play it is Lady Wishfort who creates most the impression of time's flow.

Not just Lady Wishfort, though, but all the characters are involved in these two actions of unraveling and emancipation. It is these two factors which form, for example, the elusive distinction between the characters of Fainall and Mirabell. Superficially, one seems to be good and the other bad, like Maskwell and Mellefont in *The Double-Dealer;* but in this play, the hero and villain behave very much alike: Mirabell has treated both Mr. and Mrs. Fainall very shoddily indeed, and his scheme for humiliating Lady Wishfort into consent is hardly what one would expect from a virtuous young man like Mellefont. At the opening of this chapter I said that Fainall's language could not be distinguished from Mirabell's. That is not strictly true. There are differences in their speech, but they are far more subtle than the distinguishing marks of the other characters, because Fainall and Mirabell, being the most intelligent characters in the play, tend to react to the external stimuli they share in the same way. We can, however, see differences:

Fainall. But cou'd you think, because the nodding Husband wou'd not wake, that e'er the watchful Lover slept? (364)

Mirabell. Well, have I Liberty to offer Conditions — That when you are dwindled into a Wife, I may not be beyond Measure enlarg'd into a Husband. (407)

Fainall describes himself as divided into two separate roles, lover and husband. He is a man who sees the outer framework of appearances and formalities as perpetually divorced from the inner, "real" nature of emotions and desires. Mirabell sees himself as a self growing into a husband. In general, he seeks a harmony between appearance and nature; though he recognizes the need for keeping a distance between them, he resists outright inconsistency.

Mirabell characterizes Fainall (whose name, of course, is significant) as "a Man lavish of his Morals, an interested and professing Friend, a false and a designing Lover; yet one whose Wit and outward fair Behaviour, have gain'd a Reputation with the Town" (368). Marwood says to him: "Truth and you are inconsistent" (366). To Fainall, dissimulation is an ordinary condition of being. "Had you dissembl'd better," he says to Mirabell, "Things might have continu'd in the State of Nature" (345). The difference between him and Mirabell is summed up neatly in their dialogue about Millamant:

Fainall. For a passionate Lover, methinks you are a Man somewhat too discerning in the Failings of your Mistress.

Mirabell. And for a discerning Man, somewhat too passionate a Lover; for I like her with all her Faults; nay like her for her Faults. Her Follies are so natural, or so artful, that they become her; and those Affectations which in another Woman wou'd be odious, serve but to make her more agreeable. (348)

To Fainall, faults are something to be hidden from outward appearance; to Mirabell, they are natural or derived from an art harmonizing with nature, and to be accepted as part of the total personality. The play as a whole criticizes, with Mirabell, appearances and forms which are not the natural outgrowths of inward, private emotions. His provisos in the contract scene are uniformly against outward forms that repress or conceal: she-confidantes (he does not provide against males), masks, cosmetics, house-to-house saleswomen who are really bawds, corseting of unborn children, and tea-tables that hide carousing. Mirabell seeks the reconciliation of appearances with the passions that give rise to them. What is frustrating him in his love for Millamant is that he cannot help loving her. He can neither disguise his love nor express it. Reason and passion are at war within him: "Motion not Method is [woman's] Occupation. To know this, and yet continue to be in Love, is to be made wise from the Dictates of Reason, and yet persevere to play the Fool by the force of Instinct" (375). Her insistence on motion, her failure to stabilize her emotions and give them permanent form keeps Mirabell in a state of flux, too.

Millamant relishes her own changeability: as Mirabell says of her, "Think of you! To think of a Whirlwind, tho 'twere in a Whirlwind, were a Case of more steady Contemplation" (375). Over and over again, she delightedly contradicts herself. She is reluctant to formalize her feelings for fear their social form would stifle her real self. "Ah!" she cries, "I'll never marry, unless I am first made sure of my Will and Pleasure" (406). Millamant's love of change is revealed in the style of her speech as well as the matter. She talks in short sentences tumbling over one another in quick succession. Millamant keeps herself uninvolved and loves to twit others who fail to do so: she reduces Marwood to impotent rage by poking fun at her desire for Mirabell (388), and she cuts Mirabell to a gasp when she shows she knows his plan to humiliate Lady Wishfort (374). She herself avoids the discrepancy between appearance and nature by having nothing to conceal.

Mrs. Marwood, on the other hand, thrives on concealment. In the conventions of the play, a disparity between known appearances and concealed nature gives power to the one who knows the secret. Marwood craves this power. Thus, she expreses her pretended aversion to men: "I am thinking sometimes to carry my Aversion further. . . . by marrying; if I cou'd but find one that lov'd me very well, and would be thoroughly sensible of ill Usage, I think I should do myself the Violence of undergoing the Ceremony."

Mrs. *Fainall*. You wou'd not make him a Cuckold?
Mrs. *Marwood*. No; but I'd make him believe I did, and that's as bad.
Mrs. *Fain*. Why had you not as good do it?
Mrs. *Mar*. O if he shou'd ever discover it, he wou'd then know the worst, and be out of his Pain; but I wou'd have him ever to continue upon the Rack of Fear and Jealousie.
(361)

It is she who devises Fainall's plan to blackmail Lady Wishfort, who "will come to any Composition to save her [daughter's] Reputation" (398). She shows the same sense of roles defining personality that Fainall has, when she says, "'Tis an unhappy Circumstance of Life, that Love shou'd ever die before us; and that the Man so often shou'd out-live the Lover" (360). Her action throughout, like Fainall's, is an attempt to give expression to her passions by the use of intrigue rather than by ordinary social expression; she turns out to be as wrong-headed as her lover.

Between Mrs. Marwood and Mrs. Fainall, there is the same kind of elusive distinction as between Fainall and Mirabell. Both are guilty of illicit affairs, but one seems innately bad, the other innately good — "a pattern of Generosity" (385). (Mrs. Fainall's affair, it should be remembered, is venial by Restoration standards; the least of female lapses was that of a widow, contrasted with the worst, Marwood's, that of an unmarried woman. The worst thing Mrs. Fainall did was to marry Fainall under false pretenses, but he married her under false pretenses, too.) Like Marwood, Mrs. Fainall is (or was) given to extremes of passion. She has, she says, "lov'd without Bounds," and now wants to hate without limits (368). Like Marwood, she tends to be indifferent to reputation, but therein lies the distinction; while Marwood's indecorum lies in giving too much freedom to her passions and hence undervaluing reputation which stands as a block to their free expression, Mrs. Fainall has learned the folly of giving too much importance to outward appearances, of committing "disagreeable and dangerous Actions" "to save that Idol Reputation" (368). She can say snidely to Marwood, "Madam, you seem to stifle your Resentment: You had better give it vent" (439). "Fy, fy," she says, brushing aside Millamant's coyness, "have him, have him, and tell him so in plain Terms: For I am sure you have a Mind to him" (409). She has learned from her own mistakes the tragedy of allowing an outward convention, her marriage, which did not grow organically from emotion, to impose itself upon and stifle her inner nature.

Lady Wishfort and the two "unnaturals," Witwoud and Petulant, are humor characters who have virtually replaced themselves by their affectations. Witwoud's wit amounts only to extravagant similes that connect things superficially, that is, his similes establish connections (his own wit to a fire, for example — 370), but the connections are not particularly meaningful. Like Witwoud's wit, Petulant's professed animosity comes to nothing. Together these two form an absurd plane of complete and empty sociality against which the main actions are reflected. They enter the final resolution, "rubbing their Eyes, — just risen from Sleep"

(437). Petulant sees the whole thing as a game: "How now? what's the matter? who's Hand's out?" Both are guilty of continual over-simplification, Witwoud in his "similitudes" and Petulant with his "All's one, let it pass." Real emotions are lost on them. They are ridiculous, all manner and no substance, as empty as balloons, and blown by whatever random stimuli come their way.

Sir Wilfull Witwoud, though equally absurd, is their opposite, all substance and no manner. He is an alien figure like Ben or Manly, who comes from elsewhere and passes through "the Town" only to go away again. Like the other alien figures, he serves to suggest an alternative way of life to that of London, in his case, a mode in which "great lubberly Brothers slabber and kiss one another when they meet, like a Call of Serjeants" (394). Lady Wishfort suggests his role as an alien by telling him, "Thou art not fit to live in a Christian Commonwealth, thou beastly Pagan" (414). His presence, by suggesting another way of life, puts the main action into a perspective that raises the play as a whole beyond the mere description of manners into a generalized statement about man in and out of society.

Miss Elinor Fuchs in a very astute treatment of the play suggests that Witwoud and Petulant and Sir Wilfull are "half-men."[10] She points out that Witwoud and Petulant are described as a pair of "Battledores" and as "Treble and Base" (390). Witwoud and Sir Wilfull constitute one tree, "a Medlar grafted on a Crab" (350), or one ass (411). Their relationship as half-brothers is significant. Petulant and Sir Wilfull make "a Pair of Castanets" (412). There is an arithmetical suggestion that Witwoud and Petulant are each worth one half of Mirabell or Sir Wilfull. As Fainall had said earlier, describing the "Cabal-Nights": "Some body mov'd that to avoid Scandal there might be one Man of the Community; upon which *Witwoud* and *Petulant* were enroll'd Members" (345). In connection with this concept of "half-men" we should remember that Mirabell establishes his final relationship with Millamant by supplying her with the second half of a couplet from Waller (405). It is as though all *four* of these men were seeking halves to complete themselves, as in Aristophanes' myth in the *Symposium.* Man, this half-man metaphor suggests, needs the completion represented by conventional forms. He needs forms not only to shield his private life, but also to give his fleeting emotions a stability and durability.

Professors Brooks and Heilman say the play represents "almost a symphonic pattern in which the theme of love receives a variety of treatments, ranging from the somber . . . to the burlesque." Mirabell and Millamant must come between extremes, an absolute social standard or none, by finding an inner standard. The irony that pervades the play suggests the deviousness of the "way of the world."[11] Miss Fuchs resorts to an even wider concept, concluding that *The Way of the World* is about different kinds of decorum. The "great decorum" achieved by Mirabell and Millamant represents a way of idealizing human potentialities by creating a civilized sensibility that is focused back on the wash of activity out of which it grew. Congreve, she says, seems to demand that life must have form, precise and elegant social forms which can fuse beauty and truth, distilling the positive qualities from a world which mixes indiscriminately wisdom and folly, honesty and falsehood, love and hate, beauty and ugliness.[12] These two interpretations set the play in the tradition of British ceremonial, the Burkean belief in forms that evolve and solidify, embodying a standard to later times. "The King," writes Pepys in 1666, "hath yesterday in Council declared his resolution of setting a fashion for clothes, which he will never alter. It will be a vest, I know not well how; but it is to teach the nobility thrift, and will do good."[13] To Congreve, as to Pepys, Charles II, and Englishmen generally, external forms can be a means of training up the self like a vine on a trellis.

Paul and Miriam Mueschke, by their careful and exact explication of lines and scenes, suggest still another aspect of the play. Very acutely, they point out that *The Way of the World* deals at its most obvious level with the fight between two pairs of adulterers for three legacies. "Congreve," they say, "is not an apologist for, but a satirist of the way of the world." The play attacks (as did *The Double-Dealer*) *both* folly and vice. The folly appears in the persons of Witwoud and Petulant. The vice shows in the contrast between a pair of adulterers (Mirabell and Mrs. Fainall) on the way to reformation and a pair of adulterers (Fainall and Mrs. Marwood) on the way to further degradation. The four standard Restoration types in the play, the rake (Mirabell), the cast mistress (Marwood), the adulteress (Mrs. Fainall), and the cuckold (Fainall), are not treated, as even in Congreve's earlier plays, with amused tolerance. They are all shown as highly intelligent; they are all made to fear and finally to suffer scandal and exposure. "Throughout *The Way of the World* every character who has indulged in illicit relations finds that his present or past adultery hampers his ability to plan for the future — that immorality cannot be quibbled out of existence."[14]

Whether one takes this moral view of the play or the more formal one suggested by Miss Fuchs and Professors Brooks and Heilman, clearly *The Way of the World* deals with much more than "manners." Even so, while these descriptions are the most complete so far suggested, I think they neglect Congreve's sense of co-ordinates that we saw in *The Old Batchelor.* In particular, they neglect the idea of emancipation in the play.

Mirabell and Millamant do not simply achieve a form — they first free themselves from an old form that no longer reflects a true state of affairs. The play comprises two actions moving, as it were, at right angles to each other. The first, which I have called an unraveling, evens out the disparities in knowledge that existed at the opening of the play so that at the end everybody knows everything. The second action, which I have called emancipation, creates from the breakdown of the old social order dominated by Lady Wishfort a new social order that grows out of the underlying emotional realities of the situation.

These two actions coalesce in the "way" of the title. "Way," in the sense of habitual manner or style, suggests that discrepancy between appearance and nature which is the ubiquitous "way" of the Restoration world; it is this "way" on which the unraveling action is based. "Way," in the sense of path or direction of motion, suggests that moving force of passions which makes existing forms change in the emancipating action of the play. The three references within the play to its title bear out the pattern. The first occurs when Fainall discovers his wife has played him false, that she married him only to cover up her affair with Mirabell. "I it seems am a Husband, a Rank-Husband," he snarls, "and my Wife a very Errant, Rank-Wife, — all in the Way of the *World*" (397); by which, I take it, he means not only marital infidelity, but the discrepancy between appearances and the true facts which he sees as a condition of existence. The second time the title is mentioned is when Fainall reassures Marwood as their relationship is revealed: "If it must all come out, why let 'em know it, 'tis but the *Way of the World*" (436). The third reference to the title occurs when Mirabell produces the crucial deed:

Fainall. Confusion!
Mirabell. Even so, Sir, 'tis *the Way of the World, Sir.* (438–439)

Both these latter "ways of the world" refer to a breakdown of the normal discrepancy between appearance and nature. These, then, are the "ways of the world": the passage of time and the discrepancy between "natural" emotions and social appearances. From these two fundamental characteristics of this world (as opposed to some Paradise), social conventions build up and break down as one generation passes on control to the next, as in the accompanying diagram.

The play, though it takes place in the canonical twelve hours, reaches

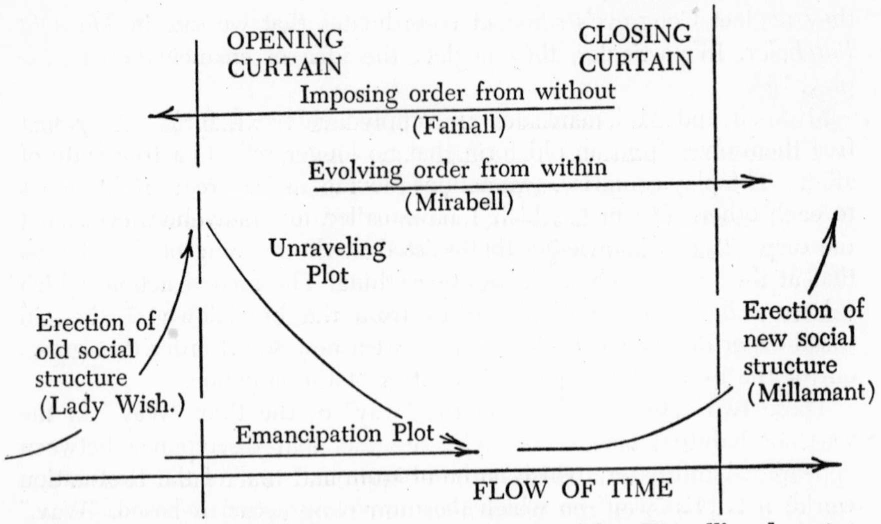

back into a past before the curtain to give us Mrs. Fainall's education and the building up of her false marriage and, in general, a complicated family structure that has become largely meaningless, no longer a reflection of any underlying emotional reality. Congreve presents this old order in Lady Wishfort, who, "Full of the Vigour of Fifty five, declares for a Friend and *Ratafia;* and let Posterity shift for it self, she'll breed no more" (345). The play reaches forward beyond the closing curtain to the possible reformation of the Fainalls' marriage, and Mirabell's statements about parenthood (408) suggest a new order created from the marriage of Mirabell and Millamant in which they are the parental figures.

Fainall's plot is an attempt to retain the old order, to use the discrepancy between reputation (appearance) and the actual facts (nature) to hold back natural evolution. Fainall is trying to build on the old order rather than on the realities which it no longer represents. Mirabell, at first, tries somewhat the same technique, though he is always trying to build toward a new order. Significantly, the technique fails. Mirabell succeeds only when he produces a "deed" that represents a fusion of the social and emotional situations. The world has two ways: the flux of emotions in time and the build-up and breakdown of discrepancies between nature and social appearances. Social forms build up until they become rigid, separate entities no longer connected to emotional realities and then break down — Mrs. Fainall's marriage, for example, or Marwood's friendship with Lady Wishfort.

The ways of the world, then, are cyclic. The play assumes two kinds of reality, public appearance (typified by family relations) and an inner, personal nature (typified by emotions). One "way" is that there is an organic flux of both inward and outward natures. Passions are quickly born, grow, and die. From them grow more slowly the outer, social relations of people (marriages and "breeding"), which in turn define and limit future passions. The other "way" is that there is and ought to be a difference (with Congreve, not necessarily a contradiction) between these two kinds of reality; one must retain a decorum and balance between them (as exemplified by the match between Mirabell and Millamant). Too much of a difference (Mrs. Fainall's marriage or her husband's blackmail) results in a situation where the social fact exerts undue restraint on the emotional. Too little difference leads to the absurdities of Sir Wilfull's behavior.

These two themes are common in Congreve's nondramatic poetry. His poems, when read as a group rather than individually, show two recurring ideas: the contrast between outer form and inner mind or soul and the contrast between the permanent and divine and the transient and mortal. A frequent image in his poetry is the sun, which, though celestial and eternal, daily dies to define the time in which we live and die. Thus, the cyclic sense of society building up and breaking down in response to changing emotional patterns is no novelty in Congreve's thought as a whole.

Appearance and nature, though the most obvious of these dualisms that build up and break down, are not the only such pair in *The Way of the World.* In the action, family structure and emotional structure, past and present, guilt and retribution, form and substance, upper class and lower class, all separate at first, then come together briefly at the end to begin to separate again. Similarly, the language separates and then fuses fancy and judgment or generalization and instance. Action and language themselves begin in Act I by being separate in the dialogue between villain and hero; they end in Act V made one in the crucial "deed." Thus, *The Way of the World* in its largest sense is about opposites separated, then joined, separated again, joined again. Behind the dynastic structure, behind even the emotional structure lies the central image of the play, so obvious it is hidden; it is the preoccupation of every character, even of every reader: the sexual union of man and woman. From this one rhythm proceed, like ripples from a splash, all the other rhythms of reality, the ways, indeed, of the world.

Nevertheless, while this cyclic, rhythmic view of reality is not altogether inappropriate to a man whose political heritage included two revolutions (1649 and 1688), it is rather strikingly reminiscent of the Romantics. Congreve is a century early — this approach belongs at the beginning of the nineteenth, not the eighteenth century. Still, as Miss

Nicolson writes of the scientific discoveries of the seventeenth century, in particular, the conception of an infinite universe: "Romanticism had come to England. Had it not been for an accident of history, the spirit we associate with 'High Romanticism' would have burst forth, I am persuaded, a century earlier than we find it. It was in bloom among the scientists; it was budding among the poets." [15] Moreover, it is a Romantic philosopher, Hegel, who most accurately describes Congreve's point of view by the concepts of *das Innere* and *das Äussere*. *Das Innere* is the essence of a thing, that we, following seventeenth-century terminology, have called its "nature"; *das Äussere* is its form or appearance. Appearance must grow from nature, but, at the same time, appearance must define an essence which is a new *Innere*.

> If the essence of nature is ever described as the inner part, the person who so describes it only knows its outer shell [viz. Fainall]. . . . In Nature as well as in Mind, so long as the notion, design, or law are at first the inner capacity, mere possibilities, they are at first only an external inorganic nature [viz. Mirabell at the opening]. . . . As a man is outwardly, that is to say in his actions (not of course in his merely bodily outwardness), so is he inwardly: and if his virtue, morality &c. are only inwardly his, — that is if they exist only in his intentions, and sentiments, and his outward acts are not identical with them, the one half of him is as hollow and empty as the other [viz. Fainall's split personality].[16]

By the same token, Witwoud, Petulant, and Sir Wilfull (the "half-men") are dead because they do not grow but exist separated from real nature.

The classic illustration of Hegel's philosophy is the seed. Initially, the seed is defined by *das Äussere,* the form of the plant that created it, just as the old social order dominated by Lady Wishfort defines — or confines — the emotional seeds of the new order to be created about Millamant. (This system is bad genetics but good philosophy.) The seed becomes the essence of a new growth at the same time that the new growth defines the essence of the next seed (Mirabell's and Millamant's posterity). Congreve's description of social structure is simply the vitalist, evolutionary version that we ordinarily associate with Shaw or Bergson or Hegel or Marx. The fundamental conflict in *The Way of the World* is vitalist — between Mirabell who looks forward to a posterity and Fainall who wants to keep a rigid, restrictive *status quo*.

Several commentators have suggested Bergson's *Le Rire* as the comic theory most obviously related to Restoration comedy.[17] His theory is simply the obverse of evolutionary vitalism: laughter is based on the substitution of the rigid and mechanical for the vital, organic, and pliant. While Fainall, though he tries to substitute forced relations for organic ones, is hardly laughable, Lady Wishfort perfectly exemplifies Bergson's point. At the same time, however, society (a form of rigidity) uses laughter as a weapon against the individual who tries to take liberties with its rigidity; for example, Manly, or, for that matter, Mirabell, who tries to evolve a new social order. Although I do not think Bergson's theory adequately describes Restoration comedy, it does suggest a valid kinship between Romanticism and the later phase of Restoration comedy, particularly Congreve's achievement. The sense of perpetual seeking, the theme of retreat, and the quasi-Byronic rake-hero that we have seen in such plays as *The Plain-Dealer* are the stock devices of Romantic writing. Congreve, as Miss Nicolson's remarks suggest, is simply an incipient Romantic, and *The Way of the World,* like so many other Romantic writings, tests art against life.

In general, there is something in an artist that makes him at the end test his art. Yeats's final poems, the late quartets of Beethoven, Mann's *Felix Krull,* and Shakespeare's last two plays all do. Indeed, Fainall refers to *The Tempest* (350). I feel sure Congreve knew when he wrote this play that this was to be his last significant writing for the new Collierized stage and so wrote a play, in part at least, about playwriting. That is, just as social orders build up and break down according to the changing emotional forces that underly them, so, in a sense, the order represented by a play — the actors, the scenes, the costumes, and so on — all builds up and breaks down according to the changing authors. We have already noticed various references to literature in the play, for example, Lady Wishfort's pastoral *Weltschmerz* or Sir Wilfull's "lingo." The most brilliant example, however, occurs when Witwoud says, as he makes his final entrance (438), "Hey day! what are you all got together, like Players at the End of the last Act?" Congreve simply picks up the play and drops it in his audience's lap. He gives the whole denouement an ironic undercutting, after the manner of *The Plain-Dealer.* We have seen, too, how Witwoud's false wit and Fainall's gambling similes contrast with Mirabell's true wit in that they impose an order from without while he evolves an order from within. Congreve calls attention to the "playness of the play" for a purpose. He wants us to see there is a parallel between Fainall's dissimulation and the dramatist's art; both use the discrepancy between an appearance and a reality for a purpose. It is the same kind of parallel one senses between Jonson and his Mosca and Face, between Shakespeare and his Prospero or Duke Vincentio or between Valentine in *Love for Love* and Congreve himself. Mirabell in life evolves an outward decorum, a harmonious order from inner nature, just as Congreve does in art.

The Way of the World, however, goes beyond the art of playwriting to art in its broadest seventeenth-century sense, meaning any human contrivance (as opposed to "nature"), and particularly human contrivances based on the systematic application of general principles. The play fairly bristles with kinds of art: manners, decorum, wit, law, gambling rules, social rituals, cosmetics, literary art, and the art of marriage as evolved in the rules of the great contract scene. "Nature," in the great Renaissance formula, "is the art of God." *The Way of the World* in effect says that life, in the special cyclic, rhythmic sense of the play, life is the art of man. Should we be surprised then, that after this play Congreve retired from the stage, or that he told Voltaire he wished "to be visited on no other footing than as a gentleman who lived a life of plainness and simplicity"? How supremely comic was that idea of the wax automaton.

16 • *The Critical Failure*

Scarcely was the century out before the critics began sharpening their axes on Restoration comedy. It is curious how in period after period these comedies have run up against some preconception that has prevented their being appreciated. In the eighteenth century, the idea was that no "immoral" actions should appear on the stage, at least not without pious condemnation. In the early nineteenth century, when Romanticism burgeoned, the leading poets stressed escape from society; they could hardly care much for a comedy preoccupied with one's proper relation to society (though some Romantic critics did find merit in these plays). In the middle and late nineteenth century, morality was in the saddle again. In the early twentieth century, Ibsenite realism (misunderstood) was the fashion. In the middle twentieth century verse drama is our ideal, and Restoration comedy is unfortunately in prose. So it goes, and yet through all these three centuries (except for the Victorian period when the plays were not staged), audiences seem to have enjoyed them despite all the confusions and condemnations introduced by the critics.

The critics' condemnations have largely been because these comedies are "immoral." The critics' confusions have largely been to praise the plays for the wrong reasons: they are good because they deal realistically with the "manners" of upper-class Restoration London. In other words, they are good as plays because they are really documents for a social historian. This, then, has been the pitiful fate of the silver age of English comedy — critical condemnation, confusion, and indifference. It is typical that in a recent colloquy of essays, two distinguished critics and myself all agreed that recent criticism of Restoration comedy has been poor, but even in this heartening unanimity, each of us had a different reason for saying so.[1] The critics have been hard on these comedies, and the pity of it is that they started so soon.

Even before *The Way of the World* was mounted, the first, or nearly the first, and certainly the most influential of the "morals" critics strutted to the critical rostrum. Jeremy Collier was only an obscure clergyman, but his views have persisted, largely unchanged, down to the present time. "This egregious jackass," as Lytton Strachey calls him, produced in the spring of 1698 a book provocatively titled: *A Short View of the Immorality and Profaneness of the English Stage: Together with the Sense of Antiquity upon this Argument.*[2] Even a charitable evaluation of the pamphlet admits that "forty per cent" of it is "irrelevant"; a less charitable view calls it "grotesque," and notes, quite correctly, "Any opinion held by any character in a play is assumed to be the author's."[3] Collier's pamphlet has five parts: the first, "The Immodesty of the Stage," dealt with indecencies in language; the second, "The Profaneness of the Stage," exposed indecencies in plot and supposed ridicule of Scripture; the third, "The Clergy Abused by the Stage," revealed the playwrights' alleged efforts "to expose not only the Men, but the Business." Although the fifth part, dealing with specific plays and "The Opinion of the *Heathen* Philosophers," was dearest to Collier's heart — he aspired to literary criticism — it was the fourth section that insured his literary reputation.

"Immorality Encouraged by the Stage," read the heading:

CHAP. IV

The Stage-Poets make their Principal Persons Vitious, and reward them at the End of the Play.

The Lines of Virtue and Vice are Struck out by Nature in very Legible Distinctions. . . . 'Tis confessed as long as the Mind is awake, and Conscience goes true, there's no fear of being imposed on. But when Vice is varnish'd over with Pleasure, and comes in the Shape of Convenience, the case grows somewhat dangerous; for then the Fancy may be gain'd, and the Guards corrupted, and Reason suborn'd against itself. . . . To put *Lewdness* into a Thriving condition, to give it an Equipage of Quality, and to treat it with Ceremony and Respect, is the way to confound the Understanding, to fortifie the Charm, and to make the Mischief invincible.

To speak freely, A Lewd Character seldom wants good Luck in *Comedy.* So that whenever you see a thorough Libertine, you may almost swear he is in a rising way, and that the *Poet* intends to make him a great Man.

In answer to the playwrights' view that they were exposing vice and folly by holding a mirror up to them, Collier said: "Take them at the best, and they do no more than expose a little Humour, and Formality. But then, as the Matter is manag'd, the Correction is much worse than the Fault. . . . It cherishes those Passions, and rewards those Vices, which 'tis the business of Reason to discountenance."[4] This was the crux of his idea, that these plays encouraged vice because vicious characters are rewarded in them, and this objection has dominated two and a half centuries of criticism of Restoration comedy.

Among Collier's early supporters were those two apostles of gentility,

Joseph Addison and Sir Richard Steele. One *Spectator* (Addison) complained:

> The poet so contrives matters that the two Criminals are the Favourites of the Audience. . . . I have often wondered that our ordinary Poets cannot frame to themselves the Idea of a fine man who is not a Whore-master, or of a Fine Woman that is not a Jilt.

Steele ingenuously suggested a remedy:

> Might not he who is now represented as a fine Gentleman, tho' he betrays the Honour and Bed of his Neighbour and Friend, and lies with half the Women in the Play, and is at last rewarded with her of the best Character in it; I say, upon giving the Comedy another Cast, might not such a one divert the Audience quite as well, if at the Catastrophe he were found out for a Traytor, and met with Contempt accordingly?

Poets, said Steele, ought to "strew the rough paths of virtue so full of flowers, that we are not sensible of the uneasiness of them; and imagine ourselves in the midst of pleasures, and the most bewitching allurements, at the time we are making a progress in the severest duties of life." [5] This great critical theory led to the absurdity of *The Conscious Lovers* (1722), his own unintentionally hilarious comedy that was to be the prototype for eighteenth-century "weeping comedy."

The modern reader may omit the priggery of the autobiography (1740) of Colley Cibber, actor and poet laureate,[6] and turn to Dr. Johnson for an instance of the eighteenth-century attitude. He, characteristically, was more blunt. "It is acknowledged, with universal conviction," he wrote of Congreve, "that the perusal of his works will make no man better; and that their ultimate effect is to present pleasure in alliance with vice, and to relax those obligations by which life ought to be regulated." [7] Finally, though, there was a glimmer of hope. In 1772, five years before Johnson's *Lives,* Oliver Goldsmith wrote his sensible "Essay on the Theatre," complaining about "mulish," "sterile" sentimental comedy.[8] Following him, Sheridan returned "laughing comedy" to the stage with his own approximations to Restoration comedy and so ushered in a brief period of tolerance.

The nineteenth century opened with urbane experimentation in the criticism of Restoration comedy by three distinguished Romantic critics. William Hazlitt, in his *Lectures on the English Comic Writers* (1819), abandoned the method of generalization and discussed the works of Wycherley, Congreve, Vanbrugh, and Farquhar play by play, without rancor and with great sanity and intelligence. He perfectly pinpointed the essential comic sense of the Restoration, the contrasts among true refinement, affectation, and ignorance.[9] In 1823, Charles Lamb published in the first series of *Elia* his famous essay "On the Artificial Comedy of the Last Century," embodying the then radical suggestion that these plays were a world to which the ordinary moral reactions of an audience ought not to apply.[10] Even more important, in 1840, Leigh Hunt published *The Dramatic Works of Wycherley, Congreve, Vanbrugh, and Farquhar*, making the plays available to the reading public. Hunt's own "Biographical and Critical Notices" advocated charity: "Our ancestors may not have been so bad as we suppose them, even upon our own principles. . . . The balance is not always settled in our favour merely by our looking grave on the matter, and showing that our virtue makes us neither merry nor charitable."[11] It was Hunt's misfortune to be reviewed in January 1841 by Thomas Babington Macaulay.

"In an essay, written," says Strachey, "in that style, which, with its metallic exactness, and its fatal efficiency, was certainly one of the most remarkable products of the Industrial Revolution,"[12] Macaulay rattled invective and condemnation, and called the plays a "systematic attempt to associate vice with those things which men value most and desire most, and virtue with everything ridiculous and degrading." The gist of his argument was thus simply a repetition of Collier, for whom Macaulay had high praise. The bulk of his article was an *ad hominem* denunciation of the playwrights themselves, often based on false evidence. He attacked also those few critics who had had the temerity to have any opinion about the plays other than immediate condemnation. "It is not the fact," he announced, brushing aside Lamb's inoffensive argument, "that the world of these dramatists is a world into which no moral enters. Morality constantly enters into that world, a sound morality, and an unsound morality; the sound morality to be insulted, derided, associated with everything mean and hateful; the unsound morality to be set off to every advantage, and inculcated by all methods, direct and indirect."[13] Thackeray objected, too. Congreve, he said, did not "teach love for the poor and good will for the unfortunate."[14] Meredith, despite his vaunted love of mirth, denounced "our so-called Comedy of Manners, or Comedy of the manners of South-Sea Islanders under city veneer; and as to Comic Idea, vacuous as the mask without the face behind it." He airily waved aside the idea that the playwright might be holding a mirror up to his audience to show them how ridiculous they were. "It would at any rate hardly be questioned," wrote Meredith, "that it is unwholesome for men and women to see themselves as they are, if they are no better than they should be: and they will not, when they have improved in manners, care much to see themselves as they once were."[15]

American readers of the Mauve Decade and after found in Barrett Wendell's criticism the same comforting moral condemnation.[16] Even after the appearance of John Palmer's historic book, William Archer, Shaw's fellow reviewer, could write in 1923 from the foreknowledge that all drama not Ibsenite was to that extent lacking, that the Restoration playwrights "depicted vice with a liquorish gusto." Restoration comedy "is constantly calling upon us for admiration of one line of conduct and condemnation, or at all events ridicule, of another. And the line of conduct it despises is relatively good, while that which it admires is consistently infamous."[17] The main line of morals criticism had not changed since Collier's day: "The Stage-Poets make their Principal Persons Vitious and reward them at the End of the Play."

The underlying assumption that the dramatist ought to administer poetic justice is a childish oversimplification; it leads to the most magnificently absurd kind of ending, as any reader of eighteenth- or nineteenth-century drama can testify, or indeed anyone who sees many Hollywood films in which "good guys" win and "bad guys" lose. The drama ought to take some account of the fact that in life good guys sometimes finish last. Furthermore, is the simple statement that the "vitious" persons are rewarded true? I think not. As between the jealous and avaricious merchant who tyrannizes over his wife and the rake-hero who cuckolds him, who is to say who is the more "vitious"?

Finally, without exception, every one of the eleven plays we have considered deals with the reform of the hero, not his reward. His initiation into true love at the end — his "reward" — marks his reclamation to virtue, and so Dryden described it: "We make not vicious persons happy, but only as Heaven makes sinners so; that is, by reclaiming them first from vice. For so it is to be supposed they are, when they resolve to marry; for then, enjoying what they desire in one, they cease to pursue the love of many."[18] The knowledge and experience the hero gained as a rake become the wisdom necessary for real virtue. The merchant, by contrast, is rigid and incurable. The statement that Restoration comedy is "immoral" is either oversimplified or false, and I am sure critics would long since have come to this conclusion were it not for a complication introduced in the early twentieth century and based on Lamb's essay. That complication is "manners" criticism.

Lamb's essay was partly an attempt to get away from the attack based on indecency of subject matter by suggesting that, in some sense, one's ordinary moral feelings were not meant to apply to Restoration comedies.

> They are a world of themselves almost as much as fairyland. Take one of their characters, male or female (with few exceptions they are alike), and place it in a modern play, and my virtuous indignation shall rise against the profligate wretch . . . because in a modern play I am to judge of the right and the wrong. . . . It has got into a moral world where it has no business, from which

it must needs fall headlong. . . . But in its own world do we feel the creature is so very bad?—The Fainalls and the Mirabels, the Dorimants and the Lady Touchwoods, in their own sphere do not offend my moral sense; in fact they do not appeal to it at all. They seem engaged in their proper element. They break through no laws, or conscientious restraints. They know of none. They have got out of Christendom into the land—what shall I call it?—of cuckoldry—the Utopia of gallantry, where pleasure is a duty, and the manners perfect freedom. It is altogether a speculative scene of things, which has no reference whatever to the world that is.[19]

Lamb's description, in its context as one of a series of essays on actors, should probably be understood, one survey of the Romantics points out, not as an ordinary critical evaluation but as a direction as to how the comedies should be *played*, "as something almost symbolic, a passionate dance-figure, or an arabesque of words and repartees. Once we step out of that region, the inhumanity of the thing becomes too apparent."[20] Lamb's essay means neither that Restoration comedy did not reflect Restoration society, nor that that society was not like later life, nor, in any broad sense, that Restoration comedy had no relation to "real" life; Lamb's essay simply says that Restoration comedy should be acted in a stylized, artificial way.

But curiously enough, even if Lamb's essay be taken as saying the plays are unreal, it produced an unexpected result. Increasingly, the plays came to be treated not as plays but as documents for a social historian—realistic descriptions of upper-class life in Restoration London. In the latter half of the nineteenth century a number of continental critics wrote on Restoration comedy with increased emphasis on the social context of the plays, partly as an answer to Lamb. Finally, in 1913, John Palmer brought forth his book *The Comedy of Manners,* to answer both Lamb and Macaulay by the flat assertion: "The excellence of Restoration comedy is, in fact, directly due to the honest fidelity with which it reflects the spirit of an intensely interesting phase of our social history." In the summarizing sections of his book, Palmer set forth a very reasonable and intelligent answer to "morals" critics:

Art is not primarily concerned with morality, but morality is the stuff of the poet's art. The artist is dealing with emotions and conduct which in the world whence he draws material are determined by positive morality. Morality is his subject, though it is not his object.

There is a higher morality than that of Jeremy Collier . . . and without in the least circumscribing the sphere of the artist one may confidently say that the highest art has invariably expressed the highest morality.[21]

Unfortunately, however, Palmer in a book, *Comedy,* published the following year emphasized only those parts of *The Comedy of Manners* which stressed the view that "manners are the principal theme." Later writers tended to follow; Bonamy Dobrée, writing in 1924, suggested that "we simply accept the life of the time, and without associating it with ourselves, derive interest and pleasure from the observation and understanding of men whose outlook on life died with their erring bodies some two centuries ago." He concluded about the plays: "If we were to try to sum up what the comedy of this period as a whole achieved, it would be to say that it gave a brilliant picture of its time rather than a new insight into man. . . . These writers never came to the condition of seeing life whole, though what they saw they perceived very clearly." [22]

The success of this approach in avoiding "morals" criticism is suggested by the remarks of T. S. Eliot's "B" in "A Dialogue on Dramatic Poetry," who pronounces the comedy:

> Impeccable. The morality of our Restoration drama cannot be impugned. It assumes orthodox Christian morality, and laughs (in its comedy) at human nature for not living up to it. It retains its respect for the divine by showing the failure of the human. . . . Our Restoration drama is all virtue. It depends upon virtue for its existence.

Another of "B" 's remarks, however, shows the price that Restoration comedy paid for this reprieve: "The question of Wycherley and the question of Shakespeare are not on the same plane. Restoration comedy is a comedy of social manners. . . . It laughs at the members of a society who transgress its laws." [23] To become legitimated, *moralisé,* the plays have paid with their significance; they since have been regarded by many critics as no more meaningful than books of etiquette.

Palmer's schism now created a number of sects of "manners" criticism. Formerly the question of "moral" or "immoral" had been simply one question. Now several others were added: Is the world of Restoration comedy a "real" reflection of Stuart court life, or is it artificial? Does that world have any relation to ordinary life? Does Restoration comedy concern itself with morality or simply with the "manners" of a coterie? Finally, then, is Restoration comedy "moral" or "immoral"? Mathematically, there are at least sixteen possible attitudes; all of them, no doubt, could be illustrated by quotations from critics. For example, of six writers, all of whom agree that Restoration comedy was a thoroughly real picture of the life of the court coterie, two find the plays moral, two immoral, and two amoral.[24] Conversely, of four critics who agree that the world of Restoration comedy is "artificial," two find the plays immoral and two amoral.[25] Professor Sherburn summarizes the final compromise that has grown out of this welter of criticism: "Nowadays it is wise to regret the grossness of situation and of repartee in these comedies and to try to recapture the fine sense of social protocol that made any unconscious singing off key — violating the pattern — amusing." [26] Behind "manners" criticism one senses always the tacit assumption that the business of literature is to portray the mores of a particular period. While that may be so, I think it is even more the function of literature to fuse the details of which it is made with some kind of human universal. To neglect the universal is to turn the writer into a social historian, and that has indeed been the principal result of Palmer's book and of the consequent "manners" criticism of Restoration comedy. The plays are commonly regarded as meaningless representatives of an outmoded frivolity.

A better result of Palmer's book was a good deal of scholarly work on the plays. In 1923, Professor Nicoll published his definitive history of the drama of the period, a book rich with stage information, play lists, datings, and the like, to which all later critics of Restoration comedy are greatly indebted.[27] Also in the twenties appeared definitive editions of the works — both plays and poems — of the leading playwrights, by Summers, Brett-Smith, Dobrée, and others.[28] Some writers, like Hotson and Harbage, turned their attention to the question whether these plays bore any real relation to English drama before the Puritan edict closing the theaters in 1642,[29] or whether they were (as the Victorians thought them), a French importation.[30] (The conclusion seems final that, although isolated situations, bits of dialogue, and particular characters were borrowed from Molière and other French writers, the major plays of the period represent an essentially English combination of Ben Jonson's realism with John Fletcher's sophistication.) Two thorough books have appeared detailing the course of the controversy that followed Collier's pamphlet in 1698.[31] In the forties and fifties, several books appeared which followed particular topics through a great many of the plays chronologically.[32] For example, Miss Elisabeth Mignon's *Crabbed Age and Youth: The Old Men and Women in the Restoration Comedy of Manners* traces the changing attitude toward old age, from derision to overawed respect. In showing the decay of high Restoration comedy into sentimentalism this kind of book serves as a useful reminder that the shorthand designation, "Restoration comedy," that I, like every other writer on this subject, use is deceptive; the comedies of 1685 are quite different from those of 1665.

This large body of criticism and scholarship, when it dealt with the background of Restoration comedy, concentrated on social background, neglecting almost entirely the intellectual background — with one salient exception. In 1929 an article appeared by Professor Guy Montgomery, who raised a question: "I should like to know whether there were not beneath those *manners*, a system of ideas, of which the manners, and incidentally, the comedy were not a 'realization.'" He went on to note that the motives *behind* a society's conduct are often more meaningful than the conduct itself would suggest. Science, he pointed out, might well be that significant background motive. Restoration comedy, therefore, should perhaps be understood as a bitter, brittle questioning (in view of the new scientific discoveries) of the old, narrow, conventional morality.[33] As I hope Chapter 6 shows, Professor Montgomery's question is quite pertinent to the whole matter of Restoration comedy.

Another notable exception to the critical failure was Miss Kathleen M. Lynch's study of the *values* (as opposed to the social history) embodied in these comedies. Her *The Social Mode of Restoration Comedy* (1926) shows primarily that these plays are in the direct tradition of English drama, not significantly influenced by Molière. The wit that shaped Restoration comedy, she argues, was both a product of and a rebellion against the seventeenth-century nondramatic tradition of *préciosité* or *secentismo:* the tradition of extravagant similes and metaphors to describe exaggerated, introspective, and idealized emotions. The style appears in such unrelated items as the intolerably dull French romances of the period (D'Urfé's *Astrée* or Mlle de Scudéry's *Artamène ou le Grand Cyrus,* for example), the artificial Caroline court-Platonism, and the poetry of Donne, Lovelace, and Suckling. Miss Lynch shows that Restoration comedy, then, was not simply an exposition of manners, but a fusion of this *précieuse* tradition of conduct with Jonsonian realism. It was simultaneously a satire on those who could not produce the *précieuse* manner and a revolt against the affectations of that manner: "Here, surely, is a variety of comic outlook possible only in the highly sophisticated society which this type of comedy represents. One may search in vain in Elizabethan drama and in the drama of Molière for a similar consistent contrast of comic standards." Miss Lynch shows she is influenced in part by Bergson's theory of the comic; namely, that an individual is ridiculous when he behaves in a conventional, mechanized manner rather than in an organic or vital way. It is in this sense, she says, that we laugh at the heroes and heroines as well as the fools. The value of her study lies in two points: first, the recognition that the authors do not unhesitatingly approve of their heroes and heroines; second, the realization that because these authors use the positive and the negative of the same standard, they rise above that standard — these plays are not just about "manners."[34]

And in the midst of all this scholarship, where were the New Critics, the *Scrutiny* group, the writers for *Horizon* and *Hound and Horn* and the rest? They were apparently scared off by an influential essay by Professor L. C. Knights, "Restoration Comedy: The Reality and the Myth," which originally appeared in *Scrutiny* in September 1937. Mr. Knights's point is that Restoration comedy shows an "attenuation and enfeeblement," not only compared to Elizabethan drama, but to the nondramatic literature of the Restoration itself. The prose in the plays is weak, "unrelated to a mode of perceiving. . . . As for the 'wit,' when it isn't merely verbal and obvious . . . it is hopelessly dependent on convention," e.g., that an intelligent husband must be jealous. "The trouble is not that the Restoration comic writers deal with a limited number of themes, but that they bring to bear a miserably limited set of attitudes. And these, in turn, are factitious to exactly the same degree as the prose is artificial and non-representative of the current non-dramatic medium." Mr. Knights also dismisses, somewhat unchivalrously, Miss Lynch's careful evidence for a complex comic standard as "factitious," and concludes: "The criticism that defenders of Restoration comedy need to answer is not that the comedies are 'immoral,' but that they are trivial, gross and dull." [35]

This comment, though hardly likely to stir up critical interest in the plays, did good in one sense: it substituted the aesthetic question for the moral question which obsessed Victorian and anti-Victorian critics. Unfortunately, Knights's essay seems also to have turned modern criticism away from the intricate art of these comedies. Mr. T. S. Eliot recently defined the critic's job as helping the reader to enjoy the piece (or equally, I suppose, to dislike it) *for the right reasons.* Modern criticism of Restoration comedy has been long on liking and disliking, but woefully short on right reasons, which have in other fields been the great achievement of modern criticism. Until we understand these plays *as plays,* there is simply no point in making moral, sociological, or aesthetic judgments about them.

Two recent books on Restoration comedy do in fact try to deal with the plays as plays. The first is Professor Thomas Fujimura's *The Restoration Comedy of Wit* (1952). He argues that the comic writers were concerned not with etiquette but with the broad concept of "wit" or "decorum," which, he says, was much more than a social ideal. It involved an intellectual ideal based on such philosophical naturalism as Hobbes's, which made for egoistic, libertine heroes and dialogue that pokes through pretenses, cant, and conventional morality. In examining the plays, Professor Fujimura confines his attention to observing two elements: the recurrent "outwitting situation involving Truewits, Witwouds, and Witlesses," and "wit play, in fanciful similitudes, raillery scenes, and expressions of skeptical, sexual, and sophistical wit." The weakness of the book is that it rests on the critical preconception that "wit comedy" has these two elements. If a Restoration comedy shows these two elements, it is a good play; if not, not. The strength of the book is that it recognizes that Restoration comedy is a comedy with some intellectual substance. It is not simply a "comedy of manners," but a comedy that grows out of the intellectual problems of its day and ours.[36]

Professor Dale Underwood's *Etherege and the Seventeenth-Century Comedy of Manners* (1957), while primarily a historical study along lines similar to Professor Fujimura's, also contains many valuable critical insights in its treatment of Etherege's three plays (particularly *She wou'd if she cou'd*), and its analysis of "the comic language." Professor Underwood, however, mainly shows that Etherege (who, he feels, invented the Restoration comic style) carried on the Jacobean tradition of Jonson and Fletcher — but with two important changes. First, moral values are shifted so that Machiavellian, libertine, and Hobbesian attitudes balance off more or less evenly with traditional, courtly, and heroic values. Second, the Restoration dramatist prefers to work at a highly intellectualized and abstract level of experience rather than at the sensuous, concrete level favored by earlier dramatists. Perhaps most important, Professor Underwood stresses "the many-sided awareness, involuted irony, indirection, and complexity of view which is the peculiar badge of comic expression in Etherege's plays."[37] His study, therefore, makes a firm step forward beyond the many too many impressionistic studies which Restoration comedy has been suffering all these years.

As even this brief summary suggests, the bibliography in this field is mountainous, but the mountain has brought forth a mouse. The great failure has been that the critics have chosen to deal mostly in mere impressions. The scholars, on the other hand, have been doing their work: they have brought out highly useful biographical and social facts; they have established accurate texts; and they have given us an understanding of the theatrical and intellectual history of the period. Critics can provide facts, too — plot parallelisms, repeated metaphors, structure, imagery, all those things that modern criticism includes in the term "meaning" — but these, for the most part, critics have neglected. Instead, with few exceptions, the critics have made what should be conclusions reached after examining the plays into preconceptions to limit examination of the plays. The comedies are said to be "immoral," or "purely social," or "artificial," or "brilliant," and then dismissed.

Etherege, Wycherley, and Congreve, however, are really quite conventional; they use symbols, images, contrast, parallelism, and the like, just as more obviously respectable writers do, and it is high time we read them as though they did.

17 • *From Charles to Charles*

The critical misreadings of Restoration comedy occur, I think, because at some pre-verbal level we all expect these plays to be Elizabethan, and we measure them by that standard. Restoration and Elizabethan plays seem equally foreign to us, the language more or less equally old-fashioned, the customs and beliefs alien, the jokes — some of them — lost on us. The critic's disappointment and confusion when he reads a Restoration comedy by Elizabethan standards leads him to dismiss it as immoral or as a trivial description of a trivial coterie. Actually, of course, the seventeenth century saw the most profound changes of modern intellectual history take place. Restoration comedy falls on the "modern" side of those changes; in a very real sense it is the first "modern" drama, and it should be read in its own non-Elizabethan frame of reference, the separation of appearance from nature and fact from value.

"Intellectual changes," however, and "frames of reference" are rather abstruse terms for rather frothy comedies. The problem is to relate intellectual changes to the plays *as plays*. Many scholars have pointed out the ways in which people in 1700 thought differently from people in 1600; unfortunately the ways that plays changed across the century are not nearly so clear. There is, however, an obvious place to look for the differences, namely, the Restoration adaptations of Elizabethan plays. The alterations the Restoration dramatists made should pinpoint for us the ways intellectual changes or changes in frames of reference affected plays as plays.

We have already seen (in Chapter 2) some of the differences in theatrical practice. Actresses appeared on the English public stage for the first time in the Restoration. The new theaters had much more in the way of curtains and scenery than did the old. The influence of classical and pseudo-classical theories of drama was stronger in the Restoration. All in all, these changes can be epitomized in the generalization that the Elizabethan theatergoer was meant to be drawn into an action; the Restoration playwright thought of his audience as cultivated, disinterested judges who watched, critically and dispassionately, a spectacle. These, however, are merely theatrical changes. Other changes were going on at a more fundamental level.

For one thing, playwrights tended to idealize reality as in heroic drama; they justified the practice by misreading Aristotle. Actually, two kinds of idealizing bracket our eleven comedies: heroic drama at the beginning of the period (and on and on and on) and sentimental comedy at the end. Sentimental comedy, Professor Bernbaum points out, tried to arouse admiration (the feeling heroics tried to exploit), not for kings and queens, but for ordinary, contemporary, middle-class people. Beneath the earlier, heroic idealizing lay a distrust of ordinary human nature; hence, ideal people were placed in remote, exotic, and romantic settings. The later, sentimental idealizing put ideal people in realistic London; it built rather on a faith in human nature[1] (which, we have seen, the lover-heroes of the later comedies tend to exemplify, too). Both heroic idealizing[2] and sentimental idealizing[3] were thought to teach by alluring examples, just the opposite of the right-way–wrong-way method the comic writers used. This tendency to idealize shows the thinking behind neoclassical drama much more than the comedies do; that thinking, moreover, differs profoundly from pre-Restoration dramatic theory.

More important, the language of Restoration drama also represented a change. Compare, for example, these two pasasges:

Blow, winds, and crack your cheeks! Rage! Blow!
You cataracts and hurricanoes, spout
Till you have drench'd our steeples, drown'd the cocks!
You sulph'rous and thought-executing fires,
Vaunt-couriers of oak-cleaving thunderbolts,
Singe my white head! And thou, all-shaking thunder,
Strike flat the thick rotundity o' th' world!
Crack nature's moulds, all germens spill at once
That makes ingrateful man! [4]

Blow Winds, and burst your Cheeks, rage louder yet,
Fantastick Lightning singe, singe my white Head;
Spout Cataracts, and Hurricanos fall,
'Till you have drown'd the Towns and Palaces
Of proud ingratefull Man.[5]

Nahum Tate has made Shakespeare's Lear rave more sensibly. That is, he has shortened Lear's ranting and made it more limited and, in the terms of the late seventeenth century, more coherent. Shakespeare's passage runs from steeples and weathercocks to the "thick rotundity of the world" to the cosmos itself, creative mother nature, "nature's moulds" and "all germens." This progression, intuitive in Shakespeare's words, is spelled out in Tate's by connectives like "louder," " 'Till," and the "Of" that links to "ingratefull Man" the "Towns and Palaces" (themselves a rationalization of Shakespeare's synecdochal "steeples" and "cocks"). The range of the progression is shortened — Tate makes no attempt to go beyond "ingratefull Man" to such abstract universals as are represented in the terms "thought-executing" or "nature's moulds."

Obviously, one cannot by a single example prove an era, but there are many historians who have pointed out that this rationalizing of language is typical, and moreover that any such change in language really symbolizes a change in thought. We have already seen (in Chapter 6) that for the Restoration thinker, appearance and nature were normally different; for the Elizabethan, appearance normally reflected nature. We have already seen (in Chapter 11) that for the Restoration thinker, fact and value were separate; for the Elizabethan, each was in a sense implicit in the other. We have seen in the several discussions of the comedies themeslves how Restoration thought shows in the plays. The last remaining problem is to see how the *changes* in thought became *changes* in drama.

The best index to these changes in drama is the large body of Restoration adaptations of earlier English drama. The adaptors worked mostly on tragedies and tragicomedies, eliminating any comic elements and enlarging the emotions to absurd dimensions. The characters were set to reasoning transparently about their feelings in neat little conflicts between love and honor. In the end, poetic justice resolves these conflicts, rewarding the good characters and punishing the bad. We have already seen one of these — Nahum Tate's rewriting of *King Lear*.

Another example is Davenant's adaptation, in early 1662, of *Measure for Measure* (1604), called *The Law against Lovers.*[6] Davenant retains the basic situation in which Claudio, the fiancé of the pregnant Juliet, is jailed under an obsolete law against seduction, enforced by Angelo, the deputy, in the absence of the reigning duke. (The duke, of course, is actually in the city, disguised as a friar, manipulating matters behind the scenes.) Isabella, Claudio's sister, pleading with Angelo, is approached by him: Will she sleep with Angelo to save her brother's life? Davenant drops the low comedy associated with Pompey and Mrs. Overdone, the bawd; for them he substitutes Beatrice and Benedick and their witty dialogues from *Much Ado about Nothing*. More significantly, he eliminates "Mariana in the moated grange," Angelo's own discarded fiancée. While Shakespeare resolved the conflict by substituting Mariana for Isabella in "the infamous bed-trick," Davenant tries a number of solutions. First, Benedick and Beatrice forge a pardon; when that fails, Benedick arouses a civil insurrection to try to free Claudio. Finally, Angelo breaks down and proposes honorable marriage to Isabella, saying he was only testing her. The duke reveals himself and pardons all. (Shakespeare's duke married Isabella and resumed rule, but Davenant's retires to a monastery.)

Although Davenant's revision does not seem to have been particularly popular, his changes suggest what, even so early as 1662, Restoration audiences wanted. The substitution of Beatrice and Benedick for the low characters shows a taste for repartee, "the witty war" between lovers (V.v), and a rejection of "low" comedy. One little incident is all that remains of the Mariana plot: Isabella says cuttingly, if Juliet wants Claudio saved, let Juliet sleep with Angelo. Juliet indignantly refuses, and Isabella chides her for demanding that same price of his sister.

> *Juliet.* Alas, we know not what is good or ill.
> *Isabella.* Perhaps we should not learn that fatal skill.
> The serpent taught it first. (IV.ii)

This is a thoroughly un-Shakespearean comment. It shows the uncertainty, the sense of testing an unknown, that shapes Restoration drama and sets it off from earlier English drama. The common action of both versions is based on testing: the duke tests Angelo and Angelo tests Isabella. (The testing of Isabella is intentional with Davenant, inadvertent in Shakespeare's version.) Shakespeare, however, uses the law Angelo enforces to test a known framework of values. These values may bend, but they spring back, affirming the proverbial "measure for measure." Davenant's title suggests the change: his play explores a set of unknown consequences following on a peculiar "law against lovers."

The action of Shakespeare's play expounds the tempering effect of mercy on justice through the awareness of personal sin. The action operates on three levels, personal, social, and cosmic. The personal conflicts exist in the minds of the individual characters, where passion rises against reason. The social conflict grows from Angelo's administration of the law and its effect on the society as a whole, even down to the clowns and bawds of the farcical scenes; the cosmic level manifests itself mostly in imagery, but also in Isabella's wish to go to a nunnery (seeking a heavenly husband), the duke's masquerading as a friar, and the discussions of death. These three levels correspond to one another by analogy, the most basic method of Elizabethan drama, its way of creating an "action" that "imitated nature."

"Action" and "analogy" are not easy to define and extensional definitions serve best; for example, Professor Francis Fergusson's description of *Hamlet:*

> The main action of *Hamlet* may be described as the attempt to find and destroy the hidden 'imposthume' which is poisoning the life of Claudius' Denmark. All of the characters — from Polonius with his "windlasses" and "assays of bias," to Hamlet with his parables and symbolic shows — realize this action, in comic, or evil, or inspired ways.

The fact that all the characters — Claudius, Ophelia, Laertes, all — are trying to find out and destroy something makes their individual actions *analogies;* these analogies in turn define the total *action.* And, as in almost any Elizabethan drama, "Stretching beyond the play in all directions are the analogies between Denmark and England, Denmark and Rome under 'the mightiest Julius'; Hamlet's stage and Shakespeare's stage; the theater and life," and so on.[7]

In view of this analogical sense also embodied in Shakespeare's *Measure for Measure,* the change of Davenant's that means most is Benedick's stirring up the civil war. To raise the personal conflict to a social level, there must be a causal link — Claudio must have a friend who starts a civil war to relate the disintegration of Angelo as individual to that of the state he rules. An analogical link is felt to be insufficient. So too, heaven exists in Davenant's play, not as a stage behind the stage of this world on which earthly events cast shadows, but rather: "We through afflictions make our way to Heaven" (V.v). Heaven exists as something one comes to after the world, as one comes to marriage after love or to a monastery after life or to civil war after injustice: they are all related primarily by a causal link. They are seen as sequences of first-second rather than as simultaneous highers and lowers. For Shakespeare's total vision, Davenant substituted a literal-minded "moral drawn from a poetic dream" (V.v).

The Restoration adapted far less of earlier English comedy than it did of tragicomedy or tragedy. Consequently, the pattern of changes is much less clear. Jonson was performed as is; indeed Dryden said that "In his works you find little to retrench or alter."[8] Shakespeare, however, and Fletcher were freely altered. Possibly Jonson's critical prestige was such that alteration was thought presumptuous; more likely the satirical and skeptical tone and the "regularity" of his comedies so satisfied Restoration audiences that alteration was unnecessary. Significantly, only one adaptation of an earlier English comedy can be called, by any stretch of judgment, a "comedy of manners" (Farquhar's *The Inconstant*) and that was written in 1702, long after the form had evolved independently. With that exception, the altered comedies are either heroic dramas or farces dealing with lower- or middle-class people. In no sense is earlier English comedy a "source" for the high comedy of the Restoration.

Nevertheless, as with tragedy, Restoration adaptations of earlier English comedies — though they do not become comedies of manners — do give a good idea of what audiences after 1660 looked for in a comedy. For example, about 1667, George Villiers, Duke of Buckingham, later to be the author of that brilliant spoof on heroic drama, *The Rehearsal,* revamped Beaumont and Fletcher's *The Chances* (1627).[9]

Buckingham's most significant changes take place in the low plot. In Fletcher's version, Constantia, a prostitute being kept by the elderly Antonio, has run away with a fiddler. Buckingham converts Antonio from a rugged, retired-military type to an impotent old lecher, who was not keeping Constantia but had hired her on a one-night basis. In the finale she blackmails him into leaving her alone, by threatening to reveal his inabilities. Thus, as in most Restoration comedies, a pretense is kept up at the end, and, as in intrigue plots generally, knowledge of that pretense gives power: Constantia can blackmail Antonio. In Fletcher's version, Constantia had been accompanied by a bawd. Buckingham individualizes this character, turning her into a pretentious Malaprop-like old lady and, *mirabile dictu,* Constantia's mother. The change perfectly exemplifies the Restoration comic idea of the relation of parents to children. Their influence is never beneficial: in this play, it is corrupting; in others, repressive. Those who appear to be guides are in nature not. The use of a girl's mother for her bawd also sets a tone of universal social corruption surrounding the action, and this is an axiom of Restoration comedy — that one operates in a very fallen age indeed. Finally, in Buckingham's ending, Constantia escapes Antonio and a young gallant agrees to keep her. In the curtain lines her new lover contrasts this arrangement to the marriage contracted in the high plot:

> Now see the odds 'twixt marry'd Folks and Friends:
> Our Love begins just where their Passion ends.

The Restoration playwright sees the world as offering two ways of life: one legitimate, represented by the marriages of the high plot; one not so legitimate, but perhaps more exciting, represented by sustained pretenses and immorality. *The Chances,* both in its old and even more in its new form, proved popular.[10]

A somewhat less popular adaptation was John Lacy's *Sauny the Scot* (1667),[11] a revision of *The Taming of the Shrew* (1596). Lacy's most striking change is a new taming episode. In Shakespeare's play, Petruchio tames Kate by the time she comes back to her father's. In Lacy's version, Kate agrees to Petruchio's statements while en route to her father's that the sun is the moon and an old man a young maid, but when she arrives, she assures her husband she was just pretending, and to spite him, will not speak a word. Petruchio resorts to a new device: he pretends Kate is dead, ties her to the bier and prepares to bury her alive, while her father and the others present seem to permit this. Kate, frightened, finally speaks, agreeing to be a proper wife. The scene has little dramatic impact, and Kate's conversion, even with the supernatural overtones of some of the speeches (393), is unconvincing. It does, however, keep up the Restoration habit of testing things, pushing them to their utmost limit. So, too, Lacy thereby hints that one's nature is hard to change — it requires the ultimate threat: one must be tragicomically "killed" and "reborn" to do it. It is easy enough, however, for Kate to change her appearance, to pretend to be a submissive wife. Gone is Shakespeare's sense that woman's nature and appearance are one; as Kate in her last speech says:

> Why are our bodies soft and weak and smooth,
> Unapt to toil and trouble in the world,
> But that our soft conditions and our hearts
> Should well agree with our external parts?

Shakespeare's Kate sees a direct analogy between the home, the political body, and the individual body:

> Thy husband is thy lord, thy life, thy keeper,
> Thy head, thy sovereign; . . .
> Such duty as the subject owes the prince
> Even such a woman oweth to her husband.

Needless to say, there is no such analogical sense in Lacy's version. All the elements are held together only by cause and effect.

Gone, too, is Shakespeare's feeling for a normality. The problem in *The Taming of the Shrew* is to return Kate to her normal social relations; being a repentant sinner, a convert, she is of course stronger in her role of wife at the end than those who never deviated. At the end of *Sauny the Scot,* the epilogue informs us "next you see the very *Tamer Tam'd,*" suggesting that the supposed normality to which Petruchio has restored Kate does not exist. Whereas in *The Taming* a passing merchant, told he is in danger because of war, is induced to disguise himself and play a suitor's father in order to fabricate a marriage settlement, in *Sauny* a "Knight of the Post," i.e., a professional false witness, is paid to do the job. For Shakespeare, normality means peace and prosperity; for Lacy, the world normally surrounding the married couples is a sustained corruption. The Knight of the Post recalls the good old days with Kate's father, whom he pretends to know. Ironically, he says: "Ay, marry, these were golden days indeed — no cozening, no cheating. The world is altered" (368).

Another comedy, a middle-class farce, adapted for Restoration performance was *Eastward Hoe* (1605), on which Ben Jonson, John Marston, and George Chapman collaborated.[12] The tone of the Jacobean play is ironic. The virtuous city people are unbearably stuffy and stodgy and a pious moral is dutifully pointed out at the end. The courtly audience for which the play was first performed probably sneered not only at the nominal villains but the nominal heroes, too. Nahum Tate wrote the Restoration version, *Cuckolds-Haven,* published in 1685.[13] His changes show the authentic Restoration tone. In the final courtroom scene, the "villains" do not reform. Instead, they buy off the alderman-hero's lawyer and accuse the alderman himself of witchcraft. The cheat fails and Touchstone, the alderman, has an opportunity for revenge, but simply laughs it off: "Well, it was a witty Practice, and I forgive them all" (44). The villains are freed — unrepentant. His daughter, who in 1605 begged Touchstone's forgiveness, in 1685 insists that he ask her to ask his forgiveness, to which her father replies, "She has Spirit for an Empress: Tell her, Wife, I desire her, to desire my Pardon." In place of the punishment, repentance, and moral of the Jacobean version, the foolish husbands of the Restoration are told: "As you came to be Cuckolds by locking your Wives up: for aught I know you may be Uncuckolded by giving them their Freedom" (44).

In every case, Tate's changes suggest one of two things: first, that there is no morality commonly practiced by society by which these actions can be judged and, second, that in the face of this uncertainty, the best thing to do is to relax, as Touchstone does, and get as much fun out of the doings as you can. Jonson and his collaborators had found bourgeois morality distasteful, something to be laughed at, but Tate saw a society in which there was no morality, stodgy or otherwise, only the hope that by letting people find their own way, they will stumble onto a workable practice.

One adaptation, though of a tragicomedy, tells us more than all the others about Restoration social comedy: Dryden and Davenant's version of *The Tempest* (1667).[14] It was immensely popular — there are twenty-three definitely known performances between 1660 and 1700. Shadwell gave it an operatic form in which it completely replaced Shakespeare's original on the stage and was played in London as late as 1838.[15] "It would hardly be an exaggeration to say that it was the favourite play of the Restoration stage," says Shadwell's editor.[16]

Shakespeare set up three plots related by analogy: high, dealing with monarchical usurpations; low, based on Caliban, the sailors, and their mock kingdom; and middle, the romance of Ferdinand and Miranda. Davenant (the Restoration version was mostly his) made no particularly meaningful changes in the high plot; in the low, he added Sycorax, Caliban's sister, and created a new, more sexual buffoonery. The interesting changes came in the middle plot; as Dryden describes them in his Preface:

> But Sir *William Davenant,* as he was a Man of quick and piercing imagination, soon found that somewhat might be added to the Design of *Shakespear,* of

which neither *Fletcher* nor *Suckling* had ever thought: and therefore to put the last hand to it, he design'd the Counterpart to *Shakespear's* Plot, namely, that of a Man who had never seen a Woman; that by this means those two Characters of Innocence and Love might the more illustrate and commend each other. (4)

Not only does Prospero have Miranda — he has Dorinda, too, who has never seen any man but her father. The prize addition is Hippolito, the "right Heir of the Dukedom of *Mantua*" (6). This young man has never seen a woman, because Prospero, convinced that women are the root of all evil and that death awaits Hippolito if he sees one, keeps him in a cave at the opposite end of the island.

In due course, Ferdinand and Miranda meet and fall in love, and Hippolito and Dorinda do the same. Hippolito, however, with the care-free spontaneity of the primitive, sees Miranda and decides he wants her too, his theory being that if one woman is good, two are better. Ferdinand, somewhat put out by this, challenges him to a duel and Hippolito very nearly dies — fulfilling dutifully Prospero's prophecy. Just as Prospero is about to execute Ferdinand for murder, Hippolito recovers by supernatural means, and all sail happily off to Italy.

Davenant's play is based on one continued joke — the contrast implied between the "enchanted island" of the play and "the Town" of his Restoration audience. The comparison occasionally becomes explicit, as when Prospero explains the dangers of men to his daughters:

Prospero. . . . Old men are tame
By Nature, but all the Danger lies in a wild
Young Man.
Dorinda. Do they run wild about the Woods?
Pros. No, they are wild within Doors, in Chambers,
And in Closets.
Dor. But Father, I would stroak 'em, make 'em gentle,
Then sure they would not hurt me.
Pros. You must not trust them, Child:
No Woman can come neer 'em but she feels
A pain full nine Months. . . . (39)

This joke — the comic contrast between what the "natural" characters know and what Davenant's sophisticated and cynical audiences know — is just the point Davenant wanted to make: his theme is the effect of knowledge, particularly sexual knowledge, and sophistication. Thus, Hippolito's spontaneity contrasts with the disillusionment and cynicism of the experienced Ferdinand. When Miranda tells Ferdinand he must show brotherly love to Hippolito, Ferdinand replies: "When you bid me love him, I must hate him" (69). Moreover, he assumes immediately that Miranda is deceiving him:

It is too plain: like most of her frail Sex
She's false, but has not learnt the art to hide it;
Nature has done her part, she loves variety.
Why did I think that any Woman could
Be innocent, because she's young?

Davenant represents knowledge as disruptive in its first effects, leading first to anarchy, but finally to a greater wisdom. Knowledge and experience imply doubt, but Davenant accepts this fact as a *felix culpa*. Civilization has its discontents, but it is worth them, for society regulates passions toward peace: "Sir, if you love you must be ty'd to one," says Ferdinand to Hippolito. Primitive, "natural" love is, by contrast, promiscuity. Thus, Hippolito replies to Ferdinand's stricture:

But, Sir, I find it is against my Nature.
I must love where I like, and I believe I may like all,
All that are fair. (65)

"Is there but one [woman] here?" says Hippolito of the island,

This is a base poor World: I'le go to th' other;
I've heard Men have abundance of 'em there. (72)

Even Sycorax, when she discovers the joys of love, wishes to "be kind" to every man she meets. Hippolito's ungoverned sexuality, his desire for all the women in the world, causes his duel with Ferdinand and his "death." His disobedience, like Adam's, brings conflict and death to his world, but, also like Adam's, it creates the possibility of redemption. Hippolito's wound, caused by Ferdinand's jealousy of Miranda, is cured by her anointing the weapon that injured him, cured, in other words, by the very love he affronted. His "death and rebirth" teach him to live in a social, imperfect world, not an "enchanted island" or earthly paradise. Just as secular love is treated in the play as the type of divine love for primitive and sophisticate alike, so sexual knowledge is treated as the knowledge of good and evil from which comes death.

The *felix culpa* of the innocents introduces deception and fighting to the island. Before Dorinda, for example, knows about sex, Prospero can say:

I'm sure
Unartful Truth lies open in her Mind,
As Crystal streams their sandy bottom show. (44)

But after Miranda has learned of love, Prospero sighs:

I find she loves him much because she hides it.
Love teaches cunning even to Innocence. (70)

Dissimulation does not exist before sexual knowledge: neither does fighting (except, of course, for Caliban's animal malice). "We," says Hippolito, "have no Swords growing in our World." In the real world of knowledge, with its deceptions and conflicts, the sophisticate is superior. Thus, Prospero calls Ferdinand "the full blown Flower,/ Of which this youth [Hippolito] was but the Op'ning-bud" (44). It is Ferdinand who dominates the final quartet:

> *Miranda to Dorinda.* If Children come by lying in a Bed,
> I wonder you and I had none between us.
> *Dorinda.* Sister it was our fault, we meant like fools
> To look 'em in the fields, and they it seems
> Are only found in Beds.
> *Hippolito.* I am o'erjoy'd
> That I shall have *Dorinda* in a bed;
> We'll lye all night and day together there,
> And never rise again.
> *Ferdinand. Aside to him. Hippolito!* you yet are ignorant
> Of your great Happiness, but there is somewhat
> Which for your own and fair *Dorinda's* sake
> I must instruct you in.
> *Hip.* Pray teach me quickly
> How Men and Women in your World make love,
> I shall soon learn I warrant you. (100)

Not the primitive, who lives on an "enchanted island," but a man — even a rake — who has learned how to deal with the facts of an imperfect world is the final hero.

For Davenant, heaven is hostile, or at best has severed its connections with the flawed mechanism of earth. Davenant laughs at attempts to realize the spiritual world in the material: the soul, says Hippolito, is "A small blew thing that runs about within us" (94). Shakespeare demonstrates through Ariel and the other spirits a harmony between the visible and invisible worlds, a harmony played upon by the magus-king. Shakespeare treats Prospero's manipulation of the island through an essentially secular knowledge as an analogy to God's manipulation of reality through Providence. Prospero's knowledge, in other words, leads him only to what he should already have known — the Christian ethic. For Shakespeare, analogy links heaven and earth, but Davenant's Prospero remarks:

> Alas! How much in vain doth feeble Art
> Endeavor to resist the will of Heaven? (83)

Like most Restoration writers (especially Milton), Davenant treats secular knowledge as the bringer of deceptions and conflicts that only further knowledge can mold into a new order.

Davenant, in this play as in *The Law against Lovers,* replaces analogical connections by causal ones. Shakespeare created in *The Tempest* a study of the dramatic manipulation of the island-reality to achieve a catharsis: a set of analogies showing Prospero as monarch, father, magus, teacher, dramatic artist, even as God. What Davenant saw was a study of the "natural man." For the Restoration writer, serious or comic, sex provided a lowest common denominator for all mankind — the animal level of man. Davenant's *The Tempest* uses the natural man's intuitive sexuality to generate an action of rivalry, to say, much in the manner of Locke and Hobbes: "Because men are naturally this way, struggles and rivalries arise and government is needed." That "because" replaces Shakespeare's "as." Where Shakespeare affirmed a belief, Davenant asks a question — and so do we. More than any other play, his *Tempest* shows why Restoration drama is closer to modern drama than to Elizabethan.

The new *Tempest* proved prodigiously popular. From the Dryden-Davenant version (1667), Thomas Shadwell made an opera in April of 1674. Shadwell's opera, in turn, provoked a parody by Thomas Duffett in November of the same year.[17] The parody poked some rather heavy-handed fun at the unreality of *The Tempest;* it translated the girl-who-has-never-seen-a-man plot to the unlikely milieu of Bridewell prison. Duffett, however, in translating the characters to whores, apprentices, Quakers, gamblers, and so on, simply recognizes explicitly what Dryden and Davenant treat implicitly: that the original plot which showed someone learning about the opposite sex meant to the Restoration a study of the "natural" man, man outside the law.

In 1702, George Farquhar, the last and least of the great comic dramatists of the Restoration, brought out *The Inconstant,* a prose adaptation of John Fletcher's verse comedy, *The Wild-Goose Chase* (1621).[18] Not only is Farquhar's play the only "comedy of manners" that is based on an earlier English source; it is the most explicit example of the difference between English comedy of 1660–1710 and earlier English comedy. The plot traces Oriana's wooing of Mirabel, a young man who has just completed an especially rakish version of the Grand Tour, and who, therefore, is especially reluctant to marry. The characters are changed somewhat. In Fletcher's version, Mirabel's father is a solemn, orderly gentleman; in Farquhar's he is a doddering old lecher. In Fletcher's version, Mirabel and Oriana each have two companions that create two subplots, while in Farquhar's, Mirabel has but one companion, Duretete, and Oriana but one, Bisarre. The important changes, however, are in the finale. In *The Wild-Goose Chase,* Mirabel, when he was abroad, had saved the life of an Italian merchant. Mirabel, after all Oriana's other schemes have failed, is told that this merchant had died and remembered his rescuer in his will. Oriana conquers by pretending to be the merchant's daughter come to deliver the bequest. She is so beautiful and so charming that Mirabel is tricked into proposing ("And yet, perhaps, I knew ye"), is caught, and carries his companions into matrimony, too. In *The Inconstant,* however, Duretete and Bisarre agree to part amicably. The incident of the merchant is done away with. Instead, Mirabel finally rejects Oriana and she, in despair, disguises herself as a page to follow him (like Wycherley's Fidelia). Mirabel picks up a pretty girl, Lamorce, at the theater, and accompanies her to her secluded house, where he is robbed by her accomplices. Oriana gets help and rescues him, and he marries her.

In short, every one of Farquhar's changes, like Tate's, tends to suggest a world of deceptive corruption outside the nucleus of love. The action in Fletcher's play is to restore Mirabel to normality. Oriana says:

> If he be wild,
> The reclaiming him to good and honest, Brother,
> Will make much for my honor; which, if I prosper
> Shall be the study of my love, and life too. . . .
> My mind tells me
> That I, and only I, must make him perfect;
> And in that hope I rest. (I.i)

This same speech in Farquhar's adaptation becomes: "Let me but get him into the bands of Matrimony, I'll spoyl his wandring, I warrant him. I'll do his business that way, never fear" (I.i). Fletcher shows a background of honesty and goodness; for instance, Mirabel's saving the Italian merchant and the merchant's rewarding him, Mirabel's own sober father as opposed to Farquhar's version of that father, Mirabel's companions' falling in love as opposed to Duretete's refusing to. The earlier play makes Oriana's love a part of the normal goodness of society. Mirabel, in marrying her, is changing from an abnormally bad behavior to the normal, good order of things. Italy is unusual and bad; Oriana and society are usual and good.

The Restoration version, on the other hand, creates the picture of universal corruption. Oriana is a special oasis of goodness—everything else, society, foreign countries, even the hero's confidant Duretete, represents a liberty of doubtful merit. For instance, when in Fletcher's play the gallants discuss the women they have seduced, they are limited to Italy, but Farquhar's gallants have had French, Dutch, and English women as well as Italian. Outside the nucleus of romantic love wait deceptions like those of Lamorce, and from those deceptions and corruptions Mirabel retreats into the haven of matrimony, described in the imagery as a prison. Thus Mirabel says in his curtain speech:

Vertue in this so advantageous light has her own sparkling Charms more tempting far than glittering Gold or Glory. Behold the Foil [*pointing to* Lamorce] that sets this brightness off [*to* Oriana]. Here view the pride [*to* Oriana] and scandal of the Sex [*to* La'm] there [*to* La'm] the false Meteor whose Deluding light leads Mankind to destruction here [*to* Oriana] the bright shining Star that guides to a Security of Happiness, a Garden and a single She [*to* Oriana] was our first fathers bliss, the Tempter [*to* La'm] and to wander was his Curse.

What liberty can be so Tempting there [*to* La'm]
As a soft, vertuous, Amorous bondage here? [*to* Oriana]

And yet the world is not so bad that Duretete cannot choose to stay in it.

Farquhar, like Lacy and Davenant, stresses causal relationships at the expense of analogical ones. In Fletcher's version, Mirabel knows the social order and his place in it and somewhat improbably agrees to return. The little world of Mirabel is made to fit the larger world of society. In Farquhar's version, the dramatist feels he must show cause. Mirabel must be driven back by his experience with Lamorce. In Fletcher's version all three rakes return; all three respond to the felt relation of the individual to his society. In Farquhar's version one returns and one does not, because only one has felt the stimulus of Lamorce's corruption. Again, the analogical relations that direct the action in the Jacobean play are replaced by causal stimuli in the Restoration play. In another way, Farquhar's play is typical of the later phase of Restoration comedy in showing two alternatives — a right way of life (the nucleus of personal emotion) and a wrong (the whirl of society) as in Mirabel's curtain speech. The pattern of two heroes, one choosing romance and the other choosing society, is the pattern of the great Restoration comedies, *The Country Wife, The Plain-Dealer,* and *Love for Love,* among others.

In short, the Restoration adaptations of earlier English plays show that Restoration drama, and particularly Restoration comedy, is *not* simply a decadent form of Elizabethan drama. Restoration comedy represents a profound change in method and manner from earlier English comedies, and the "morals" and "manners" criticisms that, tacitly or overtly, compare Restoration drama invidiously to Elizabethan drama simply lead nowhere. The differences are too fundamental. Professor Underwood, in his examination of the Machiavellian and libertine tradition in Etherege's plays, points to the movement away from immediate sensuous data to categories and classes of experience.[19] Our examination of adaptations suggests two other specific differences.

First, Restoration comedies, unlike Elizabethan or Stuart plays of any kind, popular or coterie, comic or tragic, assume that society is bad in the special sense that, in society, appearance does not, indeed, should not correspond to nature. These comedies, however, go much farther, and this is what makes them different — they assume, often tacitly, that whether society is bad or not is simply not worth worrying about. The special thing, the new thing about Restoration comedy is that society is regarded as less important than and irrelevant to personal, emotional relationships. The rake-hero, like the rest of the people in the play, manipulates the difference between appearance and nature to gain his antisocial ends. His real self remains uncommitted either to society or to emotions. In the later comedies, the lover-hero, unlike the rest of the people in the play, finds love, and love unites for him appearance and nature. He wins complete candor and complete commitment — but only to his love, not to his society as a whole.

Second, Restoration comedy questions; earlier English comedy affirms. Even the supposedly decadent comedies of the Jacobean and Caroline coterie theaters satirize from the point of view of a known and accepted set of values. Perception is not a problem, except for the most disordered characters. The immediate sensuous data about a thing establish its place in "the great chain of being" and hence its value. Facts, in other words, directly imply the values associated with the facts.

For the Restoration writer, however, sensuous data are "secondary qualities," illusions obscuring the solid facts. Facts must be approached through logical and scientific classes that strip off sensuous data. Facts, moreover, do not imply values. Values lack authority and must be understood as merely personal emotions. Because facts were thought obscured and values separated from facts, Restoration comedy became concerned almost to the exclusion of anything else with perception. The social conventions which are the sensuous data of the comedies are in a scientific sense "secondary qualities." They mask the essential facts and values, and the characteristic tropes of Restoration comedy serve to peer through the mask. Conversion down and the language of split-man observation get through to the facts; the right-way–wrong-way simile probes the values.

These tropes do not put an event in an all-embracing set of cosmic analogies as Elizabethan and Stuart metaphors characteristically do. Instead, they systematize and classify experience "scientifically." It is probably this change that the critics are really lamenting. The language of Restoration comedy does not — cannot — relate one event to another through an all-inclusive world-view as the language of earlier English drama did. Neither, for that matter, can the language of a modern play, even one explicitly trying to be cosmic, such as T. S. Eliot's *The Cocktail Party*. The fact that we cannot relate all the different aspects of experience to one another is simply a side-effect of science, a condition of modern existence. Science demanded that facts be stripped of their values and their sensuousness as the price of progress. A scientific view of the universe does not therefore help us to relate events in terms of value or sensuous characteristics as the pre-Restoration, pseudo-scientific view did. Fortunately or unfortunately, the world-view embodied in Restoration comedy is the causal one of science, not the analogical one of Shakespeare. And this is our second distinction between Restoration and pre-Restoration comedy. Restoration comedy lost the cosmic implications the analogies of language and action made in earlier comedy. As such it became the first "modern" drama.

Thus, just these six adaptations have all pointed to two kinds of dramatic changes: first, changes to show society, because it necessarily involves pretense and disguise, as more corrupt, and to show the characters' indifference to that corruption; second, changes to limit the social and cosmic analogies of a given event and to stress the causes and results of the event. Restoration comedy is "modern" in the sense that these changes imitate the change from the analogical, metaphorical world-view of the Renaissance to the scientific, cause-effect world-view of the later seventeenth century and our own.

It is common for writers on Restoration comedy to point to certain Jacobean and Caroline comedies as forerunners of the so-called comedy of manners, because they deal with the upper classes and have witty, freethinking lovers, the woman as emancipated as the man, and free and graceful dialogue. If I am correct in saying that Restoration comedy is fundamentally different from Tudor-Stuart drama, then even these so-called forerunners should lack these two elements of the Restoration comedy that distinguish it from earlier English drama: indifference to social corruption and concentration on causes and effects as opposed to social and cosmic analogies. Fletcher's *The Wild-Goose Chase* is the most commonly cited of these forerunners, and we have already seen how it differs from the real Restoration comedy based on it.

Another play often called a forerunner of Restoration comedy is Philip Massinger's *A New Way to Pay Old Debts* (1625).[20] There are two plots in Massinger's play, both based on the character of Sir Giles Overreach, a grasping, heartless financier, who is building up an empire in land by any means, fair or foul, mostly foul. One plot shows him trying to break up his daughter Margaret's romance and marry her above her station to Lord Lovell. The other shows Lady Allworth helping Overreach's nephew Wellborn, a good-hearted wastrel (supposedly a forerunner of the rake-hero), to get his lands back from the financier. Thus both plots affirm traditional social values.

The play has the two-sided structure of a morality play. The forces of good, Lady Allworth and Lord Lovell, stand for traditional values and nobility; like good angels they fight for the young people, Wellborn, Margaret, and Allworth, against the deviltry of Sir Giles and his aides. Like a morality, the action grows from the foreknowledge of cosmic good and evil. Thus, Overreach refers to his activities as his "religion," and Lovell to Sir Giles's recounting of them as "a devilish matins"; Sir Giles's treacherous aide Marall is answered as "devil," "tempter," when Wellborn resists his urgings to suicide; Lovell cries at the final retribution, "Heaven's hand is in this." (These are only a few examples from a stream of such metaphors running through the play.)

Overreach's deviltry takes two related forms. First, he tries to reverse the traditional social structure by replacing the landed aristocracy, by reducing decayed nobles to servants, and by marrying his daughter above her station. (Overreach's character is derived from the historical Sir Giles Mompesson, who, significantly, also came to a bad end.) Second, while Overreach seeks material wealth and titles, he denies the spiritual wealth of virtue and nobility. Intellectually, he justifies this reversal by denying to "words" (i.e., any intangibles) the importance of things. "Friendship is but a word," he snarls,

> I would be worldly wise; for the other wisdome,
> That does prescribe vs a well-gouerned life,
> And to doe right to others as our selues,
> I value not an Atome. (II.i)

He dismisses chastity: "Words are no substances" (III.ii). He cares not for reputation, but duels nevertheless, not to keep his honor, a mere "word," but to enforce his wrongful acquisition of things.

Over and over, the play states that spiritual and material nature ought to coincide and normally do. Overreach appears evil to all and is so in nature; the nobility, Lovell and Lady Allworth, are reputedly — and actually — virtuous and noble. The abnormal condition is shown, first, as Wellborn's lack of material wealth to match his inner nature, his birth and merit; and, second, as Allworth's inability to translate his hidden love for Margaret into the visible form of marriage. The action of the play is to achieve normality by matching appearances to inner, spiritual nature. Overreach must be shown that his mad cry, "Is not the whole world included in my selfe?" is wrong, that

> Some vndone widdow sitts vpon mine arme,
> And takes away the vse of 't; and my sword
> Glew'd to my scabberd with wrong'd orphans teares,
> Will not be drawne,

in other words, that the spiritual and material fact are one. It is not enough that the wastrel Wellborn be restored to wealth. "I had a reputation," he remarks at the end of the play,

> and, 'till I redeeme it
> Some noble way, I am but halfe made vp.

Appearance must be matched to nature on the personal, social, and cosmic levels.

There are Restoration elements. *A New Way to Pay Old Debts* is like a comedy of manners in the complexity of its plot, in its emphasis on a social problem, its rake-hero, its pair of "witty lovers," and in its use of the characteristic Restoration device of intrigue, chains of cause and effect in which the causal power comes from a difference in the knowledge people have. But the use of pretense or intrigue is limited. Compared to the sense of reversed values, it plays a small part. Even when Overreach pretends to be reconciled to his nephew, both know it is a cheat. It is the same with the "good angels." They deceive Sir Giles but only to let him deceive himself by replacing substance with appearances as he characteristically does. These pretenses are justified because, as Lady Allworth says, "My ends are good." The intrigues are meaningful only in the context of the values the play asserts.

As in *Measure for Measure,* the play tests these values, but reaffirms them. The material fact corresponds to the spiritual, and appearance corresponds to reality. Furthermore, the action develops by analogy on the three levels usual in Jacobean writing: personal — the love-affairs and the shattering of Overreach's mind; social — the problem of retaining the landed aristocracy; and cosmic — the supernatural ending. *A New Way* simply lacks the Restoration tone. It is not surprising, therefore, that the Restoration was the one period in the stage history of the play when it was ignored. It had only one known performance from 1660 to 1700.[21]

James Shirley's *Hyde-Park* (1632)[22] is also often spoken of as an early comedy of manners. There are three plots, all ending at a horse race in Hyde Park. First, Mrs. Bonavent, whose husband has been lost at sea, finally marries her suitor, Lacy. On their wedding day, Bonavent returns and Lacy resigns his bride. In the second plot, Mrs. Carol is a reluctant beauty; her suitor Fairfield, by simulating reluctance, wins her. In the third, one Trier is the favored suitor of Julietta. To test her virtue, he introduces to Julietta the rakish Lord Bonvile, who promptly flirts with and propositions her. She resists, and Trier proudly announces he was simply testing her virtue. To his discomfiture, she promptly throws him over and accepts Bonvile as an honorable suitor.

Here again, there are Restoration elements. Lord Bonvile constitutes a rake-hero; Carol and Fairfield are a pair of witty lovers. The humor consists of witty sexual similes, and the play treats realistically the doings of the upper class. Furthermore, the play tests the canons of behavior by the Enoch Arden story and that of the doubting suitor. Yet this play found little more favor in the Restoration than Massinger's; there are only two known performances in the Restoration period.[23] In effect, the pieces are right, but the glue wrong: the events of the plot are held together in the virtuous atmosphere established by the Bonavent plot. All the people in the play ooze goodness, saving only the trivial Rider and Venture. The play even asserts that one is wrong to suspect that people will not be virtuous. Bonavent errs in suspecting that his wife would deceive him; Trier loses for testing Julietta's honesty:

> *Julietta.* He that shall doubt my virtue, out of fancy,
> Merits my just suspicion and disdain.
> *Lord Bonvile.* Oh fie, Frank! practise jealousy so soon!
> Distrust the truth of her thou lov'st! suspect
> Thy own heart sooner. (V.ii)

In only one unusual way does the play show a real Restoration touch: in the sustained comparison of the horse-and-foot race to the love-chase. This conversion downward of human emotions to animal pursuit is sustained in the play by the setting, by many metaphors, and by the sudden reversals in the horse race corresponding to those in the three love-races. This one metaphor supplies what little there is of authentic Restoration tone.

A third candidate for a prototype of Restoration social comedy is James Shirley's *The Lady of Pleasure* (1635).[24] It is often so described, but there are no known performances between 1660 and 1700. It, too, has two plots. In the high plot, Celestina, an enchanting sixteen-year-old widow, adopts a rich outward show of expensive gaieties but rejects dishonorable proposals. At the same time, Lady Aretina Bornwell begins to indulge herself in gallants and costly pleasures. After she seduces one of her gallants, and her scholarly nephew Frederick, who has been corrupted by her example, makes incestuous proposals to her, and her husband tells her his estate is running out, the remorseful Aretina reforms. She retires to the country with her unwitting husband and her conscience. "Her reform," Professor Underwood notes, "like the resolution of most pre-Restoration comedy dealing with the epicure, is an unambiguous reaffirmation of the established social and moral order."[25]

There are some Restoration elements: the play deals with the upper class, emphasizes wit and the love-duel; there is even a cuckolding. But the play as a whole is more Elizabethan in character. It grows from an analogical comparison between the two ladies, Aretina and Celestina. (The names are significant, as well as the fact that their first encounter must take place through the barrier of French.) In the show and pretense of court life, Aretina is too free with her money for her limited wealth and rank, whereas Celestina's estate will bear splendor. Similarly, Aretina is too free with her gallants for her limited stock of virtue: she ends by committing adultery. Celestina's largeness of soul permits her to accept the advances of men without falling. Wealth and station in the play belong to inward virtue—"The truest wealth shines from the soul" (8). The play assumes in the Elizabethan way that the spiritual fact corresponds to the material, that appearance does not belie nature. One must, however, give appropriate value to each. Celestina can thus declare, "I say my prayers, yet can wear good clothes" (30), whereas the fop says: "'Tis sin enough to have your clothes suspected" (56). Aretina corrupts her scholarly nephew away from his delight in the harmony of nature to a concern with appearance only, a kind of discord in his knowledge (25). The highest compliment paid to Celestina is, "You are all composed of harmony" (94). The curtain lines of the play are:

> Music! And, when our ladies
> Are tired with active motion, to give
> Them rest, in some new rapture to advance
> Full mirth, our souls shall leap into a dance.

The play asserts as its final value the harmony between material facts represented by the dance and spiritual facts represented by the soul. The social events are treated as having cosmic implications.

The most un-Elizabethan, the most Restoration-like touch is the lack of retribution for Aretina's hidden guilt. The cuckolding creates an epistemological problem: the husband does not know he has been deceived, and yet he need fear no shame, for the fop does not know he has seduced Lady Aretina, who was disguised. This version of the Platonic problem of Gyges' ring sheds a thoroughly skeptical light on the assumption throughout the rest of the play that the spiritual fact and the material manifestation of it are one. Aretina herself remarks on looking in a mirror: "'Tis a false glass; sure I am more deformed. . . . My soul is miserable" (92). She finally repents: "Pardon, heaven, my shame, yet hid from the world's eye" (99). This admission and testing of the difference between appearance and nature, the spiritual and material fact, and the assumption that this difference can persist indefinitely give the play what little it has of Restoration tonality.

We have considered only six Restoration adaptations, hardly as exhaustive a treatment of the subject as needs to be made; particularly lacking is a treatment of Continental sources. Yet just these six plays, by the sheer force of their repetition, point insistently at two fundamental changes in comedies between 1642 and 1660. First, for the Stuart playwright, society, though it might be imperfect, was reformable; society for the Restoration playwright was in the nature of things corrupt, because it demanded the separation of appearance from nature. Being corrupt, it also became irrelevant to the real candor of one's emotional life. Second, the Restoration playwright did not explore by analogy and metaphor the social and cosmic implications of an event; he was interested rather in the event itself and in its causes and consequences. We have considered four Stuart plays commonly called forerunners of the Restoration comedy of manners and seen that they lack these two specific distinguishing characteristics.

Between Charles the Martyr and Charles the Merry comes a watershed. The Tudor-Stuart playwrights are on the medieval side of it; the writers of Restoration social comedy are in modern times. If we read Restoration comedy the way we read Elizabethan drama we will see only the vestige of a great theater gone, not a new beginning. Yet if we agree to grant a "willing suspension of disbelief" to the Elizabethan world-picture, we ought to grant it, too, to the Restoration writers' assumption that all things are not as they should be, a belief surely less foreign to us. Just as more modern literature, confronted with Darwin or Freud, groped, so they, faced with Descartes and Hobbes, sought an ethic in immorality.

18 . *Forms to His Conceit*

We are now in a position to summarize and to resign these plays to their fate on the stage. We have examined the eleven comedies of Etherege, Wycherley, and Congreve; we have seen they share two themes, the separation of appearance from nature and of fact from value; we have looked at the intellectual context of the plays; we have seen the critical failure. We have found the true historical situation of Etherege, Wycherley, and Congreve, namely, that in an age of wrenched and shifting values, they were groping artistically for an ethic. They found it in the harmonizing of appearances with nature through idealized personal emotion. Their comedies are not simply about "manners." On the contrary, the plays have real intellectual substance and meaning; since they do, they are not immoral either, for they are true to the purpose of literature, "the pleasure of understanding." One cannot, however, enjoy that pleasure by treating these plays like Elizabethan plays. There are superficial similarities, but the differences are far more profound, as the Restoration adaptations of earlier English plays show. These changes are revealed by the action, but more obviously by the language. In a very real sense, understanding the comedies of Etherege, Wycherley, and Congreve begins and ends with their language.

The linguistic feature that strikes one most immediately is the large number of similes as opposed to metaphors. The "like" and "as" are essential because the implicit metaphorical correspondences of the Elizabethan world-picture are no longer so strongly felt in the Restoration. Many of these similes compare sex to food, drink, dueling, sport, lawsuits, in short, anything but sex. These similes simply realize linguistically the actual disguises and sublimations society demands in sexual matters. The similes, of course, run to other things besides sex, but sexual or nonsexual, they all tend either to convert down or to convert up, either to make some noble or abstract quality into a tangible, often ignoble, "natural" thing or to translate things merely physical into neoplatonic religious imagery. A third kind of comparison is the right-way–wrong-way simile which, in comparing two things, really contrasts right and wrong ways of comparing them. This simile grows into a whole dramatic structure in which the various plots contrast alternative ways of life.

One "right" way (that is, a socially or ethically more correct or more successful approach to life) is set off against one or more "wrong" or limited ways. The somewhat complacent sense that the "right" way works out better than the "wrong," though it is often undercut ironically, is at bottom the comic equivalent of the sense of poetic justice in the serious drama of the period. Still another trope important to Restoration comedy is the language of split-man observation in which the speaker splits himself into actor and spectator by commenting dispassionately on his own actions in terms of general and universal principles.

All these figures of speech meet in the "mirror" theory of comedy, according to which the stage should serve as a mirror of the audience. Conversions up represent on the stage that fine old human tendency in the audience to trick out the basest actions in the noblest motives; conversion down simply strips off the nobility. In this mirror theory, both actors and audience are split into actor and spectator. That is, the actor in the stage-mirror acts and is at the same time the spectator of the audience; so the spectator watches the actor, while he is aware of his own actions in the real world. Restoration staging carried out this theory by setting up audiences as watchers of scene and spectacle, much more than they were for earlier English drama. The Elizabethan theater, popular and "priuat," treated the spectator as someone to be drawn into the action; even the elaborate and spectacular Stuart masques made the audience serve as the actors of the piece. In a Restoration play, however, the author is apt to call attention specifically to the stage as stage, to deliberately destroy the illusion and thus to call attention to the mirror of the stage, by cracking it.

The mirror theory, moreover, establishes a connection between the plays and the morality that critics have so worried about. The play represents a wrong way — the reflection of the audience — in order to let the audience infer a right way, "by considering the Deformity of [the hero's] Blemishes, [to] become sensible how much a Finer Thing he wou'd be without 'em." [1] At the heart, then, of the comic sense of these plays is what we have called the "right-way–wrong-way simile." The wrong way is the play's humor: the discrepancy between appearance and nature. In the early plays the right way is represented simply by the marriage of the hero — a happy ending that represents a realizable ideal. In the later plays the contrast between the right way and the wrong way becomes the contrast between two successes: the happy ending for the lover-hero (we might call him the "hero in value") as opposed to the more limited happy ending for the rake-hero (the "hero in fact"). Horner and Harcourt are examples, as are Freeman and Manly, Bellmour and Vainlove, or Fainall and Mirabell.

Thus, our eleven plays begin by being simply antiheroic. The playwright balances the idealizing conversions of the heroic manner against the conversions down of low farce. Etherege's first play, *The Comical Revenge* (1664), plays a set of variations on the theme of love as hostility, ranging from the heroic "wound of love" inflicted by the loved one's eyes to, at the lowest level, venereal disease. Etherege's second play, *She wou'd if she cou'd* (1668), less explicitly antiheroic, contrasts the liberty of sophisticated social forms which free inner desires as opposed to the restraint of forced social forms which confine the "natural man." His third — and finest — play, *The Man of Mode* (1676) develops the same idea even further. The play presents a kind of ultimate modishness as a way of harmonizing social restrictions and "wild" natural desires.

Wycherley, though he too begins with antiheroicism, develops quite differently from Etherege. His first play, *Love in a Wood* (1671), deals with the confusions caused by social conventions and restrictions; the play compares these confusions at a high, heroic level with those at the level of low London life, and shows them resolved in both cases by letting the "natural" self come out from behind its shell of appearances. Wycherley's second play, *The Gentleman Dancing-Master* (1672), contrasts appearances forced on nature with appearances that evolve from nature. His third play, *The Country Wife* (1675), marks a new departure: it contrasts social pretenses that only seem to free one with honest, irrational, ingenuous actions that are really free, a wisdom of means as opposed to a wisdom of ends. His fourth play, *The Plain-Dealer* (1676) goes still farther, setting off against each other two worlds: this limited, social world as opposed to the unlimited, impossible world of ideals.

Congreve goes on from the point at which Wycherley left off in *The Plain-Dealer*. His first play, *The Old Batchelor* (1693), shows man as surrounded by choices, particularly the choice represented by *The Plain-Dealer* between the limitations of reality and the unrealizable infinity of ideals. *The Double-Dealer* (1693), Congreve's second play, deals with natural goodness as opposed to the folly and vice of suppressing or overexpressing the self. His third play, *Love for Love* (1695), distinguishes far more successfully between the specious rationality of society on one side and on the other the irrationality of "real" reality, the fusion of "real" natures. *The Way of the World* (1700), his last play, develops just exactly what the title says: the cyclic nature of this world where social forms build up and break down as they grow from, harden over, and finally stifle the "natural" emotions that underlie them.

Thus, all these comedies develop two basic themes: first, the separation of appearance and nature, and second, the separation of reason, society, and natural law, the realm of "solid" facts on the one hand from faith, personal emotion, and supernatural and religious matters on the other. These comedies, sophisticated and jaded as they are, end like a phallic orgy in some Mycenaean village square, with a marriage; and these marriages, like the primal marriage of the heaven-father to the earth-mother, symbolize the closing of a gap, albeit the more abstract gap between appearance and nature and between rational fact and irrational value.

Having made that epitome, I have done all that I can do to convince you that the plays are meaningful, and I would sign off at this point, were I not writing about plays. It seems to me, however, that the literary critic who deals with drama has an added responsibility that other literary critics do not have, namely, to suggest ways in which his purely literary insights can be re-created into *viva voce* dramatic action. The critic's leap into abstraction derives much of its value from being the basis for the producer's realization of the concrete.

The critic at his desk senses the unity of the play by an explicit awareness of certain central themes about which the play takes form. The producer must make his audience in the theater feel the same essential unity, in Hamlet's phrase, "his whole function suiting with forms to his conceit," that is, his conception of the play. (In it, let us hope, the critics have proved of some use.) Within that conception, acting, blocking, lighting, sets, and all the theatrical specifics should co-operate to give the audience in the limited time of performance a sense of the unity of the play about its themes. Necessarily, of course, in realizing this unity, each play presents its own problems, and each company must decide on the details of production for itself. The first principle in all cases, however, is the same. Everyone working on the production of the play should agree that every detail must contribute to the central concept of the play and through it to the total, unified effect. Any detail, no matter how charming in itself, must be excluded if it does not work within the context of the play as a whole. The individual talents of producer, actor, or choreographer should unite in subordination to their single product.

Though it may seem to be elaborating the obvious, the producer's first problem is to select a play that fits the means of production at his disposal. In these days of arena theaters, outdoor theaters, platform stages, and the rest, the producer's means vary widely, and some plays will inevitably fit his means better than others. I once saw, for example, an outdoor production of *Love for Love,* though *Love for Love* is a very "indoor" play: all the action takes place in interiors and the atmosphere of the play as a whole should be one of confinement and closure — a social box from which only Valentine, Angelica, and Ben escape. Most of the difficulties in the production seemed to come from this original mistake of producing *Love for Love* outdoors. From an aesthetic point of view, the atmosphere of the theater pulled away from the atmosphere of the play. The presence of trees and hedges and other "natural" surroundings made the whole play seem artificial and destroyed the balance the play represents between naturalness and conscious artificiality. The large playing area tended to engulf the characters, though in a Restoration comedy the characters should always dominate their surroundings. There were practical difficulties, too. The actors, being out of doors, were forced to speak so loudly that the sheer effort of making themselves understood slowed down the pace of the repartee and pitched the play perilously close to the edge of monotony. All in all, the producer, who knew he had an outdoor theater, should not have picked *Love for Love.* If he wanted to do a Restoration play, he could have used Wycherley's *Love in a Wood* or Etherege's *She wou'd if she cou'd,* or Farquhar's *The Recruiting-Officer* or *The Beaux' Stratagem,* any one of which has a more outdoor atmosphere in which rustic surroundings have a part in the symbolism of the play. An arena or platform stage is even harder than the outdoors on a Restoration comedy; all the plays emphasize the scenic, two-dimensional quality of the action. Possibly directors for theaters in the round would do best to leave Restoration comedy alone.

The producer's next step should be toward a library, to establish a script. The so-called "acting editions" and other easily available editions are often full of mistakes: speeches wrongly assigned, acts and scenes wrongly divided, wordings changed, expurgations made, and so on. Second, while in the library, the producer would do well to find out what the play is about. This is a step many producers seem to hesitate to take, but it is really quite useful. Without some understanding of "the play's metaphysical core," as G. Wilson Knight calls it, there is no criterion for deciding about cuts, grouping, blocking, sets, and the like. The producer's knowledge of contrasts and themes, in short, the meaning of the play, must control his choice of details so that, as Knight says, "the grouping and action continually reflect, not the passing incident only, but its relation to the whole."[2] Producers and directors should read any book they can find that will add to their understanding of the plays.

Without exception, Restoration comedies are too long for modern performance, and the producer is faced with the problem of what and how to cut. The usual Restoration comedy is made up of two or more fairly intricate plots, and the temptation is strong to reduce the play by eliminating one of them. As we have seen, however, it is the contrast between these separate plots that develops the meaning of the play. Cutting one of these contrasting plots or incidents would almost certainly spoil the unity and balance of the theatrical experience as a whole. The producer should force himself to go through the tedious business of line-by-line cutting.

The first and most obvious things to cut are the dances. With the exception of the final dance in *The Way of the World,* the dances in the plays dealt with in this book are expendable. Originally a concession to seventeenth-century taste, they add virtually nothing to a twentieth-century audience's appreciation of the play. If the dances are to be kept, they ought not to be stiff and silent and terribly "modern"; they should have action in them and a neoclassic sense of pattern. Ideally, they should move the characters about in such a way as to develop symbolically the movements of the play as a whole.

Another set of fairly obvious things to be cut are the local jokes, the innumerable witticisms based on places or topics that were once intrinsically funny. Just as the mere mention of Brooklyn convulses a modern audience, references to "Spring-Garden" or "Will's" apparently delighted Restoration theatergoers. They fall on indifferent ears today. While some of these jokes should be left in to give the feeling of reality and contemporaneity that is an important part of the atmosphere of Restoration comedy, most of them can and should be cut. Where a local joke involves something important, the producer should feel free to insert in the script an explanatory phrase. He might, for example, change plain "Will's" to "Will's coffee-house." Alternatively, the producer might substitute the modern equivalent — if and only if it does not involve an obvious anachronism. For example, the joke in *Love for Love* based on the card game "losing Loadum" might be rephrased to "backwards rummy," a modern equivalent that is not obviously out of place. The producer should, of course, avoid cutting any lines that contribute substantially to the meaning and effect of the play as a whole — even if those lines are not particularly funny or "theatrical." He should be careful about cutting long speeches, too, for they serve to break up the staccato effect of the usual two-sided repartee. Beyond these limitations, the producer should simply try to make his Restoration comedy as funny and lively as possible.

As with all drama in the theater, the sets, lighting, and other details of production should contribute to and reinforce the effect of the play as a unified experience. They should represent in physical form "the play's metaphysical core." As we have seen in our eleven plays, one of the dominant themes of Restoration comedy is the complex relation between appearance and nature, and it is this theme the set designer can stress. The set for a Restoration comedy ought to give a sense of the complex dialectic between the outer layer of sense-impressions and the "solid" underlying core of personal and private life. The designer should give us a sense of the flatness of appearances and the roundness and depth of nature. One way of doing this — and I am sure there are many others — is to rely most heavily on flats and backdrops for the set. Only when absolutely necessary should a three-dimensional structure be permitted on the stage, for it will detract from the solidity that in Restoration comedy belongs only to the characters. Notice that Restoration customs help here; it was not customary to leave a room full of furniture. A servant was summoned to bring in chairs as they were needed. The modern producer would be wise to do the same. These plays are preeminently plays of character, and the set should enable us to see the roundness and depth and universality of the character against the illusory quality of his local and temporary surroundings. An Ibsenite respect for the solidity of things is completely out of place in Restoration comedy. As is often done in productions of Gilbert and Sullivan, the designer should create the impression in the audience's mind of an *intentionally ineffective illusion.* Small, obviously flat flats should represent solid objects, trees, bushes, urns, columns, and the like. Interiors should be bare and small, so that the characters dominate the scene. In 1957, I saw one highly successful Restoration set (by "Motley" for the Playwrights' Company production of *The Country Wife*): stylized, transparent flats with columns and such painted on them were raised and lowered with the curtain up.

It seems almost needless to say it, but a fourth-wall conception of drama will be fatal to the artificiality necessary in a production of Restoration comedy. Obviously, for interiors, the set in any theater with a proscenium arch will have to represent three walls of a room, but in such a case the director should always try to make the audience aware that the illusion of reality is just that — an illusion. The production must stress the feeling that the play is a mirror of the audience, that it only partly represents a reality of its own. The actors ought to be as aware of the audience as the audience is of them. Asides ought always to be given to the audience, and a good deal of the wit-play should be spoken out across the footlights. Play it, in other words, like a modern musical comedy. The audience ought constantly to be aware of the artificiality of the theatrical situation and the relation of its pretenses to those of the characters. Lines in the play referring to plays as such should be stressed, for the "playness of the play" functions, as we have seen, as an important symbol for the difference between social appearance and real nature.

There is very little, I think, that can be said of lighting a Restoration comedy. As in any comedy, the lighting should generally be flat, even, and bright. Effects of light and dark and deep shadows are out of the question, although an occasional shadow on one of the flats or backdrops would do no harm — it would help to establish the set as a mere "appearance."

The production as a whole should be set in an artificial framework corresponding to the prologue and epilogue of the Restoration performance. The prologue and epilogue themselves might be used to create this artificial setting, or a modern prologue and epilogue might be written for the purpose, or one might use such a device as a pair of footmen ostensibly lighting "footlights." What is needed is some action that insists, "This is a play; don't be fooled by it," yet, if it is of any length, something that begins the play with a definite suggestion of what it is all about. In short, everything the producer or director add to implement the unity of the written play should develop the effect I have called "intentionally ineffective illusion."

Costumes ought to carry out the same theme, the contrast between appearance and nature. We should be made to sense the essential nature of the individual under the welter of appearances, periwig and doublet and cravat, or the gown and headdress of the ladies. Unlike the set, however, the costume and wig ought to be solid and heavy, for these are the appearances the character presents to the world and wants to have treated as reality. Solidity of costume contrasts with solidity of character and gives a necessary sense of depth, the layers of personality all equally "real." The lighter and more farcical characters should wear light pastels, hero and heroine solid light colors, older people solid and darker colors. Make-up can help in these distinctions. Those characters whom I have described in the discussion of the plays as substituting appearance for nature ought to be very heavily made up. Their faces should acquire a pale, masklike quality to contrast with the more natural make-up of the other characters. Both the acting and costuming of the fop call for a touch of effeminacy. The best examples for the costumer and make-up man are the portraits of the period, by Lely and Kneller and Van Dyck and particularly the magnificent engraving of Charles II by David Loggan; they all bring out the essential personality from under the ponderous weight of Restoration costume and wig, giving a sense of the dialectic between the individual and what his society imposes on him.

Properties can be invaluable in suggesting this solidity of character. Hand props should be solid like costumes, though solid furniture would probably detract from the solidity of character. It might be well to scale down slightly both furniture and hand props so that the actor seems large for his surroundings, for almost always the characters of a Restoration comedy are in part types: their names, such as Trapland, Scandal, or Mrs. Frail, suggest that these people are to be thought of as enduring types somewhat larger than life. Slightly undersized properties can help re-create this literary value on the stage.

Masks and mirrors are important because they emphasize the difference between appearance and nature. Most Restoration comedies call for them in the text, but the producer should be alert for opportunities to include them wherever possible. A large mirror should be a part of any Restoration interior, and the actors should adjust their clothing and wigs frequently by it. Pocket and hand mirrors should be in almost constant use. On virtually every occasion when a feminine character appears or is about to appear on the street or out of doors she should carry a mask that she puts up to her face in the manner of a lorgnette.

Although acting Restoration comedy almost deserves a book in itself, one thing is clear. The naturalism of ordinary modern acting is as out of place as the fourth-wall convention is out of place in the production as a whole. A Restoration comedy is a stylized performance of very conscious theatrical artistry, and attempts to keep up an illusion of reality are quite unsuited to its performance. The actor must not think of himself as representing a person who responds to each stimulus in an organic, lifelike way. Restoration characters are built upon principles, and the actor must recognize the principle appropriate to the character he is acting and act with it always in his mind.

There are in general two types of people in a Restoration comedy: "humor" characters and nonhumor characters, and the actor's first task is to decide which he is playing. Humor characters are, for example, in *Love for Love,* Mr. Foresight and Sir Sampson, Don Diego and Paris in *The Gentleman Dancing-Master,* Pinchwife in *The Country Wife,* Oldfox and the Widow Blackacre in *The Plain-Dealer,* Heartwell in *The Old Batchelor,* and in *The Way of the World,* Witwoud and Petulant. The humor character tends to be simply the embodiment of one idiosyncrasy that shapes everything else the character does. The actor playing a humor character must establish in his mind the idiosyncrasy on which the character is founded, and let that one-dimensional conception color his every word and action. "I am an old, crack-brained astrologer, and therefore I react to this situation by these three criteria." The actor of a humor character should keep in mind Congreve's statement: "Our *Humour* . . . is a Colour, Taste, and Smell Diffused through all; thô our Actions are never so many, and different in Form, they are all Splinters of the same Wood." [3]

An actor who is acting a nonhumor character faces a different problem. Nonhumor characters include most of the heroes, heroines, gallants, wits, valets, and maids that form the texture of Restoration comedy. These characters, as we have seen in the discussions of the plays, operate by the interaction of appearance and nature. They are in a constant dialectic between clothing, posture, manners, pretense, disguise, and affectation on the one hand and their personal, private lives on the other. The actor must so carry out the part that the audience becomes intensely aware of this separation of appearance and nature. Instead of trying to run the emotional gamut and respond to each stimulus differently, the actor should assign any action or speech to one of three situations, each requiring its own type of acting. In the first, the appearance or manner dominates the action. This occasion includes most ordinary Restoration banter and repartee. The actor should assume a series of obviously contrived postures, use stiff, artificial gestures, speak directly to the audience as much as possible, and give his voice as affected a tone as he can contrive. In the second situation, the character is responding sincerely and naturally, openly expressing his real nature. Love scenes between hero and heroine, plotting and scheming, or urgent actions of any kind usually fall into this category. In the third situation, the most difficult to act, the character is feeling strongly, but is restrained by outer circumstances. The opening scene of *The Way of the World,* with its tense dialogue between Fainall and Mirabell, is a perfect example of this situation. This compromise level of acting calls for the style of the "appearance situation," but the actor should let a tension show in his voice and manner that reveals the pressure of "natural" emotion on appearance. The two polar situations — complete appearance and complete nature — these the actor must distinguish by widely different gestures, manners, and tones of voice, so that the audience feels the separation of the character's outward self from his inward self and, through this characterization, feels the appearance-nature theme of the comedy.

Two special acting situations come up. The first includes the "natural" characters such as Ben in *Love for Love,* or Sir Wilfull in *The Way of the World.* These characters should be played almost entirely on the level of spontaneous emotional expression — the situation I have been calling "natural." They represent people outside the central group without the style and aplomb of the central characters, and the actor who plays them must emphasize this fact. The characters ought to be so "natural" they almost become monotonous — but not quite. Occasionally such characters acquire humors as Ben does in *Love for Love* or Manly in *The Plain-Dealer.* In such a case, the actor must combine the "naturalness" of the one type with the single-minded idiosyncratic character of the other in the proportions he judges best. Humor should be strong in Ben, for example, but "nature" should dominate in Manly. The second situation that does not fit the categories I have suggested is that of "real" people, such as the orange-woman and the shoemaker in *The Man of Mode* or Trapland the scrivener and Buckram the lawyer in *Love for Love*. These people represent the "real" world of business or trade outside the coterie, and they ought to be played accordingly. They should appear very realistic, solid, even ponderous, to contrast with the elegant affectations of the central characters. These "real" or "natural" people are the only ones in Restoration comedy to be acted realistically.

The acting, by these devices, can help realize the separation of appearance and nature. This, the more dramatic of the two themes of Restoration comedy, is easier to develop in theatrical terms than the other, the separation of the "practical," social world from the irrational, intuitional world of personal emotion, which is less dramatic and more "literary." In part, the acting, by making a sharp distinction between behavior for appearances' sake and "real" behavior, will inevitably help to bring this theme out. Blocking can help, too, by associating one area of the stage with the rational, social world and another with the irrational. In any case, though, it is only through details like these that actor, director, producer, and all the others associated with the production of a Restoration comedy — indeed of any drama — can make the printed play into a complete experience in the living theater. To do so, however, there must be a continual realization of the "meaning" of the play, its "metaphysical core." Theatricality must not be thought of as a separate attribute unrelated to the thematic structure of the play as a whole. In the case of Restoration comedy, two continuing themes must be kept in mind: first, the dialectic between appearance and nature, and second, the separation of fact from value. The production of a Restoration comedy must be a re-creation of these two themes on the stage. It is in this sense that I hope this study justifies the application of the dead and solemn hand of criticism to eleven delightfully frivolous Restoration comedies. It is in this sense that I hope this criticism is not an end, but a beginning.

Notes

CHAPTER 1. GROUND RULES

1. W. M. Thackeray, "Charity and Humor" (1852), *Miscellaneous Papers and Sketches* (Boston and New York, 1895), p. 454.
2. Emmett L. Avery, *Congreve's Plays on the Eighteenth-Century Stage* (New York: Modern Language Association, 1951); pp. 150–160 discuss nineteenth- and twentieth-century performances. See also, by the same author, "*The Country Wife* in the Eighteenth Century," *Research Studies of the State College of Washington,* X (1942), 141–172; "*The Plain-Dealer* in the Eighteenth Century," *ibid.,* XI (1943), 234–256.
3. Leigh Hunt, "Biographical and Critical Notices," *The Dramatic Works of Wycherley, Congreve, Vanbrugh, and Farquhar* (London, 1840), p. lxxxviii.
4. G. Wilson Knight, *Principles of Shakespearian Production* (London: Faber, 1936), pp. 49, 54.
5. The latter half of *Dramatic Essays of the Neo-Classic Age,* ed. Henry H. Adams and Baxter Hathaway (New York: Columbia University Press, 1950), will show the trend, particularly the essays of Diderot and Beaumarchais. August Wilhelm von Schlegel, "Lectures on the Dramatic Art and Literature" (1809), Lecture XIII, *Sämmtliche Werke,* ed. Edward Böcking, 12 vols. (Leipzig, 1846), V, 233.
6. *Dialogues of Plato,* trans. Benjamin Jowett, 5 vols., 3d ed. (Oxford, 1892), *Symposium,* 223.
7. Søren Kierkegaard, *The Journals,* cited in *A Kierkegaard Anthology,* ed. Robert Bretall (Princeton: Princeton University Press, 1946), p. 134.
8. "On Wit and Humour," *Coleridge's Miscellaneous Criticism,* ed. Thomas M. Raysor (Cambridge: Harvard University Press, 1936), p. 444.

CHAPTER 2. SCENES AND HEROES

1. Alfred Harbage, *Shakespeare and the Rival Traditions* (New York: Macmillan, 1952).
2. Elizabeth G. Scanlan, "Tennis Court Theatres in England and Scotland," *Theatre Notebook,* X (1956), 10–15. Elizabeth G. Scanlan, "Reconstruction of the Duke's Playhouse in Lincoln's Inn Fields, 1661–1671," *ibid.,* X (1956), 48–50. Edward A. Langhans, "Notes on the Reconstruction of the Lincoln's Inn Fields Theatre," *ibid.,* X (1956), 112–114.
3. Richard Flecknoe, *A Short Discourse of the English Stage* (1664), reprinted in Joel E. Spingarn, *Critical Essays of the Seventeenth Century,* 3 vols. (Oxford: Oxford University Press, 1908), II, 95.
4. *The Diary of Samuel Pepys,* ed. Henry B. Wheatley, 8 vols. (London: Bell, 1926), II, 294.
5. Hyder E. Rollins, "A Contribution to the History of the English Commonwealth Drama," *Studies in Philology,* XVIII (1921), 227–333; and by the same author,

"The Commonwealth Drama: Miscellaneous Notes," *ibid.*, XX (1923), 52–69. Leslie Hotson, *The Commonwealth and Restoration Stage* (Cambridge: Harvard University Press, 1928).

6. See Alfred B. Harbage, *Annals of English Drama, 975–1700* (Philadelphia: University of Pennsylvania Press, 1940), for the years 1642–1660 for a list of drolls and other plays written in the interregnum.
7. See Alfred B. Harbage, *Cavalier Drama* (New York: Modern Language Association, 1936), pp. 13–16, 149–153, for an excellent discussion of changes in the stage and stage practices.
8. F. W. Bateson, "Contributions to a Dictionary of Critical Terms: I. 'Comedy of Manners,'" *Essays in Criticism,* I (1951), 89–93. For the translation of *ethos,* see René Rapin, *Reflections on Aristotle's Treatise of Poesie,* trans. Thomas Rymer (London, 1694), Part I, sec. xxv, p. 38.
9. "Preface to *Troilus and Cressida,*" *Selected Essays of John Dryden,* ed. W. P. Ker, 2 vols. (Oxford: Oxford University Press, 1926), I, 213.
10. Dale Underwood, *Etherege and the Seventeenth-Century Comedy of Manners,* Yale Studies in English, vol. 135 (New Haven: Yale University Press, 1957), generally, and in particular, pp. 143–159.
11. Harbage, *Cavalier Drama* (n. 7), pp. 72, 88; see also pp. 80, 250, 255–258. See also Kathleen M. Lynch, *The Social Mode of Restoration Comedy,* University of Michigan Publications in Language and Literature, vol. III (New York: Macmillan, 1926).
12. Harbage, *Cavalier Drama* (n. 7), pp. 28–71.
13. "Preface to *Annus Mirabilis*" (1667), *Essays of John Dryden* (n. 9), I, 18.
14. A. E. Parsons, "The English Heroic Play," *Modern Language Review,* III (1938), 2. Torquato Tasso, "Del Poema Eroico," *Opere,* 5 vols. (Milan, 1824), III, 20–22, 140–143.
15. Montague Summers, *Shakespeare Adaptations* (Boston: Small, Maynard, 1922), pp. 175–254.
16. *Ibid.,* "Introduction," pp. cv-cvi.
17. Hazelton Spencer, *Shakespeare Improved* (Cambridge: Harvard University Press, 1927), pp. 74–75.
18. Samuel Johnson and George Steevens, *The Works of Shakespeare,* 10 vols., 2d ed. (London, 1778), IX, 566.
19. Sir Francis Bacon, *The Advancement of Learning* (1605), Bk. II, cap. iv, ed. William A. Wright (Oxford: Clarendon Press, 1900), pp. 100–101.
20. Sir Philip Sidney, "Defense of Poesie," *Complete Works,* ed. Albert Fueillerat, 5 vols. (Cambridge University Press, 1923), III, 8.
21. Aristotle, *Poetics,* cap. XV, 11, XXV, 2–3, and XV, 1, ed. W. Hamilton Fyfe (London: Heinemann, 1927), pp. 56–59 and 100–101 (Loeb Classical Library). See also *Aristotle on the Art of Poetry,* trans. Ingram Bywater (Oxford: Clarendon Press, 1920), pp. 5–7, 85–86, and 55, and Lane Cooper, *Aristotle on the Art of Poetry* (New York: Ginn, 1913). I am greatly indebted to Professor J. Peterson Elder of the Harvard Classics Department for his perceptive assistance on this point.
22. René Rapin, *Monsieur Rapin's Reflections on Aristotle's Treatise of Poesie . . . Made English by Mr.* [*Thomas*] *Rymer* (London, 1694), Part I, sec. x, p. 14; Part II, sec. iv, p. 80.
23. *Aristotle,* trans. Bywater (n. 21), p. 43.
24. John C. Hodges, *The Library of William Congreve* (New York: New York Public Library, 1955).

25. *Dramatic Essays of the Neoclassic Age,* ed. Henry Hitch Adams and Baxter Hathaway (New York: Columbia University Press, 1950), p. xi.
26. "Premier Discours de l'Utilité et des Parties du Poème Dramatique," *Théatre de Pierre Corneille,* ed. Voltaire, 12 vols. (Paris, 1764), XII, 232–236.
27. Cecil V. Deane, *Dramatic Theory and the Rhymed Heroic Play* (Oxford: Oxford University Press, 1931). Mervyn L. Poston, "The Origin of the English Heroic Play," *Modern Language Review,* XVI (1921), 18–22. Reuben A. Brower, "Dryden's Poetic Diction and Virgil," *Philological Quarterly,* XVIII (1939), 211–217.
28. Brower, in *Philological Quarterly,* XVIII, 211–217, and John Arthos, *The Language of Natural Description in Eighteenth-Century Poetry,* University of Michigan Publications in Language and Literature, vol. XXIV (Ann Arbor: University of Michigan Press, 1949).
29. Dryden, *Selected Essays* (n. 9), I, 63.

CHAPTER 3. THE COMICAL REVENGE

1. John Downes, *Roscius Anglicanus* (London, 1708), p. 25. *The Letterbook of Sir George Etherege,* ed. Sybil Rosenfeld (Oxford: Oxford University Press, 1928), pp. 1–28.
2. John Palmer, *The Comedy of Manners* (London: Bell, 1913), p. 67. Thomas H. Fujimura, *The Restoration Comedy of Wit* (Princeton: Princeton University Press, 1952), p. 95. Clifford Leech, writing of *Marriage à la Mode* in "Restoration Tragedy: A Reconsideration," *Durham University Journal,* XLII (1950), 109.
3. William Empson, *English Pastoral Poetry* (New York: Norton, 1938), p. 47.
4. John Wilcox, *The Relation of Molière to Restoration Comedy* (New York: Columbia University Press, 1938), p. 73n.
5. My references are to page numbers in *The Dramatic Works of Sir George Etherege,* ed. H. F. B. Brett-Smith, 2 vols. (Oxford: Basil Blackwell, 1927), I, 1–88. They may be related to other editions by the following table:

   Act I, sc. i: 1–2; sc. ii: 2–8; sc. iii; 9–11; sc. iv: 11–13.
   Act II, sc. i: 13–16; sc. ii: 17–22; sc. iii: 22–29.
   Act III, sc. i: 29–30; sc. ii: 30–33; sc. iii: 33–34: sc. iv: 35–36; sc. v: 36–40; sc. vi: 40–44; sc. vii: 44–46.
   Act IV, sc. i: 46–47; sc. ii: 48–49; sc. iii: 49–51; sc. iv: 52–56; sc. v: 56–57; sc. vi: 58–59; sc. vii: 60–62.
   Act V, sc. i: 62–66; sc. ii: 66–75; sc. iii: 76–78; sc. iv: 78–81; sc. v: 81–86.
6. Dale Underwood, *Etherege and the Seventeenth-Century Comedy of Manners,* Yale Studies in English, vol. 135 (New Haven: Yale University Press, 1957), p. 56.
7. Du Fresnoy, "Observations on the Art of Painting," trans. John Dryden, *Works,* ed. Sir Walter Scott and George Saintsbury, 18 vols. (Edinburgh, 1882–1893), XVII, 363.
8. Underwood, *Etherege* (n. 6), chap. iii.

CHAPTER 4. SHE WOU'D IF SHE COU'D

1. *The Diary of Samuel Pepys,* ed. Henry B. Wheatley, 8 vols. (London: Bell, 1926), VII, 287.
2. Thomas Shadwell, "Preface to *The Humorists, A Comedy*" (1671), reprinted in Joel E. Spingarn, *Critical Essays of the Seventeenth Century,* 3 vols. (Oxford: Oxford University Press, 1908), II, 152.

3. Dale Underwood, *Etherege and the Seventeenth-Century Comedy of Manners,* Yale Studies in English, vol. 135 (New Haven: Yale University Press, 1957), chap. iv, discusses the form and structure of the play at length and with considerable subtlety. This chapter also has a number of insights into the imagery and significance of the play. Though Professor Underwood's approach differs from mine, our conclusions, not unsurprisingly, sometimes agree.

4. My references are to pages in *The Dramatic Works of Sir George Etherege,* ed. H. F. B. Brett-Smith, 2 vols. (Oxford: Basil Blackwell, 1927), II, 89–180. They may be applied to other editions by means of the following table:

 Act I, sc. i: 91–98; sc. ii: 99–104.
 Act II, sc. i: 104–110; sc. ii: 110–118.
 Act III, sc. i: 118–126; sc. ii: 126–129; sc. iii: 129–143.
 Act IV, sc. i: 143–149; sc. ii: 149–159.
 Act V, sc. i: 160–179.

5. G. Wilson Knight, *The Shakespearian Tempest,* 3d ed. (London: Methuen, 1953), p. 293.

6. Cleanth Brooks and Robert Heilman, *Understanding Drama* (New York: Holt, 1948), p. 442. The quotation refers to *The Way of the World* but is widely applicable to Restoration comedy.

7. Andrews Wanning, "Some Changes in the Prose Style of the Seventeenth Century," (Cambridge, Eng., 1938, unpub. diss. on deposit in the Harvard College Library), p. 313. This statement also refers to *The Way of the World* but applies equally to Etherege's language. Professor Wanning's chapter is entitled "The Language of Split-Man Observation," a useful term generally for the language of Restoration comedy, and one to which we shall have frequent reference.

CHAPTER 5. LOVE IN A WOOD

1. The dating of the play is discussed in *Plays,* ed. William C. Ward (London, 1893), pp. 3–5. See also Allardyce Nicoll, *A History of Restoration Drama, 1660–1700* (Cambridge: Cambridge University Press, 1928), pp. 225–226. The source for the anecdote about the Duchess of Cleveland is John Dennis, Letter, "To the Honourable *Major* Pack. Containing some remarkable Passages of Mr. *Wycherley's* Life" (September 1, 1720), reprinted in *The Critical Works of John Dennis,* ed. Edward Niles Hooker, 2 vols. (Baltimore: Johns Hopkins Press, 1939), II, 409.

2. My references are to pages in *The Complete Works of William Wycherley,* ed. Montague Summers, 4 vols. (London: Nonesuch Press, 1924), I, 65–150. They may be related to other editions by the following table:

 Act I, sc. i: 73–79; sc. ii: 79–87.
 Act II, sc. i: 87–95; sc. ii: 95–99; sc. iii: 99–100; sc. iv: 100–102.
 Act III, sc. i: 103–115; sc. ii: 115–118.
 Act IV, sc. i: 119–124; sc. ii: 124–126; sc. iii: 126–134.
 Act V, sc. i: 134–146; sc. ii: 147–149.

3. James U. Rundle, "Wycherley and Caldéron: A Source for *Love in a Wood,*" *PMLA,* LXIV (1949), 701–707.

4. Bonamy Dobrée, *Restoration Comedy: 1660–1720* (Oxford: Clarendon Press, 1924), p. 83.

CHAPTER 6. DISGUISE, COMIC AND COSMIC

1. Ashley H. Thorndike, *English Comedy* (New York: Macmillan, 1929), p. 341.
2. William Empson, *English Pastoral Poetry* (New York: Norton, 1938), pp. 11–13.
3. Theodore Spenser, *Shakespeare and the Nature of Man*, 2d ed. (New York; Macmillan, 1955), p. 14.
4. Edmund Spenser, "An Hymne in Honovr of Beavtie" (1596), lines 132–133, 139–140.
5. *Ibid.*, lines 141–144, 148–150.
6. *Ibid.*, lines 157–158.
7. A. P. Rossiter, *English Drama from Early Times to the Elizabethans* (London: Hutchinson's University Library, 1950), chap. viii.
8. Basil Willey, *The Seventeenth Century Background* (London: Chatto and Windus, 1934), chap i, sec. 3.
9. Richard Hooker, *Of the Laws of Ecclesiastical Polity* (1594), Book I, sec. iii.
10. *The Diary of Samuel Pepys*, ed. Henry B. Wheatley, 8 vols. (London: Bell, 1926), II, 88 (Sept. 1, 1661.)
11. Gilbert Burnet, *History of His Own Time*, ed. Osmund Airy, 2 vols. (Oxford, 1897), I, 473.
12. Leigh Hunt, "Biographical and Critical Notices," *The Dramatic Works of Wycherley, Congreve, Vanbrugh, and Farquhar* (London, 1840), p. xi. Hunt gives Voltaire as his source, but Voltaire does not mention the story. Wycherley's modern editor says, "Although the reference to Voltaire may be incorrect, there can be no doubt as to the truth of the story which is alluded to in contemporary manuscript satires." (*The Complete Works of William Wycherley*, ed. Montague Summers, 4 vols. [London: Nonesuch Press, 1924], I, 36.)
13. "Letter from Thomas Henshaw to Sir Robert Paston," John Ives, *Select Papers Chiefly Relating to English Antiquities* (London, 1773), p. 39.
14. Burnet, *History* (n. 11), I, 476.
15. Anthony Hamilton, *The Memoirs of Count Grammont*, ed. Gordon Goodwin, 2 vols. (London: A. H. Bullen, 1903), II, 82–83.
16. Gilbert Burnet, *Some Passages of the Life and Death of the . . . Earl of Rochester* (London, 1696), p. 27.
17. *Memoirs of Count Grammont* (n. 15), II, 207–208.
18. *Ibid.*, II, 84–92. *The Diary of Samuel Pepys*, ed. Henry B. Wheatley, 8 vols. (London: Bell, 1926), IV, 336 (February 21, 1664/5).
19. *Memoirs of Count Grammont* (n. 15), I, 116.
20. *The Dramatic Records of Sir Henry Herbert*, ed. Joseph Q. Adams, Cornell Studies in English (London: Humphry Milford, 1917), p. 56.
21. The anecdote is recounted by Hamilton's editor, Gordon Goodwin, *Memoirs of Count Grammont* (n. 15), II, 247–248; it also appears in Peter Cunningham's *The Story of Nell Gwyn* (New York, 1887), pp. 162–163. Both writers are apparently quoting from the same seventeenth-century source.
22. John Sheffield, Earl of Mulgrave, later Duke of Buckingham, "A Short Character of Charles II, King of England," reprinted in *The Dramatick Works of his Grace, George Villiers, Late Duke of Buckingham*, 2 vols., 3d ed. (London, 1715), II, 241. Burnet, *History* (n. 11), II, 468.
23. "Maxims of State, Applicable to all Times Written by the Right Honourable the Marquiss of Hallifax," in *The Dramatick Works of . . . George Villiers* (n. 22),

Maxim XXI, vol. II, p. 249. These maxims, however, are not by Halifax, but the authorship is not important for the purposes of the present study. Miss H. C. Foxcroft, *The Life and Letters of Sir George Savile, Bart.*, 2 vols. (London, 1898), II, 449–450, attributes this maxim to Henry St. John, Viscount Bolingbroke. Halifax's later editor, Sir Walter Raleigh, does not discuss the problem.

24. "A Character of King Charles II," *The Complete Works of George Savile, Marquess of Halifax,* ed. Sir Walter Raleigh (Oxford: Clarendon Press, 1912), p. 192.
25. Two examples occur in the "Preface to *Troilus and Cressida*" and the "Preface to *Albion and Albianus,*" *Selected Essays of John Dryden,* ed. W. P. Ker, 2 vols. (Oxford: Oxford University Press, 1926), I, 227, 270.
26. "A Parallel of Poetry and Painting" (1695), *Selected Essays* (n. 25), II, 147–148.
27. *The Spectator,* nos. 62 (May 11, 1711) and 63 (May 12, 1711).
28. See Horace, *Epistle to the Pisos,* trans. James Harry and Sara Catron Smith, in *The Great Critics,* ed. J. H. Smith and Edd Winfield Parks, 3d ed. (New York: Norton, 1951), p. 123.
29. Sir Philip Sidney, "Defense of Poesie," *Complete Works,* ed. Albert Feuillerat, 5 vols. (Cambridge: Cambridge University Press, 1912–1926), III, 5.
30. Edmund Bolton, "Hypercritica: or a Rule of Judgement, for Writing or Reading our History's" (1618), *Critical Essays of the Seventeenth Century,* ed. Joel E. Spingarn, 3 vols. (Bloomington: Indiana University Press, 1957), I, 107. Sir William Alexander, Earl of Stirling, "Anacrisis, or A Censure of Some Poets Ancient and Modern" (1634), Spingarn, I, 182.
31. Thomas Nashe, *Pierce Penilesse his Supplication to the Diuell* (1592), *Works,* ed. Ronald B. McKerrow, 5 vols. (London: A. H. Bullen, 1904–1910), I, 213.
32. John C. Hodges, *The Library of William Congreve* (New York: New York Public Library, 1955), p. 68.
33. "Letter to Charles Cotton," *Complete Works* (n. 24), pp. 185–186.
34. Sir William Temple, "Of Poetry" (1690), Spingarn (n. 30), III, 80, 100–101.
35. John Sheffield, Earl of Mulgrave, "An Essay upon Poetry" (1682), Spingarn (n. 30), II, 287, 291.
36. William Wotton, "Reflections upon Ancient and Modern Learning" (1694), Spingarn (n. 30), III, 212.
37. Thomas Shadwell, "Preface to *The Humorists, A Comedy*" (1671), Spingarn (n. 30), II, 153.
38. John Webster, *Academiarum Examen* (London, 1654), pp. 88–89.
39. Richard Flecknoe, *A Short Discourse of the English Stage* (1664), Spingarn (n. 30), II, 95.
40. John Bunyan, *Grace Abounding and Pilgrim's Progress,* ed. John Brown (Cambridge: Cambridge University Press, 1907), "The Author's Apology for his Book," p. 138.
41. Joseph Glanvill, "Essay concerning Preaching" (1678), Spingarn (n. 30), II, 277.
42. *The Tatler,* no. 167 (May 4, 1710); *The Spectator,* no. 156 (August 29, 1711).
43. Thomas Sprat, *The History of the Royal-Society of London* (1667), Spingarn (n. 30), II, 116, 118.
44. See Richard F. Jones, "Science and English Prose Style in the Third Quarter of the Seventeenth Century," *PMLA,* XLV (1930), 977–1009.
45. *Meditations on the First Philosophy,* Meditation VI: "Of the Existence of Material Things," *The Philosophical Works of Descartes,* trans. Elizabeth S. Haldane and G. R. T. Ross (Cambridge: Cambridge University Press, 1912), p. 191.

46. Dante, *Purgatorio,* xviii, 49–54, *The Divine Comedy of Dante Alighieri,* trans. Charles Eliot Norton, rev. ed., 3 vols. (Boston and New York: Houghton, Mifflin, 1902), II, 137. *Summa Theologica,* i.3.5.

47. *The Canons and Decrees of the Council of Trent,* ed. T. A. Buckley (London, 1851), Session XIII (1551), Canons XI and II.

48. Louis I. Bredvold, *The Intellectual Milieu of John Dryden* (Ann Arbor: University of Michigan Press, 1934), pp. 1–19.

49. John Locke, *An Essay concerning Human Understanding* (1690), ed. Alexander Campbell Fraser, 2 vols. (Oxford, 1894), Book IV, chap. xii, sec. 11: Book II, chap. xxiii, sec. 11.

50. Bernard de Fontenelle, *A Plurality of Worlds . . . Translated into English by Mr. [John] Glanvill* (London, 1688), p. 7.

51. Joseph Glanvill, *Scepsis scientifica* (1664), "Address to the Royal Society," chap. ix, chap. xxi, p. 133.

52. Thomas Hobbes, *Leviathan,* Book I, chap. i, "Of Sense," *The English Works of Thomas Hobbes,* ed. Sir William Molesworth, 11 vols. (London, 1840), III, 1. *Treatise of Human Nature,* chap. ii, *English Works,* IV, 8.

53. Edwin A. Burtt, *The Metaphysical Foundations of Modern Physical Science* (New York: Harcourt, Brace, 1927), pp. 5, 73–74, 108, 236–237.

54. Alfred North Whitehead, *Science and the Modern World* (New York: Macmillan, 1925), pp. 79–80.

55. *[John] Aubrey's Brief Lives,* ed. Oliver Lawson Dick (Ann Arbor: University of Michigan Press, 1957), p. 152.

56. "On Reason and Religion," *The Dramatick Works of . . . Buckingham* (n. 22), II, 182.

57. Dale Underwood, *Etherege and the Seventeenth-Century Comedy of Manners,* Yale Studies in English, Vol. 135 (New Haven: Yale University Press, 1957), pp. 102–103.

58. Andrews J. Wanning, "Some Changes in the Prose Style of the Seventeenth Century" (Cambridge, Eng., 1938, unpub. diss.), pp. 328–329. This admirable work is on deposit in the Harvard College Library, and I am quoting by the kind permission of Professor Wanning.

59. John Dryden, *The State of Innocence,* II.i, *The Works of John Dryden,* ed. Sir Walter Scott and George Saintsbury, 18 vols. (Edinburgh, 1882–1892), V, 133.

60. Hodges, *Library of William Congreve* (n. 32).

61. *The Letterbook of Sir George Etherege,* ed. Sybil Rosenfeld (Oxford: Oxford University Press, 1928), p. 226 (June 23/July 3, 1687) and p. 187 (August 11/21, 1687).

62. *Ibid.,* p. 62 (January 9/19, 1685/6).

63. *The Complete Works of William Wycherley,* ed. Montague Summers, 4 vols. (London: Nonesuch Press, 1924), IV, 241–242.

64. Wycherley to Pope (January 19, 1707/8), *The Correspondence of Alexander Pope,* ed. George Sherburn, 5 vols. (Oxford: Oxford University Press, 1956), I, 39.

65. *The Mourning Bride, Poems & Miscellanies,* ed. Bonamy Dobrée, The World's Classics (Oxford: Oxford University Press, 1928), p. 204.

66. *Comedies by William Congreve,* ed. Bonamy Dobrée, The World's Classics (London: Oxford University Press, 1925), p. 5.

67. *Ibid.,* pp. 7–8.

CHAPTER 7. THE GENTLEMAN DANCING-MASTER

1. My references are to pages in *The Complete Works of William Wycherley,* ed. Montague Summers, 4 vols. (London: Nonesuch Press, 1924), I, 151–233. They may be related to other editions by the following table:

   Act II, sc. i: 172–185.
   Act I, sc. i: 157–164; sc. ii: 164–172.
   Act III, sc. i: 185–198.
   Act IV, sc. i: 199–215.
   Act V, sc. i: 216–231.

2. "Little Briar-Rose," *Folk-Lore and Fable: Aesop, Grimm, and Andersen,* ed. Charles W. Eliot, The Harvard Classics, vol. 17 (New York, 1909), pp. 146–149. See also Joseph Campbell, *The Hero with a Thousand Faces* (New York: Bollingen Foundation, 1949), pp. 63, 243.

CHAPTER 8. THE COUNTRY WIFE

1. William Hazlitt, "On Wycherley, Congreve, Vanbrugh, and Farquhar" (1819), *Works,* ed. P. P. Howe, Centenary Edition, 21 vols. (London: Dent, 1930–1934), VI, 76.
2. George Nettleton, *English Drama of the Restoration and Eighteenth Century* (New York: Macmillan, 1914), p. 80.
3. Kathleen M. Lynch, *The Social Mode of Restoration Comedy,* University of Michigan Publications in Language and Literature, vol. III (New York: Macmillan, 1926), pp. 169–170, is one example.
4. Sir Richard Steele, *The Tatler,* no. 3 (April 16, 1709).
5. Henry Ten Eyck Perry, *The Comic Spirit in Restoration Drama* (New Haven: Yale University Press, 1925), p. 43.
6. L. J. Potts, *Comedy* (London: Hutchinson's University Library, 1948), p. 55.
7. My references are to pages in *The Complete Works of William Wycherley,* ed. Montague Summers, 4 vols. (London: Nonesuch Press, 1924), II, 1–88. They may be related to other editions by means of the following table:
   Act I, sc. i: 11–21.
   Act II, sc. i: 22–34.
   Act III, sc. i: 35–37; sc. ii: 37–50.
   Act IV, sc. i: 50–54; sc. ii: 54–59; sc. iii: 59–68; sc. iv: 68–70.
   Act V, sc. i: 70–73; sc. ii: 73–75; sc. iii: 75–77; sc. iv: 78–87.
8. Robert W. White, *The Abnormal Personality* (New York: Ronald Press, 1948), p. 278.
9. Bonamy Dobrée, *Restoration Comedy: 1660–1720* (Oxford: Clarendon Press, 1924), p. 94.
10. F. W. Bateson, "Second Thoughts: II. L. C. Knights and Restoration Comedy," *Essays in Criticism,* VII (April 1957), 65.
11. *Ibid.*

CHAPTER 9. THE MAN OF MODE

1. My references are to pages in *The Dramatic Works of Sir George Etherege,* ed. H. F. B. Brett-Smith, 2 vols. (Boston and New York, 1927), II, 182–288. They may be related to other editions by means of the following table:

Act I, sc. i: 189–204.
Act II, sc. i: 205–210; sc. ii: 210–218.
Act III, sc. i: 219–224; sc. ii: 225–233; sc. iii: 233–244.
Act IV, sc. i: 244–257; sc. ii: 258–263; sc. iii: 264.
Act V, sc. i: 265–274; sc. ii: 274–287.

2. Dale Underwood, *Etherege and the Seventeenth-Century Comedy of Manners* Yale Studies in English, vol. 135 (New Haven: Yale University Press, 1957), p. 79.
3. Professor Underwood (*ibid.*, pp. 90–91) goes so far as to say that Dorimant is following Harriet to the country more for a "ruin" than a romance.
4. Letter to Mr. Poley, January 2/12, 1687/8, *The Letterbook of Sir George Etherege,* ed. Sybil Rosenfeld (Oxford: Oxford University Press, 1928), p. 309.

CHAPTER 10. THE PLAIN-DEALER

1. *The Complete Works of William Wycherley,* ed. Montague Summers, 4 vols. (London: Nonesuch Press, 1924), II, 89–196. My references are to pages of this edition; they may be related to other editions by means of the following table:

Act I, sc. i: 105–118.
Act. II, sc. i: 119–140.
Act III, sc. i: 140–158.
Act IV, sc. i: 158–166; sc. ii: 166–176.
Act V, sc. i: 177–180; sc. ii: 180–189; sc. iii: 189–192; sc. iv: 192–196.

2. John Dennis, "Decay and Defects of Dramatick Poetry" (1725?), *Critical Works,* ed. Edward Niles Hooker, 2 vols. (Baltimore: Johns Hopkins Press, 1939), II, 277.
3. John Dryden, "The Author's Apology for Heroic Poetry and Poetic Licence" (1677), *Selected Essays of John Dryden,* ed. W. P. Ker, 2 vols. (Oxford: Oxford University Press, 1926), I, 182. This passage is sometimes cited in favor of the proposition that this play is an attack on Restoration society; the word "general" ought to be underlined.
4. William Hazlitt, "On Wycherley, Congreve, Vanbrugh, and Farquhar" (1819), *Works,* ed. P. P. Howe, 21 vols., Centenary Edition (London: Dent, 1930–1934), VI, 78.
5. Leigh Hunt, "Biographical Notices," *The Dramatic Works of Wycherley, Congreve, Vanbrugh, and Farquhar* (London, 1840), p. xvii.
6. Macaulay, see below, p. 202, Chap. 16. George Meredith, *An Essay on Comedy* (London: Constable, 1919), pp. 30–31.
7. W. Heldt, "A Chronological and Critical Review," *Neophilologus,* VIII (1923), 118. Felix E. Schelling, "The Restoration Drama I," *The Cambridge History of English Literature* (Cambridge: Cambridge University Press, 1912), VIII, 145. See also Schelling, *English Drama* (London: Dent, 1914), p. 264.
8. Louis Cazamian, *A History of English Literature* (New York: Macmillan, 1927), II, 46.
9. Joseph Wood Krutch, *Comedy and Conscience after the Restoration* (New York: Columbia University Press, 1924), p. 46.
10. George Nettleton, *English Drama of the Restoration and Eighteenth Century* (New York: Macmillan, 1914), p. 83.
11. William Archer, *The Old Drama and the New* (New York: Dodd, Mead, 1929), p. 31.
12. Jean-Jacques Rousseau, "Lettre sur les Spectacles," *Oeuvres,* 20 vols. (Paris, 1817), VIII, 53 and generally.

13. John Wilcox, *The Relation of Molière to Restoration Comedy* (New York: Columbia University Press, 1938), p. 96.
14. *Ibid.*, pp. 100–101.
15. Bonamy Dobrée, *Restoration Comedy: 1660–1720* (Oxford: Clarendon Press, 1924), p. 87.
16. Henry Ten Eyck Perry, *The Comic Spirit in Restoration Drama* (New Haven: Yale University Press, 1925), pp. 49–50.
17. George Granville, Lord Lansdowne, "A Letter with a Character of Mr. *Wycherley*," *The Genuine Works in Verse and Prose*, 3 vols. (London, 1736), II, 112–113.
18. Dryden, "Discourse concerning Satire," *Essays* (n. 3), II, 85.
19. Thomas H. Fujimura, *The Restoration Comedy of Wit* (Princeton: Princeton University Press, 1952), pp. 147–149.
20. Kathleen M. Lynch, *The Social Mode of Restoration Comedy*, University of Michigan Publications in Language and Literature, vol. III (New York: Macmillan, 1926), pp. 172–173.
21. Alexander H. Chorney, "Wycherley's Manly Reinterpreted," *Essays Critical and Historical Dedicated to Lily B. Campbell* (Berkeley: University of California Press, 1950), p. 164.
22. Fujimura, *Restoration Comedy* (n. 19), p. 150.
23. Dobrée, *Restoration Comedy* (n. 15), pp. 87–88.
24. Søren Kierkegaard, *Fear and Trembling*, trans. Walter Lowrie (Princeton: Princeton University Press, 1941), pp. 19–20.
25. Ernst Cassirer, *Essay on Man* (New Haven: Yale University Press, 1944), p. 150.
26. Epigrams LXXIX and XXI, *Works* (n. 1), IV, 117 and 111.
27. William Empson, *The Structure of Complex Words* (London: Chatto and Windus, 1951), pp. 192–194.
28. Andrews Wanning, "Some Changes in the Prose Style of the Seventeenth Century" (Cambridge, Eng., 1938, unpub. diss., see n. 58, Chap. 6) title, chap. 4, sec. 5.
29. Leigh Hunt (n. 5), "Biographical and Critical Notices," p. xxx.
30. Wanning, "Some Changes" (n. 28), pp. 311, 431.
31. *The Plays of William Shakespeare*, ed. Samuel Johnson and George Steevens, 2d ed., 10 vols. (London, 1778), I, 204–205.
32. Ernest Bernbaum, *The Drama of Sensibility* (Boston: Ginn, 1915), pp. 4–6.
33. *Ibid.*, p. 66.

CHAPTER 11. A SENSE OF SCHISM

1. Thomas Hobbes, *Treatise of Human Nature*, chap. ix, part 13, *English Works*, ed. Sir William Molesworth, 11 vols. (London, 1839–1845), IV, 46.
2. John Dryden, "Preface to *An Evening's Love or The Mock Astrologer*" (1671), *Selected Essays*, ed. W. P. Ker, 2 vols. (Oxford: Oxford University Press, 1926), I, 143.
3. Sir John Vanbrugh, "A Short Vindication of *The Relapse* and *The Provok'd Wife*," *Complete Works*, ed. Bonamy Dobrée and Geoffrey Webb, 4 vols. (Bloomsbury: Nonesuch Press, 1927), I, 206–207.
4. René Rapin, *Monsieur Rapin's Reflections on Aristotle's Treatise of Poesie . . . Made English by Mr.* [*Thomas*] *Rymer* (London, 1694), Part II, sec. xxv, p. 131.

5. *The Mourning Bride, Poems & Miscellanies,* ed. Bonamy Dobrée, The World's Classics (London: Oxford University Press, 1925), p. 275.
6. "A Short Vindication of *The Relapse* and *The Provok'd Wife*" (n. 3), I. 206.
7. Thomas D'Urfey, Prologue to *The Fool Turn'd Critick* (London, 1678).
8. T. S. Eliot, "The Metaphysical Poets," *Selected Essays,* 2d ed. (New York: Harcourt, Brace, 1950), p. 247.
9. Douglas Bush, *The Renaissance and English Humanism* (Toronto: University of Toronto Press, 1939), pp. 54–55, 85–86.
10. Arthur O. Lovejoy, *Essays in the History of Ideas* (Baltimore: Johns Hopkins Press, 1948), pp. 315–317.
11. Basil Willey, *The Seventeenth Century Background* (London: Chatto and Windus, 1934), chap. i, sec. 1.
12. Perry Miller, *The New England Mind: The Seventeenth Century,* 2d ed. (Cambridge: Harvard University Press, 1954), p. 14.
13. John Calvin, *Institutes of the Christian Religion* (1536), I.xvi.4, trans. John Allen, 2 vols. (Philadelphia, n.d.), I, 186.
14. Sir Walter Raleigh, Preface to *The History of the World* (London, 1614), *Works,* 8 vols. (Oxford, 1829), II, v–vi. See also *Sir Walter Raleigh: Selections from His Writings,* ed. G. E. Hadow (Oxford: Oxford University Press, 1917), pp. 40–41.
15. Marjorie Nicolson, *The Breaking of the Circle* (Evanston: Northwestern University Press, 1950), p. xviii.
16. *Ibid.,* p. xviii.
17. Joseph Glanvill, *Scepsis scientifica* (London, 1664), b3ᵛ. John Locke, *An Essay concerning Human Understanding* (1690), ed. Alexander Campbell Fraser, 2 vols. (Oxford, 1894), Bk. IV, chap. vi, sec. 11.
18. Thomas Burnet, *The Theory of the Earth* (London, 1684), Bk. II, chap. iv, pp. 210 and 205.
19. Bernard de Fontenelle, *A Plurality of Worlds . . . Translated into English by Mr.* [*John*] *Glanvill* (London, 1688), p. 10.
20. Blaise Pascal, *Pensées,* ed. Victor Giraud (Paris, 1924), no. 793.
21. Burnet, *Theory of the Earth* (n. 18) IV.ix, p. 208.
22. Basil Willey, "The Touch of Cold Philosophy," in *The Seventeenth Century: Essays by and in Honor of Richard Foster Jones* (Stanford: Stanford University Press, 1951), p. 373.
23. Sir Thomas Browne, *Religio Medici,* I.x, *Works,* ed. Geoffrey Keynes, 6 vols. (London: Faber, 1928–1931), I, 15.
24. Herschel Baker, *The Wars of Truth* (Cambridge: Harvard University Press, 1952), pp. 8–9.
25. John Bunyan, *Grace Abounding and Pilgrim's Progress,* ed. John Brown (Cambridge, 1907), p. 267. Hobbes, "Philosophical Rudiments," chap. xv, part 14, English Works (n. 1), II, 216.
26. Fontenelle, *A Plurality of Worlds* (n. 19), p. 10.
27. Willey, *Seventeenth Century Background* (n. 11), chap. i, sec. 1.
28. *Hamlet,* IV.v.124–125.
29. *Richard II,* III.ii.54–55.
30. Quoted in J. E. Neale, *Elizabeth I* (Garden City: Doubleday Anchor Books, 1957), p. 388.
31. George Chapman, *The Revenge of Bussy D'Ambois,* IV.i.137–146, *Dramatic Works,* ed. John Pearson, 3 vols. (London, 1873), II, 152.

32. "Contemplation of the State of Man," *The Whole Works of the Right Rev. Jeremy Taylor,* ed. Reginald Heber, 11 vols. (London, 1828), III, 500.
33. *Paradiso,* xxxiii, 91–95, *The Divine Comedy of Dante Alighieri,* trans. Charles Eliot Norton, rev. ed., 3 vols. (Boston: Houghton, Mifflin, 1902), III, 255.
34. Joseph Glanvill, *The Vanity of Dogmatizing* (London, 1661), p. 68.
35. Burnet, *Theory of the Earth* (n. 18), IV, ix, 203–210.
36. John Dennis, "On Poetical Justice" (1712), *Critical Works,* ed. Edward N. Hooker, 2 vols. (Baltimore: Johns Hopkins Press, 1939), II, 20.
37. Henry Vaughan, "They are all gone into the world of light."
38. Anon., *A Comparison between the Two Stages* (1702), ed. Staring B. Wells (Princeton: Princeton University Press, 1942), p. 1.
39. *The Tatler,* no. 42 (July 16, 1709).
40. *Paradise Lost,* IV, 313–318, 738–740, 765–768.
41. R. H. Tawney, *Religion and the Rise of Capitalism* (New York: Harcourt, Brace, 1926), pp. 277, 279.
42. Edwin A. Burtt, *The Metaphysical Foundations of Modern Physical Science* (New York: Harcourt, Brace, 1927). Alfred North Whitehead, *Science and the Modern World* (New York: Macmillan, 1925).
43. Willey, *The Seventeenth Century Background* (n. 11); Baker, *The Wars of Truth* (n. 24).
44. Dale Underwood, *Etherege and the Seventeenth-Century Comedy of Manners* Yale Studies in English, vol. 135 (New Haven: Yale University Press, 1957), pp. 8–9, 95–101, and generally.
45. Marjorie Nicolson, "The Telescope and Imagination," *Modern Philology,* XXXII (1935), 233–260.
46. *Paradise Lost,* XII, 469–478.
47. Wylie Sypher, *Four Stages of Renaissance Style* (Garden City: Doubleday Anchor Books, 1955), pp. 212, 239.
48. Romans vi.1-2.
49. Romans v.20.
50. *The Tatler,* no. 33 (June 25, 1709).
51. John Dryden, "Preface to *An Evening's Love, or The Mock Astrologer*" (1671), *Selected Essays* (n. 2), I, 143–144.
52. *Paradise Lost,* XII, 587.
53. *King Lear,* I.ii.128–135; *Othello,* I.iii.322–324.
54. Underwood, *Etherege* (n. 44), p. 63n.
55. Dryden, *I The Conquest of Granada,* I.i.206–209.
56. Sir Thomas Browne, *Religio Medici,* I.x, *Works* (n. 23), I, 20.
57. *The Letterbook of Sir George Etherege,* ed. Sybil Rosenfeld (Oxford: Oxford University Press, 1928), p. 327 (February 13/23, 1687/8).
58. *The Works of Sir George Etheredge: Plays and Poems,* ed. A. W. Verity (London, 1888), pp. 397–399.
59. *The Complete Works of William Wycherley,* ed. Montague Summers, 4 vols. (London: Nonesuch Press, 1924), III, 41.
60. Epigrams CCLXII, LXXXVI, *Works,* IV, 137, 118.
61. *Works,* IV, 206.
62. Letterbook (n. 57), p. 305 (December 19, 1687).

63. Act III, scene i. *The Mourning Bride, Poems, & Miscellanies,* ed. Bonamy Dobrée, The World's Classics (London: Oxford University Press, 1928), p. 112.
64. *Ibid.,* p. 204.
65. John C. Hodges, *The Library of William Congreve* (New York: New York Public Library, 1955).
66. *The Mourning Bride* (n. 63), p. 378.

CHAPTER 12. THE OLD BATCHELOR

1. "A Letter with a Character of Mr. Wycherley," *The Genuine Works in Verse and Prose,* 3 vols. (London, 1736), II, 112–113.
2. Samuel Johnson, "William Congreve," *Lives of the English Poets,* ed. George B. Hill, 3 vols. (Oxford: Clarendon Press, 1905), II, 219.
3. John C. Hodges, *William Congreve the Man* (New York: Modern Language Association, 1941), p. 44.
4. Kathleen M. Lynch, *A Congreve Gallery* (Cambridge: Harvard University Press, 1951) adopts Professor Hodges' (n. 3) proofs.
5. Voltaire, *Letters concerning the English Nation (1728–31)* (London: L. Davis and C. Reymers, 1760), p. 149. For reasons unknown, the anecdote does not appear in French editions.
6. Lynch, *A Congreve Gallery,* pp. 66–67. See also Bonamy Dobrée, "Congreve's Life," in *Variety of Ways* (Oxford: Clarendon Press, 1932).
7. The edition to which I refer is: *Comedies by William Congreve,* ed. Bonamy Dobrée, The World's Classics (London: Oxford University Press, 1925), pp. 13–109. The numbers in the text refer to pages in this edition, but they may be related to other editions by the following table:

   Act I: 25–36.
   Act II: 37–51.
   Act III: 51–67.
   Act IV: 67–90.
   Act V: 90–108.

   I have not listed scenes in Congreve's plays because they vary widely in the several current editions of the plays. Congreve himself dropped the sensible English style of scene division (the scenes changing with the acts or with a change of locality), which he had used in the early quartos, and in the definitive *Works of Mr. William Congreve* (1710) he adopted the French style (in which the scenes change with the entrance and exit of each character). Thus, for example, in *The Old Batchelor,* in Act IV alone, there are twenty-two scenes in Dobrée's edition, which follows the *Works* of 1710, four in Bateson's and Summers' editions, which follow the quarto, and six in the Mermaid edition.
8. Henry Ten Eyck Perry, *The Comic Spirit in Restoration Drama* (New Haven: Yale University Press, 1925), p. 61.
9. Johnson, "William Congreve" (n. 2), p. 216.
10. Richard Steele, *The Tatler,* no. 193, July 4, 1710.
11. Johnson, "William Congreve" (n. 2), p. 216.
12. Dobrée, *Variety of Ways* (n. 6), pp. 82–83.
13. F. W. Bateson, *The Works of Congreve* (London: Peter Davies, 1930), p.xvii.
14. *The Mourning Bride, Poems, & Miscellanies,* ed. Bonamy Dobrée (London: Oxford University Press, 1928), 98–99.
15. Wylie Sypher, *Four Stages of Renaissance Style* (New York: Doubleday Anchor Books, 1955), generally, and esp. pp. 180–185.

CHAPTER 13. THE DOUBLE-DEALER

1. *The Letters of John Dryden,* ed. Charles E. Ward (Durham: Duke University Press, 1942), Letter to Walsh, December 12 [1693], p. 63.
2. Macaulay, "The Comic Dramatists of the Restoration," *Works,* 12 vols. (London: Longmans, Green, 1898), IX, 373.
3. The edition to which I refer is: *Comedies by William Congreve,* ed. Bonamy Dobrée, The World's Classics (London: Oxford University Press, 1925), pp. 111–212. The numbers in the text refer to pages in this edition, but they may be related to other editions by the following table:

   Act I: 123–135.
   Act II: 136–150.
   Act III: 150–169.
   Act IV: 169–192.
   Act V: 192–211.
4. Bonamy Dobrée, *Restoration Comedy: 1660–1720* (Oxford: Clarendon Press, 1924), pp. 129–130.

CHAPTER 14. LOVE FOR LOVE

1. *A Midsummer-Night's Dream,* V.i.7ff.
2. The edition to which I refer is: *Comedies by William Congreve,* ed. Bonamy Dobrée, The World's Classics (London: Oxford University Press, 1925), pp. 213–332. The numbers in the text refer to pages in this edition, but they may be related to other editions by the following table:

   Act I: 219–240.
   Act II: 240–261.
   Act III: 261–286.
   Act IV: 286–311.
   Act V: 312–331.
3. "*Mr.* Congreve, to *Mr.* Dennis *Concerning Humour in Comedy,*" *ibid.,* p. 7.
4. Samuel Johnson, *Lives of the English Poets,* ed. George Birkbeck Hill, 3 vols. (Oxford: Clarendon Press, 1905), II, 218.
5. Coleridge, "On Wit and Humour," *Coleridge's Miscellaneous Criticism,* ed. Thomas M. Raysor (Cambridge: Harvard University Press, 1936), p. 443.
6. *The Mourning Bride, Poems & Miscellanies,* ed. Bonamy Dobrée, The World's Classics (London: Oxford University Press, 1928), p. 286.
7. Allardyce Nicoll, *A History of Restoration Drama, 1660–1700* (Cambridge: Cambridge University Press, 1928), p. 231.

CHAPTER 15. THE WAY OF THE WORLD

1. Lytton Strachey, "Congreve, Collier, Macaulay, and Mr. Summers," *Portraits in Miniature and Other Essays* (London: Chatto and Windus, 1931), p. 49.
2. John C. Hodges, *William Congreve the Man* (New York: Modern Language Association, 1941), p. 68.
3. The edition to which I refer is: *Comedies by William Congreve,* ed. Bonamy Dobrée, The World's Classics (London: Oxford University Press, 1925), pp.

333–442. The numbers in the text refer to pages in this edition, but they may be related to other editions by the following table:

Act I: 343–359.
Act II: 360–377.
Act III: 377–400.
Act IV: 400–421.
Act V: 421–441.

4. F. W. Bateson, *The Works of Congreve* (London: Peter Davies, 1930), p. xvii.
5. Paul and Miriam Mueschke, *A New View of Congreve's Way of the World,* University of Michigan Contributions in Modern Philology, no. 23 (Ann Arbor: University of Michigan Press, 1958), p. 37.
6. Curt Sachs, *World History of the Dance,* trans. Bessie Schoenberg (New York: Norton, 1937), pp. 408–410, 414–424.
7. Elizabeth Mignon, *Crabbed Age and Youth* (Durham: Duke University Press, 1947), p. 123.
8. Mueschke, *A New View* (n. 5), p. 30.
9. *Ibid.,* p. 32.
10. Elinor C. Fuchs, "The Moral and Aesthetic Achievement of William Congreve" (Cambridge, Mass., 1955, unpub.), p. 71. This excellent study is on deposit in the Archives of the Committee on History and Literature, Holyoke 10, Harvard University.
11. Cleanth Brooks and Robert Heilman, *Understanding Drama* (New York: Holt, 1948), p. 446.
12. Fuchs, "Moral and Aesthetic Achievement" (n. 10), pp. 49–50.
13. *The Diary of Samuel Pepys,* ed. Henry B. Wheatley, 8 vols. (London: Bell, 1904), VI, 11 (October 8, 1666).
14. Mueschke, *A New View* (n. 5) pp. 13–14, 25.
15. Marjorie Nicolson, *The Breaking of the Circle* (Evanston: Northwestern University Press, 1950), p. 180.
16. George Wilhelm Friedrich Hegel, *Encyclopaedia of the Philosophical Sciences,* sec. 140, trans. William Wallace, 2d ed. (Oxford: Clarendon Press, 1892), p. 253. See also *Science of Logic,* Vol. 1, Bk. II, sec. 2, chap. iii–c, trans. W. H. Johnston and L. G. Struthers, 2 vols. (London: Allen and Unwin, 1929), II, 154ff.
17. Henri Bergson, *Laughter,* trans. Cloudesley Brereton and Fred Rothwell (New York: Macmillan, 1915). Louise Mathewson, *Bergson's Theory of the Comic in the Light of English Comedy,* University of Nebraska Studies in Language, Literature, and Criticism, vol. V (Lincoln, 1920). Kathleen M. Lynch, *The Social Mode of Restoration Comedy,* University of Michigan Publications in Language and Literature, vol. III (New York: Macmillan, 1938). Although Miss Lynch does not discuss Bergson directly, her own theory of Restoration comedy bears obvious relations to *Le Rire,* and Bergson is listed in her bibliography.

CHAPTER 16. THE CRITICAL FAILURE

1. John Wain, "Restoration Comedy and Its Modern Critics," *Essays in Criticism,* VI (October 1956), 367–385. F. W. Bateson, "Second Thoughts: II. L. C. Knights and Restoration Comedy," *Essays in Criticism,* VII (April 1957), 56–67. Norman N. Holland in "The Critical Forum: Restoration Comedy Again," *Essays in Criticism,* VII (July 1957), 319–322. Mr. William Empson contributes a factual comment in "The Critical Forum: Restoration Comedy Again," *Essays in Criticism,* VII (July 1957), 318.

2. London: S. Keble, R. Sare, and H. Hindmarsh, 1698.
3. W. Heldt, "A Chronological and Critical Review of the Appreciation and Condemnation of the Comic Dramatists of the Restoration and Orange Periods," *Neophilologus,* VIII (1922–23), 39–59, 109–128, 197–204. Heldt's critical history is definitive and invaluable. Although he lists "morals" critics earlier than Collier (p. 44), he considers them insignificant. The "less charitable view" is Lytton Strachey, "Congreve, Collier, Macaulay, and Mr. Summers," *Portraits in Miniature and Other Essays* (London: Chatto and Windus, 1931), pp. 43, 44.
4. Collier, *A Short View* (n. 2), pp. 140–141, 211, 286–287.
5. *The Spectator,* no. 446 (August 1, 1712); no. 51 (April 28, 1711). *The Tatler,* no. 98 (November 24, 1709).
6. *An Apology for the Life of Mr. Colley Cibber,* ed. Robert W. Lowe, 2 vols. (London, 1889), I, 265ff.
7. Samuel Johnson, "William Congreve," *Lives of the English Poets,* ed. George B. Hill, 3 vols. (Oxford: Clarendon Press, 1905), II, 222.
8. Oliver Goldsmith, "An Essay on the Theatre; or, A Comparison between Laughing and Sentimental Comedy," *Westminster Magazine,* December 1772.
9. William Hazlitt, "On Wycherley, Congreve, Vanbrugh, and Farquhar," *Lectures on the English Comic Writers* (1819), *Complete Works,* ed. P. P. Howe, Centenary Edition, 21 vols. (London: Dent, 1930–1934), VI, 70.
10. *Works of Charles and Mary Lamb,* ed. E. V. Lucas, 7 vols. (London: Methuen, 1903–1905), II, 141–147.
11. Leigh Hunt, "Biographical and Critical Notices," *The Dramatic Works of Wycherley, Congreve, Vanbrugh, and Farquhar* (London, 1840), p. lxii.
12. *Portraits in Miniature* (n. 3), p. 45.
13. Macaulay, *Edinburgh Review,* January 1841, "Comic Dramatists of the Restoration," *Works,* 12 vols. (London: Longmans, Green, 1898), IX, 340, 345.
14. Thackeray, "Charity and Humor" (1852), *Miscellaneous Papers and Sketches* (Boston and New York, 1895), p. 451.
15. George Meredith, *The New Quarterly Magazine,* April 1879, *An Essay on Comedy and the Uses of the Comic Spirit* (London: Constable, 1919), pp. 17, 18–19.
16. Barrett Wendell, *The Temper of the Seventeenth Century in English Literature* (New York: Scribner's, 1904), p. 338.
17. William Archer, *The Old Drama and the New* (New York: Dodd, Mead, 1929), pp. 31, 175.
18. John Dryden, "Preface to *An Evening's Love or The Mock Astrologer*" (1671), *Selected Essays,* ed. W. P. Ker, 2 vols. (Oxford: Oxford University Press, 1926), I, 143–144.
19. *Works* (n. 10), II, 142–143.
20. Oliver Elton, *A Survey of English Literature, 1780–1880,* 4 vols. (New York: Macmillan, 1920), II, 355. See also Walter E. Houghton, Jr., "Lamb's Criticism of Restoration Comedy," *Journal of English Literary History,* X (1943), 61–73.
21. *The Comedy of Manners* (London: Bell, 1913), pp. 22, 289, 290.
22. Bonamy Dobrée, *Restoration Comedy: 1660–1720* (Oxford: Clarendon Press, 1924), pp. 26, 171.
23. T. S. Eliot, "A Dialogue on Dramatic Poetry" (1928), *Selected Essays,* 2d ed. (New York: Harcourt, Brace, 1950), pp. 33, 40–41.
24. Moral: Heldt, in *Neophilologus,* VIII, 203, and Ernest Bernbaum, *The Drama of Sensibility* (Boston: Ginn, 1915), p. 6. Immoral: Arthur E. Case, "The Comedy of Manners," *British Dramatists from Dryden to Sheridan* (New York: Houghton Mifflin, 1939), pp. 151–152, and George Nettleton, *English Drama*

of the *Restoration and Eighteenth Century* (New York: Macmillan, 1928). Amoral: Malcolm Elwin, *The Playgoer's Handbook to Restoration Drama* (London: Jonathan Cape, 1928), p. 24, and Henry H. Adams and Baxter Hathaway, *Dramatic Essays of the Neo-Classic Age* (New York: Columbia University Press, 1950), p. xii.

25. Immoral: David Daiches, *Literature and Society* (London: Gollancz, 1938), p. 114, and Felix E. Schelling, *English Drama* (London: Dent, 1914), p. 268. Amoral: Bartholow V. Crawford, "High Comedy in Terms of Restoration Practice," *Philological Quarterly*, VIII (1929), 346, and Willard Smith, *The Nature of Comedy* (Boston: Richard G. Badger, 1930), pp. 52–53.

26. George Sherburn, "Restoration Comedy," in *A Literary History of England*, ed. Albert C. Baugh (New York: Appleton-Century-Crofts, 1948), p. 763.

27. Allardyce Nicoll, *A History of Restoration Drama, 1660–1700* (Cambridge: Cambridge University Press, 1923); references in this study are to the fourth edition, 1952, or the second, 1928.

28. *The Dramatic Works of Sir George Etherege*, ed. H. F. B. Brett-Smith, 2 vols. (Oxford: Basil Blackwell, 1927). *The Complete Works of William Wycherley*, ed. Montague Summers, 4 vols. (London: Nonesuch Press, 1924). *The Complete Works of William Congreve*, ed. Montague Summers, 4 vols. (London: Nonesuch Press, 1923). *Comedies by William Congreve*, ed. Bonamy Dobrée, The World's Classics (London: Oxford University Press, 1925). *The Mourning Bride, Poems & Miscellanies*, ed. Bonamy Dobrée, The World's Classics (London: Oxford University Press, 1928).

29. Leslie Hotson, *The Commonwealth and Restoration Stage* (Cambridge: Harvard University Press, 1928). Alfred B. Harbage, *Cavalier Drama* (New York: Modern Language Association, 1936).

30. Sir A. W. Ward, *A History of English Dramatic Literature to the Death of Queen Anne*, 3 vols. (London, 1875), III, 461–477. Dudley Howe Miles, *The Influence of Molière on Restoration Comedy* (New York: Columbia University Press, 1910). Kathleen M. Lynch, *The Social Mode of Restoration Comedy*, University of Michigan Publications in Language and Literature, vol. III (New York: Macmillan, 1926). John Wilcox, *The Relation of Molière to Restoration Comedy* (New York: Columbia University Press, 1938).

31. Joseph Wood Krutch, *Comedy and Conscience after the Restoration* (New York: Columbia University Press, 1924). Sister Rose Anthony, *The Jeremy Collier Stage Controversy: 1689–1726* (Milwaukee: Marquette University Press, 1937).

32. Gellert S. Alleman, *Matrimonial Law and the Materials of Restoration Comedy* (Wallingford, Pa., 1942). Elizabeth Mignon, *Crabbed Age and Youth* (Durham: Duke University Press, 1947). John Harrington Smith, *The Gay Couple in Restoration Comedy* (Cambridge: Harvard University Press, 1948).

33. Guy Montgomery, "The Challenge of Restoration Comedy," *Essays in Criticism*, University of California Publications in English, I (Berkeley: University of California Press, 1929), 137–138, 139–140, 147.

34. Lynch, *The Social Mode* (n. 30), p. 7. See also Henri Bergson, *Laughter*, trans. Cloudesley Brereton and Fred Rothwell (New York: Macmillan, 1913), and Louise Mathewson, *Bergson's Theory of the Comic in the Light of English Comedy*, University of Nebraska Studies in Language, Literature, and Criticism, vol. V (Lincoln, Nebraska, 1920).

35. L. C. Knights, "Restoration Comedy: The Reality and the Myth," *Explorations* (New York: G. W. Stewart, 1947), pp. 154, 155, 168. See, by the same author, *Drama and Society in the Age of Jonson* (London: Chatto and Windus, 1937), p. 292.

36. Thomas H. Fujimura, *The Restoration Comedy of Wit* (Princeton: Princeton University Press, 1952).
37. Dale Underwood, *Etherege and the Seventeenth-Century Comedy of Manners*, Yale Studies in English, vol. 135 (New Haven: Yale University Press, 1957), p. 161 and generally.

CHAPTER 17. FROM CHARLES TO CHARLES

1. Ernest Bernbaum, *The Drama of Sensibility* (Boston: Ginn, 1915), pp. 2, 4–5.
2. René Rapin, *Monsieur Rapin's Reflections on Aristotle's Treatise of Poesie . . . Made English by Mr.* [*Thomas*] *Rymer* (London, 1694), Part I, sec. x, p. 14.
3. *The Spectator*, no. 249 (December 15, 1711).
4. *King Lear*, III.ii.1–9.
5. Nahum Tate, *The History of King Lear* (1681), III.i, reprinted in Montague Summers, *Shakespeare Adaptations* (London: Jonathan Cape, 1922), p. 206.
6. Hazelton Spencer, *Shakespeare Improved* (Cambridge: Harvard University Press, 1927), p. 58, n. 13, discusses the dating, and on p. 73, the stage history of this adaptation. Sir William Davenant, *Dramatic Works*, ed. James Maidment and W. H. Logan, 5 vols. (London, 1874), V, 109–211.
7. Francis Fergusson, *The Idea of a Theater* (Princeton: Princeton University Press, 1949), pp. 140–141, 105. Theodore Spencer, *Shakespeare and the Nature of Man*, 2d ed. (New York: Macmillan, 1955) and E. M. W. Tillyard, *The Elizabethan World-Picture* (London: Chatto and Windus, 1943), discuss the Renaissance-medieval sense of metaphorical correspondence between universe, political body, and individual.
8. Robert Gale Noyes, *Ben Jonson on the English Stage, 1660–1776* (Cambridge: Harvard University Press, 1935), p. 28
9. *The Chances, The Works of Beaumont and Fletcher*, ed. Arnold Glover and A. R. Waller, 10 vols. (Cambridge: Cambridge University Press, 1926), IV, 174–245. George Villiers, Duke of Buckingham, *Dramatick Works*, 2 vols., 3d ed. (London, 1715), II, 99–150. The adaptation is dated and the two versions compared in A. C. Sprague, *Beaumont and Fletcher on the Restoration Stage* (Cambridge: Harvard University Press, 1926), pp. 31–32, 221–227.
10. Emmett L. Avery, "A Tentative Calendar of Daily Theatrical Performances, 1660–1700," *Research Studies of the State College of Washington*, XIII (1945), see Index, pp. 225–283.
11. John Lacy, *Dramatic Works*, ed. James Maidment and W. H. Logan (London, 1875), pp. 311–398. My references are to page numbers in this edition; the description in the text will, I believe, enable the reader to locate a quoted passage in other editions. Spencer, *Shakespeare Improved* (n. 6), pp. 83, 85, discusses the dating, and on pp. 274–281, the changes.
12. Ben Jonson, ed. C. H. Herford and Percy Simpson, 11 vols. (Oxford: Clarendon Press, 1925–1952), IV, 487–619.
13. Nahum Tate, *Cuckolds-Haven or an Alderman No Conjurer* (London: J. H. and Edward Poole, 1685).
14. Summers, *Shakespeare Adaptations* (n. 5), pp. 1–104. The dating is given in the Introduction, pp. xli–xliii. References in the text are to page numbers in this edition; they may be related to other editions by the following table:
    Act I: 9–24.
    Act II: 24–43.
    Act III: 43–66.
    Act IV: 66–91.
    Act V: 91–104.

15. Avery, "A Tentative Calendar" (n. 10), see Index. See also Summers, *Shakespeare Adaptations* (n. 5), pp. xli–xliii.
16. *The Complete Works of Thomas Shadwell,* ed. Montague Summers, 5 vols. (London: Fortune Press, 1927), I, civ.
17. Reprinted in Summers, *Shakespeare Adaptations* (n. 5).
18. *Beaumont and Fletcher,* ed. Arnold Glover and A. R. Waller (n. 9), IV, 314–390. George Farquhar, *The Complete Works,* ed. Charles Stonehill, 2 vols. (Bloomsbury: Nonesuch Press, 1930), I, 215–278.
19. Dale Underwood, *Etherege and the Seventeenth-Century Comedy of Manners,* Yale Studies in English, vol. 135 (New Haven: Yale University Press, 1957), pp. 159–161.
20. Philip Massinger, *A New Way to Pay Old Debts,* ed. A. H. Cruickshank (Oxford, 1926).
21. Robert H. Ball, *The Amazing Career of Sir Giles Overreach* (Princeton: Princeton University Press, 1929), p. 33. See also Avery, "A Tentative Calendar" (n. 10), Index.
22. *The Dramatic Works and Poems of James Shirley,* ed. William Gifford and Alexander Dyce, 6 vols. (London, 1833), II, 457–541.
23. Avery, "A Tentative Calendar" (n. 10).
24. Shirley, *Works* (n. 22), IV, 1–100. References are to page numbers of this edition; they may be related to other editions by the following table:
    Act I: 5–23.
    Act II: 24–40.
    Act III: 41–62.
    Act IV: 63–81.
    Act V: 81–100.
25. Underwood, *Etherege* (n. 19), p. 155.

CHAPTER 18. FORMS TO HIS CONCEIT

1. Sir John Vanbrugh, "A Short Vindication of *The Relapse* and *The Provok'd Wife,*" *Complete Works,* ed. Bonamy Dobrée and Geoffrey Webb, 4 vols. (Bloomsbury: Nonesuch Press, 1927), I, 206–207.
2. G. Wilson Knight, *Principles of Shakespearian Production* (London: Faber, 1936), pp. 34, 37–38.
3. "*Mr.* Congreve, to *Mr.* Dennis, *Concerning Humour in Comedy,*" *Comedies by William Congreve,* ed. Bonamy Dobrée, The World's Classics (London: Oxford University Press, 1925), pp. 7–8.

Index

Accidents. *See* Appearance and nature
Acting: as image, 67, 90, 92, 162–163; of Restoration comedy, 239–241. *See also* Play itself; Plays
Action of Restoration comedy: definition of term, 213–214; discovery, 155, 180–195; education of idealists, 105–107; emancipating, 180–195; marriage of a rake, 3–4; penetration, 69; rake reformed, 61, 94, 203; therapy, 91, 94, 162, 171, 203; therapy of audience, 114–115. *See also* Immorality; "Morals" criticism
Actor, as image of world, 60
Adams, Henry H., 243, 245, 259
Adaptations, Restoration, 211–225
Addison, Joseph, 51, 158, 201
Adulteress. *See* Characters
Adultery, 29–35, 73–75, 133–134, 149–155, 167, 192–193, 200–203
Advancement of Learning, 15
Aeneid, 13
Affectation: in acting Restoration comedy, 240–241; in characters, 61, 80–84, 125, 150–153, 167, 187; clothing as, 87–88; Congreve on, 61; confining, 69; contrasted to dissimulation, 50, 67, 137; Etherege on, 59–60, 95; a folly, 34–37, 69, 102, 187, 190, 233; in language, 51–52; of morals, 35, 75, 80; as necessary evil, 95, 102; not in Paradise, 123; as reality, 5, 162, 170; sex as, 87–88; as vice, 98; of wit, 39, 152, 190; Wycherley on, 60. *See also* Appearance and nature
Agrippa von Nettesheim, Henry Cornelius, 54
Alien figure (character), 173–174, 191
Alleman, Gellert S., 259
Analogy: definition of term, 213–214; as dramatic technique, 213–230; as explanation of universe, 118; reduced use in Restoration, 35, 38, 44; Tudor-Stuart use, 26, 127, 216
Angel, Edward, 67
Animal images, 30, 98, 102, 156–157
Annus Mirabilis, 13
Anthony, Sister Rose, 259
Antiheroic elements in Restoration comedy, 9, 19, 21–27, 35, 41, 44, 79–80, 85, 88, 114, 125, 141, 211, 233
Antitheses: antiheroic in comedies, 27; between general and particular, 138–139
Antony and Cleopatra, 46
"Apology for Heroic Poetry," 96, 108
Appearance and nature: defined, 4–5; in language, 50–54, 71, 139, 143–145; in production of Restoration comedy, 237–240; confusion of, a folly, 33–37, 39–44, 65–70, 76–77, 81–83, 87–88, 102, 132–133, 149–153, 154–155, 190–191, 233
in intellectual climate: Congreve on, 61; Descartes on, 54; Elizabethan view, 46–47; Hobbes on, 55–56; Locke on, 55; medieval view, 47, 56; Romantic view, 196; scientific view, 53–58, 63, 127, 233–234; seventeenth-century view, 45–63, 212; Shakespeare on, 46–47, 62; skeptical tradition, 54
separation of: affectation as, 45, 57–58, 62–63, 104, 171, 233–234; appearance easy to change, nature hard, 61–62, 216; basic theme of comedies, 4, 27, 28, 102–105, 132–138, 148, 149–156, 167–172, 178, 188–191, 193–195, 231, 233–234, 240–241; essential quality of society, 32–33, 116, 167–174, 176–179, 194–195, 223–224; requires skill, 101–109; as villainy, 188–189
united: in early seventeenth-century drama, 227, 229; in heroic drama, 25; in Paradise, 94, 122–124; in "right way," 82–83
Aquinas, St. Thomas, 54, 117
Arcadia, 13
Archer, William, 97, 203
Argalus and Parthenia, 10
Aristophanes, 191
Aristotle, *Poetics,* 12, 16–18

Arms and the Man, 62–63
Arran, Charles Butler, Earl of, 128–129
Artamène ou le Grand Cyrus, 13, 207
Art and nature, 61, 123, 187, 197–198. *See also* Nature
Arthos, John, 245
Astrée, 207
Attitudes toward Restoration comedy, 3, 199–209, 223, 231
Aubrey, John, 56
Audience, Elizabethan and Restoration contrasted, 9–11, 210
Averroës, 54
Avery, Emmett L., 243, 260, 261

Bacon, Sir Francis, 15, 45
Baker, Herschel C., 120, 125
Ball, Robert H., 261
Baroque style, 126, 146
Bateson, F. W., 12, 77, 145–156, 175
Beau (character), 161
Beaumont, Francis, and John Fletcher, 214–215
Beaux' Stratagem, The, 235
Beethoven, Ludwig van, 197
Behn, Mrs. Aphra, 131
Bendo, Alexander, 48
Bergson, Henri, 196–197, 207
Bernbaum, Ernest, 113, 211, 258
Bernini, Giovanni Lorenzo, 45
Bible, 126
Birds, 30, 41, 90, 93, 105, 147
Blackfriars Theater, 10
Blank verse, 11
Body images, 141
Bolton, Edmund, 51
Bracegirdle, Ann, 131
Bredvold, Louis I., 249
Brett-Smith, H. F. B., 206
Briar-Rose, Little, 250
Brief Lives, 56
Brooks, Cleanth, 191, 246
Brower, Reuben A., 28, 245
Browne, Sir Thomas, 120, 128, 130, 169
Bruno, Giordano, 125
Buckingham, George Villiers, second Duke of, 38, 53–54, 56–57, 58, 214
Buckingham, Mary Fairfax, Duchess of, 48
Bumpkin. *See* Characters
Bunyan, John, 45, 53, 120
Burke, Edmund, 192
Burnet, Gilbert, Bishop of Salisbury, 47, 48, 59, 247
Burnet, Thomas, 119, 122–123, 130
Burtt, Edwin A., 56, 125
Bush, Douglas, 117
Business images, 31, 79, 90, 133
Byron, George Gordon, sixth Baron, 197

Calderon de la Barca, Pedro, 41, 45, 64
Calvin, John, 118
Cambridge History of English Literature, The, 96
Campbell, Joseph, 250
Candor: and appearance and nature, 128; in Paradise, 122–124; as "right way," 98, 116, 224; vs. society, 224, 230. *See also* Appearance and Nature; Knowledge
Caroline drama, 13, 230–231
Case, Arthur E., 258
Cassirer, Ernst, 252
Castlemaine, Lady, Barbara Villiers, 38, 48, 49, 97
Catherine (of Braganza), Queen, 47, 48
Cato, 158
Causality, dramatic interest in, 213–230. *See also* Science
Cavalier: attitudes, 117, 119; characters, 21, 22, 27, 41; drama, 12–13
Cazamian, Louis, 251
Cervantes, Miguel de, 6, 45
Chances, The: Beaumont and Fletcher, 214–215; Buckingham, 214–215
Chaplin, Charlie, 109
Chapman, George, 9, 121, 216–217
Characters of Restoration comedy: adulteress, 29, 73, 133–134, 151–156, 167, 192; affected ladies, 35, 61, 80–84, 125, 150–153, 167, 187; alien figure, 173–174, 191; beau, 161; bumpkin, 22–23, 31, 165–167, 176; Cavalier, 21, 22, 27, 41; clergyman, 133, 135, 200; cuckold, 27, 73, 76, 133, 150–151, 192, 203; dupe, 22–23, 132, 170; father, 168–169; fool, 22–23, 32, 39–40, 64–67, 102, 113, 132, 190–191; fop, 65–66, 80–81, 86–88, 102, 176; gossip, 87, 170; "half-men," 191, 196; hero, 25–26, 34–35, 65–69, 75, 86, 91–94, 108–109, 112–113, 126, 135, 157–159, 162–165, 171–172, 174, 176, 187–189, 240; heroine, 30, 42, 65–69, 82, 92–94, 137–138, 162–165, 183–186, 189, 240; "hero in fact," 108–109, 135–137, 232; "hero in value," 87, 112–113, 136–137, 232; "humor," 167–168, 239; hypocrite, 61, 125, 155–160; lover-hero, 34–35, 77–78, 87, 211, 224, 232; merchant, 10, 48, 61, 79, 133,

167–168, 203; *miles gloriosus,* 132–133; misanthrope, 96–109, 132, 134; mistresses, 22, 27, 88–89, 137, 189–190, 192; "natural," 165–167, 171, 176, 180, 191, 218, 240–241; nonhumor, 239–240; older people and parents, 33, 65–67, 89–90, 168–169, 206, 215; pastoral, 101, 107–108; presocial, 165–167, 181; Puritan, 39–40, 103, 133; realistic, 89, 167–168, 241; servant, 140–141, 240; "sign-post," 89; suprasocial, 161, 164, 165, 166, 167, 170–173, 174; upper class, 26, 228; villain, 75, 104, 109, 155–160, 176, 187–189; widow, 23, 103, 181, 186–187, 190; wit, 39, 150, 154, 190; witty lovers, 12, 26, 33–35, 66–70, 227, 228. *See also* Rake

Charles I, 11, 230

Charles II: as dissembler, 49–50, 121; and forms, 192; and Hobbes, 55, 56; mentioned, 3, 10, 54, 230, 238

Chekhov, Anton, 6

China scene (*Country Wife*), 77

Chorney, Alexander H., 98

Christian humanism, 125

Cibber, Colley, 130, 201

Clergy: abused on stage, 200; characters, 133, 135, 200

Cleveland, Barbara Villiers, Duchess of, 38, 48, 49, 97

Clothing, 192, 240. *See also* Images

Cockpit theatre, 11

Cocktail Party, The, 224

Coleridge, Samuel Taylor, 6, 165

Collier, Jeremy, 175, 187, 197, 199–200, 202, 203, 206

Comedy: Bergson on, 196–197, 207; eighteenth-century, sentimental, 85, 101, 113, 160, 200, 206, 211; of manners, 7, 9, 12, 85; mirror theory of, 115–116, 200, 211, 232; morality of, 6; ritual origins of, 109, 182, 234; Tudor-Stuart, 224. *See also* Drama; Restoration comedy

Comical Revenge, The. See Etherege

Comparison between the Two Stages, A, 254

Confidential Clerk, The, 179

Congreve, William: "Concerning Humour in Comedy," 61–62, 165, 239; influenced by Wycherley, 98, 131, 149; library, 17, 51, 59, 130; life, 131–132; poems, 61, 115, 130, 167, 195; prose style, 138–140

Double-Dealer, The: full discussion, 149–160; summary, 233; mentioned, 174, 188, 192

Love for Love: full discussion, 161–174; summary, 233; mentioned, 5, 183, 197, 223, 234–235, 236, 239, 240–241

Mourning Bride, The: 130, 146, 157

Old Batchelor, The: full discussion, 131–148; summary, 233; mentioned, 56, 98, 149, 152, 157–159, 163, 167, 172–173, 193, 239

Way of the World, The: full discussion, 175–198; summary, 233; mentioned, 27, 96, 116, 131, 146, 149, 197, 199, 239, 240

mentioned: 5, 7, 38, 58, 63, 111, 113, 116, 131, 132, 137, 138, 139, 140, 144, 145, 146, 147, 148, 149, 151, 153, 155, 157, 158, 159, 160, 161, 165, 166, 167, 171, 172, 173, 174, 175, 176, 177, 178, 179, 180, 186, 192, 195, 196, 197, 198, 201, 202, 209, 231

Conquest of Granada, The, 127–128

Conscious Lovers, The, 201

Contract scene, 183–185

Conversion down. *See* Language of Restoration comedy

Conversion up. *See* Language of Restoration comedy

Co-ordinate system, 15, 144–148, 158

Corneille, Pierre, 17–18, 45

Cosmetics, images, 186, 198

Cosmic images, 153, 173

Coterie drama, 8–12, 45, 205, 210, 223

Council of Trent, 54, 59

Count Grammont, The Memoirs of, 49, 59, 247

Country Wife, The. See Wycherley

Country: characters, 22–23, 31, 165–167, 176; as marriage, 34; contrasted to town, 29–35, 42–43, 66, 76–77, 82, 87, 93. *See also* Nature

Cowley, Abraham, 54

Crawford, Bartholow V., 259

Criticism of Restoration comedy. *See* Attitudes

Critique de l'Ecole des femmes, 100

Cromwell, Oliver, 45

Cuckolds: characters, 27, 73, 76, 133, 150–151, 192, 203; forcing nature, 81–82

Cuckolds-Haven, 217

"Cult of chase," 136, 163, 167, 185

Cunningham, Peter, 247

Dacier, André, 17, 59

Daiches, David, 259

Dances, 182, 236. *See also* Images: dancing
Dante, 13, 54, 122
Darkness, 43–44, 105, 156
Darwin, Charles, 230
Davenant, Sir William, 11, 13, 212–214
Davenant, Sir William, and John Dryden, 217–221
Deane, Cecil V., 245
Death-and-rebirth, 26, 216. *See also* Ritual
Deception, 32–33, 57, 75, 116, 167–174, 176–179, 194–195, 223–224. *See also* Appearance and nature
Decorum, theme of, 192, 198, 208
Deeds as plot device, 180–181, 195
"Defense of Poesie" (Sidney), 16, 51
"Degree," Restoration sense of Renaissance concept of, 23, 26
Dekker, Thomas, 9
Dennis, John, 96, 123, 165
Descartes, René, 45, 54–55, 58–59, 230
de Scudéry, Madeleine, 13, 207
Diogenes, 170
Dionysus, 109. *See also* Ritual
Disease: compared to heroic "wound of love," 23–24, 85, 142, 233; love as, 24, 25, 31, 41, 79–80, 90, 140, 166
Disguise: cosmic, 45, 57, 63; court pastime, 47–50, 62; episodes in plays, 23, 39, 64, 73, 98, 101, 133, 167, 177, 216, 229; human nature as, 42, 58, 61, 240; in similes, 231; in society, 138, 225, 231; as "wrong way," 116, 135. *See also* Appearance and nature
Dissimulation: and affectation, 50, 67, 137; and character, 58, 106–107, 155; a folly, 137; and intellectual climate of Restoration, 45, 57, 63; a necessity, 42, 47, 50; not in Paradise, 94, 123; and science, 61, 128; result of sexual knowledge, 220; society as, 36–37, 75, 90, 123, 136, 171, 194–195, 223–224; a villainy, 188–189. *See also* Appearance and nature
Divine Comedy, The, 13, 54, 122
Dobrée, Bonamy, 42, 75, 101, 138, 153, 206, 252, 255
Donne, John, 45, 119, 207
Don Quixote: Cervantes, 6; D'Urfey, 187
Dorset Garden Theater, 64, 86
Double-Dealer, The. See Congreve
Downes, John, 20
Drama: Cavalier, 12–13; coterie, 8–12, 45, 205, 210, 223; Ibsenite, 203, 237; theory of, 7; Tudor-Stuart, 9, 12–13, 27, 47, 58, 127, 210, 223–224, 230–231. *See also* Comedy; Heroic drama; Tragedy
Dramatic history, place of Restoration comedy in, 9–13, 210–229
Dreiser, Theodore, 127
Drury Lane Theater, 73, 132, 149
Dryden, John: *Annus Mirabilis,* 13; Congreve's reading of, 17; *Conquest of Granada,* 127–128; essays, 12, 13, 15, 17, 19, 25, 51, 96, 98, 108, 114–115, 126, 203, 214; letters, 149; *Marriage à la Mode,* 21; *State of Innocence,* 58–59; *Wild Gallant,* 20; mentioned, 45, 53
  and Sir William Davenant, 217–221; and Henry Purcell, 19
Duels, 23–24, 31, 41, 90
Duffett, Thomas, 221
Dupes, 22–23, 132, 170
d'Urfé, Honoré, 207
D'Urfey, Tom, 115–116, 187

Eastward Hoe, 216–217
Eighteenth-century comedy, 85, 101, 113, 160, 200, 206, 211
Elizabeth I, 9, 50, 121
Elizabethan drama, 9, 12, 27, 47, 58, 127, 210, 230–231
Eliot, T. S., 117, 179, 205, 208, 224
Elton, Oliver, 258
Elwin, Malcolm, 259
Emotions: contrasted to social appearances, 4–5, 36, 42, 84, 116, 169, 176–198, 233, 241; fulfilled by social appearances, 69, 84, 95, 176–198, 233; substitutes for personal God, 130. *See also* Passion
Empson, William, 21, 45, 109
"Enchanted island," as Paradise contrasted to town, 110
Enchanted Island, The (Dryden and Davenant), 217–221
Epictetus, 170
Epilogues, 238
Essay of Dramatic Poesy, An (Dryden), 19, 214
Etherege, Sir George: *Letterbook,* 59, 95, 128–130; life, 20; poems, 59–60, 129
  Comical Revenge, The: full discussion, 20–27; summary, 233; mentioned, 28, 38, 40, 59, 71, 80, 85, 112, 128
  Man of Mode, The: full discussion, 86–95; summary, 233; mentioned, 7, 57, 85, 112, 116, 126, 128, 136, 139, 150, 157, 241

She wou'd if she cou'd: full discussion, 28–37; summary, 233; mentioned, 60, 71, 111, 112, 137, 209, 235
mentioned, 5, 7, 19, 20, 21, 24, 25, 26, 27, 28, 30, 31, 50, 57, 63, 70, 72, 81, 86, 87, 88, 89, 90, 93, 94, 95, 147, 170, 174, 209, 223, 231
Evelyn, John, 54

Fact and value, separation of, 118–124, 128–130, 212, 224, 233–234, 241
Faerie Queen, The, 13
Faith, contrasted to reason, 117, 120, 129
Family relations, contrasted to emotional relations, 169–170, 176–198
Farquhar, George: *The Inconstant,* 214, 221–223, 225; mentioned, 201, 235
Felix culpa, 126, 219
Fergusson, Francis, 213
Fideism: dramatic use of, 130; growth of, 116–117, 120
Fishing: love as, 24, 41; sex as, 31
Flecknoe, Richard, 10, 52
Fletcher, John: relation to Restoration drama, 13, 101, 206, 209, 214; style, 138; *The Wild Goose Chase,* 221–223, 225
Fletcher, John, and Francis Beaumont, 214–215
Folly: as confinement, 32, 69, 108, 171; as over-expressing self, 95, 149–153, 154–155, 233; over-wisdom as, 78; as "right way," 82, 108–109, 112, 171–174; substitution of appearances for reality, 33–37, 39–40, 50, 64–67, 69–70, 95, 102–103, 132–133, 149–153, 154–155, 190–191, 233; and villainy, 154–155. *See also* Appearance and nature; Characters
Fontenelle, Bernard de, 55, 59, 119, 120, 130
Food images, 61, 79, 136, 142
Fools, 22–23, 32, 39–40, 64–67, 102, 113, 132, 190–191
Fops, 65–66, 80–81, 86–88, 102, 176
Freud, Sigmund, 4, 74, 142, 230
Fruit, 89
Fuchs, Elinor, 191, 192
Fujimura, Thomas, 97–98, 208–209, 245, 252

Galileo Galilei, 45
Gambling images, 24, 31, 40–41, 198
Games as images, 95, 157, 198
Gascoign, Sir Bernard, 48
"Genteel comedy," 12
Gentleman Dancing-Master, The. See Wycherley
Gentillet, Innocent, 62
Gilbert and Sullivan, 237
Glanvill, Joseph, 53, 55, 119, 122
Godolphin, Sidney Godolphin, Earl of, 131–132
Godolphin, Henrietta, Duchess of Marlborough, 131–132
Gogol, Nikolai, 6
Goldsmith, Oliver, 201
Goodwin, Gordon, 247
Gossips, 87, 170
Graham, Martha, 182
Grammont, The Memoirs of Count, 49, 59, 247
Grand Cyrus, Le, 13, 207
Granville, George, Lord Lansdowne, 97–98, 131
Greville, Fulke, first Lord Brooke, 54
Gwyn, Nell, 10, 20, 49

"Half-men" (characters), 191, 196
Halifax, George Savile, first Marquess of, 50
Hall, Jacob, 38
Hamilton, Anthony, 49, 59, 247
Hamlet, 121, 163, 213–214, 234
"Happy ending," 15, 84, 107–109, 234
Harbage, Alfred B., 9, 12–13, 206, 244
Hart, Charles, 20
Hathaway, Baxter, 243, 245, 259
Hawking, sex as, 24, 31
Hazlitt, William, 73, 96, 201
Hegel, George Wilhelm Friedrich, 196
Heilman, Robert, 191, 246
Heldt, W., 96, 258
Henrietta Maria, Queen, 11, 49
Henry IV, 11
Henry V, 62
Herbert, George, 45
Herbert, Sir Henry, 247
Heroes. *See* Characters
Heroic drama: described, 13–19, 114, 157; influence on Restoration comedy, 9, 21–27, 35, 41, 44, 79–80, 85, 88, 114, 125, 141, 211, 233
Heroic images, 42, 74, 85
Heroines. *See* Characters
Heywood, Thomas, 9
Histriomastix, 11
Hobbes, Thomas: on appearance and nature, 55–56; and Charles II, 55–56; and Congreve, 59; definition of laughter, 114; libertine tradition, 125, 209;

political theory, 221; mentioned, 45, 70, 230
Hodges, John C., 17, 59, 248, 255
Hollywood, 15, 203
Homer, 13
Hooker, Richard, 47
Horace, 51
Horizon, 207
Horse-race, courtship as, 228
Hostility, theme of, 23–24, 30–31, 42, 74, 90, 142, 231, 233. *See also* Images; Love; Marriage; Sex
Hotson, Leslie, 206, 244
Houghton, Walter E., Jr., 258
Hound and Horn, 207
Houses, 34, 142–143
"Humor" characters, 167–168, 239
Humorists, The, 28
Hunt, Leigh, 3, 96, 111, 202
Hunting, love as, 31, 41
Huyghens, Christian, 45
Hyde-Park, 227
Hypocrisy: in characters, 35, 61, 66, 125, 155–160; as theme, 39–40, 63, 102, 105, 163. *See also* Affection; Appearance and nature; Pretense

Ibsenite drama, 203, 237
Idealism, contrasted to naturalism, 22, 44, 82–85, 108–109, 121, 130, 173, 233
Idealizing: heroic, 13–19, 21, 42, 211; and reality, 108–109, 121, 130, 233; sentimental, 85, 113, 211. *See also* Paradise
Iliad, 13
Images: acting, 67, 90, 92, 162–163; animal, 30, 98, 102, 156–157; birds, 30, 41, 90, 93, 105, 147; body, 141; business, 31, 79, 90, 133; china, 77; clothing, 32, 66, 88, 89; cosmetics, 186, 198; cosmic, 153, 173; dancing, 65, 182–183, 236; darkness, 43–44, 105, 156; deeds, 180–181, 195; derived from character, 173; duels, 23–24, 31, 41, 90; fishing, 24, 31, 41; food, 61, 79, 136, 142; fruit, 89; gambling, 24, 31, 40–41, 198; games, 95, 157, 198; hawking, 24, 31; heroic, 42, 74, 85; horse-race, 228; houses, 34, 142–143; hunting, 31, 41; law, 31, 90, 103–105, 157, 183–186, 198; light and dark, 43–44, 105, 156; literary, 151–152, 187, 197; local, 236; part of "meaning," 3, 209; military, 23–24, 30–31, 74; mirror, 66, 87, 103, 156, 239; neoplatonic, 23, 142, 164, 172; pastoral, 42–43, 187; penetration, 69, 154–155; play itself as, 33–34, 67, 100, 104, 115–116, 197, 232, 237; plays, 33–34, 104, 136; pressing, 68; stage itself, 232; surfaces, 154–155; swindling, 31, 40; three-dimensional, 144–148, 172; travel, 147; vegetable, 157; vessel, 172–173; weight, 36, 141, 172; wounds, 24, 80, 85, 233. *See also* Disease; Hostility, theme of; Love; Marriage; Mask; Money; Religious images; Sex
Immorality of Restoration comedy, 3–4, 72, 199–206, 209, 231. *See also* "Morals" criticism; Rake-hero
Inconstant, The, 214, 221–223, 225
Indecency in Restoration comedy, 4
Inside and outside. *See* Appearance and nature
Intrigue: Restoration convention of, 176, 177, 194–195; a "wrong way," 43, 173
Irony: to suggest deviousness of society, 181, 192; breaking dramatic illusion, 197; in endings, 94–95, 232; in religious images, 93, 141

Jacobean drama, 12, 47, 127, 210, 223–224, 230–231
Jacobean style, 139
James II, 20, 49
Jealousy, 68–69, 90
Jerusalem Liberated, 13
Johnson, Dr. Samuel: on Congreve, 131, 138, 140, 146, 165, 201; on *King Lear,* 14–15
Jones, Richard F., 248
Jonson, Ben: *Alchemist, The,* 197; *Eastward Hoe,* 216–217; playwright identified with inventive character, 197; relation to Restoration comedy, 206, 209, 214; *Volpone,* 197; mentioned, 9, 38, 45, 112

Keats, John, 175
Kepler, Johann, 45
Kierkegaard, Søren, 6, 108, 164
King Arthur, 19
King Lear: Shakespeare, 14, 127, 211; Tate, 14, 211–212
Kneller, Sir Godfrey, 238
Knight, G. Wilson, 5, 30, 235
Knights, L. C., 8, 207
Knowledge, theme of, 122–124, 126–127, 161–163, 170–171. *See also* Candor
Krutch, Joseph Wood, 97, 259

Lacy, John, 215–216
Lady of Pleasure, The, 228–229
Lamb, Charles, 12, 45, 201–202, 203–204
Land, as opposed to sea, 110, 165, 171
Langhans, Edward A., 243
Language: "natural," 53; influence of Puritans, 53; influence of science, 53–58, 224–225; theories of, 51
Language of Restoration comedy: antithesis, 27, 138–139; blank verse, 11; changed from earlier drama, 125, 211–212; conversion down, 27, 79–80, 116, 127, 128, 140–141, 172, 228, 231–232; conversion up, 25, 42, 78, 116, 141–142, 172, 231–232; nouns, increased use of, 57; right-way–wrong-way simile, 70–72, 110, 114–117, 129, 139, 172–173, 231; shifts in meaning, 125; similes, 57, 228, 231; of split-man observation, 36, 111, 139, 148, 232. *See also* Images; Love; Marriage; Sex
Lansdowne, George Granville, Lord, 97–98, 131
Laughter: as natural, 152; theories of, 114–115, 196, 207
Law, images of, 31, 90, 103–105, 157, 183–186, 198
Law against Lovers, The, 212–214
Lawrence, D. H., 4
Leech, Clifford, 245
Lely, Sir Peter, 238
Liberty, theme of, 29–36, 127–128, 161–162, 174, 233. *See also* Love; Marriage
Light and dark, 43–44, 105, 156
Lincoln's Inn Fields Theater, 161, 175
Literature: function of, 3–4, 206, 231; images of, 151–152, 187, 197
Local jokes, 236. *See also* Realism
Locke, John: on appearance and nature, 55; Congreve's reading of, 59, 130; in *Love for Love,* 164–165; and mechanistic universe, 119; and political theory, 221; mentioned, 45
Loggan, David, 238
London, 31, 108, 211. *See also* Town
Lope de Vega, 45
Love: as acting, 162–163; as birding, 41; as business, 90; as confinement, 142–143; as cock-fight, 90, 105; as disease, 24–25, 41, 79, 85, 90, 140, 166, 233; disturbing influence of, 24, 66; as duel, 90; as fighting, 41; as fishing, 24, 41; as gambling, 41; as hawking, 24; as horse-race, 228; as house, 34, 142; as hunting, 41; as lawsuit, 90; as madness, 161–163, 172; as "way of world," 191; as witty war, 213; as wound, 24, 80, 85, 233. *See also* Money; Religious images; Sex
Love for Love. See Congreve
Love in a Tub. See Etherege, *Comical Revenge*
Love in a Wood. See Wycherley
Lovejoy, Arthur O., 117
Lovelace, Richard, 12, 207
Lovers: as heroes, 34–35, 77–78, 87, 211, 224, 232; witty, characteristic of Restoration comedy, 12, 26, 227, 228; witty, characters, 12, 26, 33–35, 66–70, 227, 228
Lynch, Kathleen M., 98, 132, 207, 208, 250, 255, 257, 259

Macaulay, Thomas Babington, first Baron, 4, 11, 96, 149, 202
Macbeth, 47, 62
Machiavelli, Niccolò, 50, 62, 125, 209, 223
Madness, 161–163, 172
Man and Superman, 62
Mañanas de abril y mayo, 41
Man of Mode, The. See Etherege
Mann, Thomas, 197
Mannerist style, 146
Manners: in acting, 240; as appearances, 57, 66; as art, 198; comedies about more than, 4, 95, 207, 231; criticism of comedies based on, 3, 4, 199, 203–206, 209, 223, 231; as social laws, 103
"Manners, comedy of": term defined, 12; mentioned, 7, 9, 85
Marlborough, Henrietta Godolphin, Duchess of, 131–132
Marlowe, Christopher, 9
Marriage à la Mode, 21
Marriage: as banquet, 136; as business, 31; as confinement, 35, 136, 142–143, 222; as country, 34; as duel, 31; as gambling, 24, 40; as imprisonment, 22, 25–26, 137; as social form, 68–70, 190; as swindling, 40; as symbol for union of appearance and nature, 69, 193–195, 234; as vessel, 172–173. *See also* Love; Money
Marston, John, 9, 216–217
Marvell, Andrew, 45
Marx, Karl, 196
Mask: enhances beauty, 78, 79; face as, 143, 155; pleasure of wearing, 163; plot device, 29, 45, 86, 133; in production, 239; woman more herself when wearing, 49, 82, 154

Massinger, Philip, 225–227
Mathematics, 54, 95
Mathewson, Louise, 257, 259
Measure for Measure, 197, 212–214, 227
Memoirs of Count Grammont, The, 49, 59, 247
Merchants. *See* Characters
Meredith, George, 12, 96, 202
Metaphysics, appearance and nature in, 47, 54–57, 61, 63, 114, 127, 196, 212, 233–234
Mignon, Elizabeth, 183, 206
Miles gloriosus, 132–133
Miles, Dudley Howe, 259
Military images, 23–24, 30–31, 74
Miller, Perry G. E., 118
Milton, John: *Paradise Lost*, 13, 45, 58, 122–126, 130; mentioned, 45
Mirrors as images, 66, 87, 103, 156, 239
Mirror theory of comedy, 115–116, 200, 211, 232
Misanthrope, Le, 44, 97, 109
Misanthrope as character, 96–109, 132, 134
Mistresses. *See* Characters
Modern: term defined, 4–5, 124, 210, 225; drama, 128, 130; Restoration comedy as, 8, 230; science, 120
Modishness, 88, 233
Molière: *Critique de l'Ecole des femmes*, 100; influence on Restoration comedy, 206; *Le Misanthrope*, 44, 97, 109; mentioned, 45
Money: as motivation, 102, 160; music as, 140; reputation as, 27; wit as, 152, 157
Montaigne, Michel de, 51, 54
Montgomery, Guy, 206–207
Morality, conventional, 75, 217, 231
Morality play, 47
"Morals" criticism of Restoration comedy, 3–4, 199–206, 223, 231
"Motley" (set designer), 237
Mourning Bride, The, 130, 146, 157
Much Ado about Nothing, 212–214
Mueschke, Paul and Miriam, 181, 185, 186, 192
Mulgrave, John Sheffield, Earl of, 52, 247

Nashe, Thomas, 51
Natural: candor, 116; characters, 165–167, 171, 176, 180, 191, 218, 240–241; dissembling, 143–147; goodness, 233; language, 53; law, 47, 122, 124; man, 29, 165, 171, 221
Naturalism, 117, 127, 169. *See also* Fideism; Idealism
Nature: art and, 61, 123, 187, 197–198; art of God, 198; as cyclic, 194–198, 233; Elizabethan sense of, 168, 213; vs. manners, 4; as physical, 75, 102, 226–227; as private life, 4, 69, 185, 193, 231, 233; sex as, 29–30, 102, 137, 166; vs. society, 4, 35–36, 42, 85, 116, 233, 241; spiritual, 226–227; suppressed or over-expressed, 150. *See also* Appearance and nature
Neale, J. E., 253
Neoplatonic images, 23, 142, 164, 172. *See also* Religious imagery
Nettleton, George, 250, 251, 258
New Criticism, 207
Newton, Sir Isaac, 45, 59
Nicoll, Allardyce, 206, 256
Nicolson, Marjorie, 118, 125, 196–197
Nokes, James, 67, 116
Nonhumor Characters, 239–240
Nouns, increased use of, 57
Novel, growth of, 58
Noyes, Robert G., 260

Old Batchelor, The. See Congreve
Older people. *See* Characters
Oldys, William, 112
Oppenheimer, Robert, 128
Optical devices, significance of, 55
Othello, 127
Outside and inside. *See* Appearance and nature

Palmer, John, 12, 203–206, 245
Paradise Lost, 13, 45, 58, 122–126, 130
Paradise: as denouement, 126, 203; love as, 25, 78–79, 91, 130; as perfect knowledge, 122–124; vs. society, 94, 110, 130, 164, 193
Parallelism, a part of meaning, 3, 209. *See also* Analogy
Parents, 168–169, 215
Parsons, A. E., 244
Pascal, Blaise, 119
Passion: natural flow of, 144, 193–195; as opposed to reason, 94, 133, 144–145. *See also* Emotions; Nature
Pastoral: characters, 101, 107–108; images, 42–43, 187; Restoration comedy as, 45
Pepys, Samuel, 10, 28, 47, 49, 192
Perry, Henry Ten Eyck, 74, 252, 255
Petrarchanism, 23
Phoenix Theater, 10

Physical reality: as opposed to spiritual, 119–120. *See also* Fact and value
Pilgrim's Progress, 45, 53, 120
Plain-Dealer, The. See Wycherley
Plato, 6, 59, 135, 170, 191, 229
Platonism, of Caroline court, 207
Play itself as image, 33–34, 67, 100, 104, 115–116, 197, 232, 237. *See also* Comedy, mirror theory of
Plays, images of, 33–34, 104, 136
Playwrights' Company, 236
Poetic justice, 15, 27, 84, 200–203, 232
Poetics, 12, 16–18
Poetry: as decoration, 52; as madness, 161–163; in *Plain-Dealer,* 106
Pomponazzi, Pietro, 54
Pope, Alexander, 38, 60, 119, 131
Poston, Mervyn L., 245
Potts, L. J., 74
Preciosité, 207
Presocial characters, 165–167, 181
Pressing, sex as, 68
Pretense: in acting Restoration comedy, 240; confuses self, 34–37, 39–40; and country, 76; play itself as image for, 33–34, 67, 100, 104, 115–116, 197, 232, 237; seventeenth-century attitude toward, 45–63, 212; and society, 32–33, 68, 83, 98, 102, 116, 171, 172, 194–195, 223–224. *See also* Appearance and nature
Primary qualities. *See* Appearance and nature
Production of Restoration comedy: contemporary, 9–12, 88; modern, 92, 107, 232, 234–241; principles of, 5, 234–241
Prologues, 238
Providence: changing definitions, 118–119; contrasted to natural laws, 124; as reality, 164
Prynne, William, 11
Pseudodoxia Epidemica, 169
Psychology, 58, 99
Purcell, Henry, 45; and John Dryden, 19
Puritans: as characters, 39–40, 103, 133; closing of theaters, 10, 206; fideistic, 116–117; language, effect on, 53; mentioned, 21, 45, 125
Pyrrho of Elis, 54

Quakerism, 130
Quem Quaeritis, 9

Racine, Jean, 45
Rake-hero: aging, 73; characteristic of Restoration comedy, 12, 26, 86, 192, 227–228; contrasted to primitive, 220; dissembles to succeed, 50, 224; finds Paradise in love, 121–122, 124, 126, 203; outgrowth of Renaissance villain, 127–128; redeemed or rewarded, 3–4, 61, 200–201, 203; a Romantic figure, 197; succeeds less than "hero in value," 113, 232. *See also* Characters
Raleigh, Sir Walter, 54, 118
Rapin, René, 16–17, 115, 260
Ratisbon, 20, 95
Ravenscroft, Edward, 131
Realism: in characters, 89, 167–168, 241; contrasted to idealism, 22, 44, 82–85, 108–109, 121, 130, 173, 233; in setting, 35, 108, 204–206, 228, 236
Reason: and faith, 117, 120, 129; and passion, 94, 133, 144–145
Recruiting-Officer, The, 235
Rehearsal, The, 53–54, 214
Religious images: denouements in terms of, 126, 203; heroic, 22, 25–26; as illusion, 105, 133, 136–137; love divine, 22, 25–26, 141–142; marks "right way" of appearance matching nature, 35, 42, 78–79, 82, 91, 93–94, 116; suprasocial, 164
Rembrandt van Rijn, 45
Reputation, 27, 57, 65, 75, 89, 170, 194. *See also* Appearance and nature
Restoration comedy: assumptions behind, 112, 230; didactic method of, 114–116, 200, 211, 233; dramatic history, place in, 9–13, 210–229; *See also* Action of; Antiheroic elements in; Attitudes toward; Characters of; Heroic drama; Images; Language of; Manners criticism of; "Morals" criticism of; Production of; Ritual elements in; Science; Structure; Themes of
Retreat from society, 174
Richard II, 62, 121
Richard III, 46, 62
Richelieu, Cardinal de, 45
Richmond, Duchess of, 48
Right-way–wrong-way simile. *See* Language of Restoration comedy
Ritual elements in Restoration comedy, 109, 182, 234
Rochester, John Wilmot, second Earl of, 48, 57
Rollins, Hyder E., 243
Romanticism in Restoration comedy, 195–196
Rossiter, A. P., 247

Rousseau, Jean Jacques, 97
Royal Society of London, 45, 53
Rubens, Peter Paul, 45
Rundle, James U., 246
Rymer, Thomas, 17, 252

Sachs, Curt, 257
St. James's Park. See Wycherley, *Love in a Wood*
Salisbury Court Theater, 10
Sauny the Scot, 215–216
Savile, George, first Marquess of Halifax, 50
Scanlan, Elizabeth G., 243
Schelling, Felix E., 251, 259
Schlegel, August Wilhelm von, 6
Science: causality vs. analogy, 117–119, 225; growth of, 117–120; influence on heroic drama, 15–16, 18; influence on language, 53–58, 224–225; influence on naturalism, 117, 127; influence on Restoration comedy, 37, 112, 207; relation to Romanticism, 196. *See also* Appearance and nature; Fact and value
Scrutiny, 207
Scudéry, Mlle. de, 13, 207
Sea, 110, 165, 171
Secentismo, 207
Secondary qualities. *See* Appearance and nature
Seneca, 170
Sentimentalism, growth of, 85, 94, 101, 113, 160, 206, 211
Separation of appearance from nature. *See* Appearance and nature
Separation of fact from value. *See* Fact and value
Servants, 140–141, 240
Sex: as business, 31; as disease, 31; as duel, 23–24, 31; as fishing, 31; as food, 61, 78–79; as gambling, 31, 40; as hawking, 31; as hostility, 27, 30–31, 74; as hunting, 31; in images, 102; as lawsuit, 31; as modishness, 88; as money, 79; as motivation, 102, 160; as nature, 29–30, 102, 137, 166; as pressing, 68; in similes, 231; as swindling, 31, 40; as "way of world," 194–195. *See also* Love; Marriage
Sextus Empiricus, 54–55
Shadwell, Thomas, 28, 52, 59, 131, 217, 221
Shakespeare, William: diction, 175; theme of public man, 46–47, 62; mentioned, 5, 9, 45, 47, 50, 58, 112, 205, 214
Antony and Cleopatra, 46; *Hamlet,* 121, 163, 213–214, 234; *I Henry IV,* 11; *Henry V,* 10, 11, 62; *King Lear,* 14, 127, 211; *Macbeth,* 47, 62; *Measure for Measure,* 197, 212–214, 227; *Much Ado,* 212–214; *Othello,* 127; *Richard II,* 121; *Richard III,* 46, 62; *Taming of the Shrew,* 46, 215–216; *Tempest,* 197, 217–221
Shaw, George Bernard, 62–63, 136–137, 196, 203
Sheffield, John, Earl of Mulgrave, 52, 247
Sherburn, George, 205
She wou'd if she cou'd. See Etherege
Sheridan, Richard Brinsley, 6, 201
Shirley, James, 227–228, 228–229
Sidney, Sir Philip, 13, 16, 51
Siege of Rhodes, The, 11
"Sign-post" characters, 89
Similes, 57, 228, 231. *See also* Images
Sleeping Beauty, 69, 182
Smith, John Harrington, 259
Smith, Willard, 259
Society: as appearances, 32–33, 116, 167–174, 176–179, 194–195, 198, 223–224; corruption of, in Restoration, 18–19, 216–217, 222–225, 230; and natural emotions, 185, 193, 233; vs. nature, 4, 35–36, 42, 85, 116, 233, 241; vs. Paradise, 164, 193; vs. personal world, 4, 69, 84, 116, 231; Restoration comedy as purely about, 204–209; retreat from, 174. *See also* Appearance and nature
Socrates, 135
"Solid": characters, 238; a "plus" word, 53–55
Spectacle, Restoration emphasis on, 10, 210
Spectator, The, 51, 53, 201, 260
Spencer, Hazelton, 260
Spencer, Theodore, 247, 260
Spenser, Edmund, 13, 46
Spiritual reality, 119–120. *See also* Fact and value
Split-man observation, language of, 36, 111, 139, 148, 232
Sprague, A. C., 260
Sprat, Bishop Thomas, 53, 57
Spring-Garden, 236
Stage: as image, 232; Restoration innovations in, 10, 52–53, 210, 232
Stage history of Restoration comedy, 3

Staging of Restoration comedy. *See* Production
State of Innocence, The, 58–59
Steele, Sir Richard, 53, 74, 138, 201
Stirling, Sir William Alexander, Earl of, 51
Strachey, Lytton, 175, 199, 200, 202, 258
Structure, right-way–wrong-way, 83-87, 109, 114–117, 126, 129, 215, 223, 231
Sublimations, 231
Substance. *See* Appearance and nature
Suckling, Sir John, 12, 207
Summers, Montague, 206, 244, 260, 261
Suprasocial. *See* Characters
Surfaces, images of, 154–155
Swift, Jonathan, 52
Swindling, images of, 31, 40
Sypher, Wylie, 126, 146

Taming of the Shrew, The, 46, 215–216
Tasso, Torquato, 13
Tate, Nahum, 14, 211–212, 217
Tatler, The, 53, 123, 126
Tawney, R. H., 124–125
Taylor, Jeremy, 122
Tempest, The: Dryden and Davenant, 217–221; Shakespeare, 197, 217–221
Temple, Sir William, 52, 59
Terence, 75
Tertullian, 117, 120
Testing, theme of, 173, 213, 227, 228
Thackeray, William Makepeace, 3, 11, 202
Theater. *See* Stage
Themes of Restoration comedy. *See* Adultery; Affectation; Appearance and nature; Deception; Decorum; Disguise; Dissimulation; Emotions; Fact and value; Family relations; *Felix culpa;* Folly Hostility; Hyprocrisy; Knowledge; Liberty; Love; Marriage; Natural; Nature; Pretense; Reason; Reputation; Science; Sex; Society; Testing; Town and country; Wit
Thorndike, Ashley H., 247
Three-dimensional images, 144–148, 172
Thurber, James, 142
Tillyard, E. M. W., 260
Town: and country, 29–35, 42–43, 66, 76–77, 82, 87, 93; and "enchanted island," 218; and Paradise, 124, 130
Tragicomedy: heroic, 13; Restoration adaptations of, 212
Tragedy: Aristotle on, 13, 18; Elizabethan and Stuart, 47, 223–224; heroic, 13; Restoration adaptations of, 212
Transubstantiation, 54, 57, 61. *See also* Appearance and nature
Travel, images, 147
Trent, Council of, 54, 59
Tudor-Stuart drama, 9, 12–13, 27, 47, 58, 127, 210, 223–224, 230–231

Underwood, Dale, 12, 23, 57–58, 94, 125, 127, 209, 223, 228, 246
Universe: anthropocentric, 120; as mechanism, 118–120; as organism, 118. *See also* Analogy; Images, cosmic
Unreal characters, 107–108
Upper-class characters, 26, 228

Vanbrugh, Sir John, 115, 130, 201, 232
Van Dyck, Sir Anthony, 45, 238
Vaughan, Henry, 123
Vega, Lope de, 45
Vegetable images, 157
Vermeer, Jan van Delft, 45
Vessel, marriage as, 172–173
Vice, as suppressing or over-expressing self, 233
Villains. *See* Characters
Villiers, Barbara, Duchess of Cleveland, 38, 48, 49, 97
Villiers, George, Duke of Buckingham, 38, 53–54, 56–57, 58, 214
Virgil, 13, 18
Voltaire, 132

Waller, Edmund, 54
Wanning, Andrews, 58, 111–112, 246
Ward, Sir A. W., 259
Webster, John, 248
Weight, images of, 36, 141, 172
Wells, Staring B., 254
Wendell, Barrett, 202
White, Robert W., 250
Whitehead, Alfred North, 45, 56, 125
Widows, 23, 103, 181, 186–187, 190
Wilcox, John, 245, 252, 259
Wild Gallant, The, 20
Wild-Goose Chase, The, 221–223, 225
"Wildness," 88–89, 101, 150, 223
Willey, Basil, 117, 119, 121, 125, 247
Will's Coffee-house, 236
Wilmot, John, Earl of Rochester, 48, 57
Wit: characters, 39, 150, 154, 190; theme of, 198, 208
Witty lovers. *See* Lovers
Wotton, William, 52
Wound, love as, 24, 80, 85, 233

Wren, Sir Christopher, 45
Wycherley, William: and Congreve, 131; *Epigrams,* 109, 129; letters, 5, 60; life, 38, as moralist, 96–109; poems, 60, 129; prose style, 139; puts "right way" on stage, 71–72; relation to Manly, 96–109
Country Wife, The: full discussion, 73–85; summary, 233; mentioned, 4, 86, 100, 104, 112–113, 116, 128, 129, 134, 139, 223, 232, 237, 239
Gentleman Dancing-Master, The: full discussion, 64–72; summary, 233; mentioned, 73, 80, 84, 100, 116, 128, 239
Love in a Wood: full discussion, 38–44; summary, 233; mentioned, 71, 105, 235
Plain-Dealer, The: change in Restoration hero, 84–85, 129, 157, 159–160, 164, 197, 223, 232; Congreve, influence on, 98, 131, 149; full discussion, 96–113; summary, 233; mentioned, 44, 116, 128, 136, 163, 173, 239, 240–241
mentioned, 7, 38, 42, 43, 44, 50, 59, 63, 64, 65, 67, 69, 70, 71, 72, 73, 74, 75, 77, 82, 84, 85, 96, 97, 98, 99, 100, 101, 104, 105, 107, 108, 109, 112, 113, 149, 201, 205, 231

Yeats, William Butler, 182, 197
York, Duke of, later James II, 49

Zola, Émile, 127